Rural Studies in Britain and France

RURAL STUDIES IN BRITAIN AND FRANCE

Edited by *Philip Lowe*
and *Maryvonne Bodiguel*

Translated by Henry Buller

Belhaven Press
A division of Pinter Publishers
London

© The editors and contributors, 1990

First published in Great Britain in 1990 by
Belhaven Press (a division of Pinter Publishers),
25 Floral Street, London WC2E 9DS and PO Box 197, Irvington, New York

All rights reserved. No part of this publication may be
reproduced, stored in a retrieval system, or transmitted by any
other means without the prior permission of the copyright holder.
Please direct all enquiries to the publishers.

British Library Cataloguing in Publication Data
A CIP catalogue record for this book is available from the
British Library

ISBN 1 85293 083 7

Library of Congress Cataloging-in-Publication Data

Rural studies in Britain and France/edited by Philip Lowe and
  Maryvonne Bodiguel.
     p.   cm.
   ISBN 1-85293-083-7
   1. Sociology, Rural–Study and teaching–Great Britain.
  2. Sociology, Rural–Study and teaching–France. 3. Rural
  geography–Study and teaching–Great Britain.   4. Rural geography–
  Study and teaching–France. 5. Regional economics–Study and
  teaching–Great Britain. 6. Regional economics–Study and teaching–
  France. I. Lowe, Philip. II. Bodiguel, Maryvonne.
  HT411.R87   1990   90-34583
  307.72′071′041–dc20   CIP

Typeset by Witwell Ltd, Southport
Printed and bound by Biddles Ltd, Guildford and Kings Lynn

Contents

List of contributors
Preface

Part I: The Rural in Context

1. The Historical and Cultural Contexts   3
   Philip Lowe and Henry Buller
2. Rural Development in Post-War Britain and France   21
   Henry Buller and Philip Lowe
3. Concepts, Definitions and Research Traditions   37
   Maryvonne Bodiguel, Henry Buller and Philip Lowe

Part II: History

4. Commentary and Introduction   55
   Geneviève Gavignaud
5. History in Perspective: Rural Studies in French Historiography   61
   Geneviève Gavignaud and Ronald Hubscher
6. British Rural History: Themes in Agricultural History and Rural Social History   76
   Gordon Mingay

Part III: Geography

7. Commentary and Introduction   93
   Mark Cleary and Hugh Clout
8. French Geography and the Rural World   97
   Gilles Sautter and Bernard Kayser

9. Rural Geography in Britain 117
   Paul Cloke and Malcolm Moseley

Part IV: Economics

10. Commentary and Introduction 139
    André Brun
11. Rural Economics in France 144
    Michel Blanc and Philippe Lacombe
12. The Development, Organisation and Orientation of Agricultural Economics in the United Kingdom 165
    David Colman

Part V: Anthropology

13. Commentary and Introduction 179
    Maryon McDonald
14. Rural Ethnology in France 183
    Martine Ségalen, Gérard Lenclud and Georges Augustins
15. The British Anthropological Tradition, Otherness and Rural Studies 203
    Anthony Cohen

Part VI: Sociology

16. Commentary and Introduction 225
    Peter Hamilton
17. The Metamorphosis of French Rural Sociology 233
    Maryvonne Bodiguel and Bertrand Hervieu
18. Recent British Rural Sociology 248
    Graham Crow, Terry Marsden and Michael Winter

Part VII: Politics

19. Commentary and Introduction 265
    Jean Charlot
20. French Political Science and Rural Problems 269
    Isabel Boussard
21. Rural Politics in Britain 286
    Wyn Grant

Index 299

List of contributors

Philip Lowe, Bartlett School of Architecture and Planning, University College London.
Henry Buller, Groupe de Recherches Sociologiques, Université de Paris X.
Maryvonne Bodiguel, Groupe de Recherches Sociologiques, Université de Paris X.
Geneviève Gavignaud, Département d'Histoire, Université Paul Valery, Montpellier.
Ronald Hubscher, Département d'Histoire Université de Picardie, Amiens.
Gordon Mingay, Department of History, University of Kent, Canterbury.
Mark Cleary, Department of Geography, University of Brunei.
Hugh Clout, Department of Geography, University College, London.
Gilles Sautter, Laboratoire d'Anthropologie Sociale, Paris.
Bernard Kayser, Département de Géographie, Université de Toulouse le Mirail.
Paul Cloke, Department of Geography, St. David's University College, Lampester.
Malcolm Moseley, Action with Communities in Rural England, Cirencester.
André Brun, Laboratoire d'Economie et de Sociologie Rurale, Institut National de la Recherche Agronomique, Arlon.
Philippe Lacombe, Ecole Nationale d'Agronomie, Montpellier.
Michel Blanc, Institut Nationale de la Recherche Agronomique, Auzeville.
Maryon McDonald, Department of Human Sciences, Brunel University, Uxbridge.
Martine Ségalen, Laboratoire d'Ethnologie Française, Musée des Arts et Traditions Populaires, Paris.
Gérard Lenclud, Laboratoire d'Anthropologie Sociale, Paris.
Georges Augustins, Laboratoire d'Ethnologie et de Sociologie Comparative, Université de Paris X.
Anthony Cohen, Department of Social Anthropology, University of Edinburgh.
Peter Hamilton, Faculty of Social Sciences, Open University, Milton Keynes.

List of Contributors

Bertrand Hervieu, Centre de la Vie Politique Française, Fondation Nationale de Science Politique, Paris.
Graham Crow, Department of Sociology and Social Policy, University of Southampton.
Terry Marsden, Department of Town Planning, Polytechnic of the South Bank, London.
Michael Winter, Centre for Rural Studies, Royal Agricultural Collge, Circencester.
Jean Charlot, Centre de la Vie Politique Française, Fondation Nationale des Sciences Politiques, Paris.
Isabel Boussard, Centre de la Vie Politique Française, Fondation Nationale des Sciences Politiques, Paris.
Wyn Grant, Department of Politics, University of Warwick, Coventry.

Preface

The countryside and rural society, their past, present and future, are major preoccupations in Britain and in France. The urbanisation of the two nations has in no way diminished this interest; if anything, it has sharpened it. With the bulk of economic and social activity concentrated in towns and cities, the countryside has come to embody largely a cultural interest in both countries. Yet for two neighbouring nations so thrown together by history and now bound by complex political and economic ties, their rural cultures could not be more diverse. The purpose of this book is to confront these cultures by juxtaposing the separate understandings that have developed of rural Britain and rural France.

Inevitably, this is a multi-layered enterprise. At one level, as we explore the variety of functions, values and images associated with rural areas, we can appreciate the diversity of rural cultures not just between the two countries but within each. At another level, particularly when contrasting British and French experiences, the separate rural cultures appear as more cohesive and characteristic. Then again, when considering each in its context, this singularity is seen to reside not in any putative autarky but in the nature of rural culture as a component of the particular national culture. Inevitably, therefore, a comparative exercise such as this alludes to, but hopefully also qualifies, national stereotypes.

British and French rural cultures increasingly interact in circumstances that are more or less conducive to the development of mutual understanding and the breaking down of stereotypes: within various fora of the European Community; through the growing consumption of French wine and cheese in Britain and, to a somewhat lesser extent, of Scotch whisky and British beef in France;[1] in a succession of commodity battles, like the notorious 'lamb wars', between producers and exporters from the two countries; in the annual summer invasion by British tourists and second-homers of the Dordogne, Auvergne and Provence, and by French teenagers attending language schools across southern England; and through countless twinnings of Clochemerle and Ambridge.

This book is the result of another such interaction, devised with the explicit purpose of promoting mutual understanding. It brings together a specific group from either side of the Channel – those whose profession is the study of rural society.[2] Thus the book is not only a confrontation between rural cultures but between academic cultures too.

At this level also there are singularities and pluralities of contexts and meanings. In preparing the book, leading British and French rural specialists were asked to prepare parallel chapters on the dominant research and intellectual themes of the past thirty to forty years in rural studies, for each of the six main disciplines of history, geography, politics, anthropology, economics and sociology. Each has different ways of analysing and conceptualising the rural world, and it is thereby subdivided as a conceptual space, not just by national boundaries, but by disciplinary boundaries too.

Britain and France also have different academic traditions and institutional structures for research and learning. Over and above the separate disciplines, these traditions and structures have strongly shaped the way rural areas have been studied in the two countries, as explored in the introductory chapters to each of the disciplinary sections prepared by leading comparativists. There is, however, a progressive internationalisation of ideas and information which has challenged both the independence and the insularity of national academic cultures. It is most highly developed in the natural sciences with their search for universalistic laws. In the social sciences, national and cultural boundaries are not so readily transcended, but most of their basic concepts and theories derive from the writings of the same small group of celebrated nineteenth-century European social thinkers. Increasingly also, the research and communication networks of contemporary social scientists are transnational.

The consequence is that particular specialists from different countries not only share a common disciplinary outlook on the world but may also be oriented to the same international journals, scientific associations, conventions and peer groups, and may increasingly be drawn into transnational collaborative and comparative research projects. The purpose and outcome of such interactions should not necessarily be a great levelling and homogenising of ideas, but should encompass the exploration and explanation of social and cultural *differences*. This is what can distinguish international exchange between social scientists not only from that between natural scientists, but also from the harmonising, conventionalising and standardising intentions of international bureaucrats and policy-makers. But here again, social scientists are several steps behind.

After all, for several years now, Britain and France have pursued policies for agriculture, regional development and environmental protection within the same transnational framework of the European Community. Indeed, the most salient policies for rural areas, particularly those relating to agriculture, are supranational in nature, emanating from Brussels. It is no longer acceptable, therefore, for social scientists investigating the forces shaping contemporary rural society to contain their analyses implicitly within the boundaries of an assumed national sovereignty, though many of them do still act in this blinkered fashion. Moreover, France and Britain face convergent problems in their rural areas, and much might be learnt from an exchange of information and ideas: on problems such as the pressures and conflicts associated with counter-urbanisation and industrial decentralisation; the ecological and social impact of increasing recreational and tourist activity; the industrialisation and intensification of agriculture and the displacement of labour from the land; and the crisis for public policy and farm adjustment of structural surpluses in key primary products. Not only are there parallel social forces at work but, within the European Community, economic influences are increasingly transnational, not only with the advent of 1992 and the completion of the single European market, but also through the growing prominence of multinational firms in such sectors as agribusiness, food and tourism.

These converging trends, however, elicit social and institutional responses that are often strongly differentiated. After all, the relationship between civil society and the state, the history of industrialisation and urbanisation, demographic structure and culture are quite distinct for the two countries. As a consequence, similar problems have a different genesis, cultural resonance and political implications. To understand and anticipate these divergent reactions, to explore the implications of common trends in separate European contexts, it is more than ever important to achieve mutual understanding of essential differences and similarities.

Notes

1. Though French exports of food and drink to Britain are double those in the reverse direction, France is now Britain's single biggest customer, accounting for 15 per cent of the latter's food exports (which is 7 per cent of France's food imports).
2. We acknowledge the financial support of the Economic and Social Research Council (ESRC), the Centre National de la Recherche Scientifique (CNRS), and the French Foreign Ministry in facilitating these exchanges.

Part I: The Rural in Context

Social scientists do not stand apart from society or history but take as their point of departure the predominant concerns of their own societies. Thus, before examining the different ways in which social scientists have perceived the rural world in the two countries, we need to consider the historical and cultural contexts in which they operate. In this introductory section, therefore, the first chapter compares and contrasts the place of the rural world in contemporary French and British history and how this has shaped distinct cultural perceptions. The second chapter then examines the specific problems and national strategies thrown up by the separate trajectories of post-war rural development in the two countries. Finally, the third chapter reviews the different ways in which rural areas and problems have been defined and conceived by the respective governments and social science communities.

1 The Historical and Cultural Contexts

Philip Lowe and Henry Buller

Industrialisation, urbanisation and rural society

France, with over twice the expanse of the United Kingdom and a more varied morphology, straddles the temperate and Mediterranean climatic zones. Naturally, therefore, it has a more diverse topography and physiognomy, and is a country of striking regional contrasts and distinctive regional systems. Over and above these fundamental geographical differences, historical experience has also set the two countries apart, not least in terms of their divergent courses of economic development.

Britain was the first country to adopt factory-based industrialisation and urbanisation, whereas France was one of the last in Western Europe to conform to this model (O'Brien and Keyder 1978; Kindleberger 1964; Bairoch and Levy-Leboyer 1981). Processes of industrialisation and economic concentration from the mid-eighteenth century onwards turned Britain which, in earlier centuries and beyond the South East had been one of the least urbanised countries in Europe, in to the most urbanised. The growth of factories drew on an extensive prior development of resource-based crafts and proto-industrial production and occurred initially in rural areas and smaller settlements, especially in the north of England, the Midlands and South Wales. With the establishment of the factory system, industry became concentrated in certain towns, which then grew very rapidly to form new urban agglomerations (de Vries 1984). The mushrooming of the industrial cities and of London during the nineteenth century sucked in not only people, but also trades and markets, and rapidly developed and expanded these.

The surrounding rural areas and those regions which did not experience nineteenth-century industrialisation suffered deindustrialisation, being emptied of much of their formerly diverse economic activity, save for agriculture. Critical to the British historical experience is the fact that capitalist relations of production had been established in agriculture prior to the emergence of industrial capitalism. By the late eighteenth century many parts of Britain already possessed a fully commercialised agriculture which was self-consciously innovative and orientated to the expanding market in food commodities presented by the burgeoning urban population (Mingay 1977; Ward and Wilson 1971). A capitalist labour process also rendered labour exceptionally mobile (Snell 1985). At the beginning of the century one fifth of the population lived in towns; by mid-century, the urban population had overtaken that to be found in rural areas; and by the end of the century four-fifths of the population was urban-based. Urbanisation and industrialisation thus produced a spatially polarised, as well as a nationally integrated, geography in which cities functioning at the core of distinct and specialised regional economies concentrated the bulk of population and commercial and industrial activity, while rural areas became dominated by a technically progressive, market-orientated agriculture (Tilly 1983).

The experience of France in the nineteenth century was in sharp contrast. During the eighteenth century, it had been the most powerful state in Western Europe. Its population of about 28 million had been almost twice that of Britain's. It had a well organised and centralised administration in sharp contrast with the British tradition of local autonomy. Under the Enlightenment, Paris had emerged as the pre-eminent centre for science and culture. The development and professional organisation of French engineering had been promoted; and the craftsmen and artisans of Paris and various provincial centres were renowned for their skill and finesse. Both British engineering and manufacture benefited significantly from French influences and know-how during the eighteenth century (Hamilton 1958; Scoville 1960).

Though the Napoleonic period extended many of the achievements of the *ancien régime* and ushered in a host of potentially modernising reforms, the Revolution and its aftermath seriously disrupted economic life and the technical progress of French industry (Trebilcock 1981). In the decade after 1789 the output of textiles fell by over a half; and, despite the increased demand for arms, even metallurgy suffered a decline (Landes 1969). Access to new technologies and the expanding international markets was interrupted by the Napoleonic wars. During this period much of the French economy underwent what Crouzet (1962) has termed a process of pastoralisation, whilst British industry surged ahead (Kindleberger 1964; O'Brien and Keyder 1978).

A key factor in the slower growth of the French economy was the relative torpor of agriculture and provincial handicrafts. The abolition of feudal title deeds converted the peasantry into a secure, petty freeholding class even more strongly attached to the pattern of fields and settlements. Farms were small and tended to grow smaller through the Napoleonic code of equal inheritance, reaching a peak of about 3 ½ million during the 1880s. There were areas of capitalist agriculture that were technically advanced, notably the Paris Basin and in northern France, but elsewhere there was little incentive and less means to effect any major changes in husbandry. A long-term effect of the Revolution was to stimulate a certain economic individualism in the peasantry, but its major manifestation was a seemingly insatiable land-hunger (Grantham 1975; Zeldin 1973; Soboul 1956). By and large, the predominant sector was mired in low returns, traditional practices and limited involvement in the market economy. The slow increases in productivity of peasant agriculture throughout the nineteenth century and the siphoning off of much of the surplus into land purchase also placed a damper on the accelerated development of the secondary sector by nullifying peasant purchasing power of industrial goods. This helped preserve small-scale rural industry. A significant feature of the peasant economy in many areas was pluriactivity which helped support a large and diverse rural population and was a mainstay of rural industry (Hubscher 1984). Secondary sector activity thus remained highly localised, fragmented and conservative. In 1871, two-thirds of the French population lived in rural areas and approximately three-quarters of all non-agricultural industrial activity took place in the countryside, most of it in workshops rather than factories (Trebilcock 1981; Carré et al. 1976; Dupeux 1974). The nineteenth century was truly the apogee of French rural society.

The economic and technological advance which did occur was very uneven. Certain industrial sectors in a few areas, notably Paris, Alsace, around St Etienne and in parts of the Nord, were very dynamic and technologically advanced and experienced considerable concentration. But elsewhere and until well into the twentieth century, France was a largely pre-industrial, economically undynamic, primarily agrarian society. Much of its commerce and manufacture was rural in character and most of its towns were small market centres closely linked to the local farming economy, though the spread of the railways through the second half of the nineteenth century was a precursor to the piecemeal establishment of a national market – a development towards which the peasant economies of the south and west proved remarkably recalcitrant (Clout 1983; Price 1983). As Cleary comments, throughout much of France, 'The exchange of labour and goods, legal and religious dealings and what little marketing of produce there was, took place within horizons that were limited by physical environment and codified by custom and tradition'. (1989, p. 9).

The country's relative economic stagnation was reflected in and compounded by its slow demographic growth. In 1800 France was the most populous country in Western Europe with 28.3 million against Britain's 16 million. By 1910 the French population had risen by less than a half (to 41.5 million), and had been overtaken by Britain's (45.4 million) which had almost trebled during the same period. By that time, France had only fifteen towns with over 100,000 inhabitants whereas Britain had forty-seven. Though France's post-war demographic boom has brought its overall population almost level with Britain's, it remains a large but relatively empty country. The national density of population is low (100 persons per sq. km. compared with Britain's 230 persons). Despite the rapid urbanisation of the post-war years, zones of dense settlement remain relatively few and far between, and the bulk of French territory remains countryside, served by villages and small market towns.

In comparing and contrasting the British and French countryside, therefore, a basic distinction is that the context for one is a densely-packed and decidedly urbanised nation, and for the other is a nation which covers much more territory and was until recently predominantly rural and agrarian. Indeed, as late as 1950, 46 per cent of the French population lived in the countryside and 28 per cent of the labour force worked the land. Britain had been in an equivalent position about a century earlier. Inevitably, these separate national contexts have shaped rural development in different ways in the two countries in the twentieth century. Thus, whereas Nan Fairbrother characterised the British as 'the least rural people in the world' (1970), French civilisation remains still, at heart, a rural one

(Bodiguel 1986). The divergent historical backgrounds have also contributed to the formation of distinct perceptions, attitudes and institutions relating to rural issues and interests. Overall, these loom so much larger in contemporary French history, culture and politics. Inevitably, therefore, they occupy a much more prominent position in the intellectual and research traditions of French social science. In contrast, British social science has its roots in the efforts of nineteenth-century reformers, moralists and statisticians to address urgent and specifically urban social problems thrown up by the alarmingly explosive, chaotic and squalid growth of Victorian cities.

The different rural lineages: capitalist agriculture and peasant society

The contrasting status of the French and British countryside in the late nineteenth century also established different starting points and separate trajectories for their development during the twentieth century. The British countryside was well integrated into the national economy as a specialised space for capitalist agriculture. The French countryside, though gradually being integrated into a national market, was still largely a series of discrete local economies, rooted in a peasant agriculture, but with considerable social and economic diversity both locally and between regions (Weber 1976). In Marc Bloch's words, rural France was a 'large and complex country' whose variety spoke of 'very profound human differences' (Bloch 1966), p. xxv).

Perhaps the most basic distinctions and sources of social differentiation were internal to the peasantry – this being an inclusive category which normally referred to all who worked the land but which could encompass rural artisans (many of whom were also involved in farming) and the inhabitants of the countryside generally (Barral 1966). Peasant agriculture itself was a complex, locally variegated amalgam of overlapping occupations. A primary distinction was between farmers and labourers, who were in turn broadly subdivided into day-labourers and rural servants. However, about half the day-labourers had their own small plots of land. Moreover, the peasant farmer was not necessarily a proprietor: many holdings were rented either on a sharecropping or cash tenancy basis, though a good proportion of those renting land also had holdings of their own and peasant farming could co-exist with large-scale land ownership. Finally, the landlords ranged from bourgeois owners of one or two farms, through squires with sizeable estates, to rich nobles with several estates. A crude regional distinction could be made between Southern and Central France where small peasant polyculture and share tenantry predominated, and the area to the north of the Loire (excluding Brittany) where well-established capitalist hierarchies of large estates, big tenant farmers and day-labourers were much more prevalent (Clout 1983).

There was not, however, the enormous concentration of landownership that was found in Britain where four-fifths of the land, most of it tenanted, was owned by 7,000 men, and just a few hundred aristocrats controlled about a quarter of the country. In France, in contrast, three-quarters of all farms were farmed directly by their owners, amounting to about 2 2/3 million peasant proprietors owning over half the land.

The extremely concentrated ownership of land in Britain was at the base of a highly stratified and hierarchical agrarian class system of landowners, tenant farmers and wage-labourers, with numerous additional and regionally specific, status distinctions internal to each of these categories (Mills 1980). The aristocratic landowners, who had constituted Britain's ruling class, remained the dominant social class in the countryside until the twentieth century (Thompson 1963). It was the unity of this class and the power it exercised which gave to the British countryside the coherence that the French countryside lacked. Its economic interests determined the way the countryside was organised and functioned. Its social and political interests also largely determined the way the countryside was presented and represented, not least through aristocratic patronage of a small army of cultural agents, including the rural clergy, the magistracy, village schools and charitable organisations; land agents, surveyors and agricultural improvers; landscape designers, architects and craftsmen; and poets, artists and naturalists.

Aristocratic control was not undisputed, however, and during the nineteenth century it was periodically challenged from below through rural unrest and agitation, which took the form of trade union conflict in the arable areas and of tenants' rights in the pastoral areas (Newby 1987). The mounting political pressures for land reform, coupled with the agricultural depression which began in the late 1870s, did eventually undermine the hegemony of aristocratic landownership. Nevertheless, in such an emphatically urbanised country, the legacy of concentrated landownership, even if somewhat diluted in the twentieth century (even now a few hundred titled families still own almost a third of the land; and 1 per cent of the adult population owns two-thirds), has meant that the land question has remained a feature of British politics right down to the present day (Shoard 1987). Indeed, conflicts over property and access to land have been perhaps the defining feature of rural politics, successively expressed in the land reform pressures of the turn of the century, intermittent struggles over public access for recreation, the development of the statutory town and country planning system in the inter-war and post-war years, periodic disputes over such matters as compensation and betterment and the supply of land for housing development, and the contemporary concern over rural conservation. The continuing currency of the land question indicates the strength of private property rights and the resilience of landed interests in British society. These interests can call on potent ideological defences (Cox, Lowe and Winter 1988). Indeed, many of the values that the British still hold regarding the countryside derive from essentially aristocratic ideals and conventions of the eighteenth and nineteenth centuries; for example, the ideals of the organic village community, of rural moral affluence, of social aesthetics, as well as the notion that a gentlemanly and stewardship ethic should attach to the ownership of land (Wiener 1981; Barrell 1980). In a somewhat modified form, their most prominent vehicle in the twentieth century has been the rural preservation movement.

Not surprisingly, some of these ideals do not find an echo in contemporary French culture. A gentlemanly ethic hardly resonates with an ideal of peasant proprietorship. But the contrast goes much deeper. Though there were great swathes of France in the nineteenth century where large landowners retained considerable power and influence, there was no real equivalent to the general and ubiquitous cultural hegemony exercised by the British aristocracy. Certainly the predominant social grouping, the peasantry, did not play such a role despite pockets of 'peasant democracy' (Barral 1968). Indeed, it was the very absence of the sort of class consciousness that so pervaded British urban and rural society which struck observers of rural France. This surely is the upshot of that otherwise erroneous, though oft quoted, libel by Marx to the effect that the peasants 'form a vast mass, the members of which live in similar conditions but without entering into manifold relations with one another . . . Thus the great mass of the French nation is formed by simple addition of homologous magnitudes, much as potatoes in a sack form a sack of potatoes'. On the contrary, strong ideological cohesion was a characteristic of peasant communities (Mendras 1976). The dominant social figures locally were those in a position to mediate between the community and the wider world – the priest, the schoolteacher, the doctor, the large landowner. In the late nineteenth century, however, various social and political elites competed to give more general expression to the social identity of the peasantry and thus exercise leadership over it regionally and nationally. Subsequently, during the middle decades of the twentieth century, the peasantry themselves developed a sense of common purpose and the means of collective action (Barral 1968, Wright 1964). In the process, a powerful peasantist ideology was forged. Thus, in contrast to the centrality of the land question to British rural politics, French rural politics in the twentieth century have been preoccupied with the social role, well-being and fate of the peasantry and their integration into a modern, urbanised economy.

In the present century, rural Britain and rural France have experienced many similar forces and events though their impact has often been different. The trend for the British countryside has been from a highly specialised space devoted almost exclusively to primary production, to a socially and economically much more diverse, post-industrial countryside. For the French countryside, in contrast, the trend has been from an occupationally diverse, socially complex, largely pre-industrial peasant society to a modern, specialised, family-based agriculture. There has been convergence in certain aspects of social and economic life, particularly marked, for example, in the organisation of farming. Nonetheless, fundamental differences remain. One way of highlighting these is to focus on two formative but separate social and political movements in the 20th century, the one distinctive to rural France, the other to rural Britain, but which have played a central and roughly analogous role in redefining the social functions of the countryside in their different national contexts. In the next two sections, therefore, we look in turn at the peasantist movement in France and the preservation movement in Britain.

The preservation movement in Britain

The organised preservation movement emerged in late-nineteenth-century Britain as part of an intellectual reaction to many of the tenets of economic liberalism and a loss of confidence in man's ability to improve nature and society through the exercise of human reason (Sheail 1976). Such a profound shift of opinion arose from a reassessment of the social and economic changes of the nineteenth century and was fuelled by moral and aesthetic reaction to urban squalor and the predicament (and unruliness) of the urban poor.

The Victorians' self-confidence was sapped by the Great Depression of the 1880s and by the intellectual crisis of the post-Darwinian years (Burrow 1966). Britain's increasingly disappointing industrial performance in the final decades of the century was matched by a growing equivocation towards industrialism itself which reflected the absorption of the urban bourgeoisie into the upper reaches of British society and its genteel value system – a value system which disdained trade and industry, which stressed the civilised enjoyment, rather than the accumulation of wealth, and which preferred social stability to enterprise (Wiener 1981). Anti-industrial values infected social criticism and were embodied in various institutions and campaigns that sought to preserve facets of traditional society and culture from the ravages of urban growth. The countryside and the traditional and harmonious social relations supposedly found therein became the object of both literary veneration and public concern (Williams 1973, Keith 1975, Marsh 1982).

The symbolic importance of the countryside grew as its economic and social importance was eclipsed. The 1880s and 1890s saw a great agricultural slump, particularly in the arable counties, as cheap food flooded into Britain from overseas. Whereas other countries, including France, moved to protect their agricultures by introducing tariffs, Britain remained unique in its dogged commitment to free trade principles in the belief that, to maintain Britain's manufacturing competitiveness, it was in the national interest to obtain food from the cheapest possible sources and thereby keep down the real cost of industrial wages (Tracy 1982). In a sense, agricultural prosperity became a victim of the increasingly fierce competition between Britain and its major rivals. What had been a vibrant sector for investment and profit became an economic backwater. Much land went out of cultivation, the rural population declined sharply and many village communities became depressed and stagnant. The cause of rural preservation was therefore given added poignancy by a sense that the traditional order of the countryside was on the verge of extinction.

The preservation movement was not simply backward-looking but was also associated with emerging patterns of recreation and leisure, linked to concerns for the physical and mental health of an urbanised population. Towards the end of the nineteenth century a whole range of outdoor pursuits became fashionable, including rambling, cycling, climbing, camping, angling, natural history and field sports. The rural preservation movement campaigned to protect from development stretches of open countryside close to urban areas, to maintain rural footpaths and rights of way, to promote public rights of access to mountains and common land, and to establish national parks. The function of rural areas was thereby redefined in part as an urban amenity. The term which came into general currency in the early decades of the twentieth century and signified this new view of rural areas was the 'countryside'. Significantly, the fiercest struggles in this redefinition of rural space were not with ordinary country people, who remained idealised but neglected, but between the conflicting recreational tastes and means of different urban strata and landed interests, such as the hunting and shooting of the gentry, plutocrats and *nouveaux riches*, the botanising and rambling of the genteel middle class, and the hiking of the working class.

A final strand in the preservation movement was the early awakening of an ecological consciousness and an understanding of the need to impose limits on the technological subjugation of the natural world. A crucial factor was a gathering sense of the vulnerability and loss of wildlife, demanding urgent countermeasures. The awesome power man increasingly possessed over nature needed to be exercised with proper restraint and care. As Peter Chalmers Mitchell, the Secretary of the Zoological Society, declared in a strong appeal to the British Association for the organised preservation of the world's fauna, 'Each generation is the guardian of the existing resources of the world; it has come into a great inheritance, but only as a trustee' (Mitchell 1912).

Such rhetoric echoed the traditional justification for aristocratic landownership, and it was not unusual for a preservation group to have a prominent member of the nobility as its patron or figurehead. The National Trust, founded in 1895 and the most prominent of these groups, had particularly strong links with large landowners so as to be in touch with potential donors or vendors of desirable properties. As landlordism fell into decline, through the combined effects of unfavourable legislation and taxation and depressed agricultural prices, the Trust came to see the greatest threat to the landscape and historic buildings of the countryside arising from the collapse of the great estates. It increasingly expressed an ethos of paternalistic stewardship which presented the traditional, private owner as the most appropriate custodian of country estates and houses (Gaze 1988).

The Victorian groups were orientated towards safeguarding specific sites but by the 1920s the pressures on the countryside were more ubiquitous (Sheail 1981). It became evident that a much more concerted effort would be needed to introduce broad legal safeguards equal to the threats posed to rural amenities. With the formation of the Council for the Preservation of Rural England (CPRE) in 1926 rural preservation emerged as a significant force in British politics. It set about lobbying vigorously for controls over urban sprawl and ribbon development, and for the creation of green belts and national parks at a time when the motor car, new trunk roads and commuter railway lines were allowing residential development to break loose from the city boundaries (Lowerson 1980).

The Central (now Country) Landowners' Association was one of the constituent organisations of the CPRE which had strong links with the traditional landowning class, seeing in them a natural ally in combating urbanisation. The need to protect agriculture and create conditions in which it could flourish was now part of the conventional wisdom of rural preservation. The preservationists tended to have a highly romantic and idealised view of farming. In a chronic state of depression, farming practices seemed to pose no threat to other rural interests and pursuits. On the contrary, it was felt that the debilitated condition of farming exacerbated many other threats to the countryside, such as urban encroachment, the decline of rural communities and the flight from the land.

The cause of rural preservation was greatly boosted by the outbreak of the Second World War. The need to preserve the British countryside was embraced, at least in principle, as part of a general commitment to a comprehensive land-use policy and promised reconstruction. It was a cause which commended itself to the government for its obvious symbolic value in helping sustain morale during a period of intense national sacrifice. Official preparations for post-war reconstruction provided unprecedented opportunities to influence the formulation of government policy. The major focus for opinions on the future of the countryside was the official Committee on Land Utilisation in Rural Areas appointed in October 1941 under the chairmanship of Lord Justice Scott, who had been Vice-President of the CPRE. The essential thesis of the Committee's report was that the rural community was at heart an agricultural community, dependent on the continuance and revival of the traditional mixed character of British farming. The assumption was that a prosperous farming industry would preserve both the rural landscape and rural communities. 'Farmers and foresters are unconsciously the nation's landscape gardeners', declared the report, adding emphatically, 'there is no antagonism between use and beauty'. The major threat to rural areas, apart from government neglect, was seen to arise from building and industrial pressures which, it was argued, threatened to mar the countryside, take land out of farming and entice labour away from agriculture.

The assumptions made by the Scott Committee had far-reaching consequences, particularly in shaping the philosophy and objectives of post-war policy for agriculture, land-use planning and conservation. Thus the Town and Country Planning Act 1947 accorded farming and forestry a pre-emptive claim over all other uses of rural land. There were two underlying motives: to regenerate agriculture and to protect the countryside from urban development. Britain, more than any other country, had relied on imported food. The war, however, clearly demonstrated the strategic importance of increased home supplies of food and timber as well as the role government could play in stimulating production, and this became the basis of post-war agricultural policy as set out in the Agriculture Act of 1947.

The French ideology of peasantism

French intellectual and political thought in the late nineteenth century also became exercised over the issue of rural decline. Though certain enthusiasts were inspired by British efforts to preserve rural amenities, wildlife and antiquities, the main thrust of the concern was not preservationist, but with what has come to be known as the rural exodus. Though rural migration had long aroused the disapproval locally of traditional sources of authority, the vanishing peasant became a subject for more general concern when the 1891 census revealed a marked decline in the rural population. At the time, there was widespread hardship in the rural areas caused by a combination of depressed agricultural prices, the undermining of pluriactivity and rural crafts through urban-industrial expansion, the ravages of phylloxera and a run of poor weather conditions. The accelerated drift to the cities precipitated a reassessment of the role of the peasantry as part of a broader political movement which came to project the peasantry as the cornerstone of national stability and strength (Barral 1968). British farming, like that in France, was in the grip of a recession and Britain too was experiencing a relentless depopulation of rural areas. But this did not arouse the degree of political concern that it did in France nor the protectionist reaction or the pro-natalist movements, and significantly, a key element in the British concern was that rural distress leading to out-migration might exacerbate urban overcrowding.

One of the main reasons that so much more attention was accorded to the plight of the peasantry was the much greater weight of the rural population and agriculture in France. The Revolution of 1848, by setting up universal suffrage, made the rural people 'the arbiters of national destiny' (Duby and Wallon 1976 p. 164). With a democratic franchise and, after 1870, a parliamentary system with constituencies drawn up to favour the rural vote, no government could secure office without winning over the bulk of the peasantry. National politicians and representatives, therefore, had to address themselves to peasants' concerns and to reflect an image of the peasantry somewhat at odds with that popularly held by many urban Frenchmen (Barral 1966). In the novels of Balzac and Zola, for example, peasants are portrayed as coarse, greedy savages and rural life is depicted as uncouth, mean and backward. But political leaders, anxious to cultivate peasant support, projected a quite different image. On the Right and amongst social and religious conservatives this tended to take the form of an agrarian rhetoric which exalted the moral virtues of peasant farming and rural life: prolific, practical and rooted in a traditional social hierarchy, the peasant family was a counterweight to the decadent, rootless culture of the urban masses. Radicals and Republicans, in contrast, glorified peasant farmers as a bastion of the eighteenth century ideal of a republic of responsible citizens controlling their own destinies and asserting their independence through the ownership of property. As new political groupings emerged, such as the Socialists, they too had to take up the refrain and attempt to weave the defence of the peasantry into their broader ideological appeal.

The peasantry took little active part in national politics until the Great Depression of the 1930s, but the professional organisation of peasants began much earlier (Barral 1968; Wright 1964). In the late nineteenth century, conservatives and Republicans promoted rival agricultural syndicate movements led by sympathetic local notables. Both sides favoured undifferentiated organisations uniting all elements of the rural population and both proclaimed the unchallengeable virtues of small-ownership. The conservative syndicates, motivated in part by a desire to insulate the peasantry from the inroads of republican ideology, rested on the concept of a single, organic *classe paysanne*, of a *monde paysan* quite distinct in its mores from the rest of French society. Another group seeking to defend the distinctiveness of the rural world was the Catholic clergy who, in a number of regions, became active defenders of local patois and culture against the spread of the French language and the culture of the 'Jacobin' secular republic.

From these different strands of propaganda, a potent 'peasantist ideology' emerged fuelled by the economic difficulties and social discontent of the peasantry themselves. The issue of pre-eminent national concern was the decline of the rural population. Concern turned to alarm as Franco-German tensions highlighted the growing numerical superiority of the German nation and when the Great War scythed the prime of a whole generation – well over half the French casualties were peasants (Dyer 1978). Through this traumatic experience, the peasantry came to be regarded as the threatened wellspring of a dwindling national vitality. In a literature increasingly tinged with rural nostalgia, peasant life was now represented as ennobling, even though touched by tragedy and suffering. Folkloric efforts were also made to preserve or revive local songs, dances and customs.

Increasingly, though, a peasantry that was fully integrated into the market economy and assimilated into national culture, through such agencies as military service and universal state education (Weber 1976), sought to assert its own needs and identity and to displace the notables who had previously dominated the organisations representing rural interests. Under the stimulus of the depression, peasantism became an organised political force through the formation of agricultural interest groups, the largest of which was the *Union National des Syndicats Agricoles*, (formed in 1934, from an older right-wing syndical organisation) and the direct political action of the *Parti Agraire* (formed in 1927) and Henri Dorgères's *Défense Paysanne* (1928) with its green-shirted youth wing. In 1934, these three organisations joined forces to form the short-lived *Front Paysan*. Previous demands for greater protectionism gave way to calls for a full-blown corporatism in which producer-run agricultural corporations would control production, restrict the ravages of free competition in a glutted world market, and also help maintain social order. This movement was, in part, a reaction to the perceived threat posed by the ascent of the Popular Front. The rhetoric of 'peasant unity' employed by the agricultural corporatists was, in turn, criticised by the Socialists and the Communists for glossing over the differences and conflicts between large and small producers and between landowners, tenants and labourers. Their rural organising efforts presented a more collectivist ideal but one which, nevertheless, emphasised peasant solidarity, though they achieved nothing like the success of the Right.

Peasantism reached its apotheosis in the Vichy period, following France's defeat and occupation. Return to the soil and the solid virtues of rural life were a central feature of Vichy's semi-fascist ideology of national renewal; and leading agricultural corporatists were drawn into government to establish a Peasant Corporation to regulate and manage agriculture (Boussard 1980). With the liberation, the Peasant Corporation was abolished but many of the reforms of the Vichy period survived, for example the procedures for *remembrement* (land consolidation) which was to transform the structure and appearance of the countryside in the post-war years. Likewise, the corporatist notion of rural syndical unity, with a single national organisation representing agricultural interests, was preserved in the *Fédération National des Syndicats d'Exploitants Agricoles* (FNSEA) set up in 1946 to represent all active farm operators. There was also considerable continuity of personnel, as many of the farming leaders who had been active in the Vichy Corporation took up leading positions in the FNSEA.

The association with Vichy, however, discredited the more reactionary and mystical aspects of peasantism, not least the notion that the defence of rural life was crucial to the maintenance of social order. But, in many respects, the Vichy period was crucial in establishing a new climate in rural France. Peasants prospered under war-time food shortages. Many gained positions of responsibility in the new, broadly-based syndicates established under the auspices of the *Corporation Paysanne*. Experience of working closely with a state attempting to alleviate food supply problems also led to a widespread, if begrudging, acceptance of the necessary evil of state intervention in agriculture. Finally, in the efforts of the Vichy government to improve rural housing, to encourage agricultural education, to overcome the fragmentation of farm holdings and to plan agricultural supply and output, one can detect the beginnings of a systematic and rational agricultural policy, one with strong technocratic overtones (Wright 1964; Cleary 1989).

In the post-war period, peasant politics have been channelled into the work of agricultural interest groups which have increasingly defined their role in professional and technical terms. A crucial bridge between the agrarian movements of the inter-war years and the agricultural organisations of the post-war period was provided by the social Catholic movement. The *Jeunesse Agricole Catholique* (JAC) had been formed in 1929, reflecting both an interest by the church hierarchy in rejuvenating Christian commitment in the countryside and the need for improved leisure and education facilities for rural youth. It grew spectacularly through the 1930s, remained active during the Occupation years and played a key role in the early post-war period. In many parts of rural France, it proved formative in the social education of a generation of young people, fostering in them a new sense of pride and citizenship (Durupt 1983).

Rural ideology in national cultures

Up to the mid-century and in their respective national contexts, the peasantist movement in France and the preservation movement in Britain were the most prominent socio-political forces seeking to define the cultural significance of rurality in the modern world. However tinged they were with retrospective regret, both helped to forge distinctive and potent rural ideologies which have outlived their progenitors. The preservation movement has been absorbed into the contemporary environmental movement which, in Britain, has a singular fixation with the protection of the countryside (Lowe and Goyder 1984). Peasant politics, likewise, were channelled into the activities of French agricultural interest groups whose professional organisations have not been loth to call forth peasantist images to pep up their demands or to give farmers' demonstrations the deliberate echo of a *jacquerie* (Mendras 1962; Muller 1982; Cleary 1989).

What the two countries have in common, though, is that as the relative economic and social significance of the countryside has declined, it has become available as a potentially powerful cultural symbol. With the growth of public concern over urban poverty, crime and violence, the countryside could be protrayed as a haven of tranquillity and a source of old-fashioned social virtues. Though imbued with much more romanticism in Britain than in France, this sense of timeless worth, the conventional view of rural areas as repositories of tradition and the function of rural settlement in binding together and rendering accessible the national territory have meant that the countryside has come to play a central role in defining national identity. In this regard, its nativistic appeal has been enhanced by the absence from the deep countryside of the ethnic and racial minorities that post-war immigration brought in large numbers to the major cities. Thus, rural France is seen as the heartland of France, its farmers are thought of as the backbone of the nation; and the farmyard cock remains the national symbol. For a country with such strong rural roots, this is perhaps not so surprising. But such cultural symbolism is not necessarily deterred by anachronism, and, despite Britain's thoroughly urbanised character and its strongly industrial past, it has been observed that 'Rural Britain holds a special place in our affections. It seems to contain all that is best in Britain and Britishness. From it we draw a sense of our history, our culture, our very identity as a nation' (Newby 1988, p. 1).

Rural images, however, have separate resonances, and, although a strong sense that the countryside is in crisis is a central and persistent feature of the preoccupation with the rural in both Britain and France, the social definition and popular conceptions of the crisis differ quite sharply. In France, it is the perceived demise of rural society, through the decline of a traditional way of life associated with the peasantry, which attracts concern, involving as it does, the loss of an important symbol of French national identity and a challenge to the security of its national territory (Mendras 1967 and 1984; Gervais et al. 1965; Beteille 1981). In Britain, in contrast, concern has been much more strongly expressed over the decline of the rural landscape and the physical fabric of the countryside, including traditional buildings and settlements (Lowe et al. 1986). Concern over social change in the countryside has been much less pronounced and has not focused on a particular social or occupational group but more on a generalised and idealised sense of a loss of rural community, typically perceived in classless terms. (The exception is in parts of Wales and Scotland where rural identities are overlaid with separate nationalistic or linguistic identities.)

These distinct rural identities and national preoccupations are in no way ephemeral but are embodied in characteristic ways in the representative and governing institutions of the two countries and in their respective languages. The basic political and administrative unit in France, for example, remains the tiny, venerable communes, the vast majority of which are rural (Agulhon et al. 1986). In Britain, likewise, the longest lived territorial unit and the focus of local patriotism is the county, and at this level there has been considerable historical continuity in the lofty paternalism of rural administration. Indeed, even though aristocratic control was replaced by electoral representation a century ago, large farmers and landowners have continued to play a prominent role in British county government (Lee 1963, Newby et al. 1978). At the national level too, the rural vote and rural representation are entrenched in the French Senate through a *département*-based electoral college system comprising representatives of all the communes. In Britain, the equivalent revising chamber, but with greater powers, is the House of Lords whose membership is overwhelmingly hereditary and aristocratic.

Terms and perspectives

The British preoccupation with an unpeopled countryside, a landscape without figures, and the French preoccupation with the peasantry are both also embodied in the respective languages. For example, there are not even English words to signify country people equal to such French ones as *les paysans*, *les ruraux* or *les campagnards*. The nearest English equivalents – peasant, rustic or countryman –

would only be used either as an affectation or in pejorative way. 'Countryman' is perhaps the most positively used word but its positive connotations are interestingly in the context of a person's detailed knowledge of land and nature, rather than his role in the social and economic life of the countryside.

In contrast, there is a host of words to describe the physical setting – the country, the countryside, the land, the landscape, the environment, the scenery, the earth, nature. Note that most of these words are emotionally charged, but positively so. Now, reflect on what charge is carried by the following colloquialisms all listed in Roget's Thesaurus as synonymous for country-dweller: yeoman, rustic, hodge, swain, gaffer, peasant, son or daughter of the soil, boor, churl, bogtrotter, yokel, hind, chawbacon, clod, clodhopper, rube, jayseed, hick, backwoodsman, bumpkin, Tony Lumpkin, country cousin, provincial, hillbilly, village idiot, ninny. Clearly if British culture values the countryside it is as a place not as a people.

French vocabulary, in contrast, has a range of standard terms not only for country people, but also for those who farm the land, for example, *agriculteur*, *cultivateur*, *fermier*, *exploitant* and *paysan*. The last, in particular, implies not only an occupation but a way of life, associated with semi-autonomous family farming and expressed in characteristic social and cultural forms. This notion of a peasant society, though increasingly anachronistic, carries a much greater sense of a distinctive, coherent and separate social order than the nearest equivalent British term – 'rural community' – which is usually used in a loose sense to refer simply to the population of an area or settlement without necessarily implying any particular social cohesion or distinctiveness.

Of course, the non-equivalence of terms does mean that some connotations and nuances tend to be lost in translation. This is not simply due to gaps in the respective vocabularies but also reveals subtle, and occasionally fundamental, differences of outlook. For example, French farmers are engaged in *l'exploitation* (i.e. cultivation) of the land and this is generally valued in a society still unequivocally committed to modernism and the idea of progress, and which appreciates the countryside as a social order and culture wrought from nature, but apparently untarnished by the capitalist exploitation of labour. In contrast, British farmers – the heirs to a long history of capitalist agriculture – are criticised for 'exploitation' of the land by a public which is more ambivalent towards modernism and more concerned with ecological decline.

Another key term which reveals much about French cultural attitudes towards the countryside is the word *'pays'* itself. If the English word 'country' presents problems for the British and the French in its dual denotation of both the countryside and the nation, then these and further problems are presented by the French word *'pays'*. Historically derived from the pre-Roman Gallic word *'pagi'* (Debolo et al. 1982), the *pays* are relatively small areas (larger than a commune but smaller than a *département*), defined – though never formally – by a combination of geographical, social and historical features. The term carries rich connotations including that of an ancient and *sui generis*, local diversity; of distinct landscapes that have been differently settled, differently farmed, differently built on, and have long been recognised and valued as unique by those brought up in them. The common derivation of *pays* and *paysan* also conveys the association of land and life in a humanised landscape as well as the rootedness of traditional society and culture. Since the time of Bonaparte and the administrative rationalisation of France, which in a number of *départements* tried to reproduce them in the configuration of *arrondissements*, the *pays* have lost much of their explanatory power in formally defining rural communities. During the post-war years of large-scale social and economic planning they were largely ignored in the face of grand, modernising, regional objectives, but partly in reaction to the dislocation that resulted, the government introduced the policy of *contrats de pays* in 1975 which provided for development contracts between the state and self-defined grouping of communes. Indeed, despite its elusiveness and its seeming atavism, the *pays* remains an integral element in rural identity.

Academics and researchers have not been unaffected by these distinct cultural perspectives. At the most basic level, for example, there is the urban bias in the social sciences in Britain which generally downplay or ignore rural issues. Occasionally, justification is sought for this neglect in passing reference to Britain's supposed social and cultural homogeneity or to the transcendency of the basic forces of social and economic change; but its gut strength derives more from an intellectual suspicion of rural nostalgia and an implicit assumption that urban social formations are prototypical and rural social formations, if they exist, are atavistic. The consequence is that much of British rural society and politics is *terra incognita*, at least to social scientists. In France, on the other hand, the social sciences have avoided this particular bias, but they have done so largely through differentiating the study of rural affairs, which inevitably has served to reproduce an ideology of the distinctiveness, the separateness, even the autarky of rural society.

In terms of the focus of research and its broad *problématique*, we can likewise discern the different national cultural perspectives at work, in the orientation of British rural studies largely towards the land question, and of French rural studies towards the peasant question. It is certainly true, for example, that a great deal more is known about the rural environment and land use in Britain than about the social processes underlying them: in particular, the social relations surrounding rural change and its distributional consequences remain opaque.

Post-war French rural studies, in contrast, have focused on the integrity of peasant society, documenting its history, its variety and its internal functioning and recording its fate with the integration of the peasantry into a modern, urbanised economy. Despite this commendable concern with human society, French rural studies have not eluded other biases arising from their particular cultural perspective. The most striking, to an outside observer, is a tendency towards deterministic accounts of rural social organisation which portray the peasantry as the prisoners of history and geography. This was most pronounced in the regional studies tradition which so influenced subsequent work in geography, sociology and anthropology and which took as its organising principle the notion of the *pays* as a binding and bounded relationship between landscape and society.

From this broad and comparative review of the rural world in historical and cultural context, we turn now to consider the separate trajectories of post-war rural development because it is the problems thereby addressed and created which have formed much of the specific national research agendas in rural studies.

Bibliography

Agulhon, M. et al., *Les Maires en France du Consulat à nos jours* Publications de la Sorbonne, Paris, 1986.
Bairoch, P. and Levy-Leboyer, M. (eds) *Disparities in Economic Development since the Industrial Revolution* Macmillan, London, 1981.
Barral, P., 'Note historique sur l'emploi du terme "paysan" ', *Etudes Rurales* 21, 1966, 72-3.
— *Les Agrariens Français de Méline à Pisani* A. Colin, Paris, 1968.
Barrell, J. *The Dark Side of the landscape: The Rural Poor in English Paintings* Cambridge University Press, Cambridge, 1980.
Beteille, R. *La France du Vide* Libraires Techniques, Paris, 1981.
Bloch, M. *French Rural History: An Essay on its Basic Characteristics* Routledge & Kegan Paul, London, 1966.
Bodiguel, M. *Le rural en Qluestion* L'Harmattan, Paris, 1986.
Boussard, I., *Vichy et la Corporation Paysanne*, Presses de la FNSP, Paris, 1980.
Burrow, J.W. *Evolution and Society: A Study in Victorian Social Theory* Cambridge University Press, Cambridge, 1966.
Carré, J.J. Dubois, P. and Malinvaud, E., *French Economic Growth* Stanford University Press, Standford, Ca., 1976.
Cleary, M., *Peasants, Politicians and Producers: The Organisation of Agriculture in France since 1918* Cambridge University Press, Cambridge, 1989.
Clout, H.D. *The Land of France 1815-1914* Allen & Unwin, London, 1983.
Cox, G., Lowe, P. and Winter, M. 'Private rights and public responsibilities: the prospects for agricultural and environmental controls' *Journal of Rural Studies* 4, 1988, 323-37.
Crouzet, F., 'Les conséquences économiques de la Révolution', *Annales Historiques de la Révolution Française* 34, 1962, 182-217.
de Vries, J. *European Urbanisation 1500-1800* Methuen, London, 1984.
Debolo, J., Laurent, L. and Maze, J. *Anciens, Actuels... les Pays* CLAR, Sens, 1982.
Duby, G. and Wallon, A. (eds) *Histoire de la France Rurale*, vol 3, Seuil, Paris, 1976.
Dupeux, G., 'La croissance urbaine en France au XIXe siècle' *Revue d'Histoire Economique et Sociale*, 2, 52, 1974, 173-89.
Durupt, M.-J., *les Mouvements d'Action Catholique Rurale* Thèse de IIIe cycle, Paris X, Naterre, 1983.
Dyer, C. *Population and Society in Twentieth Century France* Hodder & Stoughton, London, 1978.
Fairbrother, N., *New Lives, New Landscapes* Architectural Press, London, 1970.
Gaze, J. *Figures in a Landscape: A History of the National Trust* Barrie & Jenkins, London, 1988.
Gervais, M., Servolin, C. and Weil, J., *Une France sans Paysans* Le Seuil, Paris, 1965.
Grantham, G.W., 'Scale and organisation in French farming, 1840-1880', pp. 293-326 of W.N. Parker and E.L. Jones (eds) *European Peasants and their Markets* Princeton University Press, Princeton, 1975.
Hamilton, S.B., 'Continental influences on British civil engineering to 1800', *Archives Internationales d'Histoire des Sciences*, 42, 1958.
Hubscher, R., 'La pluri-activité: un impératif ou un style de vie?' in *La Pluriactivité dans les Familles Agricoles* A.R.F. Editions, Paris, 1984.
Keith, W.J. *The Rural Tradition* Harvester Press, Hassocks, Sussex, 1975.
Kindleberger, C. *Economic Growth in France and Britain: 1851-1950* Harvard University Press, Cambridge, Mass., 1964.

Landes, D. *The Unbound Prometheus* Cambridge University Press, Cambridge, 1969.
Lee, J.M. *Social Leaders and Public Persons: A Study of County Government in Cheshire since 1888* Oxford University Press, Oxford, 1963.
Lowe, P. and Goyder, J., *Environmental Groups in Politics* Allen & Unwin, London, 1984.
Lowe, P., et al. *Countryside Conflicts: The Politics of Farming, Forestry and Conservation* Gower, Aldershot, 1986.
Lowerson, J. 'Battles for the countryside' pp. 258-80 of F. Gloversmith (ed.) *Class, Culture and Social Change: A New View of the 1930s* Harvester Press, Hassocks, Sussex, 1980.
Marsh, J. *Back to the Land: The Pastoral Influences in Victorian England from 1880 to 1914* Quartet, London, 1982.
Mendras, H. 'Politisation, dépolitisation, repolitisation du milieu rural' pp. 251-65 of G. Vedel (ed.) *La Dépolitisation, Mythe ou Réalité*, Presses de la FNSP, Paris, 1962.
— *La Fin des Paysans* SEDEIS, Paris, 1967, and Actes sud, Paris, 1984.
— *Sociétés Paysannes* A. Colin, Paris, 1976.
Mills, D.R. *Lord and Peasant in Nineteenth Century Britain* Croom Helm, London, 1980.
Mingay, G.E. (ed.) *The Agricultural Revolution: Changes in Agriculture 1650-1850* A. & C. Black, London, 1977.
Mitchell, P.C. 'Zoological gardens and the preservation of fauna' *Annual Report of the British Association*, 1912, 478-87.
Muller, P. 'Comment les idées deviennent-elles politiques? La naissance d'une nouvelle idéologie paysanne en France', *Revue Française de Science Politique* 32, 1982, 90-108.
Newby, H. *Country Life: A Social History of Rural England* Weidenfeld & Nicolson, London, 1987.
— *The Countryside in Question* Hutchinson, London, 1988.
Newby, H. et al. *Property, Paternalism and Power: Class and Control in Rural England* Hutchinson, London, 1978.
O'Brien, P. and Keyder, C., *Economic Growth in Britain and France: Two Paths to the Twentieth Century* Allen & Unwin, London, 1978.
Price, R. *The Modernisation of Rural France: Communications Networks and Agricultural Market Structures in Nineteenth Century France* Hutchinson, London, 1983.
Scoville, W.C., *The Persecution of Huguenots and French Economic Development, 1680-1720* University of California Press, Berkeley, 1960.
Sheail, J., *Nature in Trust* Blackie, Glasgow, 1976.
— *Rural Conservation in Inter-war Britain* Clarendon Press, Oxford, 1981.
Shoard, M. *This Land is Our Land: The Struggle for Britain's Countryside* Grafton Books, London, 1987.
Snell, K.D.M., *Annals of the Labouring Poor: Social Change and Agrarian England 1660-1900* Cambridge University Press, Cambridge, 1985.
Soboul, A., *Les Campagnes Montpelliéraines à la Fin de l'Ancien Régime* Paris, 1958, thèse complémentaire.
Thompson, F.M.L., *English Landed Society in the Nineteenth Century* Routledge & Kegan Paul, London, 1963.
Tilly, C., 'Flows of capital and forms of industry in Europe, 1500-1900', *Theory and Society* 13, 1983, 123-42.
Tracy, M. *Agriculture in Western Europe — Challenge and Response 1880-1920* Granada, London, 1982.
Trebilcock, C. *The Industrialisation of the Continental Powers* Longman, London, 1981.
Ward, J.T. and Wilson, R.G., (eds) *Land and Industry: The Landed Estate in the Industrial Revolution* David & Charles, Newton Abbot, 1971.
Weber, E. *Peasants into Frenchmen. The Modernization of Rural France, 1870-1914* Stanford University Press, Stanford, Ca., 1976.

Wiener, M.J., *English Culture and the Decline of the Industrial Spirit 1850-1980* Cambridge University Press, Cambridge, 1981.
Williams, R. *The Country and the City* Chatto and Windus, London, 1973.
Zeldin, T. *France, 1848-1945* vol. 1, Clarendon Press, Oxford, 1973.

2 Rural Development in Post-War Britain and France

Henry Buller and Philip Lowe

Despite their very different experiences during the Second World War – the one occupied, divided, its economy shattered, the other isolated, under regular attack and unable to feed itself – the war's end heralded for both France and Britain major social and economic change, nowhere more than in their rural areas.

Although historians and economists disagree over the extent of French economic decline in the inter-war years (Caron 1979, Malinvaud et al. 1972), the country's economic condition after its liberation was extremely precarious. The deprivations of the war and the systematic dismantling of the French economy by the occupying German forces can be held only partly to blame. France remained by and large a rural nation. In 1900, one in every two working people was in agriculture. By 1950 the figure was still well over one in four (compared with under one in ten in Britain). In that same year, just over half the French population lived in rural areas (compared with less than a quarter in Britain).

The contrast with the highly industrialised and urbanised Great Britain of the time could not be greater. Having already seen the bulk of its rural population emigrate towards the major urban centres in the nineteenth century, Britain emerged from the war not only with an unusual sense of national unity and optimism but also with the basis for an efficient and modern agricultural sector – large land holdings, a substantially reduced agricultural labour force and a strong domestic market.

Given such differences, the achievements of France in the thirty years immediately following the war seem all the more impressive. Her agriculture progressed to the extent that, within twenty-five years, France was able to stand as the second largest exporter of agricultural produce in the world. The French countryside, while retaining much of its pre-modern appearance, was transformed both economically and socially by what, in the agricultural sector at least, has been called the 'silent revolution' (Debatisse 1963).

The British countryside too has had its 'quiet revolution' (Ambrose 1974) but it has been a fundamentally different one, concerned with national social and economic change, although British farming has also undergone a technological revolution. Whereas the function of much of French rural space has become more exclusively agricultural in the post-war period, with the elimination of artisanal and small-scale industrial activity and the undermining of rural services by depopulation, in Britain farming has been relegated to one of a number of ultimately competing rural interests. Finally, although both countries have until recently concurred in seeking to expand agricultural production, there have been, since the war, fundamental differences in the general policy-making stance toward rural areas. In Great Britain, rural planning policy has been guided by two overriding principles, the protection of the countryside and the containment of urban growth. In France, rural areas, by contrast, have been seen, almost universally, as potential development zones.

Post-war rural France: the end of the peasantry

Variously described as the French 'economic miracle' (Caron 1979) or the 'thirty glorious years' (Claval 1988), the period between the end of the Second World War and the beginnings of the world economic crisis of the 1970s saw France rush headlong into modernity. The reconstruction and modernisation of France was predicated upon two major requisites: the transformation of agriculture and state intervention in economic management and regional planning. These were catalysed by a fortuitous confluence of national aspirations, post-war economic aid, the availability of cheap imported oil (France being particularly ill-endowed with domestic energy sources) and state planning initiatives. In the transformation of the agricultural sector, one would also point to the role of the young farmers' movement.

It was not until around 1950 that French agriculture regained its pre-war productivity levels, and the first important changes related more to the context in which farmers operated. On the one hand, rural depopulation once again steadily accelerated and took a new dimension. While earlier waves of outmigration had predominantly involved landless labourers and artisans, the renewed rural exodus began to affect agriculture itself in a major way, and the decline of the working farm population reached 3 per cent (or 160,000) per annum in the 1950s.

On the other hand, agriculture began to be seen by post-war policy-makers, keen to reconstruct the French economy, in a new light; not simply as a domestic food supplier but as an important economic sector. Under Marshall Aid, significant mechanical investment was made, particularly in tractors. In 1950, there was approximately one tractor to every fifteen farms in France whereas in Britain there were ten (Clout 1984). The first National Economic Plan of Jean Monnet, which ran from 1947 to 1953, was chiefly oriented towards heavy industry but nevertheless set specific productivity targets for agriculture aimed at impelling farmers to become surplus producers. In a context of world food shortages, new markets were being opened up, and were needed as France lost its status as a world colonial power. The Treaty of Rome, signed in 1957, was a crucial development which implicitly assigned a key export role to French agriculture.

Yet, while the context and the productivity of agriculture were beginning to change significantly by the early 1950s, the farming community as a whole remained a fairly conservative force. It lacked sufficient technical and mechanical know-how or indeed initiative, was still beset by fragmentation and weak market organisation, remained poor and economically disadvantaged, and saw itself threatened by and isolated from major changes in French society. Clearly a more active state role, beyond the determination of product prices, was required to integrate the agricultural sector into the modernising French economy (Gervais et al. 1976). Increasingly, the demands for such a role were coming from the emerging rural youth movement.

Above all, agriculture remained dominated demographically by elderly family farmers (even by 1960, one in five farmers was over 65) and structurally by small, mixed production units (1,774,000 farms in 1960). Only in the north and around Paris had a specialised commercial agriculture developed. Wishing to continue in agriculture, but also to participate in the modernisation of France, the younger generation were often frustrated by their lowly economic status as family workers and the extreme difficulties they faced in succeeding to the family farm. As French agriculture began to move into surplus, the burgeoning rural youth movement, inspired and led initially by the *Jeunesse Agricole Chrétienne* (JAC) and later the *Centre National des Jeunes Agriculteurs* (CNJA), sought major improvements in rural conditions and a fuller contribution from rural people to national life. This demanded a fresh approach towards agriculture. The state already intervened in certain sectors (notably wheat prices) but although its intervention was aimed ostensibly at family farmers, the main beneficiaries were the large, commercially oriented producers of the Beauce and Paris Basin. During the difficult years of the 1950s, which saw the end of French interests in Indo-China and the Algerian War, however, the old guard of French agriculture swung sharply to the Right in an attempt to hang on to the status quo and in fear of the possibility of land nationalisation. But with the advent of the Fifth Republic under de Gaulle, a fresh and dynamic approach to rural reform was initiated under the auspices of the Agriculture Minister, Edgar Pisani, drawing its inspiration largely from the CNJA. The leadership of the CNJA had come to recognise that not all peasants could remain on the land and that the migration of some farmers was essential if those who remained were to survive and prosper (Cleary 1989). This proved the rationale for state-supported agricultural restructuring.

A set of agricultural acts emerged between 1960 and 1962 (the most important being the 1960 *Loi d'orientation agricole* and the 1962 *Loi complémentaire*) which, more than anything, prompted the transformation of the nation's agriculture and set the tone for the productivism that is still in place today. They are sometimes referred to as the 'agricultural charter of the Fifth Republic' but behind their many social and economic provisions was a pragmatic assessment of the prerequisites for French agricultural domination of the recently established European Community. Though the aim was to create a progressive competitive agriculture, the legislation ultimately and intentionally avoided the central and persistent contradiction of French agriculture – its family-farm base. Even by 1973, only 12 per cent of French farms employed permanent farm-workers outside the family, although 25 per cent employed temporary workers. Any acceptable reform had to be compatible with the persistence of this form of farming. What the new policy sought to achieve was the elimination of the many small and marginal farms to allow an overall increase in the average size of holdings, and the consolidation and modernisation of the medium-sized family farm. Significantly the legislation which introduced a mechanism for a more rational redistribution of land released by the rural exodus was also meant to curb land accumulation.

The agriculture acts of the early 1960s introduced a series of measures and policy instruments amongst whose aims were those to 'establish parity between agriculture and other economic sectors' and 'to compensate family farming for its natural and economic disadvantages relative to other economic activities' (Act of 5 August 1960). Underlying these intentions was the hope, and it was little more than a hope, that the French agricultural population would continue to decline at a high rate. Already, between 1929 and 1955, the number of farms had dropped from 4 million to just over 2.25 million. Behind the Fifth Republic's 'Charter' was the hope that the decline would continue to under 1 million (a figure it has yet to reach).

The measures and policies introduced in the early 1960s served three basic aims: the structural reform of land holdings; the demographic renewal of the farm population; and the social reform of conditions of work and employment in the agricultural sector. Additional measures encouraged farmers to cooperate in the acquisition and use of agricultural machinery. As if to illustrate the continued importance of the family unit in agriculture, the most common arrangements under these latter provisions concern links between fathers and sons.

As a result of these acts, agriculture became integrated into national economic management. In each *département*, a state-appointed agricultural office was to oversee the implementation of policy. The productivist and increasingly mechanised agricultural sector moved further and further into surplus production. As France's *'petrole vert'*, its contribution to the Gross National Product grew dramatically in real terms, though proportionally it fell. In 1913, when agriculture accounted for 37 per cent of the French working population, it produced 29 per cent of the GNP. By 1938 the figures had fallen to 31 per cent and 21 per cent respectively. By 1974, the 11 per cent of the nation's active population still in agriculture contributed just 6 per cent of the GNP. Increasing substitution of capital for labour has reduced the farm workforce (by around five million since the war) and has substantially raised the standard of living of those who have remained.

Most significantly, however, the reforms initiated in the 1960s and augmented by successive administrations, have transformed the role of the farmer both within French society, and, more importantly, within rural society. Despite their commitment to a family farming structure, the laws of the 1960s sounded the death knell for the traditional peasantry, its way of life and culture (Mendras 1964, Gervais et al. 1965).

The relative tardiness of France's agricultural transformation delayed the economic and functional diversification of the French countryside. For twenty years following the war, the economic development of rural areas was interpreted almost solely in terms of agricultural modernisation. The sole exceptions were the various development agencies established in the late 1950s in some southern regions, such as the *Compagnie nationale d'aménagement du Bas-Rhône-Languedoc* (Laborie 1985). For the most part, a kind of unstated Darwinism prevailed, which, practically if not rhetorically, was devoid of sentimentality towards the French countryside and its shrinking rural communities. Depopulation was encouraged because the farm population was considered excessive and the buoyant urban economy needed and could absorb the excess. The result was disruptive social change in both rural and urban France.

Partly in reaction, the 1960s saw the extension of state planning to encompass the objectives of economic decentralisation and regional development to produce a more balanced pattern of national growth, one not so exclusively centred on Paris. The social provisions of agricultural reform legislation themselves demanded retraining and alternative, off-farm employment opportunities for those leaving agriculture. Moreover, specific countermeasures were needed if formerly marginal farming regions were not to be rendered completely unviable through agricultural competition and continuing depopulation. Such areas as Aveyron and parts of the Massif Central were being emptied of people, their landscapes abandoned after centuries of cultivation.

Early French experience with *l'aménagement du territoire* (land use planning), however, focused upon the stimulation of regional economies, usually concentrated upon major provincial centres, and only the most favoured or accessible rural areas benefited as a result of 'knock on effects' from urban centres (Le Coz 1973). Mounting evidence of the enervating impact of depopulation on marginal rural regions (*Documentation Française* 1972) and increasing calls for a more integrated approach to rural regions (Marquart 1973) led to the gradual promulgation, from the late 1960s onwards, of a rural development programme which, though implicitly covering agriculture, nonetheless cast its economic net wider than traditional primary activities. Thus the key 1967 *Loi d'orientation foncière* became the first piece of legislation to introduce the term 'rural planning'. Conceived as a response to the gathering crisis of depopulation and rural decline (Madiot 1987), the programme later responded more directly to the growing demand for local development and the devolution of planning decision-making. Thus from a narrowly sectoral orientation, French rural planning has gradually assumed a more local orientation and one more inclusive of the range of physical development issues.

At the national level, French rural planning has evolved, over the last twenty-five years, into a growth-oriented enabling mechanism for often state-led economic and infrastructural development. This was characterised, until 1982, by the strong verticalisation of the planning process and the integration of local land-use policies with national and regional development objectives. The formation of the agency for regional planning the *Délégation pour l'aménagement du territoire et à l'action régionale* (DATAR) – in 1963, the establishment of 'external state agencies' – such as the *Direction départementale de l'agriculture* and the *Direction départementale de l'équipement* – at the local level, and, finally, the setting up of a national planning code have all contributed to the predominant sense of top-down spatial and economic management.

Beside the goal of agricultural growth, contemporary (i.e. post-1960s) rural policy-making has had two principal objectives: the diversification of the rural economy and the rational allocation of rural land use. The first has been addressed through a succession of regional policy-mechanisms, heavily supported by state funding and frequently integrated into national economic planning. Beginning in the 1950s with the various development agencies of the Rhône, Corsica and others, the next major policy initiative was the creation in 1967 of the four rural renewal zones of Bretagne/Manche, Limousin, Auvergne and the mountainous regions covering in all some 27 per cent of the French land area and including one third of the country's farms. In 1973, it was complemented by the mountain policy for all communes over 600m. The area covered under this policy amounted to 9 million hectares or one fifth of France. In addition to these broad designations, which were primarily intended to encourage development projects, a series of local development planning mechanisms has been successively introduced (Buller 1988, Houée 1989), including the *Plans d'aménagement rural* in 1970 (ACEAR 1978), the *Contrats de Pays* in 1975 (Chadeau 1978) and the *Chartes Intercommunales* (Champagne 1987), which replaced the *Plans d'aménagement rural* in 1983. Individual communes, often too small to act on their own as agents of economic development, have been encouraged to collaborate in formulating and implementing policy, either through the *Chartes* and *Contrats* or through the establishment of special intercommunal agencies.

The rational allocation of land use, the second branch of an emerging rural policy, has been achieved through structure and local plans, the *Schema directeurs d'aménagement et d'urbanisme* and the *Plans d'occupation des sols*. Since 1982, the land-use planning system, originally set up in 1967, has been greatly devolved (Stevenson 1986), giving considerably more power in land allocation and development control to individual commune mayors. Although the land allocation process in France has never been as important in rural policy-making as it has in Great Britain, where it is the principal tool of non-agricultural rural policy-making, the increasing adoption of local plans by French rural communes following decentralisation is bound to promote a growing debate, within individual communes, about the deployment of land.

With societal modernisation, the distinction between rural and urban has become blurred though this has occurred much more recently than in Great Britain where counterurbanisation and industrial decentralisation are well established. Not only are these processes more novel in France, but also, given the nation's size, their impact is less immediately apparent except in the hinterlands of the major conurbations. Nevertheless, since the population turnaround first became evident in the 1970s, a 'profound change' has taken place in rural France (Chapuis 1986), resulting in part from the agricultural modernisation and rural development policies outlined above, yet in part also from the effects of secular economic and social changes observable throughout the Western world. Between 1975 and 1982 rural population actually increased for the first time in a century, by almost 1 per cent per year. Nevertheless, the geographically restricted impact of such growth has yet to reverse the *désertification* of the marginal zones of rural France.

More important, however, has been the change in rural socio-economic composition it has wrought. For the French, the most fundamental consequence is that farmers are now a minority, and a dwindling minority, within rural communes. From being half the rural population in 1962, they represent today less than a quarter of rural residents (DATAR 1988). Linked to the industrialisation of the countryside, blue-collar workers have become the largest social group (Mathieu 1985), representing, in 1982, 32.7 per cent of all rural households (Chapuis 1986). During the general period of labour-shedding between 1975 and 1982, rural communes showed non-agricultural job growth rates that were twice as high as those for urban areas, with, most dramatically, a 3 per cent growth in manufacturing against an urban decline of 11 per cent (DATAR 1988). Also of significance is the growing number of service and tertiary sector workers in rural areas. Although two-thirds of all tertiary employment is still urban-based, it is growing faster in rural communes (18.4 per cent between 1975 and 1982) than in urban ones (14.5 per cent for the same period; DATAR 1988).

The rural revival is still relatively new and fairly localised in France and its social and political implications are only just beginning to be felt (as in the 1989 municipal elections, for example). Inevitably, it has had its negative effects (Brun 1986). Indeed, it has been predicated upon the reduced role and importance of the farmer in French rural society, a reduction that neither the farming community nor, perhaps, the nation as a whole has yet really come to terms with (Kayser 1984). For some commentators, the autonomy and cohesiveness of a rural society dominated by agriculture is being replaced by a segregated and diversified society in which class divisions are becoming more overt (Jollivet 1974); in which traditional occupational hierarchies have given way to stratification based on different lifestyles and consumption patterns; and in which explicit conflicts over economic direction and land-use priorities are becoming more common (Lamarche et al. 1980). Such changes are, however, familiar to observers of British rural society. Without descending into sentimentality, many French commentators are aware that the *fin des paysans* has also meant the end of much of the distinctiveness and originality of rural France.

Post-war rural Britain: towards a middle-class territory

In stark contrast to the French experience, in which a traditionally diverse, largely pre-industrial, rural economy and society finally disappeared, giving way to a specialised, modern agricultural sector, rural Britain has moved from a post-war situation where most of the countryside was oriented largely to primary production to one of great social and economic plurality in which agriculture, though still the dominant land use, is no longer anywhere the dominant function of rural regions. Although the beginnings of a similar re-diversification are emerging in certain parts of France, notably those close to the major urban centres, the current social and economic heterogeneity of rural Britain denotes a process of post-war transformation that has been, in many respects, the inverse of that in France.

Despite the fact that both nations shared similar post-war aspirations and indeed broad policy goals – for example, the nationalisation of certain key industries, state support for a productivist agriculture, the establishment of a universal welfare system and a concern to redress imbalances in regional economic growth – certain very fundamental differences account for the divergence of rural development trajectories. The first was the state of British agriculture and its anticipated function in the immediate post-war period. The second was the relative dominance, in both economic and population terms, of urban Britain and the consequences for economic and physical planning. The final major difference lay in the 'symbolic' role of the British countryside and the emergence of environmental considerations in rural policy-making. Underlying all three, and marking a distinct break with traditions of decentralised administration and minimal state intervention, was the emergence of the central state, under the catalysis of war-time experience, as the principal 'architect' of rural policy, which in both stimulating agriculture and offsetting the differences in social and economic conditions between urban and rural populations, has transformed the fabric of rural society.

Britain had long since ceased to be a rural nation. Indeed, by the turn of the century, the emerging preservation movement had begun to refer to rural Britain as something already vanishing and in need of urgent protection. By 1950, some 78.5 per cent of the British population lived in urban areas and agriculture accounted for only 6 per cent of the nation's workforce and of GDP, which made Britain by far the most urbanised and least agricultural country in Europe.

As in France, the inter-war years had been lean ones for farmers. Indeed British agriculture had been in a chronic state of depression since the 1880s and could supply only a third of national food requirements (Whetham 1978). Such dependency on imported food suddenly became a question of national survival with the outbreak of war. Agriculture was therefore placed on a war footing with strict market regulation of all crops, guaranteed prices and central purchasing. In each county, War Agricultural Executive Committees were established, mainly comprising leading local farmers, to supervise the drive for greater production and to encourage, cajole and if necessary compel farmers to cooperate. Farming boomed and, as the war ended, farmers held their breath for fear of a return to the conditions of the 1920s and 1930s. The episode, though, had clearly demonstrated the strategic necessity of increasing home supplies of food and timber, as well as the role government could play in stimulating production (Self and Storing 1962).

Already, by the late 1940s, British farms were large by European standards – on average, two-and-a-half times their French counterparts – and the agricultural workforce was much diminished – a third of the number per agricultural area as in France. Productivity and mechanisation levels were correspondingly much higher. Most farms, for example, had a tractor and the use of combine harvesters was becoming common in the cornlands of the East. The state-led modernisation of British agriculture that followed the war, therefore, was less to do with socio-structural change, though this undoubtedly happened, than with market management and political support. Post-war agricultural policy induced a dramatic rise in productivity and, in doing so, facilitated further labour force reductions and the gradual dissociation of modern agriculture from rural society (Newby 1979; Bowers and Cheshire 1983).

The 1947 Agriculture Act, the linchpin of post-war agricultural policy, formally established a system of annually-negotiated guaranteed prices for almost all staple products. On the one hand, this protected farmers from market fluctuations and cheap imports while encouraging them to produce more. On the other, it enabled the state both to manage the expansion of the agricultural sector and to maintain cheap prices to the consumer. A system of deficiency payments preserved a delicate balance between the state's overall management of the sector and the autonomy of the individual producer. Research and extension services accompanied guaranteed prices to encourage increased output and, particularly in the uplands, following the 1946 Hill Farming Act, various grants and subsidies were provided to support farming and the modernisation and rationalisation of holdings (Self and Storing 1962).

Initially, expansion of output was encouraged regardless of public cost but as post-war food shortages receded, the emphasis switched to encouraging increased efficiency, particularly of labour, and containing the costs of price subsidies. On entry to the EEC in 1972, Britain became subject to the explicit protectionism of the Common Agricultural Policy. With the abandonment of one of the basic principles of British trading policy since the repeal of the Corn Laws – that there should be an open door for imports of cheap foodstuffs – the burden of guaranteed prices shifted from the Exchequer to the consumer, through higher food prices.

The economic impact of post-war govenment support for British agriculture has been scarcely less dramatic than for France. Output has expanded enormously. Britain is now self-sufficient in temperate foodstuffs and has emerged as a significant food exporter. The growth in yields has been outstripped by the increase in productivity; and some three-quarters of the workforce have been shed as farming has become ever more mechanised and capital-intensive. Production has been concentrated on fewer and fewer, large-scale specialised enterprises. The number of farms has fallen by about a half. Thus, the United Kingdom still has by far the largest average farm size in the EEC (69.3 hectares compared with 28.2 hectares in France, in 1986). One consequence, though, of the sharper decline in the number of agricultural workers than of farmers is a resurgence of family farming. Three-quarters of British farms now employ no full-time hired workers at all, which represents a definite convergence with the rest of Europe. But most of Britain's family farmers are highly specialised, technically sophisticated producers and with the exception of Northern Ireland and the crofting counties of Scotland (where turn-of-the-century land reforms effectively created peasant proprietorships), Britain remains apart in its lack of a class of small farmers (Cox, Lowe and Winter 1986).

Thus, although Britain and France shared a similar post-war drive towards a more productive agricultural sector – and France has surely gone further and had much further to go in this direction – the principal differences between them lie, first, in the circumstances of their agricultural sectors in the immediate post-war period and, secondly, in the early and wide-ranging intervention of the British state in regulating and promoting agricultural development.

Britain also emerged from the war with a far more focused notion of the function of its countryside, defined in terms of the demands of a largely urbanised nation. The primary one was domestic food supply, but the preservation and open air movements had also established as a prominent social objective the protection of the countryside, its landscapes and wildlife, for their cultural, scientific and recreational value. Post-war policy for land-use planning, nature conservation and amenity protection implicitly accepted the role of farmers as the guardians of the countryside. The major threat to its integrity and its agricultural potential was seen to come from unchecked and haphazard housing sprawl and industrial development. Two of the major objectives of the comprehensive land-use planning system established in 1947 were, therefore, to protect agricultural land and to contain urban growth. While agricultural activities escaped the coverage of planning control, other economic activities were largely deflected from rural areas by a very restrictive system of development control. What non-agricultural development that occurred was channelled into selected and concentrated locations. Thus as agricultural productivity began to rise sharply, there were few alternative employment opportunities for the rural working class to prevent further depopulation and community disintegration. The new prosperity which state support brought to agriculture did not ensure a place in the sun for farm-labourers: their wages lagged consistently behind the average for industrial workers and mechanisation steadily squeezed them off the land (Newby 1977).

The reduction in the farming population has been more than matched by the movement of middle-class commuters, retirees and second-homers into the countryside. Growing affluence and car-ownership have enabled more and more people to realise their dream of a home in the country. Tight planning controls around the major cities and the construction of motorways have pushed housing pressures further out into free-standing towns and villages and more remote regions. By the mid-1970s, even such classic areas of out-migration as mid-Wales and the Scottish Highlands were experiencing net population growth, though many isolated settlements still suffered decline.

Migration into the countryside has been very much a movement of middle-class owner-occupiers with their own transport. The operation of the planning system has reinforced the selective effect of people's private means, as those who have settled in the countryside have sought to use the preservation procedures of the planning system to safeguard their own residential amenity. The great exodus from the cities, though still continuing, gathered momentum in the 1960s and peaked in the 1970s. This massive population movement has disrupted established social hierarchies and provoked new divisions and tensions in rural communities (Newby 1979). The ex-urban newcomers have none of the political quiescence of the rural working class, and have challenged the political and social leadership of farmers and landowners. Gradually they have taken over many of the established institutions of rural society and have created new ones reflecting their interests and particular visions of the rural community. Indeed, many of the rural issues which have arisen in recent years derive from the expectations which the middle class have taken with them into the countryside – such as the expectations of urban standards of service provision and an unchanging countryside.

The provisions of the post-war Welfare State also facilitated this social transformation. The fact that at the war's end the vast bulk of the British population was living in urban areas and that social problems of poverty and poor health were more clearly visible there, determined the way in which social policy evolved not least for rural areas. Although the Welfare State, established in the immediate post-war period, was predominantly oriented towards the urban population, its provisions were intended to benefit everyone. The National Health Service, social security and standardised service provision all directly boosted the quality of life for rural residents. Though access to them was undoubtedly easier in the towns, these universalistic and cross-subsidised social provisions eliminated most of the inconveniences and disparities traditionally associated with rural life, and thus made rural living a potentially much more attractive proposition, not least for mobile ex-urban migrants.

Underlying these various social policies, however, was a predisposition towards centralisation and an implicit belief in the 'trickle down' effects of benefits to outlying populations (Cloke 1983). In general terms, centralisation policies – whether concerned with accommodating residential growth in designated areas, or stimulating the economic renewal of market towns, or 'rationalising' service provision to improve cost-effectiveness – have reinforced the ultimately divisive social and economic changes set in motion by post-war affluence and protectionist rural planning policy (Lowe, Bradley and Wright 1986). Those wealthy or mobile enough have been indirectly subsidised in locating beyond the 'rational' limits of journey-to-work zones, beyond the immediate range of access to commercial centres and far from the catchment areas of concentrated public housing and educational facilities. In doing so, they have introduced new resource demands, closer to those of urban Britain.

Economic diversification has followed several steps behind and has arisen less through deliberate policy measures than as the indirect consequence of the social diversification of rural areas and employment decline in the primary sector as well as through wider processes of economic restructuring (Bradley and Lowe 1984). The beginnings of the urban-rural shift in UK manufacturing activity have been dated from the late 1950s (Fothergill and Gudgin 1982). The greatest relative shift occurred in the late 1960s and early 1970s and though they experienced some absolute loss of manufacturing jobs during the recession of the late 1970s and early 1980s, rural areas continued to increase their share of national employment in manufacturing. The most favoured regions for this 'ruralisation of industry' have been southern England and Wales (Fothergill et al. 1985, p. 151), with small towns being favoured locations. Firms are typically small, often branch plants, involved in light manufacturing and find it advantageous to locate in rural areas because of such factors as space availability, an amenable, low cost, labour force and an attractive residential environment (Healey and Ilbery, 1985).

Though manufacturing employment had outstripped agricultural employment in rural areas by 1981, the source of work for most rural residents as for urban residents had become the service sector (Hodge 1986) and evidence was emerging that some types of service employment were growing faster in small towns and rural areas than in the largest urban centres (Crawford et al. 1985). The growth of a residential middle class has drawn into country towns employment in personal and commercial services, as well as in public administration to add to the traditional employment in tourism, retailing and the rural professions. The availability of pools of relatively cheap female labour has also encouraged the decentralisation of some administrative and clerical work. In addition, favoured rural areas, especially in North Wales, East Anglia, the South and the South West, because of their accessibility, environmental attractions and availability of highly skilled manpower, have drawn in employment in scientific, technical and financial services.

The shift of manufacturing and service employment to rural areas has been largely unplanned. Government recognition of the economic plight of depressed rural regions, nevertheless, has a comparatively long history in Britain: the formation of the Development Commission in 1909 predates the creation of the, albeit much broader-based DATAR in France by over fifty years. Yet, it was not until the mid-1960s that the problems of declining rural areas became a specific focus of regional economic and industrial policy, following on belated official recognition that continued rural depopulation posed a major threat to the very viability of remote rural communities and also linked with government concern over the rise of Celtic nationalism.

The success of the initiatives pursued by a number of development agencies in diversifying rural employment and housing opportunities at the local level has been widely recognised (Buller and Wright 1990), though one might add two qualifying observations. First, given the broad aims of post-war rural policy in Britain, the increasingly marked reluctance of central government to redress market forces has meant that specific rural development programmes have tended to be short-term and remedial in their effects rather than creating significant opportunities for sustained economic diversification. Under the Thatcher government, deference to market forces and reliance on private capital have become the touchstones of public policy, and rural development agencies have been obliged even more to accommodate themselves to private sector initiatives. The contrast with the French approach to rural development planning is stark. The unique combination, characteristic of post-war French economic management, of private capital investment taking its lead from state initiatives and plans has led in recent years to a wide range of rural development measures offering not only financial assistance but also increased policy-making autonomy to rural communities.

In Britain, largely because of EC constraints, agriculture remains the only major productive sector where the state intervenes systematically to structure market forces. But even here, the opportunity to pursue social objectives through the support mechanisms has been eschewed. Indeed, the second qualifying observation would be that British rural development policies, again in stark contrast to the French experience, have existed in isolation from agricultural policy-making. Attempts to unite the two – most notably in the Rural Development Boards of the late 1960s and early 1970s (which were inspired by the French SAFERs) – have been marked by their failure. In Britain, the two policy communities have remained distinct in all but certain upland areas, where integrated rural development practices have only recently begun to be applied – often, significantly, with the stimulus emerging from the need to reconcile local economic development with environmental protection.

More generally, it is environmental rather than social concerns which have emerged as the major challenge to agricultural intensification. As we have seen, the rural preservationists of the inter-war and early post-war years regarded farming as a force for conserving and protecting the countryside. Few anticipated the rapid transformation in agriculture practices that was to occur. As the scale of the post-war revolution in agriculture became apparent there was a shift in emphasis in preservationist circles from a focus on urban and industrial pressures as the main threat to landscape and wildlife to a preoccupation with the destructive effects of changing farming and forestry practices and technologies (Lowe et al. 1986). With the social transformation of rural areas, such criticisms were increasingly voiced by middle-class, rural residents. And, with the advent of the modern environmental movement, the aesthetic, natural history and amenity concerns of the earlier preservationist movement have been subsumed within a wider ecological critique of modern, intensive agriculture which has raised questions concerning its long-term sustainability and its consequences for environmental health.

Thus the period since the mid-1970s has seen the end of unchallenged agricultural expansionism and a new readiness to 'take on' powerful agricultural interests. To the environmental challenge has been added political criticism of the costs of agricultural support, the embarrassment of overproduction, the issue of farm animal welfare and public alarm over food purity. A sense of crisis and lack of direction have characterised agricultural policy throughout most of the 1980s. Elements of a post-productivist agriculture, though, are beginning to take shape, with farmers being paid in Environmentally Sensitive Areas, Sites of Special Scientific Interest and some set-aside schemes to maintain or recreate landscapes and wildlife habitats; with the possibility that stronger pollution safeguards will necessitate a shift to less intensive farming methods; with organic farming being canvassed as an extensification option; and with farmers generally being encouraged to be more market-and consumer-oriented and more alert to any opportunities to develop their land for new leisure and commercial uses. The social functions of rural space are thus being redefined with greater emphasis on its consumption role.

A rapprochement?

In the final decades of the twentieth century rural Britain and rural France find themselves undergoing broadly similar processes of dramatic change. Chapuis (1986) refers to 'profound change' which has 'astonished even the most optimistic', while DATAR (1988) highlight a 'profound and lasting transformation'. North of the Channel, commentators are talking of a 'rural renaissance' (Pacione 1984) and a process of 'rural rejuvenation'. Newby (1979) refers to a rapid and far-reaching transformation while Blunden and Curry (1985, p. 13) claim that 'change in the countryside is taking place more quickly, more dramatically and with greater consequences than ever before'. The essence of this change is the move away from a contryside dominated physically, economically and socially by productivist agriculture.

The principal differences between the two nations relate more to the different starting positions and time-scale of this diversification process than to its present-day effects. Both have seen wide-scale counterurbanisation forces at work in recent decades (Champion 1989). In Britain, the urban-rural population shift began after a long period of urban concentration and has been part of a general evolution of settlement structure within the tight constraints of a physical planning system oriented towards urban containment. In France, the counter-urbanisation process began significantly later and, in its essentially peri-urban character, coincided with rather than superseded the general phase of France's late urban expansion. In both countries, however, counterurbanisation and the sense of rural renewal this has engendered have masked the continuing depopulation from rural areas and the associated class displacement. Post-war rural change has undoubtedly been much more traumatic in France which has squeezed into one generation the transition from a pre-industrial to a post-industrial countryside that in Britain occurred over several generations. The result has been social dislocation on a greater scale registered in the lives of individuals, families and communities. In Britain, however, with the bulk of the population so thoroughly urbanised and removed from any rural roots, counter-urbanisation has engendered more pronounced tensions with indigenous populations.

Accompanying social diversification in both nations has been economic diversification. Yet, whereas in France, this process has been an intended consequence of recent, targeted policy measures that have from the outset incorporated agriculture into their developmental objectives, in Britain the dispersal of manufacturing and service employment has been largely unplanned and certainly not coordinated with the goals of argicultural or rural policy. Current British government policy in deregulating the land-use planning system to facilitate market-led economic development has not been the cause of a rural restructuring process that began twenty to thirty years previously. That process has been intrinsically linked to and in part stems from, the social recomposition of rural Britain. Yet, a similar conclusion in France, supported by evidence of the growing predominance of blue-collar workers in rural communes, hides the still limited spatial effect of diversification in that country. British rural, social and economic development has touched even the remotest areas resulting ultimately in a far more profound diversification of British rural space. Therefore, despite their broadly equivalent urban populations today, only France has been able to retain its fundamental rurality as a nation, but for how much longer?

Bibliography

Ambrose, P., *The Quiet Revolution: Social Change in a Sussex Village 1871-1971*, Chatto & Windus, London, 1974.
Blunden, J. and Curry, N., (eds), *The Changing Countryside*, Croom Helm, London, 1985.
Bowers, J.K. and Cheshire, P., *Agriculture, the Countryside and Land Use* Methuen, London, 1983.
Bradley, T. and Lowe, P. (eds) *Locality and Rurality: Economy and Society in Rural Regions* Geo Books, Norwich, 1984.
Brun, A., France: rural development in a dynamic context, in *European Review of Agricultural Economics*, 13 (3), 1986, 309-26.
Buller, H., *French Rural Planning Policy*, End of Grant Report to the ESRC, London, 1988.
Buller, H. and Wright, S., (eds), *Rural Development: Problems and Policies*, Avebury, Aldershot, 1990.
Caron, F., *An Economic History of Modern France*, Methuen, London, 1979.
Chadeau, A., 'Les Contrats de Pays', in *Moniteur des Travaux Publics*, 1978, 49.
Champagne, G., 'Les Chartes intercommunales', in *Revue de Droit Rural*, 1987, 156, 357-369.
Champion, A.G. (ed.), *Counterurbanization: The Changing Pace and Nature of Population Deconcentration* Edward Arnold, London, 1989.
Chapuis, R., *Les Ruraux Français*, Masson, Paris, 1986.

Claval, P., 1988, La France des grandes organisation, in X, de Planhol, geographie Historique de la France, Fayard, Paris, 473-531.
Cleary, M., *Peasants, Politicians and Producers*, Cambridge University Press, Cambridge, 1989.
Cloke, P. *An Introduction to Rural Settlement Planning* Methuen, London, 1983.
Clout, H., *A Rural Policy for the EEC?*, Methuen, London, 1984.
Cox, G., Lowe, P. and Winter, M., *Agriculture: People and Policies* Allen and Unwin, London, 1986.
Crawford, P. Fothergill, S. and Monk, S., *The Effects of Business Rates on the Location of Employment* Industrial Location Research Group, Department of Land Economy, University of Cambridge, 1985.
DATAR, *Nouvelles images de la France rural*, Datar, Paris, 1988.
Debatisse, M., *La revolution silencieuse*, Calmann-Levy, Paris, 1962.
Documentation Française, *La transformation du monde rurale*, Travaux et Recherches de Prospective, No. 26, 1972.
Forthergill, S. and Gudgeon, G., *Unequal Growth*, Heinemann, London, 1984.
Gervais, M., Servolin, C. and Weil, J., *Une France sans paysans*, Seuil, Paris, 1965.
Gervais, M., Jollivet, M. and Tavernier, Y., *La France rurale*, 1914 *A nos jours*, Seuil, Paris, 1976.
Healey, M.J. and Ilbery, B.W. (eds), *The Industrialization of the Countryside* Geo Books, Norwich, 1985.
Hodge, I., *Countryside Change: A Review of Research* Economic and Social Research Council, London, 1986.
Houée, P., *Les politiques de developpement rurale*, Economica, Paris, 1979.
Jollivet, M., (ed), *Sociétés paysannes ou lutte de classes au village*, Volume 2 of *Les collectivités rurales françaises*, A. Colin, Paris, 1974.
Kayser, B., 'Subversion des villages française', *Etudes rurales*, 93/94, 1984.
Lamarche, H., Rogers, S. and Karnooth, Cl., *Paysans, femmes et citoyens*, Actes Sud, Paris, 1980.
Laborie, J-P, et al., *La politique française d'aménagement du territoire de 1950 à 1985*, Documentation Française, Paris, 1985.
Le Coz, J., 'Niveaux de structuration de l'espace rural Française: les Plans d'aménagement rural', *Bulletin de la société Languedocienne de géographie*, 7 (2), 1973, 135-68.
Lowe, P., Bradley, T. and Wrights, S. (eds), *Deprivation and Welfare in Rural Areas* Geo Books, Norwich, 1986.
Lowe, P. et al. *Countryside Conflicts* Gower, Aldershot, 1986.
Madiot, Y., 'La politique d'aménagement du territoire entre les exigences de solidarité et d'efficacité', *Revue de droit rural*, 153, 1987, 197-200.
Malinvaud, E., Carré, J.J. and Dubois, P., *La croissance française*, Seuil, Paris, 1972.
Marquart, D., 'Une politique de conversion rurale', *Amenagement du territoire et développement régional*, 6, 1973, 243-68.
Mathieu, N., 'Un nouveau modèle d'analyse des transformations en cours: la diversification-spécialisation de l'espace rural français', *Economie rurale*, 166, 1985, 38-44.
Mendras, H., *La fin des paysans*, Paris, 1964.
Newby, H. *The Deferential Worker* Allen Lane, London, 1977.
— *Green and Pleasant Land*, Hutchinson, London, 1979.
— *Country Life: A Social History of Rural England*, Cardinal, London, 1987.
Pacione, M., *Rural Geography*, Harper & Row, London, 1984.
Self, P. and Storing, H. *The State and the Farmer* Allen and Unwin, London, 1962.
Stevenson, C., Recent developments in French planning law, *Journal of Planning and Environmental Law*, October 1986, 720-26.

Whetham, E.H., *The Agrarian History of England and Wales*, VIII, 1914–1939, Cambridge University Press, Cambridge, 1978.

3 Concepts, Definitions and Research Traditions

Maryvonne Bodiguel, Henry Buller and Philip Lowe

Just as distinct conceptions of 'rural' are embedded in the social, economic and cultural history of Britain and France, so the definitions of 'rurality' or rural 'space' employed by officials and social scientists have been similarly conditioned by separate national traditions. They have reflected changing political, and economic considerations, different institutional priorities, and statistical and geographical factors. Moreover, whereas the French approach has been explicit, deductive and universalistic, the British approach has been implicit, inductive and contextual. Undoubtedly, this partly reflects national stylistic differences in the relationship between ideas, social inquiry and state policy; with the French more formalistic, abstract and statist, and the British more pragmatic, empirical and liberal. But the effort and importance given to defining the rural in France also reflect the much greater salience accorded it as a significant social and spatial category.

Contemporary social and economic trends in Great Britain, most notably regional economic restructuring and counterurbanisation, have led to a newly emergent academic interest in rural change (Lowe et al. 1989). In France too, scholars and policy-makers are finding themselves increasingly obliged to reassess their ideological attitudes to the rural world in the light of social and economic changes which have undermined the distinctiveness of rural society and have created a sense of crisis in French rural studies (*Association des Ruralistes Français* 1987). To fully understand the notion of 'rural' in Britain and France, one needs to look therefore at both the operational and practical conceptions of the countryside and the ways in which academic traditions have addressed rural space and rural issues.

French rural space

The demographic approach

The statistical definition of rural space in France is virtually a century old and, despite occasional revision, has remained a vitally important research and administrative tool. Rural communes are defined as those which are physically distinct from urban agglomerations and have no more than 2,000 inhabitants living within any single built-up area (a contiguous 'built-up area' being in turn defined as that where the distance between houses does not exceed 200 metres). The rural population is then taken to be all the inhabitants of the rural communes. To take into account demographic and other changes, the French *Institut National de la Statistique et de l'Economie* (INSEE) has regularly adjusted this basic criteria of definition (Bontron 1976). In 1965, INSEE formally defined specific 'urban units' composed of a town centre, its suburbs and the adjoining rural commues that were judged to lie within the town's zone of attraction. Later, in 1975, by taking account of such factors as daily commuting distances, the proportion of the non-agricultural rural population and the number and size of industrial, commercial and administrative units, INSEE defined the *Zones de Peuplement Industriel ou Urbain* (ZPIU). In incorporating a number of rual communes within each ZPIU, INSEE created the distinction between these and the 'profound rural' communes. One of the effects of these revisions, however, has been to compromise the comparative strength of rural census data particularly in the study of rural socio-economic change.

The census of 1982 showed a rural population growth in France of 6.2 per cent between censuses, against an overall national growth rate of 3.2 per cent and an urban population growth of only 2.2 per cent. Such rural growth has, nevertheless, been very uneven. Of the 31,545 rural communes (there being 36,433 communes as a whole in mainland France), only those with over 200 inhabitants registered growth. The remainder continued to decline, suggesting the existence of some form of population density threshold below which a rural population cannot really sustain itself. Even in the expanding communes, however, it is apparent that natural increase has not been the principal cause of population growth. Nine communes out of ten continue to show a negative natural increase and an aging of the population. A general residential movement from urban areas to rural hinterlands and the growth of commuting to urban centres have been associated with considerable socio-economic change. In numerical terms, blue-collar workers today form the single most dominant group in rural areas (38.4 per cent) followed by farmers (21.2 per cent), white-collar workers (15.8 per cent), artisans and shopkeepers (11.6 per cent) and finally farm workers (3.5 per cent).

In France, the town is spreading out into the countryside and a more diversified rural society is being recreated in the process. In the long term, the concept of rural space and its distinctiveness with respect to urban space becomes less and less clearly definable. What is important, in an international comparative context, is less the precise definition of rural space than the uses to which that definition has been put and the relative importance of rural space in national political agendas.

The political approach

In France, the notion of rural space rests within the institution of the French commune. In the Middle Ages, the commune epitomised local autonomy with charters being awarded by the king or local notables to the urban bourgeoisie. The parish, an altogether separate territorial unit, remained under the direct control of either the local nobility or the Church. From the seventeenth century onwards, this communal autonomy was gradually reduced by an increasingly centralised monarchy, which progressively assumed control of the fiscal, legal and military aspects of the French state. The 1789 Revolution was the culmination of this centralising tendency. Under the desire to homogenise the French state and invoke and maintain national unity, the commune was integrated into the state apparatus as the basic administrative unit of the nation, allowing both the diffusion of national ideology and policy and the representation of local interests.

The original Act of 1789 made no distinction between communes; mayors and municipal councillors were to be elected by the same procedures in all (Agulhon et al. 1986). During the revolutionary period, however, and subsequently throughout the nineteenth century, the relative constitutional status of communes was frequently modified as the result of successive national political upheavals. Under the First Empire, for example, mayors in communes with under 5,000 inhabitants were elected democratically while those in the larger communes were nominated by the Prefect. In 1831, under the July Revolution, mayors and deputy mayors in communes with more than 3,500 and in the principal towns became subject to appointment by the King. Only with the Commune Charter of 1884 was any real homogeneity and durable municipal law achieved. For several years, though, under the Vichy regime, a legal distinction between communes was re-established, with rural communes, seen as the heartland of peasant France, retaining their franchise while the larger communes lost all local democracy (Agulhon et al. 1986).

Over the last two centuries, the status of the French commune has thus altered according to the whim of authoritarian or democratic central governments:

> The general trend has been to see local democracy as more perilous for a conservative power in those communes having a large population or occupying a strategic position (such as principal towns). By contrast, local democracy has appeared more acceptable in villages either because of the preconceived idea that rural areas contained only relatively docile politicians or because a single dominant elected representative in the person of the mayor of a small rural commune could not but be accepted. (Agulhon et al 1986, p. 30).

The statistical definition of rural communes has thus emerged from the differential notion of French communes developed by successive central authorities as a consequence of their own relationship to the nation as a whole. Within this differentiation, the concept of the small rural commune and the political and social representation that it implies has remained remarkably stable. After 1789, the urban, rather than the rural, population was seen as the more politically troublesome. As as result, small rural communes were, until very recently, regarded as little-changing and reassuring substrata to the nation, unaffected by an encroaching and turbulent modernity.

Acknowledging the political and symbolic differences between communes has ultimately allowed the reconciliation of a strongly centralised French state with the reality of a national territory subdivided into 36,433 administrative units. At a national level, the law has had to allow for local diversity but to contain that diversity within a broadly universal mould. Consequently, as a defined social entity, the town exists no more than the countryside. 'Administrative law ignores the town' wrote Jaques Moreau (1989), drawing attention to the fact that under French law neither 'urban' nor 'rural' exist in legal terms. The Urban Code, for example, despite its name, is universally applicable, though specific procedures can be adapted to particular demographic conditions.

Thus, alongside the semi-homogeneous administrative apparatus of the French state, the small rural commune has remained, characterised by a particular status afforded it by central authority. It is still an administrative unit, of course, as are all communes, but in addition to that ubiquitous function, the French rural communes are units of political and social memory, a crucial element in justifying the coexistence of a highly centralised French state with durable and compatible local democracy, particularly a local democracy founded upon such small territorial and, occasionally, demographic units. The rural communes also possess a vital historical function. While the central state has led the nation as a whole into modernity, the rural commune has retained its symbolic role as the heartland of an essentially rural nation. The ideological derivation of the notion of the countryside in France emerges in a large part from the administrative status and role of the rural commune.

The British countryside

The political approach

In Great Britain, the term 'rural' has always been far less precise. Implicit, rather than explicit, it has been used in a predominantly pragmatic manner, adjusting to different social, political and economic circumstances as the need arises. Formal definition has always been avoided and the criteria for identifying particular areas have been largely specific to individual policy fields and narrowly functional to the objectives of the policy concerned. The result has been an accretion of areal designations, for conservation, for landscape protection, special agricultural assistance and rural economic development, superimposed upon one another with no attempt to correlate their boundaries. Not even the basic units from which designations are constructed are comparable: Rural Development Areas (to combat rural unemployment and depopulation) for example, follow parish boundaries; Less Favoured Areas follow farm boundaries; and most conservation designations follow geographical features.

If, throughout recent British history, certain territorial units have seemed to persist, notably parishes, towns, counties and boroughs, they have done so under continually changing circumstances and definitions. From the Middle Ages to the nineteenth century, the administration of territorial units passed from a feudal structure to the establishment of locally-elected representatives. The most enduring administrative division through this period was that between the towns and the rest, only the former benefiting from royal charters and the constitution of distinct local authorities.

During the nineteenth century, county boroughs and urban districts emerged – around the provision of public health facilities and other urban amenities and infrastructure – as the basis of modern local government, with the former covering the major towns, and cities and the latter mainly the country towns (but also many larger villages). The administration of the remaining areas was supervised by the Justices of the Peace, often greater or lesser landowners nominated by the Crown's representative in each county, the Lord Lieutenant. Indeed, in contrast with France, where the Revolution had enshrined the commune, the British landed aristocracy jealously protected their local patronage in the counties. An 1872 law on public health created a formal distinction between urban and rural districts for the first time, based upon the provision of water supplies and household drainage. The Local Government Act of 1888, with its subsequent laws on rural and urban districts, is generally considered the milestone in advancing local rural democracy, by establishing the basis for elected county and district councils. It was, though, carefully drawn to ensure the separation of town and country and to insulate county government from urban radicalism.

Although some functionally rural settlements were thereby designated as urban districts, and though many rural districts close to urban centres took on more and more of a suburban character during the first half of the twentieth century, the coverage of rural district councils was almost conventionally taken to constitute rural Britain for many administrative and investigative purposes.

Throughout the twentieth century, the British system of local government has undergone considerable functional evolution (Keith-Lucas and Richards 1978). In the main, the provision of basic utilities has been transferred to specialised, national and regional bodies, with local government concentrating on the provision of a range of public and welfare services. In addition, with the evolution of building and land use regulations culminating in the 1947 Town and Country Planning Act, local authorities have been accorded the role of determining the physical development of their areas.

Local authorities also have general responsibilities for promoting the wellbeing and prosperity of their areas, and urban councils in particular have traditionally used the planning acts and related legislation to assume a leading role locally in economic and social development. While not usually so *dirigiste*, rural councils have likewise used land use planning as the vehicle for rural policy-making. In this, the British notion of 'planning' and of 'planners' themselves differs considerably from that in France. British planners, specifically trained in planning schools (for which there is no real equivalent in France), are eclectic and polyvalent in contrast to their French counterparts who are, for the most part, trained largely in law. Their responsibilities include not only physical land use decision-making but also environmental protection and resource management. Moreover, in the absence of national planning regulations, the British system is predominantly discretionary.

The reorganisation of local government in 1974 swept away any remaining vestiges of a formal urban-rural distinction. The initial proposal was for a system of uniform city-regions, but the reaction from the counties ensured that they, at least, remained largely intact. Pressures for administrative rationalisation nevertheless meant that at a sub-county level, many urban and rural district councils were amalgamated and former county boroughs were subsumed. The outcome was sizeable district councils combining town and country (varying in size from, for example, Bristol – with a population of 422,000 – to Radnor, with a population of only 18,670) and the disappearance of the old rural district councils. Even before reorganisation Britain had easily the largest second tier units of local government worldwide (Humes and Martin 1961); and after reorganisation the average population for lower tier authorities in Great Britain was 120,000 compared with 1000 in France (Widdicombe Committee 1986).

The demographic approach

The convenient rural classification furnished by pre-1974 local government categories had long since lost much of its social validity through demographic and regional economic change. Its removal, coupled with the emergent academic interest in rural studies led scholars, statisticians and planners to look for substitute definitions. Low population density has long been taken as the most objective statistical rural measure (Hoggart and Buller 1987) but many analysts have sought a satisfactory functional classification instead. Green (1971), for example, defined rural areas as those regions lying beyond the attraction of major urban centres while Coombes et al. (1982) have categorised rural areas in a negative sense as the tracts left over once the functional city-regions and their hinterlands have been fully delineated from travel-to-work and retailing catchments. Such definitions, however, leave the rural as a shrinking, residual category. But, in turn, the clearly delineated urban hierarchies on which the notion of city-regions was based have been undermined by urban-rural shifts in manufacturing and service employment and the emergence of complex, non-radial, travel-to-work patterns.

The countryside can no longer be equated simply with particular types of land use or economic activity. Neither can rural areas be characterised by any particular or unique social or cultural behaviour (Hoggart and Buller 1987). With the ready availability of computerised census data and more sophisticated analytic techniques, therefore, rural scholars have sought more precise and objective measures of the incidence of key rural social issues. Partly in reaction to the proliferation of urban social indicators – seen by some rural interests as a factor in unfairly skewing the distribution of central funds to urban areas – there has been interest in a more diagnostic indicator of the complexity and varying intensity of rural problems than such simple and traditional rural measures as population density (Walford 1986).

Perhaps the most prominent has been Paul Cloke's index of rurality (1977) which employed eight variables, largely from the census, covering population structure, employment, housing and location, to classify the former rural districts according to their degree of rurality. A principal components analysis was used to 'prevent any subjective valuation of variables'. According to their overall scores, the districts were allocated to one of four quartile categories: extreme rural, intermediate rural, intermediate non-rural and non-rural. The index has been widely used and has been replicated following the 1981 Census (Cloke and Edwards 1986). It combines factors which might be considered intrinsic, such as population density, occupational structure and remoteness from urban centres, with others such as standards of household amenities and the proportion of the population over 65, which might be regarded as merely contingent to rural character. Indeed, like several other attempts to define the rural, prompted by the exigencies of collecting, analysing and comparing area-based statistics, it seeks to establish a reproducible and coherent empirical referent or scale but without any greater claims to its ontological status.

In the continuing absence of a formal delineation of the British countryside, it is not surprising that the Office of Population Censuses and Surveys has recently fallen back on a physical definition of urban and rural. Enumeration districts were categorised as one or the other depending on a judgement as to whether the majority of the population lived in or outside the built-up area. On this basis, wards were classified on a wholly urban to wholly rural scale depending upon the proportion of the two different enumeration districts they comprised (Craig 1988).

Finally, it should be noted that the ESRC established a Rural Areas Database in 1985 to assemble a wide variety of social, economic and environmental information relating to rural areas. Although it was hoped that 'in due course' it would 'act as a lobby seeking to urge agencies responsible for collecting data to adopt a more comparable definition of key variables and spatial units' (Walford et al., n.d.), its policy on what data it would accept was suitably catholic, if not promiscuous:

> The Rural Areas Database is not seeking to impose a 'hard and fast' definition of what is and what is not a rural area, nor by implication what are and what are not rural data. A broad approach is being taken so that potentially interesting and relevant information is not omitted and users are able to employ the definitions that they feel to be appropriate to their needs (Walford et al n.d.).

Rural studies in Great Britain

It is inevitable that Britain and France should have different rural research traditions. France is a country where rural communes form a key element of the national identity and whose rural roots are still very strong, whereas Britain sees its rural areas in terms of how they fulfil the needs of a long urbanised nation. Given these differing contexts, rural research cannot possibly have the same significance in the two countries. In France, it has been research into the nation's very heartland, and has been preoccupied largely with the peasant question. In Great Britain, rural research has been more closely linked to policy-making, especially on land use and the environment.

The study of the British countryside has always been at least implicit in certain disciplines, notably geography and history. Thus the concern of nineteenth and early twentieth century geographers for regions, human responses to natural conditions, settlement evolution and agricultural systems focused in large part upon the rural world. However, these were not, in themselves, rural studies, and only one social science discipline in Britain has adopted an explicit rural orientation – agricultural economics. Created, in part, by the Ministry of Agriculture, largely to help provide a scientific rationale for the modernisation of the agricultural sector, agricultural economics was set up in a number of universities from the 1930s onwards and today stands as the sole institutionalised rural discipline (Whetham 1981). Significantly, as originally conceived by Ashby and Orwin, amongst others, the discipline was to have been a broad-based rural science. During the post-war period, however, it became narrowly entrenched in econometrics, thereby losing any claims it might have had to represent wider rural concerns. In any case, agricultural economics has only ever represented one specific economic sector, agriculture. Its importance in the development of a broader rural studies lies not so much in its own direct input as in the manner in which it has provoked others, both from within its ranks and outside, to cast the research net wider to include the rural economy and society in a larger sense.

A second early factor in the emergence of rural studies in Great Britain was more explicitly sociological, though it remained essentially marginal to mainstream British social thought. From the 1930s onwards, but most importantly following the Second World War, a specific body of social anthropology emerged in the form of community studies (Kuper 1973). Strongly influenced by the German Tönnies and the American Redfield, and within a tradition of structural-functionalism, British community studies sought to examine traditional rural ways of life, in order to understand how the various institutions of rural areas fitted together to form a functioning whole – in particular, how family and kinship structures complemented economic activity on the land. Mainly conducted in upland farming areas, these studies also recorded the response of local communities to external social and economic pressures which were seen to be undermining rural culture and traditions. These community studies formed, during the 1950s and early 1960s, the backbone of rural social studies, and although undertaken by social anthropologists rather than sociologists *per se*, they effectively represented the nearest thing Britain had at the time to a rural sociological tradition, one characterised by a certain pluridisciplinarity but one undoubtedly lacking in either precise methodology or sufficiently profound sociological analysis (Bell and Newby 1971).

Whereas the 1960s saw the important growth of urban sociology, social anthropology and the community studies approach came under increasing criticism. Not only did it become seemingly irrelevant, in the face of widespread social and economic change, to consider rural communities as relatively isolated units as had been the method of many community studies, but the methodological eclecticism of the approach, both in its concept of the notion of community and in its analysis of community functions drew the fire of those impressed by the rigour and theoretical nature of urban social analysis.

Although the end of the 1960s saw, to some extent, a parting of the ways between functionalist social anthropology and sociology, the former had, through the community studies tradition, paved the way for members of the latter to reconsider the relationships between agricultural organisation and rural social structures and to make the all important bridge between agrarian economic and broader social relations through an analysis of property relationships. This new focus subsequently emerged as the central preoccupation of British rural sociology in the 1970s. Pioneered by Newby and his colleagues at the University of Essex and strongly influenced by Weber, what was initially a sociology of agriculture subsequently developed into a wide-ranging analysis of the changing social structure of lowland Britain. Though continuing to remain marginal within sociology as a whole, and being more a sociology of rural Britain than an explicit rural sociology, the work of Newby and others has been crucial in injecting conceptual rigour into British rural studies and elevating them into a more coherent and intellectually-respected, academic field.

Somewhat paradoxically, but perhaps confirming an ingrained urban bias, this burst of activity and theorising in rural sociology in the 1970s had a greater impact outside of sociology than within. In particular, it has greatly influenced practitioners in those eclectic and traditionally empiricist disciplines, including geography, planning and environmental science, who have taken an interest in rural *problems*. Such a pragmatic approach to rural (and, for that matter, urban) studies in Britain is often fuelled by applied policy concerns related to local administration. The decentralised system of local government in Britain imparts considerable interest and vitality to issues of local policy making and politics. In addition, what in effect are the largest and most bureaucratic units of local government in the world furnish a ready demand for applied policy studies related to local administration and the associated training of local government professionals. Various policy-related disciplines have emerged in universities and polytechnics to satisfy just these managerialist demands – for example, town planning, housing administration, environmental health, transport studies and leisure management.

The professionalisation of rural local government has lagged somewhat behind that of its urban counterpart, but one of the earliest fields where it emerged was that of land use planning, which came to enjoy a reciprocal relationship especially with regional geography (Steel 1987). In the 1960s and 1970s a more extensive professionalisation of rural administration was boosted by a number of factors, including a general trend towards corporate planning and management throughout local government; the growth of the rural middle class; the reorganisation of local government in 1974; and the growth of a number of rural quangos. These factors together stimulated a considerable demand for rural policy research and professional training.

Coincidentally, a wave of new campus-based universities was established in regional centres often with large rural hinterlands, expanding substantially the potential research base for the examination of rural Britain. The initial focus on land use issues allowed for the early dominance of geography and planning, but departments of environmental science, anthropology and sociology also made notable contributions. Indeed, although land use policy has remained a fundamental preoccupation of British rural studies, the 1970s saw the growth of interest in other rural issues, notably deprivation, welfare, mobility, employment, housing, rural services, recreation, and environmental protection. The broadening agenda has stimulated both an interest in the fundamental social and economic processes underlying rural change and a new pluridisciplinarity in rural research. These developments were marked by the formation in 1979 of the Rural Economy and Society Study Group bringing together sociologists, anthropologists, political scientists, planners and geographers. What, as commonly agreed, was missing from the first decade of British rural studies, was a sufficiently strong theoretical underpinning for the critical analysis of social and economic change. The predominance of geographers and the importance of applied research had, to some extent, marginalised the role of theory. The 1980s therefore witnessed the continued expansion of rural studies but concurrently, and paradoxically, a re-examination of the pertinence of a distinctively rural subject matter. These developments can be pursued through the successive volumes of the Rural Economy and Society Study Group (Bradley and Lowe 1984; Lowe, Bradley and Wright 1986; Cox, Lowe and Winter 1986; Bouquet and Winter 1987; Buller and Wright 1990; Marsden and Little forthcoming). After years of expiricism, therefore, rural scholars have begun to place rural change within broader processes of social and economic transformation. Four major research themes are currently observable: the political economy analysis of general economic change and its impact upon rural areas; the re-examination of the social and economic relations of space; the role of the local state in rural political management, and the recomposition of rural society in the face of capital restructuring. Although, on the one hand, these broader research themes are, to some extent, devaluing the uniqueness of the countryside as a domain in which distinct causes and effects are discernible, in their concentration upon locality – as the focal point of change – current rural studies have implicitly strengthened the value of rural areas within the agenda of social science research.

French rural research

The French rural research tradition stands in considerable contrast to that of Britain. Characterised by an intellectual rigour, an enduring pluridisciplinarity and the constant search for total social explanation, whatever the particular disciplinary starting point, French rural studies emerged from the flourishing social science climate of the inter-war years, and have grown continuously since then.

The social sciences of the inter-war period were strongly influenced by Durkheim, whose belief that sociology could form the key federative discipline for the humanities was promulgated through the journal *l'Année Sociologique*. Believing that society could never be understood by subdividing it into discrete academic subject areas, Durkheim and his disciples saw sociology bringing to history, geography, ethnology and economics a unifying perspective that would facilitate the understanding of broader social phenomena. His ambition that sociology should annex these other disciplines was never realised. Rather, research into the understanding of the overall cohesion of society and the explanation of that cohesion became the ultimate object of all the various social science disciplines though the first actually to adopt this new orientation was undoubtedly history.

After the victory of 1918 and the return to France of Alsace and the University of Strasbourg, a research team was formed which included the historians Bloch and Febvre, the psychologist Blondel and the sociologists Halbwachs and Le Bras (Gavignaud, chapter 5 below). Inspired by Durkheim, this team extended the idea of the unity of the social sciences, with the historians, in particular, turning to geography, sociology, economics and ethnology to support their new conception of historical analysis. Although this new approach provoked substantial division amongst the French historians at the time, the intellectual determination of this pluridisciplinary group, keen to extend the acceptance of a more social and economic form of historical analysis, led to the foundation, in 1929, of the key journal *Annales d'histoire économique et sociale* whose contents were never simply restricted to the study of the past. 'There is only one science of man through time', wrote Marc Bloch in 1941, illustrating the underlying conception of the *Annales* school, 'one that needs to continually link the study of the dead with that of the living' (1941).

This multi-disciplinary group sought to consolidate the social sciences by whatever means they could, but the various component disciplines were not all in a position to play equal roles in the process. Sociology had yet to prove that it could exist as an independent discipline (being taught, until 1958, only as a part of moral philosophy) while psychology had yet to carve its own distinctive furrow. History, however, though well established, was being torn apart by the political upheavals of the time and was consequently receptive to new directions. It was historians therefore who began to apply these novel theoretical and methodological insights to their analysis of the historical past.

One cannot explicitly link the *Annales* school to any one particular theoretical current. The journal reflected an attitude rather than any specific doctrine, an attitude that entailed using a variety of analytic instruments, from whatever source, that would enable the comprehension of social reality, under the principle that the time period under study did not necessarily dictate the choice of appropriate methodology. In creating what was effectively a common methodological and disciplinary pool from which to draw, the scholars of the *Annales* school freed themselves from the strict ties of a single, encompassing theory. As such, they had a major influence in subsequent social science research during the 1950s and 1960s, where the disciplinary and methodological eclecticism of their approach, coloured at one and the same time by Durkheimian rationalism, Weberian relativism and Marxism, had a particularly strong impact on French rural studies. In 1948, the *Annales* school gained institutional importance with the foundation, on its initiative, of the *Ecole Pratique des Hautes Etudes* whose 6th Section translated the *Annales* approach into specific research programmes. This 6th Section became, in 1975, the *Ecole des Hautes Etudes en Sciences Sociales* providing further endorsement of the durability and continued relevance of the *Annales* approach to the social sciences. At the same time, however, it revealed the increasing rivalry amongst the social science disciplines for the pole position of academic hegemony.

The University of Strasbourg was very much the focal point of the inter-war consolidation of the social sciences. Dominated by Durkheim's analytical method, his scientific rigour and his desire for 'total explanation', and close to the German border, the university had long been an important location for Franco-German academic interchange. Having previously taught in Berlin, the German sociologist Simmel joined the staff at Strasbourg, remaining there until his death in 1918. Although Alsace, and the university were returned to France in that year, both Bloch and Halbwachs were able to take up temporary teaching posts in several German cities. German sociology at the time was particularly fertile. Both Simmel and Tönnies had been engaged in the study of forms of social life (the latter's *Community and Society* had appeared in 1887), creating a research theme that spread rapidly into France. Both had heavily borrowed from historical methods in their own research into social explanation, a technique the Strasbourg group was later to adopt so effectively. The works of Max Weber, hitherto ignored in France, first appeared in an article by Halbwachs published in 1925, two years before the foundation of the *Annales*.

A final influence was undoubtedly Marx and, in particular, the explanatory power of his notion of total society. Coincident with the Russian Revolution, his influence was especially strong, and although the majority of academics concerned had only briefly, if at all, adhered to communism *per se*, all were able to draw upon the theoretical and methodological insights of its founder.

The historians of the time were nevertheless reluctant to make any hard and fast choice between the Durkheimian search for scientific objectivity and Weberian relativism in questions of value and meaning. Neither were they ready to adopt exclusively the rigours of Marxist analysis. Instead, they preferred to select from all, what they needed for their particular research goals while striving to maintain a scientific basis for their work, often by the use of quantification and statistical analysis.

The influence of Marxism was strongly felt in the newly emergent economic history of the inter-war period which, in becoming an essential element in the explanation of the interaction of social phenomena, replaced the more political analysis favoured by traditional historians. The Marxism employed, however, was generally diffuse and undogmatic: a methodology rather than an explanatory framework, allowing Bloch, for example, to study feudal society in class terms and Labrousse, who combined the influence of Marx's *Capital* with that of the work of Simiand, to investigate prices and incomes fluctuations in eighteenth-century France. In all, this academic permeability to a diverse range of different theoretical approaches and their sometimes simultaneous employment, has been a characteristic feature of the French social sciences since this early period. Durkheimian determinism, like that of Marx, was, in general, an excess to be avoided.

Durkheim always supported the hegemony of sociology as the key federative discipline. The historians, for their part, thought otherwise. Only retrospectively, they argued, could the various elements of social explanation be successively arranged. Only from the 'distance' afforded by historical analysis, could the social 'whole' be successfully encompassed. Time itself, they claimed, provided the essential comparative medium for social explanation and only by bringing a sense of time to social analysis could the political and social upheavals of the epoch be sufficiently interpreted. These claims found particular accord with those social science specialists engaged in rural research.

If French rural studies have failed to develop a specific theoretical framework of their own, they have been largely characterised by the theoretical eclecticism and pluridisciplinarity of the *Annales* school. However, like the *Annales* school, that pluridisciplinarity was one initially dominated by history. As the French land area is 90 per cent rural, and, immediately after the war, contained over half the French population, it was not surprising that French historians found themselves naturally focusing upon rural societies. The first village monographs, produced by historians, began to appear towards the end of the 1950s, to be followed by the large-scale regional monographs a little later.

At the beginning of the 1960s, the sociologist Henri Mendras sought to establish the basis of a typology of French rural communities by selecting a sample of villages contained within several monographic studies. In doing so, he effectively confirmed the existence, for the first time, of a distinct rural sociology group within the *Centre National de Recherche Scientifique*, the state funded national research body. Following in the footsteps of the *Annales*, in its use of the multiple resources of the social sciences as a whole, the emergent rural sociology school similarly sought broad social explanation within a rural setting. All that distinguished it from history was the use of different data sources: the one dependent upon archives and documents, the other on direct contact. Both were nonetheless dependent upon other social sciences as the resultant works demonstrated.

The hegemony that ultimately emerged was not the result of one discipline's predominance over another, but lay rather in the focus of social science research on the social world. If the twentieth century has been marked, in France, by the dominant theoretical and methodological position of history and sociology, the preoccupation with social explanation transcends not only these two disciplines but has also emerged as a crucial concern in geography, ethnology, economics and political science.

Geography, having been linked for a long time to history in university teaching, has, to some extent, suffered from the high profile activity of its pedagogic cohabitant, though geographers have always been represented in, and have drawn from, the intellectual debates and currents of the post-war social sciences. Occupying a key position between sociology and history, and like them avoiding theoretical conflicts, human geography sought to keep man's relations to the physical environment in perspective, an increasingly onerous if limited task given the trend in the social sciences towards the analysis of major contemporary social issues. The result has been a growing crisis of identity in French geography, one that has revealed the dangers in too much pluridisciplinarity in the social sciences of the loss of conceptual and methodological originality and the gradual disappearance of any specific field of study.

Significantly, the problems of academic distinctiveness, first encountered by geographers, are now being faced by virtually all the rural disciplines. Thirty years of pluridisciplinarity have substantially hindered the independent theoretical and methodological development of individual social sciences, no more so than in rural economics; an amalgam of a discipline, economics, and a field of study, agriculture, though one which, as its name suggests, is still considered as a broad rural science.

The descendant of nineteenth century agronomy, rural economics has been characterised, according to Michel Petit (1986), by 'an empirical and pragmatic attitude, open to eclecticism, and by a clear understanding of its subject, making it aware of the interrelations between the political, economic, technical and social dimensions of the issues under study: in short by an acute receptivity to pluridisciplinary work'. Rural economics was an important accompaniment to the other social sciences in its own particular approach to the study of the rural world.

However the discipline has been constrained by the tension between the 'globalising' preoccupation of agronomists and the continuing need to conform to the scientific rigour of applied economics. The marriage between hard science, on the one hand, and social and political analysis, on the other, has not been easy. This debate, internal to rural economics, has highlighted the troublesome intellectual status of the social sciences: while a withdrawal into disciplinary individualism leads to more simplistic explanations, greater pluridisciplinarity can mean that the resultant 'pot pourri' suffers from theoretical and methodological blandness.

Certain scholars today would undoubtedly like to see a further retreat from pluridisciplinarity, believing that partial theoretical insights can bring more to a discipline than those drawn from a multitude of different and not always appropriate sciences. Perhaps one of the reasons that French ethnology is currently so strong and well structured, while other rural disciplines face crises of identity and intellectual status, is that only ethnology has been able to maintain its specific research individuality and its well-defined field of study.

Ethnology, in the 1920s, was also associated with the *Annales* school: one of its founders being the Durkheimian Marcel Mauss. Like the other social sciences at the time, ethnology fell under the spell of the hegemony of social explanation and in doing so moved ever closer to sociology. Indeed, it became difficult, in the postwar years, to tell the difference between those monographs produced by some ethnologists and those by some sociologists. Both sought similar objectives while employing the same methodologies. Today, however, ethnology is increasingly defining its own particular research agenda. Summarising the pluridisciplinary studies of the 1960s, Cuisenier (1988, p. 217) maintained:

> In 15 years, from 1960 to 1975, the French experience has been that, in order to grasp the cultural identity of chosen communities within wider society, one had to go beyond the simple juxtaposition of different disciplinary approaches, yet no social anthropology emerged that was capable of providing, even in the most basic sense, suitable categories of analysis to integrate and articulate the various disciplinary treatments.

In the explanatory hegemony of wider social explanation, the influence of Marxist analysis was particularly important in the 1950s and 1960s, when conditions – including the still tangible impact of two world wars and the problems of analysing a rapidly changing society – were especially favourable for its widespread acceptance. During this period, and up until the 1980s, the aim of the social sciences was to produce durable theoretical explanations for this social transformation by drawing from the resources of different disciplines. The withdrawal from that disciplinary and theoretical eclecticism observable today, reflects contemporary social and political realities. The latent economic crisis, deprivation, unemployment and internal political division have all tempered the fascination for global theoretical explanations of social change as they have tempered unequivocal belief in the merits of progress.

Thus, the traditional, 'globalising' *problématiques* have been reassessed and in their stead, rural social research, like the social sciences generally, has moved towards more partial, thematic issues and a more relative cultural analysis. The consequence has been to push ethnology and micro-sociology to the fore, and to allow the return of a more political form of analysis.

The economically determinant Marxist vogue of the 1960s reduced the importance of political analysis, long dear to historians with its emphasis on key events, institutions and governments. As a result, political science, with few exceptions, became limited to the study of national policy-making, election results and agricultural trade unionism (Boussard chapter 20, below). Today however, with the return to a more local research focus, political science has regained some of the ground lost to the grand theories as political organisation, local and central power relations, administrative constraints and the role of law emerge as new research interests.

French rural studies, over the last 40 years, demonstrate many of the difficulties of necessary coexistence within the social sciences. In establishing a 'rural' field of study, one that lends itself to pluridisciplinarity, scholars have sought a form of social explanation that, in its breadth, is itself partly integrated into the functioning of social systems. Such research, into the laws of change and into typologies of rural societies, has confronted the diversity of social organisation and the complex theoretical and methodological problems involved. Should one now withdraw into disciplinary individuality? What is the correct balance between disciplinary development and the need for an equally important interdependency amongst the social sciences? These questions remain fundamental to the scientific status of the rural disciplines.

Not only do France and Great Britain have very different attitudes to their respective countrysides, but they have approached the academic study of rural space and rural issues in fundamentally different ways. Intellectual on the one side, pragmatic on the other, the one turned towards conceptual speculation, the other to action and management. We return, inevitably, to the traditional images of the two countries. However, one must avoid the assumption of any innate incompatability. It is clear that the administrative organisation of each has played a major role in defining the 'scientific' approach to rural studies. If, in Great Britain, the university has played a major role in rural management and policy analysis, it is because links between policy-making and research are a great deal closer than they are in France where there is little specific training for rural policy-makers. Furthermore, French public servants, generally trained within the exclusive environment of the *Grandes Ecoles*, are 1frequently condescending in their attitudes towards academic inquiry. Effective coordination between university research and policy practice remains, in France, a long-desired goal.

Nevertheless, today, France and Great Britain find themselves facing remarkably similar rural issues (agricultural change, service withdrawal, environmental degradation and socio-economic change) and each can draw significant insights from the other. The following pages bear witness to this effort.

Bibliography

Agulhon, M., Girard, L., Robert, J. and Serman, W., *Les Maires en France du Consulat a Nos Jours*, Publications de la Sorbonne, Paris, 1986.

Association des Ruralistes Francais, 'Les études rurales sont-elles en crise?', *Bulletin de l'ARF*, no. 41–42, 1987.

Bell, C. and Newby, H., *Community Studies*, Allen & Unwin, London, 1971.
Bloch, M., *Apologie Pour L'Histoire ou le Metier D'Histoire*, Armand Colin, Paris, 1941.
Bontron, J.-C., 'Le fait rural en France. Propos critique sur sa définition', pp. 123-42 of *Réflexion sur l'espace rural français*, Université de Paris I-ENS-Fontenay, 1976.
Bouquet, M. and Winter, M. (eds.), *Who from Their Labours Rest: Conflict and Practice in Rural Tourism*, Avebury, Aldershot, 1987.
Bradley, T. and Lowe, P. (eds.), *Locality and Rurality: Economy and Society in Rural Regions*, Geo Books, Norwich, 1984.
Buller, H. and Wright, S. (eds.), *Rural Development: Problems and Practices*, Avebury, Aldershot, 1990.
Cloke, P., 'An index of rurality for England and Wales', *Regional Studies*, 11, 1977, 31-46.
Cloke, P. and Edwards, C., 'Rurality in England and Wales, 1981', *Regional Studies*, 20, 1984, 289-306.
Coombes, M.G. et al., 'Functional regions for the population census of Great Britain', in D.T. Herbert and R.J. Johnston (eds.), *Geography and the Urban Environment: Progress in Research and Application*, Wiley, Chichester, 1982.
Cox, G., Lowe, P. and Winter, M. (eds.), *Agriculture: People and Policies*, Allen & Unwin, London, 1986.
Craig, J., 'An urban-rural categorisation for wards and local authorities', *Population Trends*, 54, 1988, 6-11.
Cuisenier, J., 'Sociologie et ethnologie' in H. Mendras and M. Verret (eds.), *Les Champs de la Sociologie Française*, Armand Colin, Paris, 1988, 207-220.
Green, R., *Countryside Planning: The Future of the Rural Regions*, Manchester University Press, Manchester, 1971.
Hoggart, K. and Buller, H., *Rural Development: A Geographical Perspective*, Croom Helm, London, 1987.
Humes, S. and Martin, E. M., *The Structure of Local Governments Throughout the World*, Martinus Nijhoff, The Hague, 1961.
Keith-Lucas, B. and Richards, P.G., *A History of Local Government in the Twentieth Century*, Allen & Unwin, London, 1978.
Kuper, A., *Anthropologists and Anthropology: The British School 1922-1972*, Allen Lane, London, 1973.
Lowe, P., Bradley, T. and Wright, S. (eds.), *Deprivation and Welfare in Rural Areas*, Geo Books, Norwich, 1986.
Lowe, P. et al., *The Countryside in Question: A Research Strategy*, Countryside Change Working Paper Series, No. 1, Department of Agricultural Economics, The University, Newcastle-upon-Tyne, 1989.
Marsden, T. and Little, J. (eds.) *Perspectives on the Food System*, Avebury, Aldershot, forthcoming.
Moreau, J., 'Les structures supra et infra citadines', *Pouvoirs Locaux*, 1 (2), 1989, 78-83.
Petit, M., 'L'Etat et le statut de l'economie rurale', *Economie Rurale*, 172, 1986, 49-54.
Steel, R.W., (ed.), *British Geography 1918-1945*, Cambridge University Press, Cambridge, 1987.
Walford, N., 'Indicators of inequality as pointers to policy', pp. 109-17 of Lowe, P., Bradley, T. and Wright, S. (eds.), *op. cit.*
Walford, N. et al., *The Rural Areas Database: Progress and Prospects*, ESRC Data Archive, Colchester, not dated.
Whetham, E.H., *Agricultural Economics in Britain 1900-1940*, Institute of Agricultural Economics, Oxford, 1981.
Widdicombe Committee, *Report of the Committee of Inquiry into the Conduct of Local Authority Business*, Cmnd 9798, HMSO, London, 1986.

Part II: History

4 Commentary and Introduction

Geneviève Gavignaud

Current rural history has inherited a long university tradition; a tradition that has illuminated the work of both British and French researchers, represented here in the papers of Gordon Mingay and Ronald Hubscher. On both sides of the Channel, the aims of historians have converged in seeking to grasp the foundations and the intrinsic character of rural society and, most recently, its operation and integration within the dominant, or wider, society.

Mingay begins his paper by considering the choice facing rural scholars in Britain between specialisation according to the period under study, or according to particular themes. The continuing publication of the multi-volume *Agrarian History of England and Wales* (under the general editorship of Joan Thirsk) presents a wide-ranging synthesis of the whole gamut of historical periods and research themes. Mingay orients his paper around the two principal axes, of themes in the history of agriculture and those concerning the history of rural society, while recognising that there is often no clear distinction between the two.

The medievalists in Britain have concentrated upon a number of, now classic, themes, including the origins and evolution of field systems; the organisation and development of the manor; and the effects of the Black Death of the fourteenth century. The last theme has attracted specialist attention from those interested in the effects of population fluctuations on agricultural change.

The changes in agriculture during the early modern period (the sixteenth and seventeenth centuries) have been a starting point for much rural history research in Britain. Some twenty years ago, Professor Kerridge suggested that the agricultural revolution had taken place not during the traditionally accepted period of 1750 – 1850 but earlier, between 1560 and 1767. He based his case on important improvements in husbandry practices and challenged the significance accorded the technical innovations of the later period. Subsequent debate over the rival claims for the two periods has emphasised the generally slow and uneven adoption of innovations and has led to the gradual abandonment of the concept of an agricultural revolution and its replacement by an appreciation of the protracted nature of agricultural change. This has informed a great deal of research drawing on an expanding range of statistical sources, into the diffusion of new techniques and practices, the causes of their uneven spatial or temporal spread, and the impact on yields.

A second basic theme in British rural history research has concerned agricultural structures. Modern research has demonstrated the slow, long-term growth of the average size of farm units during the eighteenth and early nineteenth centuries and this has led to a reassessment of the parliamentary enclosures of 1760–1830. Long neglected as a subject of research, the enclosures have recently been restored – with the aid of computers and specialised land-tax analysis – to the prominence they enjoyed amongst agrarian historians more than fifty years ago. A new generation of scholars has reopened the debate concerning the fate of the small landowners, but still there remains uncertainty and debate over the extent and incidence of their decline during the eighteenth century and its causes: whether due to a supposed growth of large estates prior to 1740; or the depressed conditions of the 1730s and 1740s, as Mingay's own research would suggest; or the advancing land market fuelled by the prosperity enjoyed by landowners and farmers after 1760; or due to the inability of small owners to meet the costs of enclosures.

Reality is always more complex than the efforts of intellectual rationalisation sometimes make it appear. Otherwise why should communal practices, such as the common fields, have survived as long as they did in certain regions of England? Have they perhaps been 'safety valves' in case of poverty, or 'insurance' against possible losses? Yelling has related their persistence to certain village types and corresponding social structures.

At the other end of the social spectrum, debate and research on dominant elites in the countryside during the modern era have focused on two controversial theories first advanced nearly fifty years ago: one by Tawney, concerning the 'rise of the gentry' between 1540 and 1640; the other by Habakkuk, concerning the 'rise of the great estate' between 1680 and 1740. Many related developments have been closely examined: including, in the earlier period, the dissolution of the monasteries, the sale of Crown lands and the deteriorating position of the aristocracy; and, in the later period, the role of marriage and inheritance, government office, estate management and landowners' involvement in urban property and agricultural and industrial enterprise. With these detailed studies, the picture now appears much more complex, though in general it can be concluded that, with an active land market, enterprising men from diverse social origins, including the gentry, but also wealthy merchants, urban businessmen and professional men, were able to accumulate land as a means of improving their wealth and status.

If these former centuries have been well cleared, sowed and harvested by British rural historians to the point at which one is able to develop a total rural vision (for example, Mingay's own work), interest in the contemporary period is altogether more recent. The years of the Great Depression at the end of the nineteenth century are clearly the best known; with several studies of prices, rents and production having contributed to an understanding of its role in the decline of the old hegemony of the landed interest. Beyond that, however, relatively little work has been undertaken by agricultural historians on the causes and consequences of the return to protectionism in 1932, or of other major developments in the twentieth century.

The use of regional and local studies has been particularly favoured by British historians: they have greatly extended the range and diversity of observed change; and have laid the foundations for more general deductions. For example, recent studies have demonstrated that local variations in medieval field systems derive from the variety of physical conditions (relief, climate and soil) rather than, as once thought, the racial origins of those who settled different regions.

From this review, it seems that British rural historians are effectively intertwining economic analysis (of rent, land tax, prices, yields) and socio-political analysis (of the formation of dominant elites and the lot of subordinate groups). Much of the work of recent decades has dealt with traditional themes, such as field systems, the spread of innovations and fluctuations in farming prosperity. The more novel themes have emerged largely in the field of social history and have included studies of rural manpower, the nature and experience of different labour fractions and occupational groups (such as child labour, farm servants, harvesters, rural craftsmen and estate agents), rural living and working conditions, and unrest and disorder. In addition, beyond the central preoccupations with agrarian structures, the social relations of landownership and technical change in agriculture, British historians have paid considerable attention to demographic behaviour and the ways of life of country people. Even if a number of subject areas have not been sufficiently explored (such as farm capital, rural housing and health conditions) this has not detracted from a general comprehension of rural society and the sources of its variation and transformation. To this end, appropriate statistical sources (including parish registers, land tax records and estate accounts) are being subjected to modern computer-based treatment. Consequently, earlier interpretations are increasingly being re-evaluated and qualified, such as the role of the Black Death in the reorganisation of the manor and Marxist interpretations of the enclosure movement. British rural history is, therefore, an active and dynamic discipline.

Ronald Hubscher's paper addresses the French tradition of rural history, and his theme is notably different from Mingay's. He stresses the importance of the nineteenth and twentieth centuries in French rural historical research and draws specific attention to methodological approaches. For the historiographic practice of rural history in France, which has tended to take place through the medium of theses for the *Doctorat d'Etat*, has given much weight to the unavoidable principles of methodology. Two major epistemological phases can be distinguished:

- that of the 1930s, strongly influenced by Georges Lefebvre's *Les Paysans du Nord*;
- that beginning in the 1950s (a key influence being Robert Laurent's thesis on vine growers in the Côte-d'Or, produced in 1955) which, through subsequent decades, became a national enterprise for contemporary historians, with the mosaic now nearing completion.

French rural history has given priority to regional, or indeed, *départemental* space, largely through a multiplicity of independent local histories. In resolving the contradiction between the wish scrupulously to respect the individuality of a place and the scientific need to assure compatibility of information, each author displays, in minute detail, his or her sources and documentary evidence. One regularly encounters, therefore, the same homogeneous statistical series, communal information and *départemental* summaries of cantonal data, the major decennial censuses and cadastral and fiscal sources, all echoing the atavistic centralisation of the French state.

Amongst the writings of contemporary historians, the political/administrative relations of *procureurs*, prefects, *conseillers généraux* and judges have been examined along with the statements of politicians, particularly during election periods, of local notables and of agricultural organisations (*Sociétés d'Agriculture*, and so on). Against these accounts, the viewpoints and opinions of working people have not been especially evident, except for during periods of election or revolt.

The heaviest statistical treatments have concerned *cadastres* and the registries of land exchange, farm leases, and mortgages kept by the *Service de l'Enregistrement*, which effectively represent the 'civil state of property ownership' and, as unique records of the landed civilisation of post-revolutionary France, they have facilitated the extensive construction of structural typologies.

Quantitative techniques, based largely upon the establishment of homogeneous series, have often been employed by French rural historians and have allowed them to identify annual fluctuations (for example, in yields or prices) or more long-term shifts (for example, in populations or structures). Statistics remain in widespread use in history – numbers in the service of thought. The method claims to be all-embracing, combining 'the use of economic analysis and an historical approach, the abstract and the concrete, structural viewpoints and a sensitivity to duration' (J. Bouvier).

To be able to trace the dynamic of change, the historian has generally chosen to define a geographical area which coincides with a centre or focus of activity, or of economic development. In areas of mixed farming, this dynamic has usually been found within the dominant agriculture (i.e. cereals); and in monocultural regions, within the specialist agriculture (e.g. viticulture). Whichever the case, the relations of production, where yields, prices and farming practices interact, mediates the impact of and modifications to agricultural structures.

Then at the surface of this complex edifice, society forms, closely moulded by the land and affected by demographic factors (population density, migrations etc.), social behaviour (family strategies, succession etc.), the network of elites and social relations (the Church, the Town Hall, etc.). Through elucidating the functional mechanisms of the society, it is possible to grasp the collective and individual efforts by which men organise and govern themselves. Following on from this, much emphasis has been placed upon permanency, upon inhibitors, upon adaptations and innovations and upon the forces of renewal and progress. Passing from infrastructures to superstructures, many studies have explored the political and cultural dimension and, in doing so, have resurrected the 'total history' dear to Marc Bloch and Lucien Febvre and the 'total social phenomenon' of Albert Soboul and Marcel Mauss.

The issue of the integration of the rural world into industrial society, the market economy, or more generally, society at large has led researchers to examine the town/country dialectic, which can be both conflictual and consensual.

In this respect, the nineteenth century can be divided in two. Before the mid-century, the still relatively slow process of economic transformation maintained a rural and agrarian society. Subsequently, however, profound changes took place (including the creation of a common, national market aided by the growing rail network and imperial prosperity) and these propelled agricultural reform more or less towards capitalism.

Consequently, a wide diversity of examples of growth processes within the national territory have emerged: for some, the focus has been the best adapted regions, generally the richest (the basins), or those which have the true advantage of position (the vine growing areas); while others have considered the isolated regions (the poor and peripheral zones). Macro-economic analysis has been made easier by the existence of works of synthesis and popularisation: including *l'Histoire économique et sociale*, edited by Fernand Braudel and Ernest Labrousse, *l'Histoire de la France rurale*, edited by Georges Duby and Armand Wallon, and *l'Histoire des Français*, edited by Yves Lequin.

The justification of the monograph is precisely that it has clarified processes of growth and decline, with the mass of individual case studies allowing the establishment of more general *problématiques*. It seems, for example, that particularly in times of agricultural prosperity, agriculture has boosted overall growth, whereas at other times, including the agricultural depression of the last quarter of the nineteenth century, it has acted as a brake on the general economy. Jean Bouvier has therefore isolated the role of agriculture in the French process of industrialisation, with agricultural backwardness both constraining the process (François Crouzet) while also being a consequence of its relatively slow pace (Louis Bergeron). Crucial factors include: the role maintained by rural industry (Ronald Hubscher); temporary migrations; and collectivist practices.

Today 'revisionist' analyses have prompted a re-evaluation of the aptly-called neglected backwaters. Thus, with respect to structures, the persistence of small-scale agriculture has shown that it is capable of adaptation and innovation. In the vine producing areas in the south of France, for example, the use of cooperative cellars and the more general pooling of resources have been crucial to the survival of the small producers. Similarly, with respect to capital, the weakness of investment is now considered less responsible for agricultural conservatism than was originally thought.

Gilles Postel-Vinay has clearly demonstrated that the larger farms have not been the only ones illustrating the progress of capitalism in agriculture. André Gueslin, in bringing the accounts of the *Credit Agricole Mutuel* to the attention of historians, has demonstrated the significant role played by the so-called 'Green' bank in France.

The issue of the land recurs. Beyond the debate between collective and private ownership, a dialectic exists between large and small property ownership. The French process of agricultural development offers, at one and the same time, the scope for both large and small agricultural enterprises. Compared to the British process, is it obsolete or simply different?

French rural history has arrived at a period of synthesis, even though certain *terra incognita* remain. Nevertheless, historians seem tirelessly ready to renew their fields of interest, while research is constantly being directed towards new issues. The bicentennial of the French Revolution has, for example, brought up again the question of peasant revolts, while, for some time, Pierre Barral and Maurice Agulhon have been concerned with the rural dimension of national political change. Furthermore, practitioners of rural history appear less pessimistic than their collegues in sociology. Rural historians have for long addressed the effects of industrial and urban influences and for them at least the demise of the peasantry does not mean the end of the countryside as an object of intrinsic interest. If the 'agricultural revolution' has forced people from the land, then it may well be, from the example of other countries (such as the USA), that a 'rural revolution' will establish a non-agricultural population within the countryside (Gavignaud 1983). The subject of rural history is moving on.

In terms of this paper's aims of comparing the British and the French rural history traditions, it appears that the coherence of French research in this field owes much to the university institution in which it has been undertaken. Researchers, at once historians and geographers, have had to respond to the methodological necessities of the *Doctorat d'Etat*. From the conceptualisation of the rural object of study, to the conclusions of individual studies, the influence of the 'founding fathers' is evident, though French rural historians have not hesitated to incorporate material derived from neighbouring academic disciplines. British rural historians are perhaps a more diverse group clustered around particular thematic specialisations or periods within the broad currents of social and economic history. They interact not just with fellow scholars but with historical geographers and ecologists and with amateur and local historians too, as well as with foreign specialists, particularly North Americans, who have made significant contributions to the understanding of British rural history.

The significance of agriculture and of rural society in French economy and society up to the twentieth century has incontestably had a major influence in directing research work to recent centuries. In contrast British historical effort has been spread much more evenly over the medieval and modern periods. Whichever the focus, the countryside, the landscape and its former inhabitants, its richness and their dramas have not lost their attraction for those who are searching for more than merely roots and less than simply ideologies; perhaps just for traces of a lost Eden.

5 History in Perspective: Rural Studies in French Historiography

Geneviève Gavignaud and Ronald Hubscher

For half a century, rural history has been one of the most valued components of the French school of history. The influence of the land and the importance of the peasant in French society, the rural ancestry of the great majority of Frenchmen, the agrarian awareness traditionally common amongst elites, particularly political elites up until the 1950s, and the significance of the countryside in the collective imagination, have ensured the importance of this field of research. There is nothing surprising in the fact that the greatest historians, and their numerous imitators, should have been particularly interested in what is after all, one of the essential components of French civilisation – from Georges Lefebvre and Marc Bloch to Georges Duby, Pierre Goubert, Ernest Labrousse, Le Roy Ladurie and Maurice Agulhon. This is one reason why the analysis of the rural 'milieu' has contributed in such a major way to the development of concepts of 'total history' and why there have been such strong links between the *Annales* school and rural history. It is easy to understand the importance of rural history in the journal, *Annales. Economies. Sociétés. Civilisations*, which has long been receptive both to the new questions that rural history has often helped to raise, and to the new interpretations that these questions have subsequently prompted. However, after an especially outstanding period from the 1960s to the 1980s characterised by a particularly rich flow of monographic publications, a certain loss of momentum seems to be discernible today.

1 The Annales School: A methodology for French rural history *Geneviève Gavignaud*

The emergence of a historical school

The *Annales* school is inseparable from the journal *Annales d'histoire economique et sociale* (which later became *Annales. Economies. Sociétés. Civilisations*), the first edition of which appeared on the 15 January 1929, edited by Lucien Febvre and Marc Bloch (Carbonell and Livet 1983). In the first foreword the two editors set out their intention to give to economic and social history the attention it deserved. They challenged the excessive compartmentalisation of history practised by established historians (the antiquarians, medievalists and modernists) and demanded a more collaborative approach, first, amongst historians themselves and, then, between historians and anthropologists, geographers, sociologists and archivists. Thus they strove to 'search out uncompromisingly the living elements and infinite variety of daily life'. The basic themes – a strong emphasis on economics, an interest in the social dimension, a long-ranging perspective and an interdisciplinary approach – were established at the outset.

These methods, new to historians at the time, germinated and flowered in a specific intellectual atmosphere – the university environment of Strasbourg in the years immediately following the First World War. Febvre and Bloch, his junior by ten years, were professors in the *Faculté des Lettres* at Strasbourg which, since 1919 and its restoration to French Alsace, had attracted teachers of exceptional quality. This was largely the outcome of rapidly furnishing the university with a strong intellectual character in defiance, first, of the Germans and, second, of the traditional theology faculties which remained. Febvre had built a solid reputation based upon his work *L'Histoire de la Franche-Comté* (1911) when he was assigned to Strasbourg. Similarly, Georges Lefebvre arrived there having already published his *Paysans du Nord* (1924). Bloch published his *Caractères originaux de l'histoire rurale française* in 1931.

From this point on, Strasbourg was a meeting place of European thought, rivalling Paris, though Dean Pfister complained in 1925 that it was the 'antechamber of the Sorbonne'. Nevertheless, this Strasbourgian efflorescence was firmly within the European intellectual avant-garde. The influence of the German school of history, from Roscher to Schmoller – who taught at Strasbourg before the war – was evident. Under the influence of these historians, a historicist perspective came to penetrate all disciplines and history and economics, in particular, were brought closer together. Meanwhile in Paris, in 1903, and under the influence of the socialist thinker Jean Jaurès, the *Commission d'histoire économique et sociale de la Révolution française* had been established.

The *Annales* school never explicitly promoted Marxist politics even though its founders and many of its readers were more or less sympathetic to the tenets of historical materialism. What characterised Strasbourgian thought during the 1920s was the 'spirit of synthesis', a subject on which the philosopher Henri Berr (from Lorraine) wrote a seminal article in 1921–22 in the journal he edited, *Revue de synthèse historique*. Berr especially appreciated what was happening in Strasbourg as he himself had been pleading since the 1890s for an 'all-embracing historical science', and Febvre and Bloch had also contributed to his journal.

Eminent historians, the first editors of the *Annales* were also, in their own words, specialists in rural history. The first edition of the journal set out its somewhat fragmented plans under the signature of Marc Bloch who, the following year, published 'The struggle for agrarian individualism in 18th Century France'.

His former students still remember his course on 'Rural Life and the French Peasantry of the Middle Ages' which dealt with and interwove agricultural systems, seigneural rights, land clearance, village society and so on. At his side, Lucien Febvre stressed the importance of the land: 'For my part, I have only ever known – and I still only know – one way of comprehending, of placing, History. And that way is to fully understand, from the outset, and through all its development, the history of a region or a province'.

A disciple of Vidal de la Blache and close to Albert Demangeon, Lucien Febvre attempted to 'remove the barrier between geography and history'. In his work *La terre et l'évolution humaine*, he incorporated a 'geographical introduction to history': between man and his environment, there are ideas; and the natural milieu almost always offers a range of possibilities from which societies are free to choose alternatives. The collaboration of Demangeon, Henri Baulig and Jules Sion in *Annales* was welcomed by Febvre for whom geography should not be limited simply to describing the background scenery of history or to providing only the introductory picture, which so many historians believed themselves obliged to paint, if only 'to satisfy the restless spirits of Voltaire and Michelet' (Carbonell and Livet 1983). With geography, Febvre introduced to history the spatial dimension, the importance of land-form and a sense of the real-world.

Other close relationships linked history to anthropology under the influence of Marcel Mauss and to sociology under the influence of Maurice Halbwachs. The Durkheim school (Espinal, Hauser and also Simiand) had already begun to use statistical methods which also drew the attention of Mathiez, Lefebvre, Labrousse and others. The interdisiplinary call had been heard and the *Annales* which included Halbwachs and Demangeon on its editorial committee, became 'a permanent conference of the human sciences' in the apt expression of Fernand Braudel.

In the meantime, Georges Lefebvre had focused his interest on the revolutionary period: his *Questions agraires au temps de la Terreur, La Grande Peur* (1932) led him in the direction of the *Société des Etudes robespierristes* and the *Annales historiques de la Révolution française*. It is in these journals that the most important of his contributions to French agrarian history are to be found.

From this point on, rural history has always had a place of honour throughout France not only because of its practitioners but also, and above all, because of its omnipresence in French civilisation. The land, as a subject, was all the more open to research as it had not, until then, succeeded in attracting much attention from observers obsessed with other forms of history. It is appropriate to note, however, that in the spirit of the *Annales*, rural history has not benefited from any particular treatment: economic and social components, statistics and real-world studies, longitudinal analyses and syntheses have all been employed. Everything has been pressed into service in order to present a kaleidoscope of all aspects of local life.

The founders of the *Annales* therefore reoriented researchers, established research teams, and initiated them on themes and programmes of research based upon a solid *problématique*. A new goal emerged in history: to know how to understand, to fully comprehend, the past and the evolution of human societies. The fundamental importance of this challenge is demonstrated by its influence on subsequent generations of historians.

A developing structural and social history

Febvre and Bloch opened history up to a more profound analysis and in doing so directed historians towards the use of the most durable facts and data bases in their field of investigation. Thus structural history was born. With the work of Ernest Labrousse, this became quantified, as numerical and statistical data sources were used to trace events and circumstances over a long-term period, typically a century. From this perspective, structures are seen to emerge. According to Fernand Braudel, 'by the term structures, observers of social processes understand an organisation or coherence of relationships that are strongly fixed between real-world realities and social forms. For us historians, a structure is, without doubt, a framework or an architecture but more importantly it is a reality which because of its longevity, does not fit easily into a simple temporal context' (Braudel 1958).

Onto these structures, abstracted from the real-world, individual circumstances or events restore the movement of life. If structure supposes deconstruction and reconstruction, the circumstance or event introduces notions of dialectic which allow one to understand the dynamic nature of structures. 'History, even structural history, remains after Simiand, in the thoughts of E. Labrousse, the history of change and of variation', maintains Pierre Chaunu (1974). Thus French historiography gave a dynamic sense to structuralism, which had moved away from the stage that Claude Lévi-Strauss had attributed to it in the human sciences, that of the so-called 'primitive' societies. Structuralism became therefore, in Jean Piaget's expression, 'genetic' (1972).

Genetic structuralism does not reduce to a linear chain of causality. Rather, it allows the possibilities of discontinuity and of rupture in dialectic evolution. All structural equilibrium is thereby precariously balanced between multiple and constantly shifting hierarchies, continuously being remoulded within the total social phenomenon (Gurvitch 1967). To resolve the false structuralist/history debate, it seemed necessary to historians to contrive certain specific historical time periods:

- The long term: that of structures, their establishment, development (or non-development), or their persistence (Fernand Braudel);
- Circumstantial time: that of the multiple oscillations of prices and incomes which affect structures in both the short and the long term, all the more so as structures themselves are, in part, composed from commodities used for sale and speculation (Ernest Labrousse).
- Social time: 'the time of history in the making' (Pierre Vilar), or the 'social period' as Fernand Braudel prefers to call it; by conceiving the temporal length of a society, one can examine the stages of that society's progression and the forces of social evolution. Pierre Goubert (1960) has made the society of the Beauvais region a reference model for this style of approach.

The primacy of agrarian structures has dominated the attention of all historians of both rural areas and the peasantry. Georges Lefebvre raised the fundamental question: 'Who possesses the land as an instrument of production?' On the origin of agrarian structures, Pierre Vilar (1961) has introduced the themes of primitive settlement and resettlement structures and the relationship of these to both the means and the relations of production. The theme entitled '*structuralo-événementialo-structurelle*' by Emmanuel Le Roy Ladurie (1960) and already used by André Siegfried (1913) and Paul Bois (1960) consists of going backwards in time in order to reintegrate an event within corresponding structures.

A large number of rural history theses have consequently emphasised notions of property and the realisation of land value; for example, in the years between 1955 and 1960, those of Robert Laurent (1955), Albert Soboul (1958) and Philippe Vigier (1961). Since the affirmation and defence of the rights of property in the Revolution, private property can be simultaneously a production structure (the land constituting the principal means of production), an economic structure (producing both a direct financial output and allowing fiscal transfers) and a social structure (the family adapting to its dimension).

While the school of agrarian socialism has attempted to develop a theory of peasant society as a counterpart to the Marxist account of industrial society, historians have preferred the reality of life to intellectual speculation. Paying close attention to the detailed evidence, they have patiently analysed French rural society and its contemporary history. Pierre Barral (1968) has thrown light on the agrarianism which characterises national politics, from Méline to Pisani. Maurice Agulhon (1970) has turned his attentions more closely to social and political behaviour to the point at which it becomes a collective consciousness. Alain Corbin (1975) has been keen to stress the importance of regional customs and attitudes. Ronald Hubscher (1979–80) has investigated the rural society of the Pas-de-Calais in its entirety. In all, it has been the quest for a history written in the soil and in individual societies. Such a history begins with the basic structure, the agricultural system, and extends, according to the teachings of Marc Bloch (1931), 'to a study of both the techniques and customs of the rural world'. It is aimed at the 'explosive enormity of the total phenomenon'. Its principle and its method are to identify the maximum number of components of social reality – including its past and its present – and to establish the links which can exist between them; though, without pretending to be capable of tying up all the loose ends.

2 A critical assessment of approaches to rural history in France
Ronald Hubscher

Between 1960 and 1987, with a particularly fruitful period during the 1970s, historical studies in France were considerably enriched by works on the rural world. During this period, hardly a year passed without the publication of some major new contribution to the understanding of the French countryside. However, it is chiefly by looking at the *thèses d'Etat*, which have tended to 'set the tone' and reflect the state of the various issues, that one can best assess the current status of rural history in France.

But first, what is 'rural' for the historian? Undoubtedly the dominant reference points have been the land and the agricultural population rather than other sectors of activity or other social categories. 'Rural' therefore connotes agriculture. This is clearly demonstrated in the titles of many *thèses d'Etat*, as the following examples show; *Paysans de l'Ouest* by P. Bois (1960), *Les Paysans du Var: (fin XIXe siècle-début XXe siècle)* by Y. Rinaudo (1982), *Les Paysans du Doubs et la Seconde République: genèse d'une paysannerie conservatrice* by J.L. Mayaud (1984), *Les Paysans Beaucerons de la fin de l'Ancien Régime aux al lendemains de la première guerre mondiale* by J.C. Farcy (1985) and *Paysans et notables du Morvan au XIXe siècle* by M. Vigreux (1987). The major place accorded to the peasantry is easily justified if one takes into account the numerical preponderance of those for whom the land – over which they either have, or do not have, control – is the principal means by which they generate their income. This axiom has been accepted not only by modern historians, such as E. Le Roy Ladurie, P. Goubert and J. Jacquart, but also by contemporary historians even including those who have passed over the fateful threshold of 1914. G. Garrier (1973), C. Mesliand (1980) and G. Gavignaud 1983, covering the peasantry of Beaujolais and Lyonnais, Vaucluse and Roussillon respectively, have all placed the nineteenth century at the core of their analyses; a century which despite industrialisation remained, symbolically, that of the Peasant Republic[1]. The title of G. Désert's thesis *Une société rurale au XIXe siecle: les paysans du Calvados, 1815–1895* (1975) is very revealing of this semantic association between 'rural' and 'agricultural'. In the same way, pluriactivity has tended to be interpreted solely from the agricultural point of view even though it is an essential component of the French rural world.

In the search for truth from observation, French historians' analyses of the rural situation appear to have relied upon a set of recognisable foci or themes, of which we might identify four. First, there is the geographical focus on a defined spatial area. Secondly, there is the economic focus on the development of activities which determine the structures of production and the connections between specific production types.

Thirdly, there is the social focus on a society closely shaped by the influence of the land. In its complex structure, one can distinguish a diversity of circumstances, linked to cross-cutting legal, economic and social positions, where the divisions between different groups are often imprecise (for example, the status of small-scale landowners who can be both owners and workers at the same time). One seeks to understand such a society by identifying the relationships between its various components and, especially, the networks of dependence formed around the land (for example, clientelism). Social stratification is either reconstructed from a local reality (e.g. R. Hubscher 1979) or alternatively is found in more general social criteria; for example, the notion of the higher, middle and *petite bourgeoisie* (eg: G. Désert 1975). Nevertheless, it is always based upon the analysis of wealth and poverty (often following the methods of Adeline Daumard) from which one can more accurately identify different social groupings.

Fourthly, there is the cultural focus. This, the most recent theme in rural history, described as 'the intangible aspects of daily life, the community "atmosphere", habits and attitudes', (M. Agulhon 1970) is nonetheless necessary if one is to understand 'peasant civilisation' in its widest meaning.

Emerging from these four basic approaches has been a double *problématique* which has underlain all the works of French rural history. On the one hand, 'rural' is the art of discrimination. Researchers have emphasised the uniqueness of the rural 'object' under study, its originality or its 'deviance' from national norms and from macro-history. This theme is often more implicit than explicit as authors have often been hesitant to incorporate their object of study in any genuine model. Nevertheless, in all cases, stress has been particularly laid upon the constants of resistance to change and constraints to development within the rural world (see, for example, Alain Corbin's *Archaisme et modernité en Limousin au XIXe siècle, 1845–1880* (1975)).

On the other hand, the 'rural' and the wider society are juxtaposed thereby raising the issue of the integration of the rural world in industrial society and the market economy. This issue has led on to the themes of town/country and dominant/dominated relations, interpreted in terms of opposition and complementarity (for example, J-C Farcy 1985; R. Hubscher, 1979–80). The process of integration, which brings inevitable changes to rural society, exposes forces of renewal and progress (the whole question of 'innovation'), as well as factors of instability and readjustment (such as migratory phenomena). Much attention has been given to evolutionary change; both that taking place relatively slowly within structures, and that more immediately visible in ruptures, cyclical fluctuations and, in particular, with respect to economic crises. Such change, which is dear to historians is palpable in a series of limited crises such as phylloxera and that affecting silk-worms and oil-producing plants. In response to the globalisation of exchanges and the establishment of unified markets, it has also seen farmers driven towards greater specialisation. It has accelerated the growing importance of the town (including the adaptation of agricultural production to new urban demands, and the invasion of manufactured products). At the same time, it has provoked the destabilisation of the rural order both in demographic terms, with the town becoming the 'consumer' of men, and in social terms, through the modification of social relationships within rural society (for example, the homogenisation of the agricultural community with the diminution of social disparities, through the outmigration of many of the rural working class and the expansion of a middle-class peasantry, based on family farming).

Thus in terms of major themes, the accent in French rural history has been placed upon divisions, upon the dynamics of change, upon the dialectics of the structure-circumstance relationship (a theme strongly supported by G. Gavignaud) and, finally, upon the village society-global society relationship, including its political/cultural aspects which have been studied in great detail by Maurice Agulhon in *La République au village* (1970) and others. At the time of the nascent democracy of the beginnings of universal suffrage, politics became a major instrument in the Republican conquest of the countryside, which took place through the vote, the town hall, and the school. Cultural assimilation, republicanism and politicisation all came together.

The rural world has been reconstructed through a series of necessary, normative analyses that have emphasised changing economy/society relations. However, the charismatic authority of the founding fathers and the research conditions in France have heavily constrained the work undertaken, which has been characterised by a certain rigidity in its conceptualisation and a tendency to be rather narrowly 'academic'.

The tradition of local or regional monographs

The predominant form in which the rural world as an object of study has been described has been the monograph, covering a *département* or region. Works which deal with the national scale are much less common but include macro-economic studies such as J.B. Viallon's *La croissance agricole en France et en Bourgogne de 1850 à nos jours* (1976) and A. Gueslin's *Les origines du Crédit agricole en France, 1840 – 1914* (1978) and *Crédit, Agriculture et Mutualisme en France des années 1910 aux années 1970* (1983, described by P. Vigier as 'a decisive contribution . . . to the understanding of rural France'), as well as Y. Grebouw's *Salaires et salariés agricoles en France de la fin du XVIIIe siècle au début du XXe siècle* (1986).

Beyond these particular cases, the procedure adopted in local monographic studies has been relatively consistent. The analysis generally progresses from infrastructures to superstructures, each element in the work articulating with the one following, producing a pattern that largely determines the following characteristic layout of a thesis:

- the natural context: a geographical description covering the climate and the land-form which, while stressing the diversity within the study area, usually concludes by defining the region as a unique and identifiable area with a specific agricultural potential. From this point, the author moves towards the notion of regional disparities, a subject which has received much attention from rural historians;
- the demographic factors: people and their distribution (population density/housing density) usually complemented by classic demographic analyses following the style of Pierre Goubert (involving birth rates, death rates, marriage, fecundity etc):
- the economic characteristics;
- the society; including the identification and analysis of social categories;
- the politics, the religion, and the culture whose interaction recent theses have examined.

In all the monographic theses, one finds recurring themes. Amongst the most common is, first, the context of agricultural production; involving an evaluation of the soil and a study of the agricultural enterprises and farming practices (including crops, productivity, yields, agricultural workforces and so on). Secondly, there is usually an analysis of land structures from the associated points of view of property ownership and land-use.

A third common theme is the study of the social relations resulting from the allocation of property ownership and types of agricultural practice (notably from the perspective of direct or indirect enterprise). The study of agricultural labour, the means of production and the production process itself has led to the examination of wealth generation within the agricultural sector through revenues (and thereby, prices), inheritance (through the analysis of accumulated wealth) and indicators of investment capability, as well as to the study of the social redistribution of this wealth.

Thus, the opening up of the countryside to a national market, the impact of the competitive economy (and the issue of the costs of production) and the effect of transformations within the global economy which have provoked, for example, the decline of home-based employment, the increasing dependence of producers on consumers and the inequality of growth within the countryside which, in turn, has contributed to regional disparities, have all been examined in local monographic studies. Fluctuations in revenue have been interpreted in terms of demographic transformation and economic mutation, with social groups either profiting or being penalised by such long-term change.

Finally, the modification of social structures and of social relations under the influence of wide-ranging pressures has been considered as well as the impact on trades union organisation, political behaviour etc. To counteract the upheavals threatened by such modifications, the dominant social classes within rural society have often sought to impose their own indigenous identity by creating an agrarian ideology (see, for example, the admirable book by P. Barral on *Les Agrariens français de Méline à Pisani* published in 1968). In the defence and promotion of traditional values, with the countryside projected as the guardian in the face of the 'corrupt' town, rural society has not been loth to adapt models from outside the rural milieu to serve its purpose. Thus the organisation of farmers as an occupational group has been marked by the rapid growth of indigenous agricultural unionism (see for example, G. Garrier 1973) while the setting up of regional representative bodies (such as the *Confédération générale des vignerons du Midi*) or national ones (such as the agricultural parliamentary group), has enabled them to act as an effective political lobby (see R. Hubscher 1985).

By way of a summary, several monographs have raised the issue of the degree of adaptation of the study region to the conditions imposed by the existence of a modern competitive economy. This, in turn, has introduced the concept of growth models. In all the works reviewed here, priority has been given to the appropriation of the land. Indeed, this is the principal focus of Gavignaud's thesis. Social relations are formed around the land, not only within rural society but within society as a whole. The land is a crucial factor in town/country relations and, for a long time, has been the preferred means whereby certain urban inhabitants, through rent relations, have sought to establish their hegemony over the country.

Why this tradition?

Why has rural history focused so specifically upon the local situation and the monographic approach? Indubitably together they form an important stage in historical research; a stage that has been given much legitimacy. One might cite, for example, J. Rougerie's *L'histoire départementalisée* published in the *Annales* in 1966, or P. Leuilliot in the preface of his *Aspects de l'économie nivernaise au XIXe siècle*, or E. Labrousse for whom 'truth is multiple, real, and therefore local' or, finally, M. Agulhon, according to whom, '*Départemental* history . . . owes its scientific worth to the minutiae of local investigations' (taken from his foreword to J.L. Mayaud's thesis, 1986). *Départemental* or regional history has generally been interpreted as differential history. Because one cannot deny the variety and the individuality of the rural world, it has been necessary to study it at the local level so as to trace the multiplicity of its contours. The rural historian has also tended to rely upon this *départemental* scale for his sources and data and for summaries of communal and cantonal information; including the major agricultural surveys which were undertaken every decade during the nineteenth century, lists of names, the cadastre, fiscal archives and so on.

Furthermore, rural history – more perhaps than other sectors of the discipline – has been influenced by the traditions of its grand forefathers in taking on board new *problématiques*, though sometimes rather too slowly and without setting aside the previous, more classical, ones. The result is that in reading rural history theses, one frequently comes across successive approaches to historical research, like so many geological strata lying obediently one on top of the other.

The influence of geography upon rural history has been significant. For a long time, the university tradition in France made the rural world the exclusive preserve of geographers. Under Demangeon, Blanchard, Sion and their followers, regional studies, which accorded a major place to the long-term evolution of landscapes, populations and conditions of production, proliferated. This strong liaison between geography and history has persisted to this day in the syllabuses of higher education, which have tended to give complementary status to the two disciplines. The relationship between the natural and the human milieu has been largely internalised by French historians; hence the inevitable physical descriptions with which all rural theses seem to begin and the importance given to a certain physical determinism in explanations of agricultural activities.

A second important influence has been the innovative approach of the *Annales* school and the enormous perspectives offered by 'total history' as advocated by Marc Bloch and Lucien Febvre and invigorated by the demographic contribution of such as Marcel Reinhard, Ph. Ariès and Pierre Goubert. However, under the inspiration of Ernest Labrousse, quantitative history – first economic and then social – has also had a strong and lasting influence upon rural studies giving them a new legitimacy. Furthermore, studies have been strengthened by long-term perspectives, of the kind first introduced by Fernand Braudel. Finally, by adopting the methods of ethno-history and by integrating the approaches of a wide range of other disciplines, rural history has been considerably enriched.

Thus, one comes to understand better the ways in which French historians have approached the rural world: an approach that has, first, incorporated a geographical awareness and, secondly, has developed a resolutely quantitative, economic and social-historical methodology (involving yields, prices, incomes, social categories and their interaction) which has combined, in various dialectic relations, Reinhardian demography, cyclical fluctuation, behavioural change, and Labrousse-inspired ruptures along with Braudelian permanent and long-term temporal perspectives; all indispensable keys for penetrating the 'prisons', the mentalities and the phenomena of human civilisation.

However, although researchers have tended to stress the quantitative approach, they have not neglected qualitative methodologies by adopting a 'prosopographical' (i.e. collective biographical analysis), and thereby a more ethno-historical, approach. In actual fact, ethnographers have pioneered a field of research not usually addressed by rural historians. While the latter have been largely content to study rural families from a demographic perspective, the former have done so from the far more valuable viewpoint of familial relationships, networks of family alliances, the mobility of women and of dowries; in short, from the perspective of accumulation and transmission leading ultimately to the analysis of private and public power within rural society. A major contribution to this approach has been made by the sociological work of P. Bourdieu who introduced the notion of symbolic capital 'based upon knowledge and gratitude' and which is 'the accumulation of a particular form of capital; that of a man's reputation or prestige'. As a genuine factor within rural society, and frequently a source of conflict, symbolic capital is 'a fundamental dimension of social life'.

Incorporating these major themes in French ethnological studies, researchers have moved into the world of personal relations, matrimonial patterns and behaviour and strategies of land acquisition, and have considered a range of diverse subjects from the role of personal relationships in political life (municipal elections becoming the specific theatre of antagonistic inter-familial competition for power and prestige) and complex structures of alliances to relations between official rights, customary rights and successionary processes, to the mechanisms by which domestic groups are perpetuated. French ethnologists have investigated, in great detail, the peasant civilisation which reached its apogee in the second half of the nineteenth century, including its rituals, its indigenous knowledge, its symbols, and its imagination.

The majority of rural historians in France have passed along these various research paths though generally prudently, as historians have often been wary of concentrating too specifically upon traditional peasant civilisation for fear of presenting the rural world as being never-changing and somehow fixed in the past. Nonetheless, recent historical works have been significantly influenced by anthropology, and rural history is becoming more and more receptive to pluridisciplinarity though whether this is in response to the demands of the subject, or is merely jumping on a bandwagon, is perhaps debatable. The traditional preoccupations of rural historians – fluctuating circumstances and other forms of change – seem outdated when compared with the more vigorous themes of sociability, violence, regional identity or the integration of the peasant into the nation.

Some have criticised rural history as being characterised by a lack of theory, though such a prognosis is challengeable. The thesis of A. Wahl (1980) sought to verify, from local case studies, the famous Weberian equation of Protestantism and economic dynamism; while G. Gavignaud has looked at changes in landownership in Roussillon in the light of theories of property and appropriation formulated in the nineteenth and twentieth centuries. More generally, theoretical concerns lie behind the interest shown by most researchers in the issues of property ownership and land use in rural areas. These are the subjects of a major ideological debate concerning the evolution of French society since the revolution, raising such questions as:-

- Is there, or is there not, a process of land fragmentation in France? Are peasants gaining the advantage over urban residents and tenants of the land in the appropriation of rural space?
- Is large-scale agriculture economically superior to small-scale agriculture?
- Has there been a triumph of agrarian capitalism in France, based upon the

widespread use of modern technology in agricultural enterprises, and has this use extended ineluctably throughout the French countryside?

Virtually all rural historians have addressed the last question and many of the regional monographs have evaluated the diversity of growth models operating in rural areas and the intrinsicality of rural development processes. Some have contradicted accepted wisdom in identifying the persistent dynamism and strength of small-scale agriculture in certain regions. This has proved the need, first, for a reappraisal of models of rural development (Hubscher 1985) and, secondly, for a research approach which addresses theoretical issues more directly if only to confirm or refute them.

Nevertheless it is true that rural historians, habituated perhaps to the relativism of the *Annales* school and to the monographic method which has tended to reject direct theorisation, have largely avoided any abstraction. Refusing to place the object of their researches into an established theoretical framework, they have tenaciously held on to the exclusive validity of their documentary sources. Le Roy Ladurie, in his introduction to *Paysans du Languedoc*, has succinctly explained the changing approach of the historian to the problem of sources. After an early analysis of *compoix* (a survey of land holdings for tax purposes), 'I was', he writes, 'thrown fairly and squarely into peasant history and had come some distance from my initial preoccupation with the "origins of capitalism". It had been a classic misadventure. I had wanted to take hold of a documentary source which would unravel the certainty of my youth. Instead, the documentary source took hold of me and inspired me . . . by its particular validity'. Is this the strength or the weakness of rural history? The debate is still wide open.

On the other hand, a number of genuine weaknesses and loopholes have been evident in works of French rural history published over the last twenty years. Although today one might understand the direction and the impact of changes which have affected rural society, historians continue to ignore movement between categories and the operation of factors which assure the preservation of established roles and positions. No thesis has yet examined this issue in all its dimensions despite the fact that it is clearly one which cannot be readily separated from the understanding of the mode of operation of agricultural enterprises, which are themselves dependent upon wider society. Similarly, the process of the formation and reproduction of small and middle-scale agricultural enterprises has also been neglected. No study has considered small-scale farms in a dynamic sense over a relatively long time period, though like the family cycle, such enterprises are subject to phases of contraction and expansion which must significantly qualify any assessments that can be made of their performance, closely linked as it is to their degree of evolution. Small-scale enterprises, moreover, remain the cornerstone of a still little understood rural society mobility, the paths of which have so far defied quantitative analysis. The absence of a typology of social mobility, both upward and downward, is very evident.

As for medium-scale farms, and the social reality of the farmers concerned, these have been particularly overlooked. The acknowledged vagueness of the term 'medium-scale' has so far discouraged analysis at this level to such an extent that one might almost wonder whether such farms possess an independent identity and whether their proprietors fit into any discernible social category. Perhaps they are only the byproduct of a process of social ascent or descent, and subdivided inheritance: we just do not know.

The dynamic study of agricultural enterprises cannot be dissociated from that of pluriactivity, the importance and extent of which in France almost all rural historians have either underestimated or have interpreted in too restrictive a fashion . Ultimately, the entire economic and social structure of the countryside needs to be re-examined in the light of this phenomenon which lies at the heart of the *problématique* of the processes of integration of rural society into wider society.

The relations between that wider society and rural society have not been sufficiently refined. Far too often, they are interpreted too simplistically in terms of subordination; the countryside being dominated by the 'parasitic' towns. Studies dealing with categories and issues of age and of sex have been far too timid, limited and partial: for example, young people are frequently ignored, while the role of the aged within the village community has hardly prompted a single study. Above all, the non-agricultural rural sector has been neglected, including such important social strata as craftsmen ('the notables of the land') and small shopkeepers.

All these omissions notwithstanding, it is the economic approach which, in spite of appearances, has been the weak link in rural studies. Productivity has not been sufficiently well analysed. Although significant inroads have been made through agricultural accounting and assessments of individual farm enterprises (G. Garrier 1973; R. Pech 1975), what are still missing are general indices, at the *départemental* level, of agricultural prices; indeed any analysis of price formation which would include an analysis of costs. The problems of credit at the local level, of indebtedness and of the financial drain on the countryside imposed by the bias in land rents in favour of the town, have been the subject of only simplistic and superficial investigations. No one has examined agricultural investments or land transfers resulting from external financial inputs and, in consequence, the evolution of farming techniques has also been overlooked. Undoubtedly, there would be technical difficulties in researching such issues and a lack of suitable sources. However, the questions should at least be raised and some thought given to the possibilities of addressing them.

At present, the regional monographs such as have been described here, are increasingly becoming a mere academic exercise, often exhaustedly presented due to the lack of suitable perspectives. The distinctive talent of the individual authors has imparted no impression and one is struck by the sense of *déjà vu*, for the same mould has been used for each.

The salvation of French rural history research can come from any one of a number of directions. First of all there needs to be an extension of the field of research by removing the constriction of 1914 (including restricted access to archives) which has sterilised in-depth work on the inter-war period, for example. A re-examination is also needed of those periods already studied in the light of new questions and *problématiques*: including the role of pluriactivity in rural families, peasant power, agricultural politics in the IIIrd and IVth Republics, and the role of the peasantry in the French imagination of the nineteenth and

74 History

twentieth centuries. Thirdly, there is a need for thematic studies at the national level, or at least at the level of a group of regions (such as on the conditions of the agricultural revolution in the 1950s and 1960s and its social and economic implications). Finally, it seems increasingly desirable to develop a genuinely comparative approach starting with a common *problématique* for European rural societies. A growing number of researchers are conscious of these new directions and are responding accordingly in their studies. This will be the means by which French rural history will finds its second breath.

Note

1 The peasantry these authors present, however, is notably less archaic than that portrayed by the American historian Weber in his stimulating yet deliberately provocative book *Peasants into Frenchmen* (1976) which, beyond the somewhat questionable notion of an autonomous rural society, covers the process of integration of peasants within the larger national community.

Bibliography

Agulhon, M., *La République au village (les populations du Var de la Révolution à la Seconde République)*, Plon, Paris, 1970.

Agulhon, M., *La vie sociale en Provence intérieure*, Paris 1970.

Barral, P., *Les agrariens français de Méline à Pisani*, A. Colin, Paris, 1968.

Bloch, M., *Les caractères originaux de l'histoire rurale française*, Paris 1931.

Bois, P., *Les Paysans de l'Ouest, des structures économiques et sociales aux options politiques depuis l'époque révolutionnaire dans la Sarthe*, Le Mans, Vilaire, 1960.

Braudel, F., '*Histoire et sciences sociales: la longue durée*' dans Annales Economie-Société-Civilisations, 1958, p. 731.

Carbonell, C.O. et Livet, G., *Au Berceau des Annales*, Presses de l'Institut d'Etudes Politiques de Toulouse, 1983, 293 p.

Chaunu, C., 'L'Economie-Dépassement et prospective' dans *Faire de l'Histoire*, sous la direction de Jacques le Goff et Pierre Nora, Paris, 1974, T. II p. 57.

Corbin, A., *Archaïsme et modernité en Limousin au XIXème siècle*, 1845-1880, Rivière, Paris, 1975, 2 vol.

Désert, G., *Une société rurale au XIXème siècle. Les paysans du Calvados, 1815-1895*, Service de reproduction des thèses de l'Université de Lille, 1975, 3 vol.

Farcy, J.C., *Les Paysans beaucerons de la fin de l'Ancien Régime aux lendemains de la première guerre mondiale*, Université de Paris X-Nanterre, 1985, 3. vol. dactyl.

Garrier, G., *Paysans du Beaujolais et du Lyonnais, 1800-1970*, Presses Universitaires de Grenoble, 2 vol., 1973.

Gavignaud, G., *La révolution rurale. Essai à partir du cas américain (U.S.A.)* Roanne, Horvarth, 1983, 192 p.

Gavignaud, G., *Propriétaires-viticulteurs en Roussillon. Structures. Conjonctures. Société (XVIIIème-XXème siècle)*, Publications de la Sorbonne, Paris, 1983, 3 vol.

Goubert, G., *Beauvais et le Beauvaisis, de 1600 à 1730: Contribution à l'Histoire Sociale de la France*, Paris, SEVPEN, 1960, 635 p.

Grebouw, Y., *Salaires et salariés agricoles en France, de la fin du XVIIIème siècle au début du XXème siècle*, Université de Paris IX, 1986, 3 vol. dactyl.

Gueslin, A., *Histoire des Crédits agricoles*, Economica, Paris, 1984, 2 vol.

Gueslin, A., *Les origines du Crédit Agricole en France*, Presses de l'Université de Nancy, 1978.
Gurvitch, G., *Traité de Sociologie*, Paris, 1967, p. 20.
Hubscher, R., "*La petite exploitation en France: reproduction et compétitivité (fin XIXème siècle-début XXème siècle)*", Annales, ESC, n° 1, janvier 1985.
Hubscher, R., *L'Agriculture et la société rurale dans le Pas-de-Calais du milieu du XIXème siècle à 1914*, Commission Départementale des Monuments Historiques du Pas-de-Calais, Arrs, 1979–1980, 2 vol.
Laurent, R., *Les Vignerons de la Côte d'Or au XIXème siècle*, Paris, les Belles Lettres, 1955, 836 p.
Le Roy Ladurie, E., *Les paysans du Languedoc*, Mouton, Paris-La Haye, 1966, 2 vol.
Marx, K., *Le Capital*, L. 3, 6ème sect., p. 565.
Mayaud, J.L., *Les Secondes Républiques du Doubs*, Les Belles Lettres, Paris, 1986.
Mesliand, C., *Paysans du Vaucluse, 1869-1939*, Université d'Aix-Marseille, 1980, 3 vol. dactyl.
Pech, R., *Entreprise viticole et capitalisme en Languedoc-Roussillon. Du phylloxera aux crises de mévente*, Publications de l'Université de Toulouse-le-Mirail, 1975.
Piaget, G., *Epistémologie des Sciences de l'Homme*, Paris, 1972, préface.
Rinaudo, Y., *Les paysans du Var (fin XIXème siècle-début XXème siècle)*, Service de reproduction des thèses de l'Universitè de Lille, 1982, 3 vol.
Rougerie, J., '*Faut-il départementaliser l'Histoire de France?*', Annales ESC, janvier 1966, n° 1.
Siegfried, A., *Tableau Politique de la France de l'Ouest*, Paris, 1913.
Soboul, A., *Les campagnes montpelliéraines à la fin de l'Ancien Régime*, Paris, 1958, thèse complémentaire.
Thuillier, A., *Aspects de l'économie nivernaise au XIXème siècle*, A. Colin, 1961, (cf. la préface de P. Leuilliot).
Viallon, J.C., *La croissance agricole en France et en Bourgogne, 1850-1970*, Arno Press, New York, 1977.
Vigier, P., *Essai sur la répartition de la propriété dans la région alpine*, Paris, 1961.
Vigreux, M., *Paysans et notables du Morvan au XIXème siècle jusqu'en 1914*, Académie du Morvan, Château-Chinon, 1987.
Vilar, P., *La Catalogne dans l'Espagne moderne*, Paris, SEVPEN, 1961, T.I, p. 393.
Wahl, A., *Confessions et comportement dans les campagnes d'Alsace et de Bade, 1871-1939*, Université de Metz, 1980, dactyl.
Weber, E., *Peasants into Frenchmen. The Modernization of rural France, 1870-1914*, Stanford University Press, Stanford, California, 1976.

6 British Rural History: Themes in Agricultural History and Rural Social History

Gordon Mingay

British rural history has a long tradition, going back more than a hundred years to the pioneering work of such writers as Thorold Rogers, Maitland, the German scholar Hasbach, and the Russian Vinogradoff.[1] Some of the books produced by a slightly later generation in the years just before the First World War became standard works, still widely used even today, notably Ernle's *English Farming Past and Present*, first published in 1912, which reached a sixth edition in 1961, and J.L. and Barbara Hammond's *The Village Labourer*, 1911, of which a fifth edition appeared as recently as 1978.[2]

The decades since the First World War have seen a mounting, and now almost daunting, flow of texts, monographs, and articles, though of course over so long a period the interests of specialists in rural history have shifted in some degree as new primary sources have become available and as contemporary concerns and historical fashions have changed. Specialisation has been almost entirely on periods, with historians concentrating exclusively on the Middle Ages or earlier periods, on the early modern centuries, or on the modern era, and many historians devote their whole attention to just one century or an even shorter span of years. Within such time periods there has tended to be concentration on particular topics, such as, for example, early breeds of sheep, the origin and development of the common-field system, changes in landownership, eighteenth-century enclosures, nineteenth-century machinery, or the farm labour-force during the First World War. A few leading figures, such as Joan Thirsk, have contributed both by examining particular topics and also by drawing together large-scale general accounts of a period, as in Volumes IV and V of *The Agrarian History of England and Wales*.[3] It should be noted in passing that volume VI of this great endeavour, covering the period 1750–1860, is currently in the press, Volume VII (1850–1914) is now in active preparation, and that volume VIII (1914–1939) appeared in 1978.[4]

A great deal of modern agricultural history has centred round one or other of a few major organising themes. One of the oldest such themes is the rise of capitalist farming, i.e. large-scale farming for the market, which was exemplified by demesne farming in the early Middle Ages and continued after the leasing out of the demesnes with the gradual expansion of the scale of individual enterprise. A second theme has been that of shifts in the balance of landownership as between different strata of landowners – the 'rise of the gentry' in the period 1540–1640, and the 'rise of the great estate' in the period 1680–1740. These supposed shifts have been at the centre of studies of landownership in the past fifty years.

A traditional view influencing the interpretation of the parliamentary enclosures of the seventy years after 1760 has been that of the expropriation of the peasantry. Following Marx, left-wing historians have seen enclosure as bringing about the destruction of small owner-occupiers and the forcing of the cottagers off the land to provide the labour force of the expanding industries of the time. This view has been challenged for at least seventy-five years, and since the 1920s a 'right-wing school' of specialists has argued that the Marxist view is unsupported by the balance of the evidence, or at least is untenable in its more extreme form. However, the evidence is insufficiently unambiguous to be conclusive, and following a rather quiescent period after the late 1930s, the controversy has now revived strongly.

Lastly, the fluctuations in population – rising in the early Middle Ages, falling in the later Middle Ages, rising again in the later fifteenth and the sixteenth centuries, levelling out and then rising very rapidly from about 1750 – have been taken as the fundamental factors influencing, for example, land hunger, decline of demesne farming, the 'price revolution' of the sixteenth century, and the basic cause of rural unemployment, poverty, and unrest in the century between 1750 and 1850.

To simplify the discussion, I will concentrate first on some of the recent themes in the history of agriculture, and then on those in the area of rural social history, while recognising that the dividing line between the two is indistinct, and that, indeed, in some areas they are very closely connected.

History of agriculture

In the history of both agriculture and rural society for the two-and-a-half centuries between 1500 and 1750 much of the most recent work is to be found in Volumes IV and V of the *Agrarian History*. The medieval volumes of the series, unfortunately, are still a long way from seeing the light of day, and much of the available recent work for the Middle Ages revolves round the further elucidation of very old themes, notably the origins of, and variations in, field systems, the nature and development of the manor and its inhabitants, the effects of the Black Death, and the relationship of changes in the size of the population to trends in agriculture and rural society. In addition to some broader studies, a number of important regional and local monographs have greatly expanded our understanding of these topics.[5] In particular, they have brought out the diversity in local conditions, and thus have emphasised the hazards involved in drawing general conclusions.

To summarise the results of all this work in a few words is therefore a difficult task. But, daring to generalise where generalisation is fraught with complexity, one may tentatively suggest the following. In regard to field systems, recent evidence reinforces the view that the many local variations are explicable largely, if not always completely, by reference to physical conditions, soil, relief, climate and the nature of the farming; the old racial theory, associating regional differences in field systems to settlers of varied origins, the Kentish system to the Romans, for instance, and the common fields of the Midlands to the Scandinavians, is now more than ever discounted. Again, recent research has confirmed that changes in the organisation of the manor, specifically the leasing out of the demesne and the commutation of labour and other customary services, were well advanced before the catastrophe of the Black Death, though such changes proceeded further, of course, in its aftermath. The effects of the Black Death, being extremely varied from one area to another, remain difficult to summarise. In some parts of the country, as in the South-West, vacant lands were rapidly reoccupied, suggesting a high degree of land hunger before the outbreaks of the plague; elsewhere marginal lands were abandoned or converted from arable to pasture, the villages so affected declining in numbers or eventually disappearing altogether, though further research confirms that villages declined for a variety of reasons both before and after the great pestilence. Further, the Black Death was of course only one of a series of calamities which afflicted the fourteenth century, with other damaging outbreaks of disease and disastrous famines periodically ravaging both humans and livestock. Lastly, the earlier growth of population and its consequences may have been seriously under-estimated by previous historians. Some present opinion considers that by the beginning of the fourteenth century the population was larger than it was to be for about another four centuries, and indeed may have exceeded five millions. Whatever the true figure, the pressure of numbers on resources remains a basic element in the analysis of contemporary conditions, just as the subsequent population reduction, to as low as perhaps 2.5 millions in 1500, forms the background to the leasing out of demesnes and the commutation of services in the later Middle Ages.

Another consequence may have been improved yields for agriculture as farm production became concentrated on the better soils and the poorer land was devoted to grazing or abandoned altogether. Fluctuations in population are also held to explain a good deal of the changing agricultural conditions of the sixteenth and seventeenth centuries. Population rose from some three millions in the middle sixteenth century to over five millions in the middle seventeenth century, and in consequence the much expanded demand for food pressed on the resources of the countryside, giving rise to spectacular price increases, especially those of grain and animal products between 1500 and 1650. After the middle seventeenth century both population and long-term price levels became more stable for the next hundred years, though with a tendency for prices to fall somewhat as the productivity of agriculture increased.

This raises the question of the extent of agricultural improvement in the early modern period, one of the major themes of modern research. Twenty years ago Professor Kerridge put forward his case for the 'agricultural revolution' having occurred, not in the traditional period 1750–1850, but rather in the early modern period. Specifically, he claims, this revolution occurred between 1560 and 1767, with 'all its main achievements' falling before 1720, 'most of them before 1673, and many of them much earlier still'.[6] The grounds for this claim he held to lie chiefly in the use of watermeadows for early spring fodder, the substitution of convertible husbandry (i.e. the alternation of arable and pasture) for permanent tillage or grass, the introduction of new fallow crops and selected grasses, and improvements in manuring and stockbreeding.[7]

To strengthen his case Kerridge was at some pains to deride the significance of the post-1750 changes, such as parliamentary enclosure, the development of new breeds of livestock through selective breeding, completely new developments in the design and making of implements and machinery, and the discovery of new fertilisers. When the two periods are compared the claims for the changes of the early modern era appear to be rather exaggerated, not least because there is much room for doubt on how widely watermeadows and convertible husbandry were in fact adopted, and because there is known to have been a lengthy period of diffusion between the first introduction of new crops and grasses and their widespread use. There is the further difficulty that the first hundred years of the 'agricultural revolution' claimed for 1560-1767 were marked by rising prices, which reached a peak in the middle seventeenth century when one might have expected improvements in agricultural productivity to be exercising a moderating influence on prices. Indeed, the long-term movements in prices are much more readily explicable in terms of an expanding market demand coming from the rising population, which too reached its peak in 1640-60, forcing up prices in an era when the supply, though no doubt expanding, was nevertheless inadequate to meet it.

It is true, of course, that the traditional 'agricultural revolution' of 1750-1850 also failed to feed an expanding population, and that prices rose for the first sixty years of this period, while from the end of the eighteenth century a former substantial export of grain was replaced by a permanent need to import. But it has to be remarked that the earlier 'agricultural revolution' had to meet the needs of a population which increased by some three million mouths, a rise of a little over 100 per cent, most of the increase occurring during the first hundred years of the two hundred-year period specified by Professor Kerridge; in the later period, 1750-1850, the increase was of the order of some twelve million extra mouths, a rise of 300 per cent, again occurring over the period of a hundred years.

But agricultural historians now, and for years past, have moved away from the very concept of 'agricultural revolution', preferring to see agricultural change as essentially a very long-term, drawn-out affair, with often protracted periods between the first introduction of an innovation and its general adoption in those areas suited to it. A case has even been made for yet a further 'agricultural revolution' spanning the middle decades of the nineteenth century, based on the introduction of new farm machinery, new types of fertilisers and new methods of subsoil drainage by pipe or tile.[8] However, these changes, too, were only partial in both extent and effectiveness, and we are left with the present concept of slow, gradual, and partial change, so that at any time areas of advanced farming existed alongside areas of backward farming. Agriculture, in fact, is an industry in which, in the past, changes could be brought in neither rapidly nor universally. And if one were to judge the achievement of an 'agricultural revolution' by the speed with which innovations were adopted and by their effective impact on output, then there can be only one period to which the title can be applied – that from about 1950 to the present.

Leaving aside the concept of 'agricultural revolution', historians in recent years have concerned themselves with two aspects of innovation: establishment of the first appearance, and spread over selected areas, of a new departure, such as the adoption of turnips and clovers in East Anglia in the seventeenth and early eighteenth centuries; and, secondly, the measurement of improvement in terms of higher yields, more productive livestock, or savings in labour. The first has been assisted by the systematic examination (nowadays employing computers) of testamentary inventories, accounts of farmers' goods, stock and crops at the time of death; the second by the collection of new statistical material, though the figures available are necessarily in some degree questionable in the era before official statistics began systematically to be collected, from 1866 onwards. The interest in measurement, though by no means new, has been influenced in more recent years by the work of American econometricians, and it may prove possible in time to obtain a more precise idea of yields (though probably not of increases in livestock).

Another subject which awaits further research is that of farm structure. A few pioneering studies have pointed to the existence of a slow long-term increase in the average size of farms, taking place over the period of the eighteenth and early nineteenth centuries, the period so far systematically investigated for a small number of landed estates.[9] It has always been assumed, of course, that engrossment occurred, but influenced by contemporary complaints on the subject, the first generation of agrarian historians supposed that the increase in large farms was a rapid one, and was closely associated with the parliamentary enclosures of 1760–1830. The modern research shows that the change was in fact much slower and more gradual, and that it appears to have had no close association with enclosure, occurring as it did in common-field and old-enclosed villages just as much as in those recently enclosed. If further research shows the change to have been widespread, then the concentration of farm acreage in larger units has important implications for the development of greater efficiency of agriculture and increases in output. Landowners, for example, took much greater care to ensure that their larger farms were operated by men of capital and experience, than they did for their smaller farms.

The study of farm implements and machinery in the modern era has made very considerable progress in the past twenty years following the pioneering work of Dr E.J.T. Collins.[10] In particular, Collins has shown that from the later eighteenth century the adoption of improved hand implements made it possible to speed up the slow and heavy work of harvesting as the scythe and hook replaced the sickle. The era of more efficient horse-driven or steam-powered machinery began with the arrival of an effective threshing machine from about 1786. Soon after 1820 such machinery included steam-powered barn equipment, horse-drawn cultivators, reapers and tedders, and steam-powered ploughing and drainage rigs. Historical geographers have extended their studies of diffusion to include farm machinery,[11] and it has been found that in general the adoption of improved machinery proceeded quite slowly, held back by such factors as cost (for steam-powered equipment), the unreliability of some early machines, the unsuitability of the English climate, terrain and field sizes for machinery, and not least, the cheapness of labour used in the traditional labour-intensive methods.[12]

A considerable volume of recent work has been concerned with the last twenty-five years of the nineteenth century, the period of the so-called 'Great Depression' in English agriculture.[13] Studies of prices, rents, farm records, and the evidence given to the Royal Commissions confirm that the depression was undoubtedly highly regional in character, being much more serious in arable areas than in pasture districts, where the effects were often slight. However, in the badly-affected areas there was a considerable turnover of farm tenants, and rents fell so low as seriously to undermine the economic position of many landowners. Since the political role and social eminence of landowners were both under attack at this time, the depression remains significant as a factor in the decline of the old hegemony of the landed interest and the emergence of universal adult franchise and the expanded political role of the middle classes.[14]

There remain some serious gaps in agricultural history, although one former weakness, the lack of studies of the marketing of farm products, is in course of being rectified in the volumes of the *Agrarian History*. Another gap is the sources of farm capital. An informal local network of lending and borrowing between members of the rural community pre-dated the growth of the banking system and was important in providing outlets for surplus funds and in helping farmers and others to overcome temporary shortages of cash. It is also known that by the time of the Napoleonic Wars the larger farmers, at least, were heavily dependent on bank loans to extend their operations. However, compared with the excellent studies made in the United States, British historians have neglected this important question.

Rural social history

Turning now to more specifically social themes, perhaps the most striking development in this field has been the revival of interest in the parliamentary enclosures of 1760–1830. Except for purely local studies, little of general importance was produced on the subject of enclosure for a lengthy period stretching from the late 1930s to the early 1960s. Indeed, a senior historian, (not a specialist in the field), even went so far as to say that as a subject, enclosure was dead, worked out, and there was nothing more to be said. But since the early 1960s, and particularly in the past few years, a generation of younger scholars led by M. Turner, J. Chapman, J.M. Martin and J.A. Yelling,[15] has yielded an important body of new work. Computer analysis of enclosure material has produced for the first time reliable estimates of the extent and chronology of enclosure: and the evidence of the land tax has been combed again (though more cautiously than before) for indications of, for example, the turnover of small owners following enclosure. Indeed, studies based on land tax records have almost approached the status of a new specialist branch of agrarian history, and especially so as the complexities of the material have become more fully appreciated. However, land tax specialists have still to take account of a new study being prepared by a Canadian scholar, Professor Donald Ginter,[16] which will show that many of the existing studies based on the land tax can no longer be considered valid.

The costs of parliamentary enclosure have also been more thoroughly studied, the results being of considerable, if arguable, relevance to the old debate on the fate of small landowners; while some historians have revived the theory, first put forward nearly eighty years ago, that the greatest period of difficulty for small landowners was not the era of parliamentary enclosure but rather the first half of the eighteenth century. That doubts still exist over the extent of the decline of small owners, why they declined, and even when they declined, is witness to the lack of direct evidence and the difficulty of interpreting such indirect evidence as is provided by price movements, the land tax, and the costs of enclosing. It is possible, for example, that the high turnover of small owners after enclosure found in the land tax records may be the result of an advancing land market fuelled by the prosperity enjoyed by farmers after 1760, rather than inability to meet the costs of enclosure; while decline of small owners in the first half of the eighteenth century may have resulted in part from the low prices in that period. Indeed, the case for decline prior to the parliamentary enclosures is reinforced by the evidence of depression conditions in arable areas during the 1730s and 1740s.[17]

English historians have always tended to concentrate on the social effects of enclosure, taking it for granted that the economic consequences – the increases in post-enclosure output – were unarguably of very substantial importance. Such a view neglected two obvious qualifications, first that parliamentary enclosures affected only a proportion (according to the latest estimates about 24 per cent) of the total acreage of England and Wales, and secondly that limitations of soil and other factors inhibited the adoption of improved methods in many villages that were enclosed. It was left to an American scholar, Professor Donald McCloskey, to attempt a more precise estimate of the effects of enclosure on farm output. This he did by taking the rise in rents after enclosure as an indication of the value of the increased output (actual output figures not being available). Collecting a large body of rent material, McCloskey concluded that the average rise was of the order of 40 per cent, though the range of rises was very wide. Rents, however, were subject to a variety of economic and social influences, large owners often charging rents below the market rate and often leaving rents unchanged over long periods, for example. There is thus no certainty that either the pre-enclosure, or post-enclosure rent, was a true market one.

McCloskey has investigated also the reasons why the common fields survived as long as they did in some parts of England (though they survived much longer in some parts of the continent).[18] His main conclusion is that farmers valued the 'insurance' that the common fields provided against losses, when a variety of crops was grown in a variety of situations across the parish, and possibly, too, on different kinds of soil. It is not clear, however, whether such an 'insurance' was more advantageous than the greater flexibility in land use that enclosures made possible, or than the ordinary small farmer achieved through combining a mixture of crops with a variety of small livestock enterprises. And the 'insurance' theory does not explain adequately why common fields disappeared early in certain parts of the country while remaining widespread in the midland counties in the eighteenth century. Here Dr Yelling's suggestion, that the survival of common fields was associated with certain types of villages and certain social structures, may be more convincing.[19]

While controversy over many features of enclosure and the common fields continues, one aspect, the effects on cottagers, has not received much attention in recent years, due in part to the lack of direct evidence. However, new studies of the rural labour force in general have been growing, as have also studies of the nature and effects of the system of poor relief, which was, of course, highly relevant to a large section of the rural poor.

The studies of farm labour have been written at two levels: broad general summaries covering the whole range of labourers' conditions and experience, and more specialised studies concentrating on, for example, a particular group like the farm servants, or certain influences, such as birth rates, death rates and family size. Of the general accounts that by Professor Alan Everitt for 1500–1640 is outstanding in a period where little of importance had previously been done,[20] while for the nineteenth century the books and articles by Pamela Horn are valuable for covering a wide range of relevant subjects including not only wages and working conditions but also child labour, education, housing, trade unionism, and poverty.[21]

For certain elements of the labour force a number of important studies have appeared in recent years. Of much interest is Ann Kussmaul's study of farm servants, the farm hands who, in contrast to day labourers, were hired by the year and lived in with the farmer. Her study traces not only their conditions of employment and mobility, but also the connections between fluctuations in the numbers of farm servants and changes in the supply and demand for farm labour.[22] There have appeared also some interesting studies of rural craftsmen, tradesmen, and professional men.[23] The nature of work on the land and the traditions which governed it have been examined in some depth in studies gathered together by Raphael Samuel, especially those concerning harvesting and harvesters.[24] And most recently K.D.M. Snell has published a major study of the farm labour of southern England in the eighteenth and nineteenth centuries. This controversial work advances a number of arguments concerning the seasonal nature of unemployment on the land, the reduced economic independence of farm-workers, the decline of female employment, and the connections between large-scale arable farming and the social effects of parliamentary enclosure – a stimulating if not entirely convincing *tour-de-force*.[25]

Studies of labour unrest have become fashionable following the publication in 1963 of the influential work by Edward Thompson, *The Making of the English Working Class*. Subsequent studies, following Thompson, include the well-known account of the 1830 riots by E.J. Hobsbawm and George Rudé, *Captain Swing* (1969), and have ranged more widely than study of the country worker to include discussions of the relationship between unrest, crime, and the character of the law and its administration.[26] Discussions of what were always the more fundamental factors in the lives of rural people, movements in birth rates and death rates, family size, and disease, have been brought together along with much other material, in major new studies which will appear in the forthcoming volume IV of the *Agrarian History*.[27] Nevertheless, it cannot be said that either rural health conditions or housing in the modern period have been thoroughly investigated at present, though some aspects, such as medical provision and model villages, have been treated in monographs. However, a spate of new work has re-examined the old subject of the poor law as it operated in country districts.[28] In general, the effect has been to raise one's opinion of the working of the old unreformed pre-1834 system of relief, and to show, in particular, that the supposed evil influence of the notorious Speenhamland system of subsidising wages was neither so pernicious nor so widespread as was once supposed. The effects of the reformed 'New Poor Law' of 1834 have similarly been subject to reappraisal and again found to be much less pervasive than formerly believed, with only a small minority of the rural poor experiencing the dreaded workhouse, while the great majority continued to be relieved in the traditional way in their own homes.

The study of landownership has revolved round two controversial theories. The first, the 'rise of the gentry' in the hundred years before 1640, is associated with the late Professor R.H. Tawney, and was based, in part, on estimates of shifts in landownership provided by the counting of manors owned by individual families. Manors, it was shown subsequently, being of varying size and value, are not a sound basis for such a calculation, but nevertheless, the extent of the changes, the causes, and their implications for landed society, for contemporary politics, and even for the survival of the monarchy, produced a controversy which resulted in a number of major works up to the late 1960s.[30] The argued shift in landownership stimulated not only studies of the gentry in a number of individual counties but also discussions of the declining groups, the dissolution of the monasteries, the sales of land by the Crown, and the causes of the deteriorating position of the aristocracy. A wide variety of conflicting viewpoints were put forward, though perhaps it might be concluded that, in an era of rising prices and rents, and of an active land market, it is not surprising that enterprising men deriving from varied social origins were in a position to improve their wealth and social status, while the less enterprising fell behind. Whether there were special reasons why men of the gentry class should have tended to gain more than others, or whether within the gentry there were both rising and declining groups, have remained unresolved issues, as have also the political consequences of what changes occurred. In recent years the controversy seems to have become dormant, to be revived perhaps when some major new work on the period appears.

The second theory is associated with Professor Sir John Habakkuk who put forward the view as long ago as 1940 that the years between 1680 and 1740 saw the rise of the great estate,[31] and it remained the orthodox view for the next thirty years. Yet the basis of the argument, like Tawney's, was fragile, depending as it did on research into only two adjoining counties situated in the South Midlands. Recent findings, especially in the more northerly counties of Lincolnshire and Cumbria, have produced a more complex picture.[32] Habakkuk argued that large landowners rose through marriage and inheritance, government office, and superior estate administration, while the lesser gentry and freeholders, shut out from these sources of gain, tended to decline. The present picture is less clear-cut: as in Tawney's period, enterprising men emerging from diverse origins could make their way towards accumulating large estates, while those who declined came from no clearly defined section of the community. Prominent among the successful newcomers were wealthy merchants, contractors and urban businessmen, and leading professional men, especially lawyers. Habakkuk has since re-stated his position in a series of articles,[33] and the debate continues.

In the interim the more general aspects of landownership in the eighteenth and nineteenth centuries were examined in two monographs by Professor F.M.L. Thompson and the present writer.[34] These studies examined the economic basis of landownership – rents, estate profits, urban property, office and investments in stocks – and also landowners' involvement in agricultural and industrial enterprise, more particularly in mining and ironworking, and the financing of river improvements, turnpikes, canals, docks and railways. Attention was also given to the political and social aspects of landownership, specifically the landowners' role in government and politics, in society, the village community and in sport. All of these features of landownership have been taken further in more specialised work, especially over the past ten or fifteen years, and a valuable section of Volume V of the *Agrarian History* also takes the subject a little further back in time to cover the period between 1640 and 1750. An important large-scale comprehensive study of aristocratic landowners for the period 1660–1914 by Dr J.V. Beckett has recently been published.[35]

Professor Habakkuk noted in his 1940 article the importance of the role played by professional land stewards (later termed estate agents) in the management of great estates, a role which was significant not only because of the value of the land entrusted to them, but also because the typical large estate was made up of scattered and heterogeneous properties which often included urban developments and industrial enterprises as well as woods and farm lands. Thenceforth the study of estate management became a substantial source of new research.[36] The land steward or estate agent, it has been found, was not only a manager of landed property, he was also important as financial adviser to the landlord, and sometimes as an agricultural innovator, pushing forward such advances as the reclamation of waste lands, subsoil drainage, and provision of superior forms of farm buildings. It is not without interest that Lord Ernle, the writer of the well-known standard work, *English Farming Past and Present*, was at one time agent to the Duke of Bedford and subsequently became the first Minister of Agriculture.

The one major attempt at a comprehensive rounded study of the rural community so far is *The Victorian Countryside*, a large two-volume illustrated collection of essays, published in 1981.[37] Similar studies to cover the period since 1900 are lacking, and indeed would be premature until more specialist basic work on the twentieth century has been done. However, in recent years agrarian historians have begun to take a look at the present century, and have laid the basis for the further work to come with Volume VIII of the *Agrarian History*, covering the period 1914 to 1939, studies of farm labour during the First World War, and more general accounts of agriculture and rural social developments since 1914.[38]

Lastly one must not overlook the rapidly accumulating body of regional and local studies. These are of many types, including the histories of substantial regions and individual counties down to those of single villages, together with accounts of local farming systems, local examples of innovations and enclosures, occupational structure, the Poor Law, and much more. Considered invidually such work is by its nature limited either in time or space, or often both, but collectively it serves, first, to remind historians of the broader scene, of the remarkable diversity in local conditions and experience in so small a country; and, secondly to provide the essential building blocks from which larger structures can be erected.

Conclusion: strengths and deficiencies

To sum up: most of the work on English agrarian history over the past twenty-five years has been concerned with elaborating and qualifying established themes – field systems, enclosure, the spread of innovations, the land tax, and fluctuation in prices and farming prosperity – themes which are as old as the subject itself. But there have been some new departures, or if not entirely new, then at least more thorough examination of topics that were formerly little investigated, such as rural housing in the early modern period;[39] the more precise measurement of changes in output, prices and rents; developments in landownership and its influence on the countryside; the changing structure of farm sizes in the eighteenth and early nineteenth centuries; the advances in hand implements and the adoption of machinery and its effects in the nineteenth century; and not least the careful investigation of the nature and life of the various groups of workers who made up the rural labour force.

The scale of such diverse and innovative research indicates that, although much remains to be done, agrarian history in England is active, healthy and progressive (not forgetting the important contributions made by American and Canadian scholars). The present strength of the subject is exhibited by the growth of the British Agricultural History Society, founded in 1953, whose current membership stands at over nine hundred, and whose journal, *The Agricultural History Review*, sustains a high reputation for scholarship. Agricultural history has always played an important part in the syllabi of British economic and social history degrees, and at present there are over fifty scholars teaching in British universities whose interests lie primarily or partly in the field of agricultural history and rural social history. These, together with a number of historical geographers, constitute the core of the Society's active members.

The membership, however, is clearly far wider than this, and includes many local and amateur historians, as well as antiquarians, students, and persons with allied interests in, for example, ecology and conservation. The Society provides a forum where many different approaches, all centring on the countryside, are brought together, and this breadth of interests may also be seen in the range of the articles published in *The Agricultural History Review*, which also occasionally publishes articles dealing with other countries, and in recent issues has featured a series of specialist papers on the regional bibliographies of the agricultural history of the United States.

Lastly, although much has been achieved, there still remain many aspects of English agrarian history which are unexplored, or at least little investigated at the present. Some of the gaps in our knowledge have been mentioned above: investigation of the spread and effect of innovations, and measurement of general trends in output and productivity; the extent of long-term changes in farm structure; the sources and adequacy of farm capital; and the nature of the rural housing problem in the nineteenth and twentieth centuries. The body of information on the post-1918 era, despite the excellent work of Edith Whetham, is at present relatively thin. There is much scope for further research here, on the post-1921 depression and more especially on the entirely new phase of agrarian history which began with the return to protection in 1932 and the subsequent growth of marketing schemes and subsidies.

There is always a reluctance among historians to come very near to the present, since the character of underlying trends and the relative importance of different changes and events are more certainly identified from a distance than near to. In the post-1914 period the role of government has loomed far larger than in any previous time, and the availability of official sources is of course a major factor in the writing of the history of the modern era. Nevertheless, there is now no reason (other than the shortage of funds for research) why the inter-war period should not be investigated in greater depth and further work undertaken on the Second World War and early post-war years. This is where agrarian historians can show awareness of the relevance of their subject and the valuable contribution it can make to the wider examination of rural life.

References

1. J.E. Thorold Rogers, *A History of Agriculture and Prices in England*, Oxford, 1866-90; F.W. Maitland, *Domesday Book and Beyond*, Cambridge, 1897; W. Hasbach, *A History of the English Agricultural Labourer*, London, 1908 (first published in German in 1894); P. Vinogradoff, *The Growth of the Manor*, London, 1904.
2. Lord Ernle (R.E. Prothero), *English Farming Past and Present*, London, 1912; 6th edn., London 1961; J.L. and Barbara Hammond, *The Village Labourer*, London, 1911; 5th edn., London, 1978.
3. Joan Thirsk ed., *The Agrarian History of England and Wales, IV, 1500-1640*, Cambridge, 1967; *idem.*, *V 1640-1750*, Cambridge, 1984.
4. Edith H. Whetham, *The Agrarian History of England and Wales, VIII 1914-1939*, Cambridge, 1978.
5. Among recent additions to medieval agrarian history are the following: Alan R.H. Baker and Robin A. Butlin, (eds), *Studies of Field Systems in the British Isles*, Cambridge, 1973; John Hatcher, *Rural Economy and Society in the Duchy of Cornwall*, Cambridge, 1970; *idem.*, 'English Serfdom and Villeinage: towards a re-assessment', *Past and Present*, 90, 1981; R.H. Hilton, *A Medieval Society: the West Midlands at the end of the Thirteenth Century*, London, 1966; Joan Thirsk, 'The Common Fields', *Past and Present*, XXIX, 1964.
6. Eric Kerridge, *The Agricultural Revolution*, London, 1967, p. 328.
7. Ibid., p. 40.
8. F.M.L. Thompson, 'The Second Agricultural Revolution 1815-1880', *Economic History Review*, 2nd ser., XXI, 1, 1968.
9. G.E. Mingay, 'The Size of Farms in the Eighteenth Century', *Economic History Review*, 2nd Ser., XIV, 3, 1962; J.R. Wordie, Social Change on the Leveson-Gower estates, 1714-1832', ibid., 2nd ser., XXVII, 4, 1974.
10. E.J.T. Collins, 'The Diffusion of the Threshing Machine in Britain 1790-1880, *Tools and Tillage*, II, 1, 1972; *idem.*, 'Harvest Technology and Labour Supply in Britain 1790-1870', *Economic History Review*, 2nd ser., XXII, 3, 1969.
11. See especially J.R. Walton, *A Study in the Diffusion of Agricultural Machinery in the Nineteenth Century*, Oxford School of Geography Research Paper No. 5, 1973.
12. For a survey of the subject see G.E. Mingay, *The Agricultural Revolution: Changes in Agriculture 1650-1850*, London, 1977, pp. 38-46.
13. See especially T.W. Fletcher, 'The Great Depression of English Agriculture 1873-96' *Economic History Review*, 2nd ser., XIII, 1960-1; P.J. Perry, ed., *British Agriculture 1875-1914*, London, 1973.
14. F.M.L. Thompson, *English Landed Society in the Nineteenth Century*, London, 1963.
15. Michael Turner, *English Parliamentary Enclosure*, Folkestone, 1980; John Chapman, 'Some Problems in the Interpretation of Enclosure Awards', *Agricultural History Review*, XXVI, 2, 1978; J.M. Martin, 'The Cost of Parlimentary Enclosure in

Warwickshire', *University of Birmingham Historical Journal*, IX, 1964; J.A. Yelling, *Common Field and Enclosure in England 1450-1850*, London, 1977.
16. For recent views on land tax evidence see Michael Turner and D. Mills, (eds), *Land and Property: the English Land Tax 1962-1832*, Gloucester, 1986.
17. G.E. Mingay, 'The Agricultural Depression, 1730-1750', *Economic History Review*, 2nd ser., VIII, 1956.
18. D. McCloskey, 'The Persistence of English Common Fields', in W.N. Parker and Eric L. Jones, eds., *European Peasants and their Markets*, London, 1975.
19. Yelling, op. cit.; for a discussion of recent work on the origins of field systems see Alan R.H. Baker, 'Discourses on British Field Systems', *Agricultural History Review*, XXXI, 2, 1983.
20. Alan Everitt, 'Farm Labourers', in Joan Thirsk, (ed.), *Agrarian History, IV*, op. cit.
21. Pamela Horn, *Labouring Life in the Victorian Countryside*, Dublin, 1976; *The Victorian Country Child*, Kineton, 1974; *The Rural World 1780-1850: Social Change in the English Countryside*, London 1980.
22. Ann Kussmaul, *Servants in Husbandry in Early Modern England*, Cambridge, 1981. See also T.M. Devine, (ed.), *Farm Servants and Labour in Lowland Scotland 1770-1914*, Edinburgh, 1984.
23. See, for example, contributions to G.E. Mingay, (ed.), *The Victorian Countryside*, London, 1981.
24. Raphael Samuel, ed., *Village Life and Labour*, London, 1975.
25. K.D.M. Snell, *Annals of the Labouring Poor: Social Change and Agrarian England 1660-1900*, Cambridge 1985.
26. See, for example, E.P. Thompson, *Whigs and Hunters: the Origin of the Black Act*, London, 1976; Douglas Hay, (ed.), *Albion's Fatal Tree: Crime and Society in Eighteenth Century England*, London, 1975; John Brewer and John Styles, (eds), *An Ungovernable People: the English and the Law in the Seventeenth and Eighteenth Centuries*, London, 1980; John Stevenson and Roland Quinault, (eds), *Popular Protest and Public Order: six studies in British History, 1790-1920*, London, 1974; E. Hobsbawm & G. Rudé, *Captain Swing*, London, 1969; A.J. Peacock, *Bread and Blood*, London, 1968.
27. An earlier discussion of his views appeard in 'The Influence of Demographic Factors in the Position of the Agricultural Labourer in England and Wales, c. 1760-1914', *Agricultural History Review*, XXIX, 2, 1981.
28. See, for examples, G.W. Oxley, *Poor Relief in England and Wales 1601-1834*, Newton Abbot 1974; M.E. Rose, *The English Poor Law 1780-1930*, Newton Abbot, 1971; Anne Digby, *Pauper Palaces*, London, 1978; B.A. Holderness, ' "Open" and "Close" Parishes in England in the Eighteenth and Nineteenth Centuries', *Agricultural History Review*, XX, 2, 1972; Anthony Brundage, 'The English Poor Law System and the Cohesion of Agricultural Society', *Agricultural History*, XLVIII, 1974.
29. R.H. Tawney, 'The Rise of the Gentry', *Economic History Review*, 2nd Ser., XI, 1941.
30. H.R. Trevor-Roper, *The Gentry, 1540-1640*, Supplement No. 1 to *Economic History Review*, 1953; Lawrence Stone, *Social Change and Revolution in England 1540-1640*, London, 1965; idem., *The Causes of the English Revolution 1529-1642*, London, 1972; J.P. Cooper, 'The Counting of Manors', *Economic History Review*, 2nd Ser., VIII, 3, 1956; J.H. Hexter, 'Storm over the Gentry', in *idem., Reppraisals in History*, London, 1961; H.R. Trevor-Roper, 'The General Crisis of the Seventeenth Century', *Past and Present*, XVI, 1967; Perez Zagorin, *The Court and the Country: the beginning of the English Revolution*, London, 1969.
31. H.J. Habakkuk, 'English Landownership, 1680-1740, *Economic History Review*, 2nd Ser., X, 1940.
32. B.A. Holderness, 'The English Land Market in the Eighteenth Century: the case of

Lincolnshire', *Economic History Review*, 2nd ser. XXVII, 4, 1974; J.V. Beckett, English Landownership in the Later Seventeenth and Eighteenth Centuries: the Debate and its Problems', *Economic History Review*, 2nd ser., XXX, 4, 1977; *idem.*, 'The Pattern of Landownership in England and Wales, 1660-1880, *Economic History Review*, 2nd ser., XXXVII, 1, 1984.

33. H.K. Habakkuk, 'The Rise and Fall of English Landed Families, 1600-1800', *Transactions Royal Historical Society*, 5th ser., XXIX-XXXI, 1979-1981.
34. G.E. Mingay, *English Landed Society in the Eighteenth Century*, London, 1963; F.M.L. Thompson, *English Landed Society in the Nineteenth Century*, London 1963. For more recent discussions see Philip Jenkins, *The Making of a Ruling Class: the Glamorgan Gentry 1640-1790*, Cambridge, 1983; R.J. Olney, *Rural Society and County Government in Nineteenth-Century Lincolnshire*, Lincoln, 1973; Eric Richards, *The Leviathan of Wealth: the Sutherland Fortune in the Industrial Revolution*, London, 1973; J.T. Ward and R.G. Wilson (eds), *Land and Industry: the Landed Estate in the Industrial Revolution*, Newton Abbot, 1971; David Howell, *The Gentry of South-West Wales*, Cardiff, 1986.
35. J.V. Beckett, *The Aristocracy in England 1660-1914*, Oxford, 1986.
36. See, for example, Susanna Wade Martins, *The Holkham Estate and its Inhabitants in the Nineteenth Century*, Cambridge, 1980; Graham Mee, *Aristocratic Enterprise*, London, 1975; J. Oxley Parker, *The Oxley Parker Papers*, Colchester, 1964; David Spring, *The English Landed Estate in the Nineteenth Century: its administration*, Baltimore, 1963; Ross Wordie, *Estate Management in Eighteenth-century England*, London 1982.
37. G.E. Mingay, (ed.), *The Victorian Countryside*, London, 1981; paperback edition, London, 1986.
38. See Edith Whetham, *Agrarian History VIII*, op. cit.; P.E. Dewey, 'Government Provision of Farm Labour in England and Wales, 1914-18' *Agricultural History Review*, XXVII, 2, 1979; B.A. Holderness, *British Agriculture since 1945*, Manchester, 1985; Pamela Horn, *Rural Life in England in the First World War*, Dublin, 1984; G.E. Mingay, *British Friesians: an Epic of Progress*, Rickmansworth, 1982. A new study of agricultural labour by W.A. Armstrong, extending to the post-1945 era is currently in the press.
39. See M.W. Barley's invaluable contributions to Volumes IV and V of Joan Thirsk, ed., *The Agrarian History of England and Wales* op. cit.

Part III: Geography

7 Commentary and Introduction

Mark Cleary and Hugh Clout

The discipline of geography has traditionally evaded clear, unambiguous definition and its practitioners in both France and Britain have tended to suffer from an inherited identity crisis which derives from its academic origins embracing both earth and social sciences. Notwithstanding the soul-searching to which members of the discipline occasionally subject themselves, the geographical community at all levels grew steadily in size between the mid-1960s and the early 1980s. Such growth and vigour has probably been stronger in Britain though the experience of both communities has in many ways been remarkably similar, and few new academic posts have been created in geography departments in either country over recent years.

The field of rural geography has not proved easy to define. Notions of 'rurality', the 'rural scene', the 'countryside', *'l'espace rural'*, *'la société villageoise'* are highly varied and mutable, intersecting with a range of terms that are well represented in other branches of geography (historical, social, economic) and in other disciplines (agricultural economics, sociology, political science). Such concerns over definition confront other disciplines, but for geographers, inured by long years of training to the endless dissection of the methodological and philosophical underpinnings of their subject, problems of definition are perhaps viewed with less gravity. Certainly the papers in this section reaffirm the long-established pragmatism of the geographical community in both France and Britain while illustrating the institutional differences which affect the practice of rural geography in the two countries.

Contrasting traditions

The academic structure of French scholarship with its traditional emphasis on the *thèse d'état* has tended to focus much research in geography on very detailed regional monographs which have frequently been much stronger on historical than contemporary material. In Britain such historical inquiry has tended to be carried out by specialist historical geographers as distinct from rural geographers. In France, however, rural geographers and historians, in sharing a common university background, are much closer to each other, and a specific historical geography tradition has never developed. Kayser's 'hour of glory' and Sautter's 'golden age' for rural geography were characterised by an implicit historical approach. Since the 1970s, the move away from such an approach and the search for others have led to a certain lack of inspiration.

The considerable time necessary to produce a *thèse d'état* perhaps explains the relative paucity of research on contemporary rural issues, though the growing interest in urban topics is another reason. The emphasis on the *thèse d'état* is changing, however, and many dissertations are now thematic rather than regional in character. Nonetheless, the importance of the *thèse* has produced a rich harvest of monographs on the *pays* of France which has no real equivalent in English geographical literature.

It is clear that the place of agriculture in rural geographical research varies in the two countries. The agricultural geography study group of the Institute of British Geographers was certainly the precursor of the rural geography study group but Cloke and Moseley make clear the extent to which British rural geographers have moved from agriculture to other aspects of the rural environment as the focus of concern.

In France, agriculture remains of key importance in rural geography as in all rural disciplines. Sautter notes the degree of conformity between land use and geographic space in the identification and mapping of agricultural structure, which formed a major part of rural geography in the 1950s and 1960s and which are still active research themes, despite the radical changes in the structure of rural employment. For him, though, the countryside is always characterised by agriculture.

Kayser, however, is more critical. Although the bulk of French rural geographers continue to be interested in agricultural issues, non-agricultural rural inhabitants and activities are of growing importance. In this, Kayser anticipates an increasing role for interdisciplinary approaches. As the rural world loses its agricultural specificity, so rural geography is moving away from its traditional preoccupations. However, like Cloke, Kayser fears that this will inevitably be accompanied by some diminution in the specific role of rural geography. Perhaps the continued concern for agricultural topics in France is a reflection of the richness and variety of work on *'la fin des paysans'* whose sociological, anthropological and political perspectives, so amply identified in companion papers, have greatly stimulated and enhanced geographical work.

A contrast in the amount of research undertaken abroad by British and French rural geographers is also apparent. Thirteen of the thirty-three *thèses d'état* completed between 1980 and mid-1984 related to areas outside France, contributing to the volume and strength of publications by French geographers working on rural themes in the Third World. Unfortunately, British geographers produce a diminishing quantity of overseas studies – a reflection, amongst other things, of the decline in funding for research abroad in the last ten years or so – though Europe continues to be a significant field of investigation.

The status and funding of research in the two traditions is being subjected to certain parallel pressures. In both countries the growing importance of commissioned work can give rise to problems of objectivity and freedom of choice; in this respect the differences between France (where research is concentrated at the

CNRS and *grandes écoles*) and Britain (where research is organised on a more *ad hoc* basis) are becoming blurred. More important perhaps is the fear that contract work may oust more 'pure' research in favour of inquiries that yield immediately quantifiable and practical results which may be of limited academic value. A separate question is how really useful is much of the applied research, and how receptive is government to its findings. Perhaps the most that researchers should realistically hope to do is to influence the discussion of policy rather than directly change policy itself.

Research on environmental management and land-use policy has figured substantially in the British tradition and has encouraged collaboration between the natural and social sciences. This kind of cooperation seems to be rather more advanced than in France. In addition, British rural geographers appear to have directed their inquiries more emphatically toward immediate policy-oriented issues than have their French counterparts, though the urge for relevance (perhaps a consequence of the 'hybrid vigour' of the subject) would seem to have infected both groups, and more so than most of their colleagues in the other social sciences. Nonetheless, publications on service provision, settlement planning, rural deprivation and allied themes are less abundant in France than in Britain. Nor, rather suprisingly, does environmental politics seem to have fired the geographical imagination in France in the way it has in Britain. But, here again, the position is changing, with a greater emphasis on such work starting to emerge from French research. Notable lacunae may still be identified, notably in the field of *l'habitat* and *droit rural*.

Common concerns

Both geographical contributions raise the question of the specificity of rural geography and the branch of geography that may be nominated as 'rural'. Moseley is keen to stress that few rural geographers in Britain are really concerned with this question – a state of nonchalance that he applauds, but which Cloke disparages. Kayser also expresses a note of deeper concern, with perhaps a fear that geographers have not been able to carve out a clear, unequivocal niche in the administrative corridors of the CNRS. Such uncertainty is not, however, the preserve of rural geographers and is shared to a greater or lesser degree by other social scientists studying rural matters. Overall, there is little consensus on the scope and definition of 'rural' topics except to acknowledge that no *appellation controlée* yet exists for rural studies.

A strong element in both traditions, and one which has emerged with particular force over the last decade, emphasises links between the specific rural locale and the broader themes of state and economy. Vital explanatory mechanisms extend far beyond particular localities and transcend conventional disciplinary boundaries. Indeed the increasing importance of 'relevant' and 'applied' work in rural geography is a product of precisely this realisation. Geographers would argue that they possess the necessary experience and methods to tackle such complex problems of scale and inter-relationships. It is the exercise of power in the rural environment that is the crucial issue – power as expressed through access to services, goods and welfare and through the domain of public policy. In this respect, the different administrative structures of the two countries provide scope for fruitful comparisons between national experiences, although old myths about centralised France and decentralised Britain would need some revision in the light of recent institutional reforms in both countries.

It is interesting to note that the French authors give greater space to questions of methodology and techniques than do the English authors. Sautter and Kayser both refer to the growing importance of quantitative methodologies and computer-based analyses in rural geography research, particularly in cartography and in the development of rural data bases. Both are clear in identifying the limitations of using statistical material in the absence of global explanation. Kayser's observations regarding the 'hard-line youth' in some senses recalls debates within British geography in the 1970s.

On the British side, Cloke and Moseley say little on methods and techniques. For thirty-odd years, British geographers adopted and employed quantitative methods often in an applied manner. In recent years, however, the methods of quantitative research and the positivist research paradigm itself have increasingly been brought into question as geographers turn more and more to socio-political analysis and the search for more holistic explanations. The emergence of a critical, policy-orientated rural geography is certainly more evident in Britain than in France.

Future developments

To judge from the position papers and the discussion they stimulated, the prognosis for rural geography is far from gloomy. For Moseley questions of relevance, policy-making and welfare have given rural geography in Britain both direction and focus; and the import of concepts, especially, as Cloke discusses, from political economy has given the speciality a new intellectual rigour and excitement. Its practitioners are many and diverse, its products are still in demand, and its place in both the discipline and in the broader institutions of education seems reasonably secure. The view from the French side appears at times more pessimistic. Kayser expresses much less certainty and security though, as Sautter points out, this reflects less on the quality and diversity of the work done by French rural geographers than on the wider recognition it receives. Ultimately, it may be a question of the shallower roots of geography in French popular culture.

A major challenge for researchers in both countries will be to chart and interpret the implications of the evolving rural (rather than agricultural) policy of the European Community. Work on part-time farming is well advanced but where is the research on business strategies in rural areas, on environmentally sensitive farming policies, on welfare and service provision, or on transportation policy? The attitudes and activities of pressure groups both within the rural sector and at the rural/non-rural interface will become increasingly important in the changing economic and social environment towards the turn of the century. It is in these areas that great scope for innovative and collaborative work lies, sufficient to ensure the future vitality of rural geography.

8 French Geography and the Rural World

Gilles Sautter and Bernard Kayser

1 Is rural geography in a state of crisis?[1] by Gilles Sautter

Is there a crisis in rural studies within geography? Certainly not with respect to the level of interest in rural issues held by geographers in France. As a field of structured and institutionalised research, however, rural geography presents less coherence now than in the past when interest in rural areas and their problems formed part of a largely undifferentiated geography. Before examining the current status of rural geography, therefore, it is necessary to review its early development, as well as the way it has responded subsequently and hesitantly to the sweeping changes in the contemporary countryside, including the methodological advances it has experienced. Mention should also be made of the particular contribution of French geographers to Third World studies, which is followed by an assessment of rural geography's institutional strengths and weaknesses.

French rural geography and the post-war period

Rural geography *per se* only really emerged in the inter-war years. At this time, and until the end of the 1950s, regional studies, which were then at their apogee with the major theses of the *Ecole Française de Géographie*, contained a significant rural element. At the same time, under the title of 'general' geography, specialist and often comparative studies multiplied. Albert Demangeon, Daniel Faucher and Lucien Gachon can be seen as forerunners in this respect. Intellectual curiosity during this period was often centred around three major themes: landscapes; the relationship between the types of agriculture and the demographic situation; and the influence of the physical environment. From the point of view of the landscape, the principal questions related to the spatial distribution and social and physical determinants of the bocage (the landscape of

---

[1] The author would like to thank Madame Violette Rey for her comments on an earlier draft of this paper.

enclosed fields) and the open field (Meynier 1958). Marc Bloch and Gaston Roupnel helped to inform this debate, which often extended into the domain of the historians: the celebrated essay of Roger Dion on the formation of the French rural landscape (1934) is as much history as it is geography.

The second major theme, also rooted in historical studies, concerned the rural population and its subsistence. This was largely a question of the relationship between technical progress, or its absence, and the demographic weight of the peasantry on the land. The central research theme, of the effects of population ceilings and thresholds and the sources of change, is well illustrated in Etienne Juillard's *'La Vie Rurale en Basse-Alsace'*. Geographical understanding of tropical rural areas was growing, however, and central to this increasingly important research field was the concept of overpopulation. The thesis of P. Gourou (1965), on the peasants of the Tonkin Delta in Vietnam, demonstrated in a striking manner the limits of an already intensive agriculture system. Typologies of the stages of intensification were put forward (Juillard et al., 1957). In certain tropical countries, Gourou (1965) identified and contrasted countless individual cases of long-fallow agriculture ('characteristic of the tropics') and systems of permanent cultivation, particularly evident in the monsoon regions of Asia. Thus the conditions for rural progress, or at least a release from constraints, were beginning to be identified, thereby heralding the approach of a new phase of research.

The third major theme during this early period – that of the role of the natural environment in the diversity of agricultural activities – was frequently held, in counterpoint to the other two, in a large number of studies. Highly diversified forms of adaptation to particular natural environments were faithfully recorded, such as the Val d'Anniviers of Jean Brunhes (1910). The discussion, however, frequently became bogged down in the seemingly endless debate on the definition of favourable or unfavourable environments. On the whole, French geographers reacted strongly to the question of the 'determinism' of natural factors. Roger Dion did so in a particularly forceful way, using historical evidence, in his work on the vine and wine in France (1959). On the other hand, with respect to this same notion of natural conditions, which today would be called ecological factors, the intellectual approach of the discipline up to the beginning of the 1960s largely precluded any genuine breakthrough in terms of analysing the functional relations between the natural environment and agricultural activity (in the broadest sense). Despite a geomorphological training, the geographers of the time were largely incapable of analysing and correctly identifying variations in soil type and vegetation.

In this golden age, marked by an atheoretical tradition, a simplicity of research direction and a fairly unified conception of the subject matter of research, two particular features might be underlined. The first was the dogged use of interpretations drawn from the distant rural past, the influence of which is always present in the contemporary landscape though, as Yves Guermond (1979) has pointed out, too great a preoccupation with the genesis of the landscape may eclipse the significance of current forces of change. Nevertheless, researchers unfailingly sought to reconstitute an original state before tracing its transformation and adulteration to the present. Almost always holders of a degree and frequently an *agrégation* (a national competitive examination) in history, rural geographers were close to historians; and the social reality of the land at the time – still steeped in traditionalism – encouraged them to be so.

The second feature was the view that this land-use reality took the form of more or less coherent spaces whose dimensions were varied yet always consistent. This had become a geographical truism. When, during the 1960s under the impact of F. Perroux and his school, the traditional concept of the region began to break down, the adjectives 'homogeneous' and 'uniform' came to qualify areas within a region under a dominant agricultural system, or at least seen from an agricultural perspective, while the term 'polarised' was applied to areas under the influence of a central urban or industrial area. I myself proposed the expression 'landscape-region' for areas of natural rural environment though one would only use it in a qualified sense today.

Yet, during the halcyon days of an uncomplicated ruralism, the conformity between types of land-use and geographic space was, nonetheless, evident. Each land-use type defined a characteristic landscape, and the geographical 'game' became that of correctly identifying these landscape types, separating out their constituent parts and, finally, determining their functional logic. On the smaller scale, rural geography was concerned with identifying the distribution of landscape/land-use types and establishing typologies. It must be stressed that, from very early on, geographers have held an implicit belief in the consistency of these landscape/land-use entities, expressed in the term *structure agraire*. At that time, however, little relevance was placed on the two significant and mutually implicit implications of such a consistency: that a characteristic pattern would be inscribed on the soil and that social relations would be based upon the possession and the use of the soil. In this, one must acknowledge the role played by André Cholley who, in 1946, first formalised the notion of a land 'combination' and used the term 'system' to characterise it.

Change in the countryside and in rural geography since the 1960s

Since the beginning of the 1960s, things have changed dramatically. Not only have the situations and facts under study changed, but so too have the academic responses to them. Now that the vast bulk of the French population live in or around urban areas, it is not surprising that research has tended to move away from the rural world to concentrate instead on urban space and urban issues. Nevertheless, as far as geography is concerned, the implied causality is a little too simple. It assumes some form of competition between the two, with rural studies the loser. But the first hints of genuine dissatisfaction with rural research, over and above a simple reorientation, had already emerged. Moreover, the countryside itself was losing its autonomy and even its independent identity, not with respect to individual towns but to urbanisation as a whole, which was leading to a standardisation of life-styles, values and social relations.

Geographers also stress the specific effects of economic integration. Farmers – while less and less consumers of their own products and less closely linked than before to the nearest urban centre – are nonetheless increasingly integrated vertically into national and European markets via specialists pathways running upwards (through production systems) or downwards (via knowledge of techniques and inputs). The consequences are evident in a large number of regions where farmers have ceased to conform to any model of local activity and have made independent choices in a more varied pattern. Technical innovation is no longer diffused through the once obligatory channels of neighbour contact but, increasingly, at a distance. Each farmer has particular links within the economic and technical universe. Landscapes have lost part of their consistency and have become merely secondary influences. The mosaic of individual choices currently open to farmers is evident in contemporary farming practice and comes close to caricature when pure-bred oxen herds and general cattle are mixed together.

Not surprisingly, rural specialists have found themselves a little confused with respect to their traditional subject matter: a specifically rural space which has increasingly eluded them. However, all is not lost. One theme still able to generate passionate research interest is the redivision of rural space – based upon new economic and social demands. On top of the countryside's loss of autonomy and identity has also come the massive development of a non-agricultural rural sector. This dimension was initially explored by researchers such as N. Mathieu and J.-C. Bontron (1973). In all its manifestations, the 'non-farm' component plays an important part within rural regions. Also profoundly diverse, the pluri-activity of farmers themselves and their families has confused agricultural research.

In summary, therefore, the countryside, as a research object, has become increasingly vague and difficult to define. Yet this does not necessarily negate its significance for geographical research, nor relegate it to a residual domain, for the old-fashioned and nostalgic. The countryside remains the exclusive location of an activity, namely agriculture, and, in consequence, poses a series of specific issues. Yet, alternatively, in becoming urbanised (in the material sense of the term), the countryside ceases to command a specific research interest. Ultimately what is important is the question of value or economic worth: the value of the agricultural capital, the value of the product itself and the value of the work paid for. The upper limit for all such values is defined by the very nature of the agricultural or forestry systems, but is always sensitive, below an albeit elastic threshold, to considerable variety. Such values, or potential values, are spread out throughout space and as such predominate over all other factors that make space more or less able to fulfil its intended function: for example, ecological particularities, inherited patterns of land-use, common law, the spatial pattern resulting from the social divisions of land and so on. The ultimate ceiling of these values determines a demographic ceiling, the effects of which also influence, though less directly, the non-agricultural rural population. Thus all the arguments relating to human population densities (whether considered low or excessive) are only really meaningful, first, with respect to rural areas, and, secondly, when considered in terms of values; values linked ultimately, and yet with several exceptions, to the harnessing of the sun's energy.

According to its value, rural space generates and receives flows of resources: on the one hand, flows of money in its diverse forms, including incomes from land benefiting urban dwellers and, inversely, investments from urban sources and the various levies which the state and local communities impose on urban wealth to equip and reimburse the countryside for the relatively low earnings of rural producers; and on the other hand, flows of people, including the rural migration towards the town and the urbanised regions and now, especially since the mid-1970s, the reverse flow of repopulation in certain rural areas. Geographical works have traced a peripheral adjunct to this theme – what is taking place in the agricultural world at the margins of the urbanised regions and the resultant migrational displacements (*Etudes Rurales*, 1973), the particular peri-urban forms of agriculture (Berger 1985), and the various ways in which the French countryside has been invaded (David et al, 1979). More ecological studies have sought to quantify energy flows in various agricultural operations. Even so, at the heart of the issue of the relations of rural space to the global economy and society, a simple assessment of what the countryside gives and receives is still completely missing.

How then has geographical research, quite apart from any intellectual reorientation, reacted to the dramatically changed rural world? The volume of studies claiming to have an interest in rural issues remains very significant, and has grown in absolute numbers in recent years even if, as a proportion of the total number of publications in geography, it has declined. There are fewer exhaustive studies of particular rural areas, but rather a search for a theme, such as a specialised farming system or form of agricultural organisation, within spatial limits often pragmatically determined for the sake of convenience or relevance to policy-making.

The natural environment remains an important consideration in a certain type of study, though since 1970, following the work of G. Bertrand and his students, the methods of analysing it have largely been transformed. Examples of the modern approach include J.-P. Métailié's study of '*Le Feu Pastoral dans les Pyrénées Centrales*' (1981), the cartographic analysis of the decline of agro-pastoralism in the French Pyrenees by C. Suffert-Carnac (1978) and the investigation of the Sidobre, devastated by mineral extraction, by Cl. and G. Bertrand (1978). A recent thesis on the fallowing of the Ariége mountain region combines a detailed analysis of vegetation successions with a study of the selective agricultural behaviour of young farmers. Works with an overtly historical theme have persisted strongly, notably influenced by Xavier de Planhol (see, for example, Pitte, 1986).

A third observation from recent theses and publications is that the geographical frontiers of ruralism have become increasingly ill-defined, reflected not least in greater interaction with the perspectives of urban geography and neighbouring disciplines. This indistinctiveness is notably demonstrable in work on small towns (B. Kayser, 1979; J.-P. Laborie, 1979), urban fringe rural space (M. Berger, 1985) and the consumption of rural space through the process of urbanisation. Within geography, particularly active fringes are to be found at the interface of studies of landscape and its protection (G. Bertrand, Y. Luginbuhl, H. Mury-Flatrès), in research on 'spatial experience' (for example, the team at Caen-Rouen, with A. Frémont, J. Gallais, etc.) and within social geography (see, for example, the works of B. Kayser and the excellent book by four predominantly rural geographers: Frémont et al., 1984). Cooperation between geographers and other disciplines has been notably fruitful with ethnographers and anthropologists, forestry researchers and agriculturalists.

Methodological developments

Behind all these works and their research directions, two major traits stand out in contemporary rural geography: first, a constant, with the continuing emphasis on the spatial approach; and secondly, a radical reorientation, with the substitution of the future, as a major pole of research, for the self-perpetuating past. No value judgement is implied here. The spatial approach remains constitutive of geography. It continues to lead ruralists to stress, from the methodological viewpoint, the use of maps and fieldwork within the landscape (which is, after all, the basic manifestation of space). For them, the map is simultaneously the means of both detecting spatial structures and seeing landscape, and synthesising their research findings.

Maps and machines: old and new research methods

The 1984 International Congress of Geography was the occasion for Pierre Brunet and his *Centre des Recherches sur la Vie Rurale* at Caen to publish their map on 'Changes in French rural areas' (1984). This extremely detailed document formed a continuation of the already long-standing research of A. Perpillou, whose maps of French agricultural land-use over time are well known. He, however, has proceeded from a more first-hand knowledge of agricultural facts and landscapes, rather than from the use of statistical data sources. Brunet's maps, in contrast, are dynamic documents which integrate and illustrate changes over a thirty-year time-scale (1950–80). Other map series, appearing at approximately the same time, have been drawn up under the direction of J. Bonnamour and under the aegis of the *Commission internationale de typologie agraire*, led by J. Kostrowcki (1984). Data is increasingly treated in a complex way, using computers and agricultural survey statistics. Various sub-categories within agricultural typologies have been created using variables capable of qualifying key features of farm businesses over time, at ten year intervals. In a similar fashion, through the collaborative effort of a team of geographers and cartographers, eighteen plates, making in all 140 maps of rural France, have recently been produced on a very detailed scale and with an accompanying text (Beguin et al., 1984). Finally, computers have greatly assisted the drawing up of maps, largely by the *Recensement Général d'Agriculture* within a *départemental* framework. Maps have thus become, typically, working tools from which completely new research is possible.

In general, computer analysis and graphics have played a major part in geographical work on rural areas over the last few years. In this regard, Rey's thesis on the spatial growth of farms (1982), which assesses the consequences of the 1962 *Loi Foncière* over a twenty-year period, is a fine example of the richness of the various sources used and of the statistical treatments available.

The conceptualisation of space

The changing intellectual status of space calls for some mention. Within geography it is no longer seen either as a simple physical support for activities and social relations, or as a kind of pre-existing and independent idealised surface on which the realities of social and economic relations are inscribed; a view still often held within the social sciences. Under current theoretical conceptualisations, and implicit in the working practices of geographers, space is an autonomous 'given' only when it is definable by temporal features, either those of geological time or of past societies. But, whether conceived as a still malleable expanse, or as an ensemble of constraints and inherited possibilities, space is integral to the organisation and functioning of rural society.

To rural geographers, space poses two sets of issues: its diversity and, more importantly, its differentiation. Rural geography was traditionally split over whether to attribute to history or the natural environment the source of this diversity. Each rural or land-use entity was regarded as distinct, meriting by its originality a particular treatment. The incorporation of such individual cases within a general theme or themes was not precluded, however. More recent texts, otherwise not so far removed from their predecessors, have put greater emphasis on the differentiating mechanisms of rural space. Yves Guermond's thesis ambitiously searches for 'general laws', using multivariate analysis, to explain and even predict systems of spatial differentiation in agriculture in the eighteen *départements* of western France (1979).

But rural space, or more precisely agricultural space, also needs to be defined by geographers with respect to various scales of reality. Formerly, and in rather simplistic terms, a researcher would choose a scale at which to work and would stick to it. The choice was generally restricted either to the region, which was by far and away the most common 'local' scale, or to a much larger area allowing continental or even planet-wide comparisons. Today, however, the situation has changed considerably. One selects a small scale (either in terms of a pre-defined spatial unit, a distinct local area, or in terms of a broader theme inscribed at the local level) and locates this within wider relational space. Alternatively, one selects a broader issue at the national or global scale and, in the search for explanation, focuses down to the level of spatial sub-units within states. These two conceptual methodologies are not always easily differentiated. The *thèse d'Etat* of J.-P. Diry on industrial farming in France (1985) and that of J.-P. Peyon on French agricultural cooperatives (1983) both clearly start at the national scale. By comparison, a regional perspective is most evident in A. Frémont's thesis on animal husbandry in Normandy (1967) which, when it first appeared, was very innovative in including a detailed account of the structure of commercialisation. G. Dorel's thesis (1985), on the problems posed by the penetration of American capitalism into agricultural production, examines in particular the 'global reproduction of the system' and the means by which firms look to Third World countries for sources of profit no longer available in the United States. In another *thèse d'Etat*, J.-P. Charvet (1985) has gone to the level of international grain commerce and the regions that supply it to examine their double role, as centres of regional production (for example, Illinois and the Beauce) and as 'geographical systems'.

Today, through the medium of space, it is the evolution of rural societies, and no longer their past, which has become the focus for research. The past, when it is examined, now tends to be looked at in terms of the present's formation. This conceptual revolution has emerged as a product of the major upheaval which has been affecting rural France now for some twenty to thirty years. The new *problématique*, that of change and the structures of change, has inspired an abundance of work. In the thesis of J. Renard, on 'contemporary changes in rural life in the Nantaise region' (1975), the theme of innovation, also dealt with in a series of articles by P. Flatrès, was given prominence. Other researchers have looked at differing rates of local dynamism in rural areas. The administrative contexts are explored both by Agnès Guellec in the *Côtes-du-Nord* (1977) and P. Limouzin in *'le dynamisme des communes rurales'* (1980). Carrière (1981) has compared and contrasted the modernisation of agriculture in the USSR and Languedoc. R. Knafou's thesis (1978) examines the impact of ski centres in the French Alps upon regional agricultural practices. Change in rural areas can also be negative in that it can lead to relative impoverishment and to population loss (Duboscq, 1983). But in contrast perhaps to other social sciences, few geographers have concentrated especially on marginal regions and declining local societies. A large number, on the other hand, have examined the densely populated countryside and its growing interaction with the complexity of the wider socio-economic system. In their dealings with this new and changing subject matter, geographers have, on the whole, lacked models and each has, to a certain degree, had to clear his or her own way forward. But this has not prevented a number of them from being appreciated, beyond academic circles, within the real world of policy-making.

Third World studies in French rural geography

The enthusiam of French geographers for the rural world has, for a long time, caused them to extend their studies beyond the confines of France itself. The increasing scarcity of theses on France and the increasing number of works on Europe is not surprising. The Iberian Peninsula in particular has attracted much research, in addition to Sardinia, the Ombrie and the Mezzogiorno. Ireland, Lapland and even Soviet Russia (see, for example, M. Maurel, 1980) have also formed the subject of French rural geography texts. However, it has been the developing countries which have attracted the most interest. Among the various reasons, the challenges and the supposed differences of the unknown and the lack of existing knowledge of these countries have both been strong motivations. A significant number of ruralists are currently, or have recently been, working in Third World contexts, whether as teachers/researchers or by being attached to one of the major research institutions of the CNRS or the *Office de la Recherche Scientifique et Technique d'Outre Mers* (ORSTOM). Much of the work, which is frequently linked to indigenous national research programmes, has been described in a volume published as a result of the International Geographical Congress of 1984 (*Espace et la société dans les pays en développement*). It is striking that, on the whole, the orientations and the issues involved in this 'external' geography do not differ very much from those encountered in work conducted within rural France (or elsewhere in Europe).

The 'processes' and the 'policies' of development, though, have become subjects for research in their own right. Agricultural planning, in particular drainage and irrigation, has emerged as a significant research theme. The large-scale phenomenon of rural mobility has been widely observed and analysed, whether it be mobility towards vacant land or areas better located with respect to markets, or towards the major urban centres. Similarly, studies have described the decision-making choices of agricultural communities, held in an economic or demographic stranglehold, between farming for export and farming for a domestic urban market; a dynamic of intensification and a dynamic of spatial extension (Pélissier, 1985). The means and conditions of technical progress is a traditional rural research theme. One popular mode of analysis, which has had to be rapidly updated, contrasts farmers' 'logic' (or one might say 'rationality') with that of the 'promoters of change'. Research has examined the various levels of dialogue displayed between the different parties involved, and the various misunderstandings which serve to keep them apart. A final theme has been the emergence, from a wide range of agricultural societies, of a common entity – the family farm, such as we know it today.

Several principal *problématiques* have aided these research goals. The oldest and omnipresent one is that of progress in all its diverse forms, starting with increases in production and farm incomes, and the factors that encourage or impede them. The second, which is well exemplified in Latin America, focuses on the dominated peasant culture and all the forms of extortion to which it is victim: the capitalist appropriation of surplus value, the gulf between rich and poor within rural society, and the monopoly control by a minority of the land and the workforce. A third *problématique* concerns the greater or lesser efficiency of social and cultural forms, their unequal adaptation to the conditions necessary for 'development', the difficulties provoked by the interaction of the modern world with traditional and inherited patterns of behaviour and the varied dynamics whereby populations and social groups advance. A final intellectual organising principle for research stresses the role and impact of the state and its agents: including, at one end of the scale, the major political and economic options and the policies adopted for regional development; at the other end, the articulation of the rural world, the means by which the state communicates with local communities and the upward and downward links which connect the two.

Between the two worlds of rural geography, that which exists in France and that which occurs elsewhere, there is therefore much more than merely similarities or a comparable spirit. Yet between the geographers of the two sides there still remains a significant distance with respect to research themes and viewpoints. At a basic level, the identification of spatial and social injustices is very much more significant in Third World research. The issue of food balances among producer populations remains more than ever a central theme (see, for example, the work on the 'Two Sahels', i.e. north-east Brazil and the Sahel of Africa – or the conference entitled 'Full Granaries, Empty Granaries' – the latter referring, in a rather prejudicial generalisation to those of Africa). Beyond the individual questions that geographers ask themselves, what also differs on both sides are the research contexts and methodologies. The general paucity of institutional source material and information inevitably constrains the field-work of researchers operating in developing countries and forces them to establish data bases. Remote sensing is becoming more important just as aerial imagery is increasingly being substituted for weak local statistical documentation (e.g. Bruneau et al., 1985). For various reasons and more so than in France, collective works have tended to become the rule in developing countries, often involving researchers from a wide range of social and agricultural disciplines.

Finally, one notes that overseas, more so than in France, researchers in rural geography frequently operate as consultants and experts, taking part, either directly or indirectly, in development planning and programmes, including monitoring and evaluating their impacts. The time has long since passed when such active roles posed questions of conscience. At least in Black Africa, different teams (in Niger and Senegal), by their long-term presence, have prompted changes in aid programmes and have sought to develop a role for themselves which is not only spatially but also temporally defined.

The institutional context of French rural geography

Several comments remain to be made on the institutional role of geographers and rural geography and on the official status of this sub-branch of the discipline. The first point is that far more researchers work in this subject area than there are rural geographers, and the so-called disciplinary boundaries are definitely permeable if not largely a fiction. While a number of Chairs of Rural Geography exist within French universities, they are generally held by older people; though it must be acknowledged that at Caen and Montpellier particularly, and also at the *Ecole Normale Superieure* at Fontenay, specialist rural groups operate. One encounters very few formally designated ruralist groups within the CNRS, and none within the departments of ORSTOM (which is otherwise wholly interdisciplinary). However, under different institutional labels, active groups do nonetheless function. Within the International Geographical Union, the French Commission on Agricultural Geography has proved an important focus for new themes and reflection. Finally, rural geographers have been active participants, alongside ethnographers, anthropologists, sociologists, lawyers and historians in the *Association des Ruralistes Françaises*. In total, the image of French rural geography is that of an activity which extends far beyond its otherwise constricted institutional framework.

Finally, one must ask whether the same conclusion would be reached if the achievements of rural geography were to be examined, from the perspective of its research findings, in terms of the contribution rural geographers have made to the knowledge of the changing rural world. Unfortunately, such a contribution is generally little recognised and indubitably underestimated. In part this has been due to the difficulties, inherent in identifying their particular contribution which, due to the discouraging volume of material and a thematic profusion which is not reducible to a few well ordered models, can confuse those not immediately familiar with the subject matter. Yet, at the end of the day, doesn't geography ultimately emerge as being like a 'homing device', opening new directions through the jumble of situation and issues which comprises the rural world today?

2 Rural geography at the crossroads of disciplines *by Bernard Kayser*

Rural geography in France has had its hour of glory. It was rural geography which, by producing the major regional theses of the first half of the twentieth century (and several since[1]), introduced to France the first valid account of the nation's countryside: its diversity, its structures and even its history.

But this geography has now run its course. The exploration of the land is almost finished. Rural geographers now work on other scales, in other ways, extending their research themes into economics, sociology, ecology and agricultural economics. More and more frequently, geographers are involved in close interdisciplinary collaborations which, though they might create problems of identity, nevertheless overcome all epistemological and methodological objections by the sheer value of the results.

Their contribution to the analysis of the rural world continues to be, in any case, particularly important and relevant, as that world is, in France as in other industrialised countries, in a state of total change; undergoing a period of rapid mutation which, with hindsight, will undoubtedly seem to have been especially brutal.

The French rural world between abandonment and revitalisation

Has French rural space emptied itself and has French rural society declined? Or cannot these two factors be otherwise interpreted as demonstrating a certain stability? Geographers, aware like others of the changing circumstances and structures of the rural world, have made their observations against the backdrop of these two fundamental questions.

One profound change for rural France has been a dramatic demographic reversal between the last two censuses (1975 and 1982). Rural communities as a whole have seen their populations grow by 0.9 per cent per year, while previously they had consistently diminished at about the same rate for nearly a century. This growth has not been restricted to communes lying adjacent to urban areas (which have grown at a rate of 1.9 per cent per annum). Even the 'remote rural' communes have, on the whole, gained population during the inter-censal years at around 0.5 per cent per year. Approximately half of these have also displayed positive natural growth.

Curiously, however, this dramatic upheaval seems to interest no one. It is as if observers cannot believe it is happening. To my knowledge, only two investigations, still to be published, have sought to understand the precise mechanisms which explain this reversal. (In the USA the non-metropolitan turnaround, which took place during the 1970s, has prompted literally hundreds of studies undertaken as much by sociologists as by geographers.)

It is the qualitative changes, however, that deserve special attention, for the village population of France is no longer what it used to be. Today, there are many more blue-collar workers (29 per cent of the active population), employees (15 per cent) and middle management (12 per cent). At 35 per cent, farmers, henceforth, constitute the minority. This, in itself, is an absolutely fundamental revolution for rural France. The traditional guardians and most often the owners of rural space, they now represent just a third of the local working population; even less if one adds to the active population, the retired people – who make up around a fifth of the total rural population. Perhaps one should say only a fifth;

[1] see the Bibliography at the end of this chapter.

because, contrary to what is often believed, there are still young people within villages: 18 per cent are under 15 years of age (cf. 21 per cent in the national population) and 27 per cent are between 15 and 35 years (cf. 31 per cent in the national population). The common caricature of the dying village is appropriate only for a small minority of villages. The majority, even if they are not always terribly dynamic, still have the means and resources.

But what has happened then in rural areas? In social relationships and in daily life, a truly 'village-level' change has taken place, due to the localised effects of modernisation, of the economic crisis, and of the globalisation of information systems. First and foremost, within the rural family, previously a bastion of tradition, the relations between individuals have undergone a fantastic change: first, through the opening up of the domestic group to the exterior world; and, secondly, through the reversal of traditional parent-children relationships whereby the plans and aspirations of the latter increasingly become a key determinant of family strategies overall.

The evolution of the village community is more complex and confusing. Sufficient stress has already been placed on the disintegration of interpersonal relations and the loss of festive occasions. The task now must be to identify instead the maintenance and sometimes the reinforcement of village sociability; for example through the evident development of local associations and the growth of mutual aid under other non-traditional forms.

Power relations have also clearly changed. It is no longer simply a question of economic or ideological power at the local level. Political power itself has been shaken, and conflicts deriving, for example, from the opposition between farmers and 'the rest', are increasingly moving beyond the immediate closed arena of village society.

Finally, spatial relationships – simultaneously indicators and expressions of change – have also dramatically altered. At one level are the relations between space and nature: at a time when society has invested rural people with the responsibility for the protection of nature, farmers have found themselves more and more forced into an increasingly artificial relationship with the ecosystem. Then, concerning living space, all horizons are expanding and the relations between village society and neighbouring towns are intensifying, while longer trip patterns are no longer exceptional. Lastly, there are the spatial relations concerning the management of the countryside. As the focus of new pressures and social demands, rural space has begun to be actively defended. Through this process, in response to regulations and indeed the land-use planning system, the community rediscovers itself, and having done so, reinforces itself. We see, in this regard, affirmation of the importance of the institution of the commune which in the face of both history and technocracy, has steadfastly refused to abdicate.

The limitations of synoptic studies

Several texts produced in recent years have given the impression that we are used to having an overall vision of rural space and rural society in France. This has been largely the fault of the chosen methodology of rural geography which, though it has brought to light useful information, has nonetheless failed to propose any general explanatory schema.

The map of changes in French rural space, prepared under the guidance of P. Brunet (1984) at a scale of 1:1,000,000, is a document of considerable interest and its lavish accompanying text has also received much attention. The major agricultural changes, identified in the course of the crucial years (1950–80) are presented effectively at the national and regional level. However there is only an indication of the peri-urban dynamic. One is still a long way from global appreciation of change. In any case, this clearly would not be representable through maps.

After the publication of the *Atlas de la France Rurale* (1968), by the sociologists at Nanterre, geographers responded to the challenge by publishing *140 Cartes sur la France Rurale* (Beguin et al. 1984). The bulk are dedicated to agriculture but several sections present the conditions of rural life, rural infrastructure and land-use planning policies. Although certainly useful and very methodically undertaken, the possible interpretations one can draw from them are limited because of the *départemental* scale and their inevitable dependence upon statistical information sources.

This issue of statistical inference is the most thorny of all. No amount of computer manipulation will ever save research from the sin of inappropriate statistics. To take a single example: the bulk of studies take as their base the 'rural communes' as a whole, such as they are defined by INSEE. Of these, some are strongly marked by peri-urbanisation, while others are still remote and untouched (see Table 8.1). Can the sum and the average derived from an amalgamation of both give a genuinely usable result?

This is clearly the weakness of the recent book by Robert Chapuis, *Les Ruraux Français* (1986), who uses statistics derived essentially from rural communes as a whole in his treatment (factor analysis of corresponding variables) and who presents his findings at the level of the *arrondissement*. But this weakness is compensated: Chapuis accompanies his maps and statistics with commentaries derived from his research experiences, his reading and his own surveys. The book reflects throughout the quality of this geographer who has learnt from his peers a mistrust of relying too completely on single sources of information, no matter how statistically rigorous they might be. Chapuis straddles two generations; that of the hard-line youth, accomplished in the spatio-mathematical game from whom he takes simple techniques, and also that of the field worker, who will accept nothing unless he can verify it in the real world.

The oldest publication of the *Group de recherche sur l'espace rural français*, called simply '*L'Espace Rural Français* (1978) was based on a multivariate analytic method of a similar type to Chapuis and it too sought to incorporate several commentaries. But, despite its title, it was limited to a few specific themes (demography, services, agriculture and so on) and could draw no conclusion; going no further than a description of 'the intertwining of diverse threads . . . which make up part of the delicate and complex fabric of rural space'.

Table 8.1 The divergent development of peri-urban and remote rural areas

	Peri-urban rural	Remote rural	All rural
	Per cent	Per cent	Per cent
Farmers in active population, 1982	11	34	20
Annual population growth (1975–82)	1.9	0.5	0.9
Housing built since 1962	40	26	34

The eclecticism of local studies

In assessing the studies produced over the last twenty years by French geographers on the rural milieu, it is a difficult task to identify and trace a reasoned and organised image of structures, dynamics and spatial differentiation. Any attempt at a synthesis is confronted by the contradictions in the *problématiques*, the variability of the themes and the eclecticism of the treatments. If all these studies produced coherent information, 'pieces' capable of being placed within the puzzle, one could use them without difficulty. However, how does one treat them when they deal with only fragments of the elements of a socio-spatial system and when they are thereby representative neither of the system as a whole, nor of the elements themselves (which are too strongly interpreted in localised terms)?

One clearly misses the 'monographs', the grand studies incorporating the evolution of a localised socio-spatial system in the rural world in all its complexity. Let us re-examine recent theses, at least those which have concentrated on a precise spatial entity (a region, a *département*, and so on). A number have devoted great effort to historical analyses in the classic sense but their authors' inspiration soon diminishes when dealing with contemporary history. Others have concentrated on the analysis of land structures, which require the fastidious study of cadastral data. Others still have documented, over hundreds of printed pages, local variations in demographic behaviour. The best have achieved some balance in the chapters and have proposed a more varied, though nevertheless inevitably incomplete, interpretation. Only one, in these terms, stands out from the rest. In this sole example the author has applied systematic methods of analysis to the viticulture of the Languedoc region and it could be given as an example to folow, if the modernist desire for formalisation had not divested it of a large part of its living flesh.

Journal articles, the results of limited or partial research studies, are often more useful than theses, as they are frequently more precise. But it is not easy to sort them rationally or to include them in an effective and analytical documentary review. The automisation of documentation and the use of data bases are only one form of the clutter of modern civilisation. Ultimately, it is through only about forty more or less recent articles that one can best draw out the current configuration of the rural world today. Amongst these articles, some have been written by geographers, others not.

It is instructive to compare particular articles presenting 'focused syntheses' of individual local societies, each published by researchers of different disciplines or at least of different orientations within their disciplines. After all, whatever he or she might be, the researcher confronted by locality (the space-society coupling within a restricted compass) can but explore 'all dimensions', thereby becoming an interdisciplinarian personified. Here then are three such articles whose authors' aims account in part for the results of their researches (see Table 8.2).

First, the ethnologist has drawn from a series of detailed studies undertaken in the Bigouden region in Brittany, an analysis of the commune of St-Jean-Trolimon 'in search of its identity'. This analysis shows how a society of landowners, small farmers and agricultural day-labourers, which opened up to the outside world towards the end of the nineteenth century, is currently experiencing an agricultural crisis, an upheaval in its social structure and a contradictory growth in the non-agricultural economy, with second-home owners beginning to play an increasingly important role.

Secondly, the geographers have presented the current issues of concern for rural communities in a state of crisis on the southern fringes of the Massif Central. They show how the domination of external powers is having an increasing effect as much on the land (forestry plantations, a regional park, installations overflowing from urban areas) as on the society – summer holiday-makers having become such a part of local life as to have completely undermined it, particularly from a cultural point of view.

Thirdly, the sociologist-ethnologist team have carried their synthesis to a detailed study of the dynamics of the relationship between land use and social structure in the commune of Barre-des-Cévennes. They show that the historical modifications to the society have distorted systems of production, to the point today where forestry plantations dominate land use, with the national park also playing a growing role.

The convergence of these authors' preoccupations, despite their separate disciplinary and institutional backgrounds and lack of reciprocal influences, is striking (see Table 8.2).

The interdisciplinary geographers

Perhaps on account of their indistinctive science, geographers naturally incline to interdisciplinary activities as fish do to water. The involvement of certain geographers, for example, in the large-scale CNRS programme entitled 'The observation of social and cultural change' has been judged beneficial not only for the programme but also for the geographers themselves. Concerning the very conception of the research programme, the geographers drew the sociologists – the original initiators of the research – into the *consideration of space*, not only as place, but also as a 'fundamental element' of change. The fact that the synthesis has been published under the title *L'Esprit des Lieux* (CNRS, 1986) is illustrative of the impact that they have been able to exert. At the same time, however, the geographers in question have themselves been influenced by the various ways of thought of the other disciplines involved – the sociologists and anthropologists

112 *Geography*

Table 8.2 Summary of the thematic contents of the three 'monographs'

Discipline	Ethnologist[1]	Geographer[2]	Sociologist/Ethnologist[3]
Locality	St-Jean-Trolimon	Espinouse	Barre-des-Cévennes
Theme			
Society/environment relations	x	xxx	xx
Economic and social history	xxx	xx	xxx
Demography	xx	xx	xx
Agricultural economy	xxx	xx	xx
Non-agricultural economy	xx	xx	xx
Land structure and farm holdings	xxx	xxx	xxx
Local power and control of space	xxx	xxx	xx
Relations with the state	xx	xxx	xxx
Social and cultural life	xx	x	x
Perspectives	xxx	x	xxx

[1] M. Ségalen (1980)
[2] B. Kayser (1977 and 1986)
[3] A. Fioravanti and H. Lamarche (1978)

and, in particular, the ethnographers. Might not the geographers begin to see themselves now as spatial sociologists and anthropologists at a medium scale?

A summary

The contribution of geographers to the knowledge of the rural world is not insignificant. Whether in traditional academic research, or in the context of applied contract research, they have held their position well in the field of rural sciences. They are considered 'indispensable' in interdisciplinary programmes and are often sought for their particular skills. For geographers have first and foremost their experience, their comparative capacity, and their sense of the land. They can also become, on demand, ecologists, statisticians, cartographers. They know how to analyse agriculture, its techniques, structures, commercial links, etc. They are masters in the knowledge of difficult land issues. They excel in statistical and cartographic studies of the rural population. They also understand perfectly the problems of tourism. They show a particular capacity, perhaps a little formalistic, in dealing with town-country relations. But they have generally circumvented certain elements without which there is no legitimate analysis. Bonnamour's exhortation that 'Priority must be given to *exhaustive studies of basic mechanisms* of rural life' (1973) has been scarcely heeded.

It seems useful therefore to draw up a list, though hasty and superficial, of the major shortcomings of the discipline with respect to rural areas. Two major and seemingly complementary lacunae are observable, largely resulting from the chosen subject matter of rural research. On the one hand, concerning the two-thirds of the active village population employed outside agriculture, one really knows very little, particularly regarding the workers living and often employed in the village and the middle management and executives. On the other hand, whereas there are numerous studies of villages, one still has only very scant knowledge of the small towns – the built-up areas, often the principal local centre within a district, whose population is often between 2,000 and 5,000 inhabitants.

Contrary to what one is often led to believe, geographers are equally reserved on the subject of the relations between rural people and their natural environment (its actual basis, its mastery, its management). They are even more discreet on the relations between rural people and 'outsiders'; studies of sociability not seeming to be their concern.

They are beginning to be interested, though not enough, in issues and phenomena of power, and village politics. Nevertheless, how can one pretend to understand a range of issues involving social dynamics (even those narrowly defined in the context of the relations between society and space) if one does not analyse social actors and their local strategies in a national framework? What remains, finally, is the so far untouched issue of 'culture'. Can daily life (which is after all a very basic expression of culture) remain outside the field of investigation if the final object is the comprehension of the *village system*?

The ambition to devise a theory of rural space and of rural societies supposes that both would be identifiable as valid 'objects' of scientific investigation. However, they constitute instead merely a segment of a globality within which they are integrated. They can be isolated theoretically only with some difficulty. One is increasingly seeing them as general observation points for examining wider social processes: observation points that have obvious advantages in their scale and transparency.

Moreover, the geographers in France who have addressed rural issues are undoubtedly amongst those who have not cared very much for theory. It is noticeable, for example, that they are less sensitive than others to doctrinal allegiances and to official jargon. To some extent, this has given them an apparent objectivity and appreciable qualities of being free thinking. But is it not also a significant weakness?

The hypotheses, the analyses, the syntheses indispensable to the progression of knowledge, necessitate a theoretical infrastructure. That geographers have done without it is one of their limitations. In these uncertain times, though, one must understand that they are still this side of the hoped-for grand explanation.

Bibliography

Association des Ruralistes Français, *La Nature et le Rural*, Colloque National, Strasbourg, 1986, 4 vol.
A travers champs. Agronomes et géographes, Paris, Ed. de l'ORSTOM, 1985.
Auriac F., *Système économique et espace: le vignoble languedocien*, Paris, Economica, 1983.
Béghin, M. et al., *140 cartes sur la France rurale*, Paris, geo-media (51 rue Dareau-Paris 14ème), 1984.
Bertrand, G. et al. 'L'élément et le système', in *Revue Géographique des Pyrénées et du Sud-Ouest*, 1986, 3, jt-sept.
Bertrand, C. et G., 'Le Sidobre (Tarn), esquisse d'une monographie', in *Revue Géographique des Pyrénées et du Sud-Ouest*, avril 1978.
Beteille, R., *La France du vide*, Paris, Librairies Techniques, 1981.
Berger, M., 'Comportements et pratiques des sociétés péri-urbaines', in *Actes du colloque les périphéries urbaines. Quelles sociétés? Quels espaces? Quels dynamismes?*, Caen, Centre de Publication de l'Université, 1985, pp. 133-139.
Bonnamour, J., *Le Morvan, la terre et les hommes. Essai de géographie agricole*, Paris, P.U.F., 1985.
Bonnamour, J., *Géographie rurale, méthodes et perspectives*, Masson, 1973.
Bonnamour, J., et al., *Les types d'agriculture en France 1970-1980. Recueil de cartes*, Fontenay-aux-Roses, Centre de Géographie Rurale de l'E.N.S. de Fontenay, 1984.
Bonnamour, J., et al., *La géographie rurale en France 1980-1984*, Fontenay-aux-Roses, E.N.S. de Fontenay (Cah. de Fontenay, n°35), 1984.
Bruneau, M. et al., *Nord-Est de la Thaïlande. Evolution de quelques composantes des milieux agricoles (1972-1982)*, Bordeaux, CEGET/CNRS, 1985, Cartes et fascicule.
Brunel, S. et al., *Asie-Afrique: greniers vides, greniers pleins*, Paris, Economica, 1986.
Brunet, F. et al., *Carte des mutations de l'espace rural français, 1950-1980* (Carte et 12 p. de texte), Caen, Centre de recherches sur la vie rurale de l'Université, 1960.
Brunet, P., *Structure agraire et économie rurale des plateaux ventiaires entre la seine et l'Oise*, Caen, 1960.
Brunet, P. (sons la direction de), *Centre des mutations de l'espace rural français 1950-1980*, Centre de recherches sur la vie rurale, Caen 1984.
Brunet, R., *Les campagnes toulousaines, étude géographique*, Toulouse, 1965.
Brunhes, J., *La géographie humaine*, Paris, Félix Alcan, 1910 (Chapitre VII intitulé: Un type d'île de la haute montagne. Le texte reprend un article de J. Brunhes et P. Girardin, dans les *Annales de Géographie* de 1906).
CNRS *L'esprit des lieux, localités et changement social en France*, Paris, 1986.
Calmes, R. et al., *L'espace rural français*, Masson, 1978.
Carriere, P., *La modernisation de deux agricultures*, Montpellier, Université Paul Valéry, 1981.
Chapuis, R., *Les ruraux du département du Doubs, éléments de géographie sociologique*, Besançon, 1982.
Chapuis, R., et Brossard, T., *Les ruraux français*, Paris, Masson, 1986.
Charvet, J.P., *Les greniers du monde*, Paris, Economica, 1985.

Chevalier, J., 'La question foncière en Basse-Normandie. Essai de géographie des rapports sociaux à propos du foncier agricole', Thèse de doctorat d'Etat, Université de Caen, 1983.
Cholley, A., 'Problèmes de structure agraire et d'économie rurale' in *Annales de géographie*, avril-juin 1946.
Deffontaines, J.P. et al., *Pays, paysans, paysages dans les Vosges du Sud. Les pratiques agricoles et la transformation de l'espace*, Paris, Institut National de la Recherche Agronomique, 1977.
David, J. et al., *Problématique et méthodes d'analyse de la rurbanisation. Le plateau de Champagnier (Isère)*, Grenoble, Université scientifique et médicale, 1979.
Dion, R., *Essai sur la formation du paysage rural français*, Tours, Arrault, 1934.
Dion, R., *Histoire de la vigne et du vin en France des origines au XIXème siècle*, Paris, Roger Dion, 1959.
Diry, J.P., *L'industrialisation de l'élevage en France: économie et géographie des filières avicoles et porcines*, Paris, Ophrys, 1985.
Dongmo, J.L., *Le dynamisme bamiléké (Cameroun)*, Yaoundé, 1981, 2 vol.
Dorel, G., *Agriculture et grandes entreprises aux Etats-Unis*, Paris, Economica, 1985.
Duboscq, P., *Les campagnes d'Aquitaine: espace et valeur dans le développement du rapport capitaliste en agriculture*, Toulouse, Université de Toulouse-le-Mirail, 1983, 3 vol.
Dufour, J., *Agriculture et agriculteurs dans les campagnes mancelles*, Le Mans, 1981.
Dugrand, R., *Villes et campagnes en Bas-Languedoc*, Paris, 1963.
Etudes Rurales, 'L'urbanisation des campagnes', Paris, jv.-juin 1973.
Fel, A., *Les hautes terres du Massif Central: tradition paysanne et économie agricole*, Paris, 1962.
Fioravanti, A. et Lamarche, H., 'Elevage, reboisement et tourisme dans une zone montagneuse désertée: Barre-des-Cévennes', *Etudes rurales* n°71-72, juillet-décembre 1978.
Fremont, A., *L'élevage en Normandie, étude géographique*, Caen, 1967.
Fremont, A., Chevalier, J., Herin, J., et Renard, J., *Géographie sociale*, Paris, Masson, 1984.
Gilbanki, G.J., *Les vignobles de qualité du Sud-Est du Bassin parisien. Evolution économique et sociale*, Paris, G.J. Gilbanki, 1981.
Gillette, C., 'Découpages de l'espace rural. L'exemple de la Bourgogne', thèse de 3ème cycle, Paris, 1978.
Gourou, P., *Les Paysans du Delta tonkinois. Etude de Géographie humaine*, Paris/La Haye, 1965 (Coll. de Réimpressions).
Guermond, Y., *Le système de différenciation spatiale en agriculture: la France de l'Ouest de 1950 à 1975*, Paris, Libr. Honoré Champion, 1979.
Guellec, A., 'L'Agriculture du Département des Côtes du Nord', Rennes, thèse d'Etat, 1977.
Gu-Konu, E., 'Tradition et modernité. La modernisation agricole face à la mutation rurale en Afrique Noire', thèsis d'Etat, Paris I, 1983.
Houzard, G., 'Aménagements et évolution des forêts: l'exemple d'Ecouves', in: *Rev. Géogr. Pyrénées et Sud-Ouest*, 2, 1984, pp. 294-300 (numéro télématique forêts).
Juillard, E., Meynier, A., de Planhol X., et Sautter, G., 'Structures agraires et paysages ruraux: un quart de siècle de recherches françaises', Nancy, *Annales de l'Est*, Mémoire n°17, 1957 (Colloque international de Géographie et Histoire agraires).
Kayser, B., 'Patrimoine et gestion de l'espace rural: l'exemple de l'Espinouse', *Etudes rurales* n°65, janvier-mars 1977.
Kayser, B. et al., *Petites villes et pays dan l'aménagement rural*, Paris Ed. du CNRS, 1979.
Kayser, B., Subversion des villages français, *Etudes rurales* n°93-94, janvier-juin 1984.
Kayser, B., 'Le village recomposé', in: *L'esprit des lieux. Localités et changement social en France*, Paris, Ed. du CNRS, 1986, pp. 41-67.

Knafou, R., *Les stations intégrées de sports d'hiver des Alpes françaises*, Paris, Masson, 1978.
Laborie, J.P., *Les petites villes*, Paris, Ed. du CNRS, 1979.
Le Bourdiec F., *Hommes et paysages du riz à Madagascar. Etude de géographie humaine*, Tananarive, 1974.
Limouzin, F., 'Les facteurs du dynamisme des communes rurales françaises. Méthode d'Analyse et résultats', in: *Ann. de Géogr.*, 495, 1980, pp. 549–587.
Mace, G., *Un département rural de l'Ouest, La Mayenne*, Mayenne, 1982.
Marchal, J.Y., *Yatenga (Nord Haute-Volta): la dynamique d'un espace rural soudano-sahélien*, Paris, O.R.S.T.O.M., 1983.
Mathieu, N., Bontron, J.C., 'Les transformations de l'espace rural. Problèmes de méthode', in: *Etudes Rurales*, 49–50, jv.-1973.
Maurel, M.C., *La campagne collectivisée: société et espace rural en Russie*, Paris, Anthropos, 1980.
Metailie, J.P., *Le feu pastoral dans les Pyrénées centrales (Barousse, Oueil, Larboust)*, Paris, Ed. du CNRS, 1981.
Meynier, A. *Les paysages agraires*, Paris, Armand Colin, 1958.
Pélissier, P., 'Techniques d'encadrement et transformations de l'Agriculture en Afrique Noire', in: *Des labours de Cluny à la Révolution Verte*, Paris, P.U.F., 1985.
Peyon, J.P., *La Coopération agricole en France: étude géographique des grands organismes coopératifs*, Paris, 1983, 2 vol. (thèse Paris I).
Pitte, J.R., *Terres de Castanide. Hommes et paysages du Châtaignier de l'Antiquité à nos jours*, Paris, Fayard, 1986.
Raison, J.P., *Les hautes terres de Madagascar*, Paris, ORSTOM/Karthala, 1984, 2 vol.
Renard, J., *Les évolutions contemporaines de la vie rurale dans la région nantaise*, Les Sables d'Olonne, Le Cercle d'Or, 1975.
'*La recherche géographique française (Structures, Thèmes et Perspectives)*', Paris, Comité National Français de Géographie, 1984.
Rey, V., *Besoin de terre des agriculteurs*, Paris, Economica, 1982.
Saussol, A., *L'héritage. Essai sur le problème foncier mélanésien en Nouvelle-Calédonie*, Paris, Société des Océanistes (Musée de l'Homme), 1979.
Ségalen, M., *De la sociabilité au réseau, ou le changement dans la continuité à Saint-Jean-Trolimon*, document C.N.R.S., inédit, 1980.
Suffert-Carnac, C., 'Les grandes unifes éco-agrologiques des Pyrénées françaises en 1970–1978. Esquisse cartographique à 1/250 000', in: *Revue Géog. des Pyrénées et du Sud-Ouest*, oct. 1978.

9 Rural Geography in Britain

Paul Cloke and Malcolm Moseley

1 Introduction

'Rural geography' has come to be recognised as a sub-discipline of geography, in Britain, only since the early 1970s. In a sense, of course, most human geography before that focused on the countryside, with a long-established concern for agricultural land use and for settlement systems – stemming in part from the classical models of von Thunen and Christaller respectively, and reflecting both the traditional economic dominance of agriculture and regional geography's emphasis on the social and economic response of rural people to the physical environment. In some senses, then rural geography (although not so called) held a dominant institutional position until the 1950s. Subsequently, with the demise of regionalism and the development of systematic studies in geography, rural geography entered a wilderness phase lasting fifteen years or so. Urban arenas dominated the attention of human geographers and rural geography wallowed in its agricultural roots, seemingly oblivious to the methodological and conceptual progress being made in urban studies (Cloke, 1985).

By the early 1970s, rural areas were of such low priority for geographic study that attention could be attracted simply by pointing out how little comparatively was known about rural change. In response, a distinct and encompassing rural geography emerged drawing together a broad range of subjects. A milestone in this process was the publication of Hugh Clout's (1972) *Rural geography: An Introductory survey* which served three important purposes:

(i) it showed that important rural studies had been taking place during the wilderness period, though not necessarily conducted by geographers. Use was made for example of the research of such as Best and Coppock (1968), Bracey (1952, 1970), Coppock (1964), Pahl (1965) and Wibberley (1959, 1967).

(ii) it melded a widely dispersed range of material into a distinctly demarcated subject area which it called 'rural geography'.

(iii) it brought together aspects of society, economy and land (Figure 9.1) although it left unsolved the problems of finding methods and concepts with which to bind these aspects into a cohesive subdiscipline (Clout 1977).

In 1974, the Institute of British Geographers wound up its 'agricultural geography study group' and replaced it with one devoted to rural geography. The following decade was a period of resurgence with geographers cashing in on claims that fundamental changes to rural society and economy were going on unnoticed by the discipline. The need for basic data on rural change became inescapable, and rural geography became something of a bandwagon both for a new generation of geographers and for that section of the research fraternity which is sufficiently footloose to switch its attentions to novel fields of study.

The literature of rural geography burgeoned during this phase (Table 9.1) and the appearance of two major journals has also signalled a maturing of the field:- the *Countryside Planning Yearbook*, published annually since 1980 and relaunched in 1988 as the *International Yearbook of Rural Planning*, and the quarterly *Journal of Rural Studies*, launched in 1985. Their editors are, respectively, the geographers Andrew Gilg and Paul Cloke.

A new phase in the development of the subdiscipline has been marked by the appearance of a number of reviews of its content and methods, notably by Cloke (1980, 1988), Clark (1982a), the Rural Geography Study Group (1986) and Munton (1986). These stocktaking exercises have raised fundamental questions concerning both the identity of rural geography and its conceptual development, and these two issues, taken in turn, form the rest of the chapter.

2 The identity of rural geography by *Malcolm Moseley*

Confusion of subject and of method

Geographers are renowned for self-consciously asking 'does geography really exist as a discipline?' And rural geographers have an extra problem: does 'rurality' provide a respectable intellectual focus? If *rurality* does offer some unity of purpose it comes from the low population density and extensive use of land typical of rural areas, these characteristics generating a number of distinctive theoretical and practical questions. And if *geographers* have something distinctive to offer in that domain, it probably stems from their tradition of looking at spatial relationships and man-environment interaction.

However, not everyone would accept that 'rurality' and 'geography' have distinctive roles to play in social inquiry. Geography has often been dismissed as 'spatial fetishism' – as lavishing excessive concern on the largely irrelevant spatial dimension of economic, social or political processes. And there is no shortage of critics who would argue that the rural-urban dichotomy is outdated and misleading. Thus,

> 'Rural geography is only the bucolic expression of those national and international forces of the mixed economy at work throughout British society' (Clarke, 1982a, p. 253).

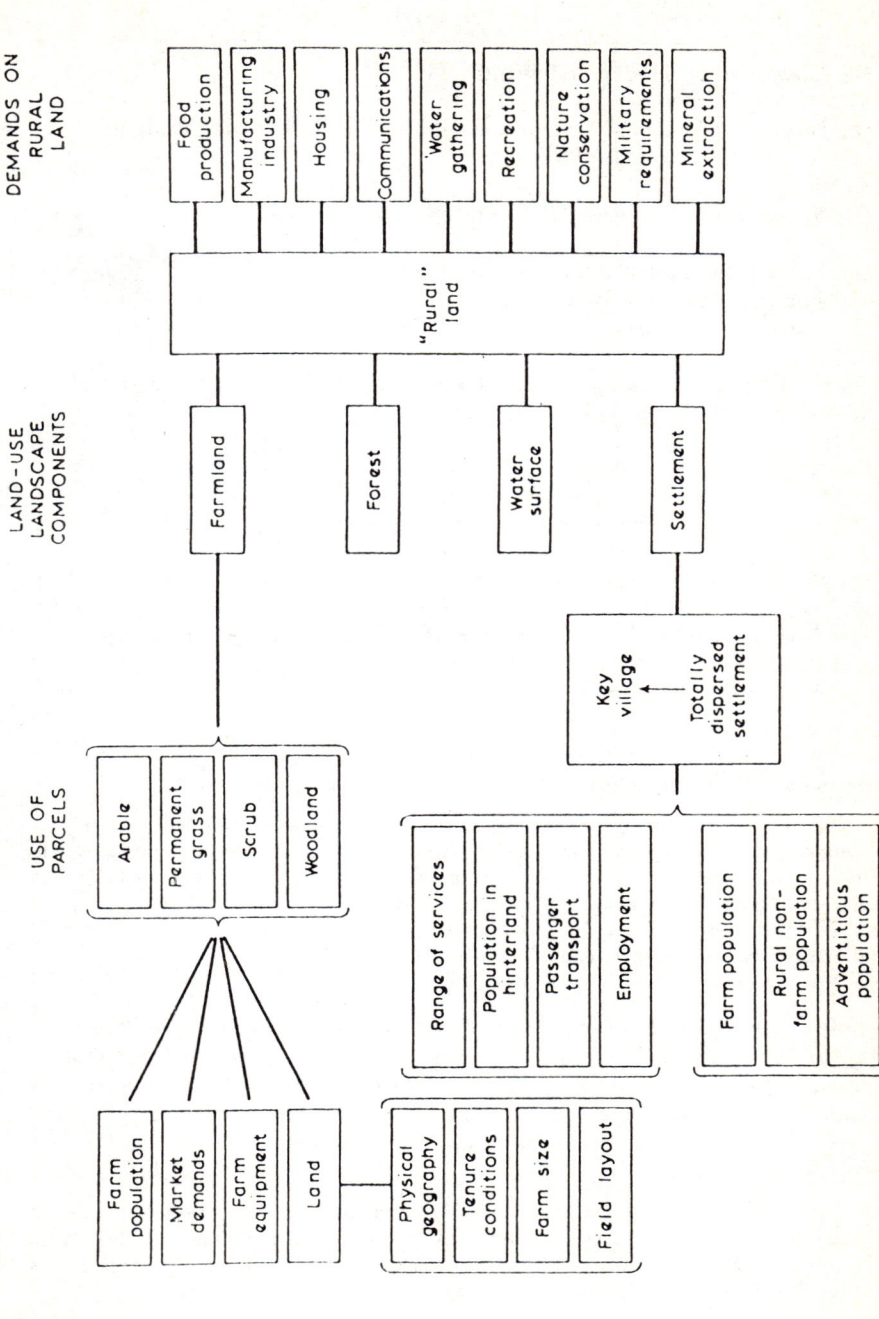

Figure 9.1 Some components of rural geography
Source: Clout (1972, 3)

Table 9.1 Some important texts used in rural geography

* *On Employment*: Hodge and Whitby (1981)

* *On Housing*: Clark (1982); Dunn et al. (1981); Phillips and Williams (1982) and Shucksmith (1981)

* *On Accessibility*: Banister (1980) and Moseley (1977)

* *On Rural Settlements*: Bunce (1982); Hodge and Qadeer (1983); Johansen and Fugitt (1984) and Swanson et al. (1979)
* *On Settlement Planning*: Cloke (1979, 1983) and Woodruffe (1976)

* *On Countryside Planning*: Blacksell and Gilg (1981); Davidson and Wibberley (1977) and Gilg (1979)

* *On Land Use*: Best (1981)

* *On Agriculture*: Bowler (1985) and Ilbery (1985)

* *On Recreation*: Patmore (1970, 1983)

* *Synthesising Texts*: Cloke and Park (1985); Gilg (1984); Pacione (1985) and Phillips and Williams (1984)

But perhaps this 'bucolic expression' need not necessarily be trivial:

> ... changes in the distribution of income or in the tax relief accorded to mortgage payments, or in the relative subsidies provided for public and private transport will affect all individuals wherever they live. However, the precise ways in which such macro-economic and political changes affect individuals, or local social groups, depend on a number of local features. It is [our] basic tenet ... that these vary between rural and urban areas consistently enough to allow generalisation.
> (Phillips and Williams, 1984, p. 3)

Not only is there considerable unease abut whether *rural* geography and rural *geography* have any truly distinctive insights to offer, there is also a lack of agreement, amongst those who call themselves rural geographers, on questions and choices of methodology and epistemology, inviting the charge that rural geography is theoretically and methodologically underdeveloped. But as Munton (1986 p.2) has argued,

> The fact that there is no agreement over which approach to adopt (whether it be based on logical positivism, a humanistic interpretation or the employment of ideas from political economy, for example) in which circumstances, or even whether approaches can be mixed, does not represent a disadvantage to intellectual inquiry...

With the focus and the method of rural geography far from being clearly defined,

Table 9.2 Subjects of rural goegraphy research 1973-81

	Percentages 1973-74	1978	1981
Agriculture	40.6	40.2	27.5
Forestry, fishing, conservation, minerals	1.6	4.0	8.7
Rural settlement	19.7	16.1	16.5
Rural population	12.0	10.3	15.1
Rural transport	3.6	4.5	4.6
Recreation and tourism	6.8	11.6	8.3
Rural development and planning	15.7	13.4	19.3
Number of research projects	249	224	218

it is tempting to be pragmatic and say simply that 'rural geography is what rural geographers do!'. In that spirit it is useful to report Clark's analysis (1982a) of several registers of the research undertaken by those academic British geographers who *considered themselves* to be rural geographers (See Table 9.2) Clark drew several conclusions about the changing nature of British rural geography over the period 1973-81:

- a *reduced* interest in agriculture, settlement and land use;
- an *increased* interest in other rural resources, notably forests, minerals and landscape, and in resource conservation;
- an *increased* interest in population, transport and socio-economic planning and development;
- an *increased* interest in rural agencies and institutions and in the applied value of research.

Going on from this, I would suggest that in the 1980s British rural geographers have tended to work in one of two very broad areas of concern: rural welfare and resource management.

Welfare of the rural population

This broad theme has been highlighted in Munton's recent review (1986, p.1)

> Today, research is concerned with the reasons for, and consequences of, social and economic change for all groups living, working and recreating in rural areas. Much attention is given, in the broadest sense, to the welfare of the rural population and the role of the State, local, national and international, in creating the framework within which that welfare fluctuates.

A possible listing of some of the major topics which have been researched, within this broad theme, is as follows:

(i) the settlement system: *not* the historical evolution of settlement patterns and their supposed geometric symmetry, but their development today and the planner's dilemma: concentrate or disperse?
(ii) population and social change – especially 'counter-urbanisation', the migration of different age and socio-economic groups, and social relationships within rural areas;
(iii) employment: especially the loss of jobs in the primary sector and the recent growth of tourism and manufacturing;
(iv) housing: especially 'unjust' access to housing and the difficulty of responding to 'local need'. Research has related, for example, to second homes, the sale of council houses and commuter and retirement in-migration;
(v) transport and accessibility: the decline of public transport, the rise of car ownership and the social inequity implied by this;
(vi) service provision: the decline of village services such as shops, schools and post offices (linked to (v), above).

As well as these six topics, we may identify two more which span the whole field:

(vii) rural deprivation: a concern for differential levels of welfare at the level of households or of areas and the degree to which 'rurality' plays a part in this;
(viii) decision-making/planning/the role of institutions: for example, local planning authorities and regional and national resource agencies such as the Rural Development Commission.

Surveying the mass of studies covered by these themes, three conclusions emerge. First, the concern is with social welfare – few rural geographers are deterred from exploring an interesting subject by the lack of a clear geographical or spatial focus. Secondly, more and more these studies are concerned with the prevailing or potential role of the state as generator or ameliorator of the various problems. Thirdly, and related to this, there may be methodological confusion, or at least eclecticism, but a common theme in the studies referred to above is their search for explanations *outside* the locality itself.

Rural resource management

Here 'resources' are defined widely to include land, minerals, water, landscape, wildlife, woodlands, etc. Some particular themes have been:

(i) land-use competition at the urban fringe – the transfer of land from agricultural to urban use;
(ii) the conflict between agriculture and the conservation of landscape and of ecosystems – e.g. the drainage of wetlands, the ploughing of moorlands, the clearance of hedgerows:
(iii) the conflict between recreation on the one hand and agriculture and/or conservation on the other;
(iv) agriculture *per se*. A recent (Bowler, 1986) review of British agricultural geography identified five broad themes:- the spatial differentiation of agriculture; agriculture and economic development; agriculture and environment; government intervention; agriculture-urban interactions. To this it is tempting to add a sixth: the behaviour of farmers and farm enterprises;
(v) landscape: its perception and evaluation.

These various studies have a strong emphasis on environmental concerns and on the role of various decision-makers, private and public, in threatening or fostering environmental quality. If two words are needed to sum them up, I would suggest 'conservation' and 'conflict'.

Conclusion

A number of conclusions emerge from this review. First, none of the British rural geographers that I know are concerned about whether they are truly 'rural geographers' rather than 'some-other-kind-of-geographer'. Pacione's diagram (Figure 9.2) indicates that the most interesting subjects of inquiry, shown in the rectangular boxes, span at least two branches of the discipline. Moreover, British rural geographers tend to be equally unconcerned about whether their research is truly rural geography rather than say, rural sociology, agricultural economics or countryside planning. I, for one, applaud this nonchalance.

Secondly, it is hard to think of any rural geographer, or piece of recent research in rural geography, not explicitly focusing on a pressing policy issue. Nearly all contemporary research is at least applicable if not applied. Again, I applaud this concern for relevance but there is room for debate about whether more fundamental research is being neglected.

Thirdly, most rural geography is now 'outward looking' when it comes to seeking explanations. As Pacione (1984) put it, 'the study of rural geography requires an appreciation of the linkages... both within and outside the immediate rural environment'; or, to quote Munton (1986, p. 2) 'a consensus seems to be emerging... that there are no theories specific to the analysis of rural problems or rural areas'. In short, while rural geographers may examine some aspect of, say, the housing market or landscape change within a small locality, few researchers would now fail to attempt a link with a broader context incorporating, for example, modern capitalism, the role of the state, and technological change.

Fourthly, going on from this, much research is now explicitly focused on conflict and the exercise of power. There is now a large body of research relating to what might be termed rural environmental politics in which the conflict between various interest groups – e.g. farmers, conservationists, government – looms large (see, for example, Lowe et al. 1986). But a concern to elucidate the nature and consequences of conflict is equally apparent in recent studies of rural housing, transport, service provision and social change. And since conflict involves winners and losers it is closely linked with a number of other fundamental themes in contemporary rural geography, notably rural deprivation and rural conservation.

Fifthly, 'British rural geographers have been reluctant to accept that there should always be as much debate over method as there is over substance' (Munton, 1986, p. 2). I sense that this may be changing and that while it would be fanciful (and in my view inappropriate) to expect a single theoretical framework to gain universal acceptance, the preceding two paragraphs indicate the direction of change.

124 *Geography*

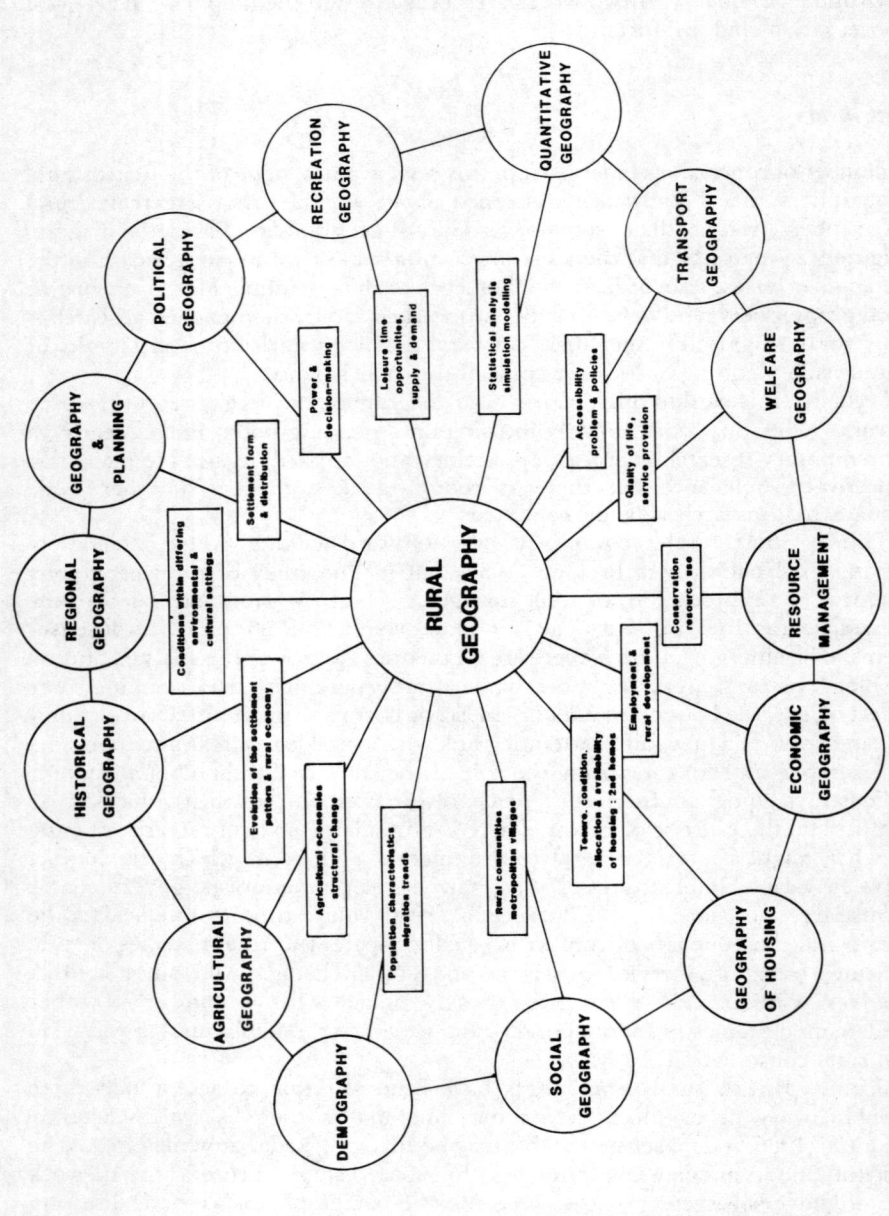

Figure 9.2 The character of rural geography
Source: Pacione, 1984

Finally, British rural geography is excessively parochial. Its practitioners stray readily into parallel areas of British rural inquiry (e.g. rural sociology or agricultural economics) but almost never into non-British rural geography; or, to be more precise, into rural geography outside the Anglo-American tradition.

3 The conceptual development of rural geography *by Paul Cloke*

This section discusses the conceptual turmoil in rural geography which has followed the considerable empirical progress made in the 1970s and 1980s, and points to some of the major emergent themes and challenges which face rural geographers in the 1990s. The decision to focus on matters of concept and theory is one which would not be shared by some analysts of rural geography, but for reasons which will become evident, the decision so to do is made unrepentantly.

By the early 1980s it had become clear that the rural geography bandwagon was losing momentum. Progress could not be sustained merely by pumping out new information on the changing rural milieu. In many ways the general appetite for information had been satiated, and new challenges were required in order to generate fresh energy. A review of potential new emphases diagnosed three deficiencies to be overcome:

(i) if rural geography was to progress by adopting an 'applied' or 'relevance' or 'welfare' approach, then some form of conceptual framework would be required on which to found the various strands of information, analysis and problem-solving.
(ii) rural geographers had been tardy and uninspired in the introduction of rigorous analytical methods for the study of countryside systems and processes.
(iii) there was a need to establish a formal applied emphasis to rural geographical research which would allow a greater degree of integration with rural planners and planning processes (Cloke 1980).

It should certainly be recorded that rural geographical research *has* become more applied and policy-oriented over the last ten years, but the advance towards theoretically-informed work is only in its infancy. This position is at least in part due to a strong instinct for institutional survival on behalf of many rural geographers. The new social theories which were gaining ground in other areas of human geography were a danger to the subjectival legitimation of *rural* geography. Such axioms as social relations being as important as spatial differentiation, and the category 'rural' being of low importance as an explanatory device, were potentially destructive to the institution of rural geography – an institution which had been carefully nurtured into an important position within geography and which was therefore to be protected at all costs against the heresies of critical social theory.

Also important in this context are the reasons why many rural geographers are interested in rural subject matter. Some, for example, have strong family connections with agriculture, and others have become interested through an appreciation of the countryside as a visual and active environment. These emphases on the land use and landscape characteristics of 'rural' tend to repel theoretical concepts which dare to minimise 'rural' as a differentiating factor. On the other hand, researchers trained in critical social theory have tended to be attracted to work in urban and regional localities where such theoretical constructs are more readily accepted.

Over the last five years or so, this situation has gradually begun to change. Spurred on by involvement in multidisciplinary arenas such as the Rural Economy and Society Study Group, by the emergence of theoretically informed, rural geography texts (notably Phillips and Williams, 1984; and Hoggart and Buller, 1987), and by the high profile attained by research projects informed by critical theories (for example connected with agricultural restructuring and rural decision-making and implementation), rural geographers have shown growing interest in political economic theory. Such progress has brought in its wake a number of key debates concerning, in particular, the continuation of positivistic approaches, the centrality of rurality, and the role of the state in rural areas. These are now briefly explored in turn.

Applied positivism?

One contentious issue centres on the temptation amongst rural geographers to cobble together a theoretical package which *both* demonstrates clearly an acknowledgement of the virtues and terminology of critical social theory *and* permits researchers to carry on much as before. The result of this package is a kind of applied positivism blithely combining political economy concepts and positivistic methods and results. For example, Andrew Gilg (1985) observes that: 'rural geographers have employed all types of approach, but the most common and widely accepted is still the logical positivist approach' (p. 4); and Richard Munton (1986) predicts that:

> ... empirical enquiry will almost certainly continue to dominate the work of British rural geographers and although much of that research may continue to depend on a logical positivist methodology, more modest claims will be made for its explanatory powers and greater attention will be paid to the contributions to be derived from critical social theory (p. 5).

Thus stemming from an innate desire to cling to positivism, there emerges a legitimating and opportunistic theoretical pluralism which may be willing to acknowledge structural explanations, but which rarely constructs research methods so as to elucidate structural mechanisms.

In some cases rural geography has been accepted as 'broadly theory-free' (Gilg, 1985, 172) and the need for a conceptual framework dismissed as a passing academic fashion. Applied positivism may be seen to obviate the need to soil the geographers' technical role with politics and ideology. This position has been criticised by Hoggart and Buller (1987) amongst others, not least because applied positivism in rural geography is neither technically neutral nor theory-free, but inclines researchers to:

> identifying the most appropriate means of 'tinkering' with existing socio-economic conditions in order to weaken the impress of malevolent trends [while failing] to recognise that the processes which brought about current maldistributions or

malpractices... are inherent in policy procedures which have to be relied on to alleviate the problems researchers have analysed. (p. 267)

Elsewhere there has been a tendency for rural geographers to put 'old hay into new barns' (Cloke, 1988). Discussions of rural deprivation illustrate this point. Here, it is very easy to juxtapose the structural acknowledgement that: 'urban and rural deprivation are manifestations of the same forces emanating from the dynamic of late industrial capitalism' (Pacione, 1984, 199, referring to Moseley, 1980) with applied positivism whereby: 'the geographer's major contribution to quality of life research, to date, has been the introduction of a spatial dimension in their work on *territorial* social indicators' (Pacione, 1984, 214, referring amongst others to Pacione, 1980, 1982). Such observations should not be taken as criticism of particular researchers; they are rather symptomatic of a widespread slothfulness in providing investigative substance to espoused theoretical tenets. Regarding the example of rural deprivation, a research agenda based on political economy concepts will have to define the problem in terms of the distributional impacts of economic restructuring and the role of the state in its facilitation.

A further example of applied positivism is much of the research on counterurbanisation and urban-to-rural industrial shifts, which in some cases have been explicitly linked, with the latter being advanced as the cause of the former. Combinations of neo-classical concepts, such as constraints on factory floorspace (Fothergill and Gudgin, 1982) and operating costs in rural areas (Keeble, 1980, 1984), have been used to concoct an account of the entire phenomenon. Such explanations have proved unsatisfactory in at least three major respects:

(i) urban-to-rural shifts in manufacturing, although demonstrating some neo-classical symptoms, were evidently underlain by more deep-seated processes connected both with capital accumulation under changing conditions, and with the new structures of capital which were appearing in response to changing conditions;
(ii) the 'urban-to-rural' description of change over-simplified the complex patterns involved. Certain localities were found to be more responsive to broad structural openings for change than were other, apparently very similar localities;
(iii) urban-rural shifts in population were not universally caused by shifting labour markets associated with manufacturing industry. Other factors – service sector employment, unemployment, retirement, alternative lifestyles, self-employment etc. (see Cloke, 1985a) – were also important.

This bankruptcy of neo-classical explanations of change when linked with positivist recording of trends (Fielding, 1982) has provided a significant impulse to the wider acceptance of political economic concepts in the understanding of socio-spatial phenomena. There now appears to be a greater willingness to develop a research agenda founded on fundamental building blocks of critical theory, namely:

– the centrality of *capital accumulation* as the driving force of social formation;
– the role of *capital restructuring* in bringing about uneven development;
– the recognition that restructuring does not occur in a social vacuum and that

social recomposition occurs both as a shaping mechanism for restructuring, and in response to it; and
- the equally valid yet less publicised recognition that restructuring does not occur in an environmental vacuum, and that *environmental recomposition* is also relevant.

As yet, progress towards reorienting research to these priorities has been slow. Phillips and Williams (1984) conclude that: 'the theoretical understanding of political economy as it affects rural areas is inadequate to develop far such a research methodology, and data are lacking with which to test empirically many propositions...' (p. 237). The degree to which these deficiencies are to be remedied will depend in no small measure on the extent to which rural geographers (alongside other rural specialists in the social sciences) are prepared to forgo their traditional 'rural' focus for other, more powerful, explanatory tools. The issue of rurality is never far removed from these debates, as it is the focus of a perpetual identity crisis for rural geographers.

The centrality of rurality

A major conceptual hurdle for rural geographers has been to place rurality in the context of critical social theory. After all, their professional niche has been predicated on an ability to exploit the explanatory power of rural characteristics, to point up differences about rural environments, to promote rural courses within geography and to sustain a flow of rural literature. This institutional momentum is difficult to reverse. Yet while the features of extensive *landscapes* dominated by farming and forestry retain a semblance of distinctive rurality, the communities that live within them have become culturally if not physically urbanised.

Thus a widening gap is occurring between land use and socio-economic characteristics in debates over the importance of those units of space that we have traditionally called rural. The priority accorded space in political economic theory has fluctuated over recent years. Dunleavy (1980, 1982) has argued that economic and socio-cultural activities in Britain are organised on an aspatial basis. Although the development of collective consumption processes may vary in different locations, these variations represent elements of differentiation of national functions and activities. This rather dogmatic position has since been tempered by those such as Massey (1985) who have emphasised that, although space may be a social construct, social relations are also clearly constructed over space, and therefore to ignore space is to ignore the arena of social construction.

Perhaps the conventional wisdom of the 1980s stems from the work of Urry (1981, 1981a, 1985) who argues that space has no general effect but that certain potential actions will be triggered by particular spatial or temporal contexts. These contexts, or localities, have reintroduced a spatial dimension as an adjunct to the core themes of social reproduction. Does it therefore follow that, by studying 'rural' localities, rural geographers can maintain an institutional identity? This question lies at the heart of the debate over rurality, yet the idea of rural localities tends to oversimplify Urry's notion. The distinctiveness of localities does not stem from rurality *per se*, or from similar frameworks of differentiation. Rather, localities are distinct because of particular forms of local social recomposition. Urry's (1984) response to the question of rural localities concludes that: 'various critical notions of different, overlapping spatial divisions of labour, of all localities as sites for the reproduction of labour-power, of variations in local social structures etc., render problematic the notion that there are distinct 'rural' localities' (p. 59). This line of conceptual argument presents a dilemma for rural geographers. It either undermines the legitimation for focusing on *rural* phenomena *per se*, or characterises such work as the investigation of secondary spatial factors. On the other hand, to ignore this critique of rurality would be greatly to diminish the potential explanatory power of critical social theory, with the attendant risk of lapsing into the applied positivism mentioned above.

Rural geographers need not get too obsessed with this issue, but they *do* have to be more honest about why they are focusing on particular locations. Phillips and Williams (1984) have outlined four potential reasons for retaining rural as an investigative unit:

(i) the need for rural studies to counterbalance the predominance of urban studies;
(ii) the pragmatic requirement for analytically convenient categories such as rural and urban;
(iii) the need to expose many of the romantic rural myths which have been fostered by an historically anti-urban social science;
(iv) the basic belief that rural areas have distinctive characteristics distinguishable from those in urban areas.

Although all of these reasons have some legitimacy, analytical pragmatism may well be the most honest answer in much of contemporary rural geography. One of the major challenges in the subject will be the extent to which geographers are willing to forgo their rurality culture and be content to work alongside other social scientists in the investigation of the mechanisms and impacts of restructuring and of the role of the state both as a catalyst of social reconstruction and as a resource allocation agency:

> In some respects, the fact that the concept of *rural* localities has been shown to be undermined by the political economy approach is of little real consequence except for the impact on the institutions of rural studies. After all, there is a clear need for comparative studies of all types of localities including those which were previously constituted as rural (Cloke 1988).

Signs of this more theoretically-informed approach are clearly visible in recent studies of agriculture (see Marsden et al., 1986) which as a particular amalgamative fraction of capital is identifiably rural because of its land usage. The next challenge for rural geographers will be boldly to adopt similar approaches in studies of restructuring and recomposition which fall outside the traditional bounds of rural specificity.

The state, policy-making and applied geography

The penchant for rural geographers to concentrate on 'applied' research has already been highlighted. Indeed one of the foremost changes in rural geographical study over the last decade has been the willingness to focus on planning and policy-making as major shaping mechanisms for rural change. Much of this work has evaluated the ability of planning to achieve various regulatory or interventionist goals, but although these issues lead directly into the political realms of accountability and societal constraint, rural geographers (unlike their urban and regional colleagues) have been reluctant to plunge into such explicitly ideological waters as those concerning power relations within the state.

The implications of the broad state-society relationships are vital for rural geographers interested in planning and policy-making in that the researchers' understanding of planning is directly contingent on a view of the state. If the state is viewed as an independent arbiter between competing interests, then planning (as an integral part of the state) will reflect this neutrality. If, on the other hand, the state has other roles, such as the facilitation of favourable conditions for capital accumulation, then planning and policy-making will reflect these functions, and expectations of a rational and neutral form of planning will be misplaced.

It would be inappropriate here to enter into lengthy discussion on the issues of power relations and the state (see Cloke, 1987, 1987a, 1988a; Cloke and Little, 1987). Obviously the different conceptualisations of power (pluralism, elitism, managerialism, structuralism etc.) are central to the detailed theoretical framework required. Equally, it is important to highlight the constraints within which policy-makers with responsibility for rural areas are operating. Two such levels of constraint have been identified (Cloke and Hanrahan, 1984):

(i) the acceptance by political and professional policy-makers of an 'art of the possible' (see Cloke and Little, 1987a, 1987b) which is determined by the state-society relationship in which it is set, and which presents decision-makers with an artificially narrow range of policy alternatives. Given a state role of supporting capital accumulation within existing social relations, this state-society constraint reduces the art of the possible to that which continues the uneven distribution of power, wealth and opportunity.
(ii) the secondary constraints arising from inter-governmental and inter-agency relations, for example:

– *central-local relations*, with the increasing centralisation of power in Britain over the last decade;
– *inter-agency relations*, with a proliferation of decision-making units, each jealously guarding its own areas of responsibility and budget, and each constrained to a greater or lesser extent by the objectives of the central state;
– *public-private sector relations*, which have become the subject of radical review with the ideologies of deregulation and privatisation having a direct impact on planning and policy-making.

One further theme of direct interest to rural geographers is the nature of the local state in 'rural' localities. Some local state theorists (for example Dunleavy, 1984) have viewed the locality as an arena for political opposition to the centre, particularly in the context of defending working-class interests against offensives by central government. Most local authorities with jurisdiction over rural areas do not fit this model. They have been shown to be broadly conservative in nature, and they have not been subject to the levels of working-class involvement that have occurred, for example, in metropolitan authorities. Does this then make the local state in rural areas distinctive from that in other locales? Once again, there should be caution in ascribing explanatory power to rurality in this context. Saunders (1984), for example, has argued that the local state in its entirety has been unsuccessful in its role as a buffer to central state goals. Indeed the institutions of local government have been so reorganised by the centre that the implementation of centrally-derived uniform policies has become easier; financial provision from the centre to the periphery has been reorganised so as to reduce local discretion in expenditure on social consumption; and an anti-state ideology has been manipulated by central government so as to reduce the expectation of welfare provision. Given these conditions, the local state covering rural areas is not so distinct.

It is nevertheless important to make explicit the conceptual framework within which studies of the local state are carried out. Dear and Clark (1981), for example, offer a viewpoint which leaves little room for significant autonomy in the local state context:

> It is only via the local state system that social and ideological control of a spatially extensive and heterogeneous jurisdiction becomes possible. In this manner, local needs are anticipated and answered, and state legitimacy ensured. Although the existence of the local state is functional for capitalism, it is also in keeping with the principles of local self-determination in a democracy (p. 1280).

Others, such as Cawson and Saunders (1983) have suggested a dualistic model whereby central state domination over the local state occurs largely in productive functions, whereas in the consumption sphere local states retain some autonomy. They identify two sectors of the state:
 (i) the corporate sector of government, located centrally and producing social investment policies
(ii) the competitive sector operating principally at the local level and producing social consumption policies.

It is within this kind of framework that local studies of power and decision-making can fruitfully be placed. Use of the political economy paradigm will demand more attention to key issues such as the nature of political conservatism at the local level; the degree to which local decision-making autonomy and discretion are available and used; the exact role played by managers and professionals in local planning and policy-making, and so on. It seems clear that the features of local states covering rural areas – political conservatism, small scale of activity, the predominance of elitism and managerialism in local decision-making, etc. – should not be explained as rural phenomena *per se*. However, these features *do* influence to a significant extent the variety of politico-cultural localities over which restructuring and recomposition are being constructed.

What future?

Rural geography has made significant conceptual progress during the 1980s, though merely catching up with what other human geographers have been involved with over a longer period of time. Perhaps all that we can say is that we are not as far behind as we used to be.

There is a danger, however, in the over-confidence bred by too speedy and too complete an espousal of the explanatory powers of political economy frameworks. It should be recognised that their use by rural researchers is currently immature and underdeveloped. What is needed now is a very careful immersion in the concepts followed by an equally careful programming of research techniques to highlight the issues raised conceptually. This will not happen if energy continues to be dissipated in the struggle to legitimise *rural* as a primary explanatory category. Instead, our interest in explaining *why* land use changes occur, and *how* the distribution and impact of interactions between economy and society are caused and facilitated, should lead us to an acceptance of the social construction of space and to research programmes which focus on wider structural phenomena in the context of familiar localities.

Rather than finishing on a note of mere exhortation, this admittedly partisan account of rual geography prefers to look forward and offer a skeletal agenda for future research. The agenda is taken from a recent discussion of rural geography and political economy (Cloke, 1988), and four areas are identified as requiring initial attention:

(i) The historical treatment of localities of interest to rural geographers has tended to be archival, if painstaking. If a political economy approach is to be pursued at all it will have to be grounded in a materialist view of the past. In particular, histories of social reproduction and reformulation will be required in order to recognise the interactive relations between economic restructuring and the host society.

(ii) The processes of economic restructuring require specific attention, with particular emphasis on the unevenness of capital expansion. Relocation, restructuring and recomposition should be analysed in terms of particular fractions of capital, and the interrelations between agriculture and other capital fractions should be fully explored. The *mobility* of capital and labour should figure prominently here.

(iii) The impacts of restructuring are also a crucial research target. Recognising that class composition and political, economic and cultural configurations in a particular locality can *shape* restructuring as well as be affected by it, there are important changes to be investigated resulting from particular interactions of the restructuring process. Changing class structures, particularly the infiltration of different fractions of the middle class (with marked impacts on local economies, political representation and so on); changing gender divisions; and changing cultural characteristics represent just some of the major issues requiring serious attention.

(iv) The recognition of the role of the state will necessitate a reformed analysis of planning, policy-making and management in these localities. Specific recognition of local power relations and mechanisms of conflict resolution should be linked with the overriding national and international contexts of state involvement. Moreover the central and local aspects of policy and power should be interrelated conceptually by means of a focus on *policy networks* and *policy communities* which transcend traditional interorganisational hierarchies.

It is perhaps this rather basic kind of programme, rather than more flashy adoptions of the paradigm which will bring rural geographers further into the mainstream of critical social science.

Bibliography

Banister, D.J., *Transport Mobility and Deprivation in Inter-Urban Areas* Saxon House, Farnborough, 1980.
Best, R.H. *Land Use and Living Space*, Methuen, London, 1981.
Best, R.H. and Coppock J.T., *The Changing Use of Land in Britain*, Faber, London, 1962.
Blacksell, M. and Gilg A., *The Countryside: Planning and Change*, Allen & Unwin, London, 1981.
Bowler, I., *Agriculture Under the Common Agricultural Policy*, Manchester University Press, Manchester, 1985.
Bowler, I., 'Agricultural geography', *Progress in Human Geography 10* no 2, 1986, 181–217.
Bracey, H.E. *Social Provision in Rural Wiltshire*, Methuen, London, 1952.
Bracey, H.E. *People in the Countryside*, Routledge & Kegan Paul, London, 1970.
Bunce, M., *Rural Settlement in an Urban World*, Croom Helm, London.
Cawson, A. and Saunders, P. 'Corporatism, competitive politics and class struggle', in King, R. (ed.) *Capital and Politics*, Routledge & Kegan Paul, London, 1983.
Clark, G., (1982a) 'Developments in rural geography', *Area 14* no 3, 1982, 249–254.
Clark, G., *Housing and Planning in the Countryside*, Wiley, Chichester, 1982.
Cloke, P.J., *Key Settlements in Rural Areas*, Methuen, London, 1979.
Cloke, P.J., 'New emphases for applied rural geography', *Progress in Human Geography* 4, 1980, 181–217.
Cloke, P.J., *An Introduction to Rural Settlement Planning*, Methuen, London, 1983.
Cloke, P.J. 'Whither rural studies?', *Journal of Rural Studies* 1, 1985, 1–10.
Cloke, P.J. (1985a) 'Counterurbanisation: a rural perspective', *Geography* 70, 1985, 13–23.
Cloke, P.J. 'Policy and planning in rural areas', in Cloke P.J. (ed.) *Rural Planning: Policy into Action*, Harper & Row, London, 1987.
Cloke, P.J. (1987a) 'Policy and implementation decisions', in Cloke P.J. (ed.) *Rural Planning: Policy into Action*, Harper & Row, London, 1987.
Cloke, P.J. 'Rural geography and political economy', in Peet R. and Thrift N. (eds) *New Models in Geography*, Allen & Unwin, London, 1988.
Cloke, P.J. (1988a) 'Planning, policy-making and state intervention in rural areas', in Cloke P.J. (ed.) *Policies and Plans for Rural People: An International Perspective*, Allen & Unwin, London, 1988.
Cloke, P.J. and Hanrahan, P. 'Policy and implementation in rural planning', *Geoforum* 15, 1984, 261–9.
Cloke, P.J. and Little, J.K., 'Policy, planning and the state in rural localities', *Journal of Rural Studies* 3, 1987, 343–352.
Cloke P.J. and Little, J.K. (1987a) Rural policies in the Gloucestershire Structure Plan I: a study of motives and mechanisms, *Environment and Planning A* 19, 1987, 959–981.
— (1987b) Rural policies in the Gloucestershire Structure Plan II: implementation and the

county-district relationship, *Environment and Planning A* 19, 1987, 1027–1050.
Cloke, P.J. and Park C.C., *Rural Resource Management*, Croom Helm, London, 1985.
Clout, H.D., *Rural Geography: An Introductory Survey*, Pergamon, Oxford, 1972.
Coppock, J.T., *An Agricultural Atlas of England and Wales*, Faber & Faber, London, 1964.
Davidson, J. and Wibberley, G.P., *Planning and the Rural Environment*, Pergamon, Oxford, 1977.
Dear, M. and Clark, G. Dimensions of local state autonomy, *Environment and Planning A* 13, 1981, 1277–1294.
Dunleavy, P. *Urban Political Analysis: The Politics of Collective Consumption*, Macmillan, London, 1980.
– 'Perspectives on urban studies', in Blowers, A., Brook, C., Dunleavy, P. and McDowell, L. (eds) *Urban Change and Conflict. An Interdisciplinary Reader*, Harper & Row, London, 1982.
– 'The limits to local government', in Boddy M. and Fudge C. (eds) *Local Socialism?* Macmillan, London, 1984.
Dunn, M.C., Rawson, M. and Rogers, A. *Rural Housing: Competition and Choice*, Allen and Unwin, London, 1981.
Fielding, A.J. 'Counterurbanisation in Western Europe', *Progress in Planning* 17, 1982, 1–52.
Fothergill, S. and Gudgin, G., *Unequal Growth: Urban and Regional Employment Change in the U.K.*, Heinemann, London, 1982.
Gilg, A.W., *Countryside Planning: The First Three Decades 1945–76*, Methuen, London, 1979.
Gilg, A.W., *An Introduction to Rural Geography*, Edward Arnold, London, 1985.
Hodge, G. and Qadeer, M., *Towns and Villages in Canada*, Butterworth, Toronto, 1983.
Hodge, I. and Whitby, M., *Rural Employment: Trends, Options, Choices*, Methuen, London, 1981.
Hoggart, K. and Buller, H., *Rural Development: A Geographical Perspective*, Croom Helm, London, 1987.
Ilbery, B., *Agricultural Geography: A Social and Economic Analysis*, Oxford University Press, Oxford, 1985.
Johansen, H.E. and Fuguitt, G.V., *The Changing Rural Village in America*, Ballinger, Cambridge, 1984.
Keeble, D.E., 'Industrial decline, regional policy and the urban-rural manufacturing shift in the United Kingdom', *Environment and Planning A* 12, 1980, 945–62.
– 'The urban-rural manufacturing shift', *Geography* 69, 1984, 163–166.
Lowe, P., Cox, G., MacEwen, M., O'Riordan, T. and Winter, M., *Countryside Conflicts: The Politics of Farming, Forestry and Conservation* Gower, Aldershot, 1986.
Marsden, T., Munton, R., Whatmore, S. and Little, J., 'Towards a political economy of capitalist agriculture: a British perspective', *International Journal of Urban and Regional Research* 10.4, 1986, 498–521.
Massey, D., 'New directions in space', in Gregory D. and Urry J. (eds) *Social Relations and Spatial Structures*, Macmillan, London, 1985.
Moseley, M.J., *Accessibility: The Rural Challenge*, Methuen, London, 1977.
– 'Is rural deprivation really rural?', *The Planner*, 66, 1980, 97.
Munton, R.J.C., 'Research in rural geography in Britain: some reflections on future directions'. Paper presented to the 2nd British-Dutch Symposium on Rural Geography, Amsterdam, 1986.
Pacione, M., 'Quality of life in a metropolitan village', *Transactions IBG* 5, 1980, 185–206.
– 'The use of objective and subjective measures of life quality in human geography', *Progress in Human Geography* 6, 1982, 495–514.

– *Rural Geography*, Harper & Row, London, 1984.
Pahl, R.E., *Urbs in Rure*, Department of Geography, London School of Economics, Geographical Paper No. 2, 1965.
Patmore, J.A., *Land and Leisure in England and Wales*, David & Charles, Newton Abbot, 1970.
– *Recreation and Resources*, Blackwell, Oxford, 1983.
Phillips, D. and Williams, A., *Rural Housing and the Public Sector*, Gower, Farnborough, 1982.
– *Rural Britain: A Social Geography*, Blackwell, Oxford, 1984.
Proudfoot, B., 'Rural geography in Britain: some aspects of rural problems and policies', in Clark G., Groenendijk, J. and Thissen, F. (eds) *The Changing Countryside*, GeoBooks, Norwich, 1984.
Rural Geography Study Group, 'Response to the request of the Institute of British Geographers' Council for information' unpublished typescript, 1986.
Saunders, P. 'Rethinking local politics', in Boddy, M. and Fudge, C., (eds) *Local Socialism?* Macmillan, London, 1984.
Shucksmith, M., *No Homes for Locals?* Gower, Farnborough, 1981.
Swanson, B.E., Cohen, R.A. and Swanson, E.P., *Small Towns and Small Towners* Sage, Beverly Hills, 1979.
Urry, J., 'Localities, regions and social class', *International Journal of Urban and Regional Research* 5, 1981, 455–73.
– (1981a) *The Anatomy of Capitalist Societies*, Macmillan, London, 1981.
– 'Capitalist restructuring, recomposition and the regions', in Bradley, T. and Lowe, P. (eds) *Locality and Rurality*, GeoBooks, Norwich, 1984.
Urry, J., 'Social relations, space and time', in Gregory, D. and Urry, J. (eds) *Social Relations and Spatial Structures*, Macmillan, London, 1985.
Wibberley, G.P., *Agriculture and Urban Growth*, Michael Joseph, London, 1959.
– 'The pressures on Britain's rural land', in Ashton J. and Roberts, S.T., (eds) *Economic Change and Agriculture*, Oliver & Boyd, Edinburgh, 1967.
Wood, A.P. and Smith, W. *Review and Directory of Rural Geography in the Commonwealth* (Discussion Paper 30, Department of Geography University of Toronto), 1982.
Woodruffe, B.J., *Rural Policies and Plans*, Oxford University Press, Oxford, 1976.

Part IV: Economics

10 Commentary and Introduction

André Brun

For a reader not specialised in agricultural (or rural) economics,[1], the distance which separates the two papers in this section might seem astonishing. The intellectual universe, the institutional environment, the historical development as well as the economic and political contexts and the natural conditions of agricultural production are profoundly different in Great Britain and France. The two papers reflect these differences, and the comparative images that they give of both their discipline and their profession seem to be very indicative of the contrasting situations in the two countries.

To help the reader place and compare the two contributions better, I will try and contrast them 'term by term' by deliberately accentuating their differences. Even at the risk of caricature, it is preferable, for the sake of the quality and relevance of future dialogue, to emphasise and come to terms with the differences rather than simply smoothing things over and erasing or ignoring them. In adopting such an approach, I will be led (and for this I apologise to readers) to giving more consideration to the French than to the English side, about which I know less.

1 Institutional hegemony versus theoretical hegemony

Going straight to the heart of the issue, one can say that established notions of who and what constitute the profession and discipline of agricultural (or rural) economics do not coincide on either side of the channel.

In the UK, the set is defined by its theoretical base. The neo-classical paradigm underlies economic science. It is the key to understanding the evolution of agriculture. It provides a coherent set of tools capable of developing answers to the questions posed by economic and political actors. One can employ its concepts and perfect its design and applications (particularly in econometrics) to answer, or at least illuminate, relevant questions of the day and, particularly over the last ten years, those relating to the operation and cost of the Common Agricultural Policy. Those who, although also studying agriculture, conduct their analyses without giving primacy to market regulation and the marginal rationality of producer and consumer, are not considered as belonging to the fraternity. The criticism and challenging of the neo-classical paradigm, therefore, are the work of outsiders, of sociologists, geographers, planners, epistemologists and so on. Thus, by comparison with the French example, the discipline appears monolithic and isolated from other social sciences, while displaying a professionalism and clearly-defined competence, in keeping with international standards in the subject.

In France, in contrast, the disciplinary/professional set seems to be largely defined by institutions chiefly as a consequence of the hegemony of one in particular, the *Département d'Economie et Sociologie Rurales* of the *Institut National de la Recherche Agronomique* (INRA), which currently has 180 researchers and practising 'engineers'. Thus, while on the British side one notices a certain theoretical hegemony within the discipline accompanied by an institutional diversity, one finds in France an institutional hegemony with a corresponding diversity of theoretical approaches, a strong reluctance to enclose the entire discipline within a single paradigm, and fluid borders with neighbouring disciplines, notably sociology (Petit 1982).

2 Differences of appreciation of the validity of the neo-classical paradigm

As heirs to the great economists who founded classical and neo-classical economic theory, British agricultural economists remain more preoccupied with demonstrating its validity, using its results and perfecting its tools for the agricultural sector, than with revealing its limitations and questioning its continued relevance to post-industrial society. Nevertheless, they have been quick to recognise that goals other than the maximisation of profit or utility are important in individual behaviour and that social costs can disrupt economic laws. They have also come to realise that the theory does not cover, or only partially covers, a number of contemporary issues (landscape, environment and so on). Consequently, they are tempted to limit their analyses to central questions of price formation and the distribution of goods and services and to have an optimistic view regarding the veracity of the relationships postulated. Even if individual actors deviate from economic rationality, 'the general behaviour at market level conforms well to the patterns suggested by the theory' (Colman, Chapter 12, below). The tools remain robust. They justify the development of a dispassionate econometrics.

For the French side, the assessments have been more diverse. As Blanc and Lacombe have suggested, a large number of rural economists are heterodox in relation to this unified conception of economic science. Acknowledging criticism of a unidimensional conception of the functioning of society, the French have adopted a more exploratory, freelance attitude, while running the risk of cutting themselves off from the international community of agricultural economists (their presence at international congresses and conferences has been weak) and of not exploiting to the full a coherent intellectual framework, elaborated and perfected by successive generations of researchers.

As observers of the rapid transition from traditionalism to modernity within the agricultural sector, they have had a passion for grand debates on the evolution of the place of agriculture in the economy and on the persistence of family farming within capitalist societies. With the development of a strong Marxist trend during the 1960s, they have been led to take into serious consideration the dialectic of history and, from this, to pose questions that neo-classical theory can no more answer than, say, those concerning the enclosure movements in Great Britain.

Furthermore, those who have not repudiated neo-classical methods have frequently been more severe in their judgements regarding the veracity and relevance of those methods and less optimistic than their British counterparts. For example, one can present the externalities that are taken to stand for the non-market effects of economic activity as exceptions to the norms of market regulation; but many French rural economists would agree instead with Claude Jessua, that such external effects have begun 'to assume ever greater significance in relation to the collective aspect of human activity. It is a perennial rule in the history of science that when a phenomenon held to be exceptional by the prevailing theory attains the same order of importance as those the theory was supposed to explain, it is time to rethink the theory and enlarge its perspective'. Others might have made the same point by arguing that the state cannot reasonably be thought of as a neutral and transcendent arbiter and calling, therefore, for a theory of the state to complement or qualify theories of market behaviour.

3 Is science neutral?

Although the question of the neutrality or objectivity of the social sciences, and in particular economic science, is not addressed in Colman's paper, and is only mentioned in passing by Blanc and Lacombe, it seems important to consider it so as to understand and, to a certain extent, justify the theoretical diversity that exists within a single discipline. This question has strongly influenced the young rural economists who, at the end of the 1950s, marked the renewal of the discipline in France. Although often ill-equipped for nurturing and contributing to this essentially epistemological debate, they could not embark upon the long career of research in rural economics that was offered them without having first identified their own position in relation to their research objective and to the state which employed them. Without going back over an often confused debate, it is worth underlining the very general agreement – well impressed on people's minds – concerning, first, the impossibility of objectivity; secondly, the non-neutrality of the social sciences; and, thirdly, the rejection of a normative attitude.

It was recognised that the use of intrinsically reductive theory, designed to explain a pre-existing reality, produces effects which themselves tend to make reality conform to the reductive model which constitutes the theory. Thus, the theory of *homo economicus* produces, to a certain extent, an 'economic man' in the same way that the theory of class struggle produces or reinforces, to a degree, the postulated class struggle. With this recognition comes a diversification of scientific approaches (non-neutrality does not imply non-scientific), reflecting a multiplicity of value systems and political preferences. Thus, risking both incompetence and isolation, a large number of French rural economists have chosen heterodox approaches.

Being ignorant of any epistemological debates in which British agricultural economists have immersed themselves, I can only reflect on the pragmatic attitude arising from the choices they have made, in Colman's account. As the neo-classical paradigm is the only reliable boat in the water, there can be no question either of changing it or of building a raft.

4 Intellectual comfort versus material comfort

It seems to me that one can invert this image of a boat and a raft when one moves from the intellectual to the material world. The peculiarities of the French research system, at least in our discipline, are such that they are often misunderstood by foreigners. Blanc and Lacombe lay considerable stress on the institutional aspects of research in rural economics and on its role in the production of knowledge.

Nevertheless, one needs to clarify certain additional points for a non-French audience:

- Research and teaching are not linked in France. Most researchers have no obligation to teach.
- The bulk of rural economics researchers are civil servants who begin their research preparing their theses, or immediately after, and who follow an unbroken research career within INRA through to retirement. The average age of the researchers, which was low during the period of rapid growth in the discipline, has risen as recruitment has diminished.
- It is almost impossible to mobilise new forces when a new research contract arises. In the majority of cases, young diploma-holders can only be attracted if a new and permanent post is created. Admittedly, research jobs can be temporary but only if the researcher wishes, after several years, to turn to new activities. This situation is the result of union pressures exercised during the 1970s to secure for temporary researchers permanent status and employment.

Once the status of researcher has been achieved, the risk of seeing oneself divested of it is almost nil. Such 'protectionism' favours intellectual audacity and heterodoxy. It is a guarantee of the freedom essential to all creativity – which partly explains the variety of approaches described by Blanc and Lacombe – but it also allows inefficiency and indulgence.

Likewise, the volume of grey matter assigned to the discipline is not very elastic. It is, in some ways, predetermined by the recruitment policies of the public research bodies and is therefore ill-suited to respond quickly to new research demands, especially as the researchers in post cannot easily be redirected to new topics.

The situation in Britain is noticeably different and conforms more closely to the theory of the market, with the numbers of academic agricultural economists having to respond to the demand for university training in the subject and the system of temporary research assistants allowing a much more flexible response to changing requirements. This time, it is the French who are reluctant to leave the boat and it is the British who are forced to build rafts to assure their material security.

5 A tendency towards convergence

Having concentrated on the differences and sometimes the distance between the two papers, I would like to finish by showing that current research trends identified in the two papers are leading to an increasing convergence.

The contemporary agricultural crisis, against a background of growing unemployment, seems to demonstrate the importance of competitiveness which leads the French to insist upon the 'autonomy of economics with respect to other social sciences' and 'the refocusing of research on more strictly economic *problematiques*' (Blanc and Lacombe, Chapter 11 below). This trend towards a more marked professionalism and rigour, supported by the change in power in France between 1981 and 1986, has satisfied both the politicians, searching for more solid arguments, and the researchers, weak from their lack of theoretical unity. Nevertheless, at the same time, it causes some to fear a too exclusive development of an instrumental and utilitarian approach.

In contrast, the crisis for the British is drawing agricultural economists out of their specialisation, to address questions of rural employment, nature conservation, alternative land uses and so on, which can be tackled only with difficulty by an approach which remains too exclusively market-oriented. The crisis seems to mark the declining importance of agriculture, the econometric analysis of which, once the high point for agricultural economists, now seems less important than problems of the environment and other questions of land use policy which demand a more pluridisciplinary approach. Whether this move of the French to more disciplinary rigour and the British to more pluridisciplinary opennesss is a trick of dialectics or a simple market adjustment, one cannot say.

Note

1 The French terms *économistes ruraux* and *l'économie rurale* are conventionally translated as 'agricultural economists' and 'agricultural economics'. Because this presumes a greater equivalence than is actually the case, we have resorted instead to a literal translation, referring to French 'rural economics' and French 'rural economists'.

References

Jessua, C.L. *Coûts sociaux et coûts privés*, Paris, PUF, 1968, p. 278.
Petit, M., Is there a French school of agricultural economics? *Journal of Agricultural Economics*, XXXIII (3), September 1982.

11 Rural Economics in France

Michel Blanc and Philippe Lacombe

A full account of the progress of rural economics over the last forty years in France would make a fine subject for a thesis. Unfortunately, the task has never been undertaken. We propose, therefore, to present an outline sketch of its development, identifying those studies and debates which, in our view, have been the most notable.

But first, what is rural economics? A vast debate exists. For our part, we take the definition given by Petit (1982) to the last conference of the International Association of Agricultural Economists: rural economics is what those who call themselves rural economists do. We will restrict our field even further by concerning ourselves solely with the activities of academics and researchers.

If these choices are somewhat pragmatic, the period under study – the last forty years – is easy to justify. In the inter-war years, as all observers of the period admit, there were no rural economists in France, with the notable exception of Augé-Laribé. Otherwise, one must go back to the turn of the century to find works worthy of interest. Thus, one can date reasonably precisely the rebirth of French rural economics: December 1948, when the *Société Française d'Economie Rurale* was formed.

The first characteristic of rural economics is the diversity of theoretical approaches adopted and the variety of subjects tackled. Both owe much to the conditions under which research has been undertaken: the institutional framework of research, on the one hand; the profound and rapid changes in the food-production sector, on the other. However, to look no further than that would be to ignore the relative autonomy of research activity. We must, therefore, show how theoretical debates have contributed towards the transformation of its *problématiques* and the entry of rural economics into the mainstream of political economy.

Having identified their theoretical reference points, it will then be pertinent to sketch out a brief list of themes tackled by rural economists and attempt to show how the subjects of investigation have evolved and diversified. At the end of this rapid excursion into the recent history of French rural economics, it will remain for us to look briefly into its future.

The institutional and social framework of rural economics

The scientific product in general, and more particularly that of economics, is not independent either of its institutional context, or of changes in the society in which it takes place.

1 The hegemony of 'agricultural engineers' and the near monopoly of INRA in French rural economic research

Undoubtedly, two factors that have strongly influenced the character of French rural economics are that the vast majority of researchers have been recruited from amongst young agricultural engineers, and that the research undertaken has largely been carried out within the Department of Rural Sociology and Economics of INRA – a body chiefly oriented to the biological sciences and their application in the agricultural sector and food production industries. This professional hegemony and institutional monopoly have historic causes.

With the expansion of industrial capitalism, higher education was invested with a new function: to train technical manpower capable of developing scientific knowledge and applying it to improve production. In France, from the beginnings of industrialization, this function was entrusted to specialist institutions, independent of the university sector – the *grandes écoles d'ingénieurs*, which have always closely associated the creation of knowledge with its dissemination. Scientific research therefore became no longer the preserve of the universities in the nineteenth century but developed additionally within specialist organizations and in laboratories attached to the *grandes écoles*, and ultimately in the larger industrial concerns. The former students of the *grandes écoles* have thereby proved to be the best adapted, by their training, to the new research functions, especially when such functions assume an applied character.

This situation, which prevailed until quite recently, was reinforced by the means by which the *grandes écoles* assured their own supremacy. Recruitment to them was based, from the beginning, on a rigorous selection procedure which manifested itself in the tendency to produce slightly fewer engineers than were needed. This, in return, engendered, a multiplication of *grandes écoles* and the development of a hierarchy amongst them. Former students' associations played a role of considerable importance in this respect. Each strove to create 'private territory' for itself in certain areas, firms and technical service departments of the state. In such a way, the *grandes écoles d'agronomie* assured themselves of a semi-monopoly in the training of civil servants for the Ministry of Agriculture and saw to it that nothing which touched this broad subject area escaped the Ministry's control. Thus 'quite naturally' when, after the last war, INRA was created, it was attached to the Ministry of Agriculture and recruited chiefly agricultural engineers.

At the same time, the growing intervention of the state in the regulation of the economy, the concentration of capital and its corollary, the displacement of centres of organizational decision-making towards the headquarters of major companies, prompted the *grandes écoles* in general to turn to economics and management teaching. The *grandes écoles d'agronomie* were no exception. Rural economics, which had always been taught there as a sub-discipline of agronomy became a specialised field of economic theory and management techniques.

When, in 1955, a department of rural economics was set up within INRA, laboratories were installed in association with chairs of rural economics at the *grandes écoles d'agronomie* and all the conditions were set for the researchers to be recruited from amongst agricultural engineers. The governing body of INRA was already accustomed to drawing from this pool for the hiring of scientists for other departments, while the holders of the chairs of rural economics saw, in the new department, an additional outlet for their students. Moreover, there was little competition from the universities whose teaching of economics was highly variable in quality, being still carried out in law faculties. The few students wishing to develop research in the subject were generally more attracted to macro-economics than to the study of a sector which, though changing rapidly, nevertheless remained the 'preserve of muddy peasants'!

Recently, however, the hegemony of the agricultural engineers in research in rural economics has been challenged. Two factors are chiefly responsible for this. Economics teaching at the universities was freed from the control of the lawyers in the 1960s and its quality has since substantially improved. High quality research teams were set up in the most dynamic universities. Work related to rural economics has sometimes been carried out there although in a scattered and discontinuous fashion. In addition, the law on research of 1982 has placed all research institutes, including INRA, under the control of the Ministry of Research and Technology. Agronomic research has thus found itself dissociated from those state apparatuses which are still under the dominance of the agricultural engineers. The procedures both for the evaluation and orientation of research work and for the recruitment of researchers for the Department of Rural Economy and Sociology at INRA are henceforth largely open to academics not having emerged from the *grandes écoles*. Below we will return to certain consequences of this change.

The hegemony of agricultural engineers in French rural economics has had a number of consequences. The engineer is, first and foremost, a technical man, who mobilises acquired knowledge from a wide range of disciplines, with a view to solving a given problem. He is also an agent of technical progress and he deeply believes that to work for this end is to advance towards a better world. He is equally a man of numbers. His work always implies precise measurement which, for him, is an incontestable guarantee of objectivity. Whatever is unmeasurable is fundamentally foreign. In addition, the engineer is a pragmatist. For him, the attainment of a concrete result counts above all else. The method employed assumes, by itself, little importance as long as it leads to the achievement of something that works well. He also has a tendency to regard all things as mechanisms whose parts have to be carefully adjusted and believes that he is there precisely in order to spot and correct possible maladjustments. Finally, his locale is most often within enterprises in the widest meaning of the term; private firms or public services.

This culture of the engineer leaves a deep impression on individual engineers. When he becomes a social science researcher, his engineering background comes through in his approach even when several economics diplomas, often rapidly gained from universities, have been added to his training. The inclination of the engineer towards pluri-disciplinarity pushes him sometimes towards heterodox currents in economics, most notably, to Marxism whose rigour of theoretical construction and ambition to account for the entirety of social phenomenon, he appreciates. Alternatively, however, his love of well-adjusted and non-dialectical mechanisms, his ease in the use of mathematical tools, and his spontaneous micro-economic conceptions attract him to neo-classical economics. Furthermore, his taste for the concrete and for measurement draw him to empiricism. Finally, his concern to be operational brings him to techniques of decision-making and the development of standards.

Paradoxically, this recruitment process by the *grandes écoles d'agronomie* has furnished a wide range of researcher profiles which have been an incontestable source of richness and dynamism. Yet this method of recruitment has also had its negative aspects. The agricultural engineers who have become researchers in rural economics have generally displayed, first, an often superficial knowledge of the history of economic theory; secondly, a rather unsure mastery of macro-economic analysis; and, finally, a marked penchant for trying to explain the particularities of the agricultural sector without endeavouring to see in them the specific manifestation of much more general phenomena.

The inclusion of rural economics within INRA – itself a 'private territory' for agricultural engineers – meant that the discipline was not inclined to develop even loose links with the university sector. Thus, it ran a grave risk of being engulfed by 'agrarianism' or agricultural fundamentalism – that gamut of doctrines which accord special virtues to agriculture and advocate favoured treatment for farmers. Fortunately, as a small minority in a research institute oriented chiefly towards biology, the economists were somewhat removed from potential pressures from the Ministry of Agriculture or the agricultural lobby – itself shaken, at the time, by severe internal struggles. In addition, the recruitment process, then having operated for a dozen or so years, gave a very particular structure to the age-pyramid of the rural economists: a very large base topped by a small and minor group of professors, barely touching forty at the beginning of the 1960s. The latter, even if they wanted it, did not have the authority closely to direct the activities of the young researchers. This was a major factor in the diversification of the interests of the researchers.

All things considered, INRA's near monopoly over the discipline proved to be advantageous for French rural economics. Its practitioners have benefited indirectly from the generous financial endowments favouring agronomic research which reflect official support for the rapid modernization of the agricultural sector. The progressive widening of the scope of INRA's interests to include the technology of food processing, food consumption, the energetics of biomass production and sylviculture encouraged rural economists to extend their interests beyond agricultural economics and become interested equally in the processing, distribution and consumption of food products, the forestry and wood processing sectors, different ways of valorising the biomass, the environmental impacts of the widespread use of certain, techniques and, finally, patterns of production. This list is, in no respect, exhaustive.

2 The effects of the changing food-production sector and the forces animating it

At the start of the 1950s, French agriculture entered a phase of rapid modernisation championed by a newly emergent movement of young farmers – some already heads of farm enterprises, the vast majority still helping on the family farm. The technical and economic dimensions of the transformation were intricately linked with, yet subordinate to, its social dimension. It was based upon the idea, at the time almost sacrilegious in the French farming world, of the necessity of the agricultural exodus to bring about a rise in the standard of living both for those who left and for those who remained. These latter saw, in the freeing of land, the increased possibilities of enlarging their holdings, of substituting capital for labour, of benefiting from economies of scale and, ultimately, of considerably increasing their own productivity. The objective therefore was to assure a collective improvement in their position by making them independent producers, neither proletarians nor capitalists, thereby enabling them, through their own labours, to aspire to new norms of consumption which would spread rapidly throughout rural society as a whole; but also, through co-operative associations, enabling them to commercialise and modernise and thus escape the 'exploitation' of dealers and suppliers.

Strongly inspired by the social doctrine of the Church, this programme also revived certain Proudhonian traditions and aspects of French radicalism. This facilitated its success not only in the bulk of traditionally Catholic regions but also in a number of areas where the Church was weak. Fundamentally reformist, it also found a degree of support amongst the higher civil servants, who, in certain offices – most notably the *Commissariat Général du Plan* – were themselves involved in economic and social modernisation of the country. It naturally received support from those governments who shared its ambitions: that of Pierre Mendès France first and those of General de Gaulle later, during the 1960s. Strengthened by this support, the young farmers' movement was able in a dozen years to take possession of the 'levers of control' for most of the farming world.

There was something of a Hugo-like epic in this movement. How could the young researchers of rural economics, emerging moreover from the *grandes écoles d'agronomie*, not feel some affinities with these young farmers, heralds simultaneously of a technical, economic and social modernisation, struggling heroically to be rid of the self-interested leadership of the large farmers? Young researchers and young farmers soon found themselves on the same wavelength. Sometimes, even personal friendships were formed between them as the aspirations of one became the research themes of the other.

Involved in the processes of modernisation, French rural economists nevertheless became aware of the dark side of the phenomenon, especially as those concerned with rural society began to investigate the broader impacts. The difficulties of the less favoured areas (*zones défavorisées*), the relative pauperisation of certain sectors of the peasantry, the domination of the food processing industries (co-operative and private) over the agricultural sector, the unequal distribution of public aid, the qualitative modification of food products, these all provoked numerous research studies. In the eyes of the no longer youthful union leaders, who now held powerful positions in professional organisations, researchers in rural economics suddenly appeared to be helping or supporting various oppositional and anti-establishment bodies such as minority agricultural unions, consumer associations and so on. Public authorities and the agricultural lobby became critical of the direction some of the research was taking, and the friendships of earlier years became soured and strained. The concentration of research effort and debate on the understanding of the 'negative' aspects of modernisation led researchers away from various issues whose importance only later emerged. The Common Agricultural Policy in particular was neglected during this period.

The coming to power of the Left in 1981 brought about an important turnover amongst political advisers. Some rural economics researchers were, for the first time, called into the ministerial office. One of them, Henri Nallet, was even agricultural adviser to the President before becoming Minister of Agriculture. Researchers thus became more aware than before of the problems experienced in the day-to-day management of food industry policy-making.

Rural economists and political economy

The conditions under which rural economic research is carried out allow one to understand the stances which rural economists have adopted towards political economy. At the risk of oversimplifying, one might distinguish three principal trends.

The novelty and the breadth of the modernisation process led the agronomists, during the course of the 1950s, to collect and process any information thought to be of relevance to the management of change. Thus, with their agricultural engineering background these rural economists first saw, in the economy, a set of techniques for making 'rational' decisions, without reference to the character and functioning of the society under study. The criteria for such a scientific approach lay in the quality of the methods used: techniques for the collection and treatment of data, private and national accounting, programming techniques, operational research, simulations, etc. These studies familiarised researchers with decision-making techniques and lent support to the strengthening and extension of a statistical apparatus which at the time was particularly weak.

These early works, realised during the setting-up of a research enterprise whose intellectual direction was still uncertain, thus consisted of empirical approaches to the mastery of economic techniques. Their limitations, however, can be clearly seen: by reducing the economy to a set of decision-making tools or to simple description, they often took for data that which should rightly have been explained. Deliberately ignoring all theoretical references, such early works have little explanatory significance. Limitations such as these rapidly led researchers to join the main currents of economic thought – neo-classicism and Marxism. But knowledge of the working environment of rural economists, outlined above, allows us also to understand the prominence of French rural economists in criticising this habitual distinction and their resultant involvement in more heterodox currents of thought.

1 The neo-classical approach

The pretension to rigour and rationality, and the operational applicability of neo-classical propositions attracted, fairly rapidly, those economists dissatisfied with their ability to explain the overall dynamics of the agricultural sector by reference to economic techniques alone.

Neo-classical analysis puts forward models of rational behaviour, from which can be constructed a representation of the whole economic structure. The justification for its rationality lies in the search for utility which determines the value of goods. From these initial presuppositions, it becomes possible to define the optimal distribution of resources according to preferences and the state of existing techniques. One can understand the attractiveness of this approach: it claims to provide an explanation of behaviour and processes while, at the same time, supplying norms of rationality. Thus, explanation and beneficial therapy are simultaneously provided. Even if such a normative conception of neo-classical economics is nowadays frequently avowed, it has nevertheless often seduced engineers who have found in economics the 'science' for social engineering. The mathematical formalisation to which neo-classical hypotheses lend themselves added to its scientific aura and had particular appeal for engineers. Armed with this model, rural economists have gone on to study the different levels of analysis for which it claims efficacy – the behaviour of producers, partial equilibria of markets, the general micro-economic equilibrium, etc – and to apply it to the gamut of issues covering price formation, market structures and the combination of production factors. The neo-classical approach has also highlighted the overall predicament of the agricultural sector; with inelasticity of demand and nil gains in marginal productivity provoking a movement of factors of production towards other sectors.

As applied economic research, work in this tradition must be attentive to real-life conditions of production and exchange, which frequently do not conform to neo-classical precepts but exhibit 'irrational' or deviant behaviour according to the model's norms. Studies within the tradition, therefore, which disclose the variations induced in the model by the peculiarities of agricultural organization, have contributed greatly to the understanding of the workings of the sector. As well as formulating a general model for the incorporation of agriculture into the economy, which has undoubtedly guided policy, explanations have also been furnished (often in terms of resistance, slowness and delays) of the operation of numerous aspects of the rural economy; for example, the mode of price setting in accordance with market structures, conditions for the mobility of factors and the successive transformations of farm businesses, and the elasticity of supply in relation to price.

The examination of the distortions induced by agrarian structures in the functioning of the reference model, has led to two principal research themes. For a first group of economists, such distortions can be identified and analysed using neo-classical tools. For example, one can try and explain, with the help particularly of the notion of opportunity cost, the difficulties, even the rationality, of the weak mobility of labour engaged in inefficient agricultural production. Sometimes, these dysfunctions are simply interpreted as being destined progressively to disappear as agriculture becomes more rationalised. Some of these economists have also proposed policy measures designed to promote a 'better working' of the agricultural economy. Such proposals are less frequent today, when there is greater interest in the explanation of the behaviour of individual agents endowed with a utility function and inserted into a network of constraints defining their situation, without any reference necessarily to the general micro-economic equilibrium. Some very varied situations of choice can thus be analysed.

For other economists, it is legitimate and desirable to explain the aforementioned dysfunctions by examining the conditions under which they exist and are reproduced. But in searching for an explanation of the genesis and reproduction of structures, norms of behaviour, preferences and performances, one soon encounters the reservations or criticisms commonly addressed to general neo-classical reasoning which invite the researcher to consider other theoretical reference points. Without considering these criticisms in any depth, it is useful to identify their principal lines.

The model claims to describe mechanisms independently of prevailing social relations, of their reproduction, or of the conflicts which they provoke. It poses an individual and universal rationality, independent of the age, the society or its historical evolution. Opposed to these presuppositions is an interpretation which identifies economic and social structuration as the basis of behaviour, and the functioning and reproduction of society. From this perspective, economic mechanisms are a product of social relations and not timeless and universal procedures of adjustment to prices. The economic actor cannot be studied independently of the socio-economic structuring in which he operates. One finds in this, moreover, a criticism which strikes at the very conception of the discipline.

The model focuses on the price link between agriculture and the rest of the economy though other relations also merit attention: externalities, power, asymmetric relations between actors and so on. Where it has been possible to take into consideration some of these other relations, price has not always proved a good indicator of the preferences of consumers confronted by the performance of producers, all the more so since consumers are habitually regarded, somewhat carelessly, as acting independently of each other. Additionally, the intermediary levels of economic organisation, located between individual actors and the general system – the sector, production systems, the state, social movements, etc. – have not been so easily absorbed into the analysis. It is precisely these intermediary levels that are experiencing considerable change and through defining technologies, modes of influence, price relations, forms of economic organisation and so on, they are profoundly altering the operating conditions of agricultural production.

One can understand, therefore, why other approaches have been adopted besides extensions of neo-classical analysis, particularly in the study of individual behaviour. Increasingly a diversification of approaches has also been stimulated by the major changes to the organisation of agricultural production, such as through the opening of markets, the development of a food industry, the interventions of the state, and the internationlisation of exchanges. The effort to understand these transformation and their direction has led to an analysis of structures and processes and their genesis.

2 The Marxist approach

During the 1970s, there was a renewed interest in Marxist analysis which had been rather neglected since the beginning of the century. On the one hand, this arose from dissatisfaction with the neo-classical approach which was felt to be reductionist and which was heavily criticised, sometimes abusively, for supposedly providing suport for liberalism; and, on the other, there was concern for a more comprehensive and more critical approach.

The dynamics of French agriculture, closely observed for more than a century since the writings of Marx, have precluded reference to the usual thesis of the general establishment of a coherent agrarian capitalism, unless as some distant future prospect. The contributions of rural economists, often jointly with development economists (and for the same reasons), have therefore consisted largely of attempts to renew the interpretation of the place of farmers in contemporary society. This has been carried out in three distinct ways.

(a) According to the first, agriculture is subject to a petty commodity mode of production which remains capable of reproducing itself. Thus it is dependent upon a worker who is also the direct owner of his means of production, who organises his own method of work and who seeks his subsistence and that of his family without being able to aspire to the accumulation of profit. This mode of production successfully resists the penetration and development of capitalism in agriculture, through the individual ownership of land and through the refractory nature of the biological and ecological forces on which agricultural production is based, which still require the individual attention of the farmer.

Such an analysis as this clearly derives from a conception of the social formation as comprising several different modes of production of which one is dominant. Stressing this coexistence can lead one to underestimate – or even ignore – the dependency relations which bind agriculture to the dominant mode of production. If one accepts that the role of the capitalist mode of production is to transform all that it comes across, it becomes difficult then to speak today of any permanence for the petty commodity mode as this is already so altered through its long-standing involvement with capitalism. In short, one insists on its permanence and coexistence when it may in fact be the transformations and dependencies which are more significant.

Such criticisms have encouraged investigations specifically of these transformations and their diversity, with a view to discovering the forms of, and consequences for, a heterogeneous agriculture existing within a social formation dominated by the capitalist mode of production.

(b) Some researchers have tried to demonstrate parallels between the situation of farmers and that of wage-earners even though the former are not the subject of a formal wage relationship. The development of ties between farmers and food-processing firms, though, can assume some of the characteristics of a wage relationship. Milk producers, in particular, find themselves under a *de facto* obligation to deliver their product to a particular industrial concern which specifies, with increasing exactitude, the technical methods of production. The rigidity of production systems is such that production must be continued. Thus, the apparent independence of producers can be interpreted as merely a formality, with the price of milk in effect corresponding to the remuneration of the work supplied. The claims of farmers, often referring to demands for a minimum wage, could also be understood in the same light.

This last point, however, is at odds with the maintenance amongst farmers of a capacity for independent initiative and at least a relative autonomy. In addition, however powerful the outside influences might be, the results of farming, far from being chiefly dependent upon the quantity of work input, are essentially determined by the scale of the efficiency of the productive apparatus held in ownership or tenancy by the farmers. The vision of farmers being drawn into a real if not formalised wage relationship appears to be relevant only in those relatively few areas where farmers are totally integrated into a food processing enterprise. In general, farmers' situations are much more diverse and recognition of this has fuelled additional interpretations in terms of social stratification.

(c) Research in this third direction has emphasised the dependence of agriculture and its transformations with regard to the dominant, capitalist mode of production, whose development excludes the presence of other modes of production. That obviously does not mean that all social forms will identify themselves with capitalism, but that they evolve under its dominant control.

Amongst farmers this control proves to be differentiated according to their differing abilities to adapt in relation to their circumstances. It is important to clarify the characteristics which ultimately define the forms of reproduction (whether simple or extended), or alternatively which ensure slow or rapid elimination. One can thus identify the different destinies of various social strata. To this end the social relations which link agricultural producers to the rest of the social formation are examined – including relations within the farming sector, but also crucially between farms and the outside world (through access to goods and services provided by external agencies). Supporters of this approach hope to propose an explanation of individual or collective strategies in the making of technical as well as socio-political choices. They also seek to identify the links between these agrarian strata or their alliances, and the varied ideologies which claim to explain the evolution of agriculture and to define its future direction.

This approach, which has the advantage of accounting for the heterogeneity of production structures and the role of the social formation in their reproduction, nevertheless encounters several difficulties. First, the criteria for defining social strata are not easily formalised in a definitive and conclusive way. Secondly, the forms of movement from one social stratum to another are not well understood. As a result, the dynamic of the whole gives rise to contradictory interpretations of the long-term development of agrarian capitalism and the place of farmers in the capitalist social formation – sometimes seen in terms of the promotion of modernised forms of artisanship, and sometimes in the permanence of a diversity of social strata. Finally, despite the general claim to unite agrarian with non-agrarian strata, indeed with basic social classes, these analyses are often restricted to an internal study of agriculture and neglect the links with the social context in which agriculture operates.

3 Heterodox currents

There remain a number of very diverse approaches involving economists of varied intellectual origins who are nonetheless united in their rejection – or, at least, their criticism – of the grand interpretive systems mentioned above. Such a negative definition, of course, brings together some strange bedfellows. It includes those disappointed with the neo-classical approach who have denounced it as being reductionist, individualistic (in the sense of ignoring the role of social structures) and ahistoric.

One also finds economists dissatisfied with orthodox Marxist analysis. Although many of them share with it a historical perspective which takes into account structures and their contradictions, they express reservations not least concerning its overriding economic determinism, the conditions for the collapse of capitalism and the advent of communism, the forms of class struggle and the role of the proletariat. Finally, in a diffuse way, the thoughts of Joseph Schumpeter have influenced many rural economists in their efforts to come to terms with the major agricultural changes of the post-war period. Notwithstanding their diverse origins, one can attempt to draw together the principal characteristics of these heterodox currents.

First, the researchers involved have given considerable attention to structural change as a product of social agency. They have aimed to give a better presentation of the diversity of socio-economic forms, their strategies, the conditions of their origin, reproduction and transformation, and the consistencies, or contradictions, which develop between them. Change and its sources are therefore considered more than are states of equilibrium, which has led to a simultaneous interest in the long and the short term. Structural transformations are inseparable from institutional and political conditions which should not be considered merely as exogenous factors. Power relations are also analysed, and concepts are proposed so as to avoid the separation of the social from the economic (for example, domination, integration, structures). Socio-economic structures, therefore, are no longer considered as being relatively secondary epiphenomena but as deeply affecting and affected by the allocation of scarce resources. Heterodox currents thus insist on the diversity and relativity of economic behaviour and mechanisms and for these to be understood in relation to their structural and historic context.

These research directions have, in fact, achieved noticeable progress in the understanding of rural economics. They have elucidated the economic and social mechanisms determining the farmers' situation in society and its evolution (e.g. the relations between agriculture and industry, the diffusion of technical progress, the development of agricultural employment, the transformation of rural societies, and the evolution of agricultural policy). Research has also been devoted to the analysis of commercial circuits and to the identification of different systems of production-processing-distribution.

The remarkable development of agricultural statistics over the last twenty years, as well as the progress achieved in the understanding of data, has reinforced studies of structures, undermining the criticism sometimes made of these researches that they are insufficiently quantified. Since the early 1960s, with more or less good fortune and always in a problematic fashion, the development of agricultural policy has largely taken research findings into account, particularly regarding structural policy, as well as aspects of financial and market organisations policy.

These currents are, therefore, very well represented in rural economics, probably more so than in any other branches of French political economy. Undoubtedly, this strong presence can be explained by the characteristics of the agricultural sector in which the technical, social and political 'facts' are closely intermeshed, where the most 'modern' organisations and the most traditional rub shoulders, and in which the intervention of public authorities is also important. The dramatic transformation of agriculture since the war, which has led certain authors to talk of an agricultural revolution, clearly invites further interpretations in terms of structures and of historical processes rather than in terms of a balance of goods adjusted by prices.

Nevertheless, these works are often challenged on their theoretical base: for example, by what principles can one define structure? Or what is the logic of the operation of the wider society to which reference is so often made? Their frequently denounced empiricism has, even so, permitted a number of people working in this area to remain sensitive to certain phenomena that others ensconced in a more rigid theoretical framework, have been condemned to ignore.

The distinctions made above have inevitably been accentuated for the purposes of this paper, and should not be seen as fixed and rigid. Each of the three approaches identified brings together neighbouring, but nevertheless, different positions with the result that the boundaries of each are not clearly defined. Additionally, one sees evidence of borrowing, or at least of results converging, from one theoretical approach to another. One can employ marginalist reasoning, for example, without accepting all the neo-classical presuppositions. The results got by one approach are sometimes studied, or supported, according to the methods of another; for example, the heterogeneity of production structures. This diversity, and its evolution over time, reflects, without doubt, a certain eclecticism in the output of French rural economists. Perhaps there is, in that, a risk of dissipation or instability, but it is also a sign of vitality which is expressed also in the proliferation of research themes.

Research themes and their evolution

1 Agricultural production

After the war, rural economists began to develop management tools adapted for farmers. With the rapid modernisation of agriculture, the question of investments and of the techno-economic choices to be made, was posed. Initially conceived as means for fine-tuning decision-making, these researches sometimes took a normative turn; seeking to determine, for example, the optimal sizes for different enterprises. But more theoretical debates were also nourished. The existence of limits to agricultural economies of scale, for example, became the subject of bitter confrontations which proved rather inconclusive. Otherwise, one examined the rationality of farmers. What economic indicators are they seeking to maximise? What relationships are established between the household and the farm? How do they view the constraints placed upon their farm business?

In recent years, studies devoted to the management of farms have been oriented in two major directions. Some believe that the farmer always has good reasons for making the choices he does. The role of management is to help him better formulate and achieve his objectives. One thereby enters the field of action-research in which the farmer is closely associated with the very conception of decision-making tools, tailor-made as it were, for each producer.

However, from the start of the 1960s, a number of those engaged in this field began to seek a better understanding of both the external factors which prompted the transformation of farm holdings and the structural obstacles which held it back. The adoption of technical change was, at that time, at the heart of numerous studies. At first, it was treated as an exogenous factor which modified the production function. Then, explanations were sought of its unequal diffusion amongst farmers. Finally, interest was focused on the conditions of its appearance and adoption. Thus, it became progressively interpreted as a variable endogenous to the economic process, described under the generic term, modernisation.

In the eyes of the vast majority of observers, this process initially required an increase in the size of farms and a reduction in the agricultural labour force. Brakes on the agricultural exodus became an important research topic. The accent was placed mainly on the individual costs of mobility which grew strongly with distance and with age. The importance of the family cycle and the works of Chayanov were rediscovered. Demographic models predicting the active agricultural population and the extent of dischargeable land were drawn up. More recently, interest has moved towards the roles assumed by women and towards a more macro-economic approach to changes in agricultural employment.

Several researchers have begun to study in close detail the processes by which land resources are redistributed with the growth in farm size. Similarly, the costs thus incurred have led to the analysis of tenure changes and their determinants. Recent work has demonstrated the twin functions of land – at the same time, both an element of inheritance and a factor of production.

Modernisation has implied an important growth in the financial needs of agriculture and the farmers' savings function was the subject of specific studies. Following that, interest blossomed in the distribution of credit to the different categories of farmer, their indebtedness, and their financial vulnerability.

Today, research on the reproduction of the agricultural labour force, the fluidity of the land market and the need for financing agricultural enterprises is concentrating more and more on the factors preventing or facilitating the transmission of farms from one generation to another. Thus the subject of succession, and all the phenomena that accompany or precede it, currently occupies a large number of researchers.

The study of the structural transformation of farm units was frequently conducted alongside that of production system modification. This latter term designated, at first, both the relations between factors of production and those between the different activities undertaken on the farm. The initial work concentrated on studying processes of farm specialisation and the break-up of the traditional polyculture-livestock husbandry. The search for economies of scale has encouraged specialisation and the man/land ratio has determined the direction it has taken; both towards milk production where it was high and towards large-scale cultivation where it was low. In parallel, the accompanying tendency towards regional specialisation also came to be studied. The multiplication of works undertaken at the regional scale led to a change in the notion of the production system, which ceased to be essentially techno-economic and micro-economic but took on instead a social and occasionally macro-economic dimension. Thus emerged the concept of the dominant production system. This corresponds, for a given product and region, to the production method judged to be the 'highest performing', which sets itself up as the social norm to be achieved.

The debate surrounding this question was intense. Some people even contested the pertinence of the concept. Others, more numerous, believed that the economic crisis was felt in the agricultural sector precisely as a crisis – or at least a questioning – of these dominant production systems, which were big consumers of industrial inputs. The stress was placed upon the deterioration of work conditions that they promoted, on their harmful environmental effects and, above all, on their difficulties of reproducing themselves without massive aid at a time when the relative prices of intermediate products and of capital goods rose, whilst their marginal physical productivity declined. The cross-sectional studies carried out showed, however, that the farms that had adopted these dominant production systems did obtain the best economic results. Clearly, this did not prove that other farms could improve their results by imitating them. For want of longitudinal data showing the evolution over time of the income of farms which had adopted different production systems, the debate could not be resolved and today has lost much of its virulence.

It has had the paradoxical merit of directing attention to the variety of production systems that exist and the status of the farmers themselves. It also stimulated research on themes previously ignored by French rural economists (such as organic agriculture, and the gathering of wild produce) and provoked renewed interest in the study of farm family incomes. With a much improved statistical base, work on the latter has been mainly devoted to the analysis of the causes of agriculture income variation over the course of time and between farms. Finally this debate on the dominant systems of production has fed a more detailed analysis of agricultural policy-making as both an outcome and a determinant of these systems.

In the 1960s, research on agricultural policy had, above all, a normative character. It was chiefly a question of prescribing measures permitting an optimal allocation of national resources. The discrepancies between the proposals of the economists and the actual decisions taken by those with political power were interpreted as being the result of the pressures of vested interest.

During the 1970s, the *problématique* radically changed, with work on policy then being largely undertaken by researchers in the Marxist tradition who conceived of policy measures as the institutional expression of compromises and shifting power relations between the different social groups involved. Consequently, appreciating the efficiency of the tools of agricultural policy in terms of what it sought to achieve did not make very great sense when the stated objectives of policy constituted only one of the elements of compromise existing at a given moment. Under such conditions, the possible non-attainment of policy objectives reflected merely a modification of the initial power relations and not a failure in goal achievement on the part of a detached public authority. So, for example, the 'crisis' of dominant production systems was not the result of a mistake emerging in agricultural policy, but only a reflection of the weakening of some of the social forces which had benefited from their diffusion.

In recent years, research on agricultural policy seems to be taking a new direction in striving to analyse the manner in which economic actors react to this or that policy measure, so as to understand its potential impact.

2 The marketing, processing and distribution of food products

The Popular Front Government, by creating in 1936 the *Office Interprofessional du Blé* (Wheat Bureau), initiated a system of public intervention in markets to guarantee a minimum price for producers. The reappearance of surpluses in beef production at the start of the 1950s raised once more the question of market organisation. A large number of studies in rural economics were devoted to this subject as well as to price fluctuations in the 'free' produce markets (notably pigs and potatoes). More recently, interest has moved towards the analysis of how markets actually operate. However, the principal studies are still carried out in the context of research on producer-to-consumer paths or chains (*filières*).

The concept of a food production chain rests in the idea that the type of economic structures prevailing at any point, from the production of agricultural raw materials at one end, to the distribution of food products at the other, depends in part upon the type of structures existing immediately above and below the point examined. The relationship between the various links in the chain are not only based upon the sale of products – some effects of dominance do emerge, which are reflected at the level of prices – but also in the technology adopted. The nature and respective strengths of the economic structures in contact with one another thus influence both the manner in which the added value and profit rate are distributed along the chain, and the change in production methods at each point. Thus, any change affecting one link becomes transmitted along the entire chain.

Initially, studies of these chains were chiefly concerned with the immediate fiscal and technological relationships being established by farmers. In particular, the study of the poultry chain became an important locus for observing the integration of agriculture into the food – processing industry. The reinforcement of cooperatives therefore appeared to some as the means to enable farmers to recuperate collectively the economic power they had individually lost of the farm level. However, several researchers saw in the cooperatives, a devalued capital which, condemned to relative immobility by existing regulations, tended to be concentrated in the first level of processing and to bring poor returns.

These initial works next led to the study of ways of distributing the gains in productivity and therefore of the valorisation of capital along the chains. The emphasis was progressively placed upon the importance of the large distribution concerns which, occupying a dominant position, managed to impose their conditions on the processing industries, whose own freedom to develop separate strategies and technological choices was thereby diminished.

3 International economic relations in the agriculture-food production sector

Research on this theme has been mainly developed since the mid-1970s, and, indeed, is the most marked contemporary shift in the orientation of French rural economists. It has been carried out, however, in a scattered fashion. Nevertheless, it is possible to distinguish a certain number of sub-themes:

- the place of agriculture in the development strategies of developing countries;
- world food markets, especially in relation to viti-viniculture and vegetable oil protein-related products;
- comparative analysis of the agricultural policy of industrialised countries and of certain market organisation and regulatory tools (notably, those for diary products);
- the study of the transformation of the agricultural production systems of a number of countries (Eastern nations, China, the USA) or of certain regions (e.g. the Latifundia systems of the Iberian Peninsula), or of certain products within the EEC (in particular, animal feedstuffs);
- more recently, new research has been aimed at the CAP, in its agro-fiscal and budgetary aspects, and at the internationalisation of production in the input sectors (fertilisers, machinery, seeds, foodstuffs).

From this perfunctory appraisal, one can nevertheless see that certain shadowy areas remain:

- there is a dearth of comprehensive comparative studies covering agriculture, policy and the food economics of the EEC countries and the larger agricultural countries of the world
- the study of the CAP as such has been neglected for too long and still occupies too few researchers;
- the movements of exchange and the transformation of production structures in the Mediterranean region have been little studied, yet the question is of considerable contemporary importance as a result of the enlargement of the EEC to include Spain, Portugal and Greece.

What future for rural economics?

With the conditions of scientific work in our field having so altered and continuing to change, one is led to wonder whether the future of rural economics lies in its dissolution, or in refining its distinctive contribution.

1 The evolution of the conditions of scientific work

The prolonged economic crisis that we are experiencing leads, undoubtedly, to diverse and sometimes contradictory interpretations, yet it also gives rise to some rather strong areas of agreement with respect to the strategies needed to cope and adapt. Thus, apart from the small minority favouring economic liberalisation, most people stress the difficulties and the lasting uncertainties of the current situation and emphasise in economic policy, therefore, performance improvement (modernisation) and adaptability. In such a perspective, social groups are far more drawn towards consensual mobilisation than to the sharpening of differences and social struggle.

Therefore, even if some prescriptions of the 'way out of the crisis' insist on necessary structural transformations, the urgency of management preoccupations as well as the uncertainties and mistrust over proposals deemed to be too radical, lead to a preoccupation with immediate economic constraints: the severity of the competition, the necessity for gains in productivity, the urgency of investments, the sensitivity of prices and markets.

In consequence, certain scientific themes, often underestimated during the 1970s and more classically economic than structural, are going to occupy the intellectual foreground. Questions of cost, performance, competitiveness, of the degree of support for domestic or foreign production, today take the centre stage with a view to assisting 'good economic management' or the positions pursued in international negotiations. The mode of price formation and costs, the imposition of quotas and their role in the remuneration and the allocation of factors, assume a prominent place, to the detriment of the analysis of economic and social structures, and their long-term transformation.

While the reduction of the relative place of agriculture in the economy may provoke a redistribution of research energies, these new preoccupations invite one to return to the more general approaches of economics, since the problems now faced by agriculture are comparable to those studied in other branches of the discipline – international economics, employment economics, public economics, industrial economics and so on. It is therefore to the concepts, approaches and results of these specialties that reference must now be made. If they were to resist this development, economists interested in agriculture would condemn themselves to an increasingly sterile isolation.

In the name of rigour and professionalism, there is renewed insistence on the autonomy of economics with respect to other social sciences, and on the refocusing of research on more strictly economic *problématiques*. While the 1970s saw the blossoming of more global, systemic, sometimes interdisciplinary studies calling upon Marxism or heterodox currents, neo-classical thought has meanwhile found, once more, an audience amongst rural economists that it had lost. Such a shift generally suits two groups: those professionally and politically responsible for policy who, confronted by difficult decisions, seek in research allegedly indisputable 'scientific' justifications for their actions; and researchers in other scientific disciplines who are left with greater scope to define their own direction.

The political switches that France has recently experienced (in 1981 and 1986) have reinforced this evolution. First, during the early years of the Socialist government, chiefly 1981–82, acute difficulties were encountered in attempting to put into practice the various reforms which had been discussed and sometimes advocated by rural economists, concerning alternative methods of allocating land uses and of managing markets; income guarantees for farmers; participation in international exchanges etc. These reform efforts have since been abandoned in favour of more traditional approaches to agricultural development. Secondly, governments of both the Right and the Left have been confronted by chronic problems for which they believe they lack sufficiently clear information concerning, notably, responses to overproduction; the degree of protection and support for the farming sector of France's main competitors; the consequences of enlarging the field of competition; ways of modernisation and so on.

These new features of the general economic and political situation have redirected the methods of the management of research. Since 1981, the organisation of research has been concentrated and subjected to a more centralised decision process. Procedures of invitation to tender, on themes justified by social demands have also been developed.

All these changes modify the conditions under which rural economists produce research. Without doubt, they lead to openings to other areas of economics and indeed to new fields. This is important for a discipline in which the risks of incestuousness have already been seen. They also reinforce a more common tendency towards cooperation with information-gathering statistical offices. Yet these changes can also focus attention on those immediate problems tackled by reductivist approaches under a very instrumentalist and utilitarian perspective of science. Under such circumstances, is rural economics going to diminish in importance and be eclipsed by other, more contemporary, branches of political economy, or can it refurbish its intellectual standing by becoming more involved in the mainstream debates of general economics?

2 The possibilities for rural economics today

Currently, the field of rural economics presents a double attraction for the wider discipline. On the one hand, it offers a vantage-point on some of the important economic problems of the day. On the other, it constitutes a field for testing the various approaches of the discipline. Let us examine each of these in turn.

(a) The characteristics of agricultural production – satisfying basic needs, utilising space, and generating diverse organisations and regulations – make it a highly important observation ground for elaborating *problématiques* on questions whose scope extends far beyond agriculture itself. Here are some examples.

The evolution of agricultural production – or in the most general sense, the elasticity of supply – remains a fundamental focus of study, not only in terms of the satisfaction of needs, which is increasingly less well achieved in numerous countries, but also in terms of the regulation of production and the costs of supporting surplus-producing countries. It constitutes a major factor in the relationships between states and in the world equilibrium. It invites the study of interactions, still not fully understood, between agricultural production, its determinants and its distribution; most obviously, of the effects of prices and of incomes; but also technical progress and the economic and social conditions of production and exchange. All of these preoccupations can give rise to a variety of approaches with regard to the elasticity of supply, comparative performance, exchange or development processes.

Agricultural production, as a user of space, contributes to the forms of populating the land and establishes diverse relationships with neighbouring activities. It is an important component of spatial planning. In addition, agriculture, probably more so than other activities, contributes to the use and production of natural resources. Whether one fears their exhaustion and degradation or is interested in the conditions and economic consequences of the progress in genetics, rural economics offers a fine opportunity for studying the relations between society and nature; what are the effective methods for managing and appropriating these resources?

The entry of food production into exchange systems has given rise to a multiplicity of organisations (private, semi-public or public) intervening in different ways and with diverse objectives in the functioning of rural economies. Through their analysis, one learns of the forms of interaction between different levels of decision-making, relating to their establishment, their activities and their effectiveness. The study of these institutions, and comparison with those in other sectors, furthers the analysis of economic organisation.

These several fields of interest concern a diverse assembly of social and geographical elements. They can invoke non-agricultural sectors but, as far as agriculture and the countryside are concerned, they assume a special sharpness which could mobilise the potential of rural economists.

(b) As a challenging observation ground, rural economics also provides occasions for testing concepts, and themes general to political economy. This testing permits one to determine the conditions and limits of their validity, or to propose possible alternatives better suited to the agricultural or rural context, but also, sometimes, to other contexts. Such proposals can thereby attain a more general significance and thus insert rural economic research into the theoretical mainstream of the discipline. Several examples, taken from contemporary scientific work, illustrate the possible fertility of rural economics in this regard.

Comparison between farms and other types of individual enterprise has revealed that economic concentration is not as generalised a phenomenon as it is often considered to be, and usually for similar reasons as prevail in agriculture. Likewise, the approach to food chains, based upon the affinities of structures identified by the study of actors and their relations, begun in rural economics, has been applied elsewhere, most recently, in industrial economics. One also notes the participation of rural economists, jointly with others, particularly development economists, in the debate between Marxists on the notion of a social formation: whether defined as the domination of one mode of production or the articulation of different modes.

On an even more general level, rural economics has made a positive contribution to debates concerning the very nature of political economy which have taken on a certain vigour in France over the last few years. After Polanyi, Godelier and others, one might summarise the central division between a formalist and a substantive definition of economics. Under the first of these, economics is the science of scarce resource allocation amongst competing needs. Thus the stress is placed on the generality and the rigour of the approach;

explanation is derived from a relatively small number of economic factors; and the independence of economics of other social sciences is emphasised. Thus, even without necessarily seeking it, a normative discourse can be achieved. Under the second, economics is the study of social relations or 'social organisation' formed by the mobilization of resources and the distribution of products. Thus the aim of economics becomes the rational explanation of social functioning in both time and space. The field of economics is thereby more complicated and encompassing than under the formalist interpretation. Economics is a social science and communication with other social sciences must be the norm (with all the problems that this entails). Such a classical debate as this is obviously not specific to rural economics but it is very much in evidence there for the various reasons highlighted above.

One could multiply such examples of the contribution and role of rural economists in wider scientific debates with political economy, but now it is surely time to try and draw several lessons from what has already been said. First, one notes interest in the need for the economic analysis of the food production process, and indeed the rural sector as a whole, from a strictly scientific viewpoint, independent of the statistical, social and emotional importance of these sectors.

Such an interest is confirmed when one compares the research conducted in other branches of political economy, or related to other sectors of society. Until very recently, communication between sub-disciplines has been poor. The recruitment processes of rural economists, the institutional compartmentalisation, the development of research methods specific to each specialist research area, have all contributed to the weakness of such cross-communication though they have not, for all that, created permanent barriers. On the contrary, large areas of mutually beneficial exchange do exist, even if they are insufficiently pursued. It appears to us, in any case, that there *is* a wider opportunity for the development of rural economics beyond any specific institutional imperatives. The potentialities are sufficiently accessible and diverse (and risky to some eyes) as to offer a challenging prospect to rural economists and their institutions in years to come.

Bibliography

Badouin, R., *Economie Rurale*, A. Colin, 1971.
Bergmann, D.R., 'Essai sur les principes directeurs d'une politique agricole française', *Economie Rurale*, N°. 34, October 1957.
Blanc, M., *Les paysanneries françaises*, Paris, J.P. Delarge, coll. Citoyens, 1977.
Boussard, J.M., *Economie de l'agriculture*, Paris, Economica, 1986.
Bye, P., Collombel, B., Schaller, B. *Inventaire des recherches sur les industries agricoles et alimentaires du département* ESR, 1973-83, INRA, Paris, 1985.
Dumont, R., *Voyage en France d'un agronome*, M.T. Genin, Paris, 1956.
Economie Rurale, 79-80 - 20 'ans d'agriculture française', 1969.
Economie Rurale, 160, March-April 1984, 'L'état de l'Economie Rurale en France':
Coujard, J.L., 'L'économie rurale: quelle(s) spécificité(s)'.
Cavailhes, J., 'Bilan de 15 ans de leadership marxiste'.
Bartoli, P., 'Sur le fonctionnement de la référence marxiste'.

Combris, P., Nefusi, M., 'Le concept d'agro-alimentaire: intérêt et limites'.
Bergmann, D.R., 'L'économie rurale en France. Essai de synthèse de la session et du bilan'.
Gervais, M., Jollivet, M. et Tavernier, Y., *La fin de la France paysanne, de 1914 à nos jours*. T. IV – de l'Histoire de la France rural, sous la direction de Duby-wallon, Paris, Seuil, 1976.
Grossman, J., *Agriculture et économie politique. Examen de quelques textes représentatifs de principales tendances de l'économie rurale française contemporaine*, September 1980, INRA-ESR, Paris, 124 pp.
In INRA – *Systèmes de production et transformations de l'agriculture*. T.1 – Essai de bilan des travaux du département d'économie et sociologie rurales, 1985:
- Mathal, P., 'Aperçu rétrospectif sur la place des systèmes de production dans quelques recherches du département'.
- Perraud, D., 'Crise agricole et crise des systèmes de production'.
- Viallon, J.B., 'Sources et méthodes utilisées'.
- Lifran, R., 'Les systèmes de production et la division sociale du travail'.
- Aubert, D., 'Politique agricole et systèmes de production'.
- Viallon, J.B., 'Le débat sur le "productivisme et l'intensification" '.
- Lifran, R., 'Le débat sur la diversité'.
- Lifran, R., Perraud, D., 'Transformation des systèmes de production et transformations sociales de l'agriculture'.
Johnson, G. *Scope of agricultural economics. Agriculture in a turbulent world economy*. Actes du 19ème Congrès de l'Association Internationale des Economistes Ruraux, Malaga, 26 August–4 September 1985.
Klatzmann, J. *Les politiques agricoles, Idées et fausses illusions*. Paris, PUF, 1972.
Lacombe, P., 'Structure of agriculture: implications for research and policy. Agriculture in a turbulent world economy', *Actes du 19ème Congrès de l'Association Internationale des Economistes Ruraux*, Malaga, 26 August–4 September 1985.
Lifran, R. *Mythes scientifiques sur la terre et les paysans*, INRA, Montpellier, 1981.
Malassis, L., 'Economie agricole, agro-alimentaire et rurale', *Economie Rurale*, n° 131, mai-juin 1979.
Mendras, H., 'L'avenir des campagnes en Europe occidentale', *Futuribles*, 1977.
Milhaud, J., Montagne, R. *L'Agriculture, aujourd'hui et demain*, Paris, PUF, 1961.
O.C.D.E. *Agriculture et croissance économique. Rapport d'un groupe d'experts*, 1985.
Petit, M., 'Is there a French school of Agricultural Economics', *Journal of Agricultural Economics*, XXXIII-3, September 1982.
Servolin, C., 'Les politiques agricoles', *Traité de Science Politique*, Tome 4, pp. 155–260. PUF, Paris, 1985.
Tracy, M., 'Excédents et échanges, dilemnes européens', *Economie Rurale*, n° 173, May–June 1986.

12 The Development, Organisation and Orientation of Agricultural Economics in the United Kingdom

David Colman

Historical background[1]

Edith Whetham's excellent account of the development of agricultural economics in Britain between 1900 and 1940 provides numerous insights into the forces which lie behind its current state and structure.[2] She traces out the genesis of the subject and the profession in terms of two separate strands: the political economy of agriculture; and farm-management economics and the application of micro-economic theory to farming practice. Of these two it was political economy which developed first, but formal emergence of the agricultural economics profession had to wait upon the much later development of farm management studies.

As Whetham records, much of the early development of British political economy was either principally concerned with agricultural problems or related to agriculture in some way. Adam Smith's book *The Wealth of Nations* in 1776 had as its main purpose 'to demonstrate that current legislation for agriculture, trade and industry was more likely to hinder than help the desired growth of wealth' (Whetham p. 2). Malthus's celebrated 'Essay on Population' had a similar free-trade, non-interventionist thrust. Amongst other things he was concerned that special schemes for assisting the poor (in the rural areas) might encourage high birth rates amongst the landless wage-earning class, which was the most vulnerable to food shortages; thus Malthus was very much concerned with 'agricultural economy'.

One of the central issues of early political economy in Britain concerned land rents. Adam Smith, David Ricardo and John Stuart Mill all considered land rents to be a monopoly price arising from the fixity of land. These economists understood that high support prices caused high monopoly rents and land prices, and that the benefits of price support are secured by farmers as landlords, or by rentier landlords. This was a central argument used by Cobden and other in their fight to repeal the Corn Laws.

The earliest Corn Laws dating back to 1361 were primarily designed to protect the interests of consumers by preventing the export of corn, thus helping to keep prices down. Later, however, the policy was reversed and the 1670 Corn Laws lifted all prohibition on exports, and at the same time instituted an early form of minimum import price/variable levy policy to protect British agriculture from foreign competition. The degree of protection varied over time but rose sharply in 1815, after the Napoleonic Wars, from which time no imports at all were to be allowed until the price of wheat exceeded 80 shillings a quarter, 'a terrible price in the money values of that day' (Trevelyan 1922, p. 152). Because grain supplies were short this policy was highly effective and imposed a heavy cost burden upon the emergent urban working class of the early nineteenth century. Political economists and social reformers of the time seized upon these high consumer costs, plus arguments about high monopoly land rents and the benefits from free trade, to join the opposition to the Corn Laws, which were finally repealed in 1846. Echoes of this successful campaign against agricultural import tariffs can still be detected in contemporary British agricultural economists' objections to the highly protectionist nature of the Common Agricultural Policy. For, acceptance of the benefits of free trade has been a central tenet of British political economy since 1846, and has been very closely associated with my own university, and the so-called Manchester School. In agricultural policy it was not until 1968, when negotiations about joining the EEC had already begun, that the UK again introduced any import levies for grain.

Throughout the nineteenth century British academic political economy was dominated by the work of Smith, Ricardo and J.S. Mill. Because the major agricultural issues of land tenure, ownership, production and trade were well covered by this mainstream of political economy, there was no separate body of agricultural economists as such. The overall tenor of the debate was in favour of free-trade and productivist in orientation, something which is still true in contemporary British agricultural economics.

Despite the intellectual stature of these nineteenth-century economists, the teaching of political economy made slow progress in British universities and comparatively few chairs in political economy were created. It was only later following the work of Marshall, Sidgwick and Jevons, and their development of marginalist neo-classical economics that the teaching of political economy became widespread in British universities. Even in these founding neo-classical works, however, the economics of agriculture had a prominent place. In Alfred Marshall's, *Principles of Economics*, which was to be the standard economic textbook for fifty years after its publication in 1890, many chapters were devoted to agricultural economy, and among chapter headings are 'The Fertility of Land, The Tendency to Diminishing Return', 'Marginal Costs in relation to Agricultural Values', 'Land Tenure', and inevitably 'Rent of Land'. Thus the economics of agriculture was centrally embedded in the work of mainstream general political economy, and this is the source of the neo-classical intellectual roots of contemporary British agricultural economics.

Given the free-trade approach to agricultural policy in Britain in the nineteenth century, and the absence of extensive attempts by government to reshape agriculture, the emergence of a distinct agricultural economics profession had to await the emergence of developments in farm management economics. Britain lagged far behind Germany, Denmark and the USA in the collection and analysis of farm costings data. It was only in the early 1900s, when a few influential individuals travelled abroad, particularly to the USA, and returned with the conviction that 'something needed to be done', that farm management economics slowly began to develop in Britain. The first major step was the establishment of the Development Commission in 1910 with specific responsibility to promote agricultural education and research and the subsequent establishment of the Agricultural Economics Research Institute at Oxford in 1913. The other major early academic centre for the development of agricultural economics was the University College of Wales at Aberystwyth, where a lectureship in Agricultural Economics was created in 1924 and a professorship in 1929. Of course the interests of both these institutions were broader than just farm management and production economics, but that was at the centre of their early work. It was from these two institutions that most of the main personalities in agricultural economics up to the 1950s emerged. Arthur Ashby who was the first Professor of Agriculture Economics at Aberystwyth perhaps deserves an individual mention. His influence was particularly important up until he left Aberystwyth in 1946 to take the Directorship of the Institute of Agricultural Economics at Oxford, and many of the leading agricultural economists who guided developments until the late 1970s had been students under Ashby's influence.

Developments in the educational and institutional structure

Much of the current institutional structure which influences the content and orientation of British agricultural economics was created in the 1920s, as part of the same movement, and influenced by the same people who inaugurated agricultural economics at Oxford and Aberystwyth. Perhaps the most important of these developments was the setting up, by the Ministry of Agriculture in 1922, of provincial advisory centres in universities and colleges. Twelve[3] of these were established in England and Wales, one in Northern Ireland and three in Scotland, a development influenced by the success of the Land Grant College system in the USA. Although these advisory centres were at first mainly staffed by scientists whose role was to advise farmers on their technical problems, it was accepted that an agricultural economist be included in the staff at each centre. However, economic analysis and advice was not initially envisaged as the major role. The agricultural economic sections of these centres each developed a set of interests suited to their separate environments. Some concentrated on advisory work, some became quite heavily involved in teaching and some pursued interests in rural sociology and history. Even so, many of them fitted awkwardly into the environment of the universities and colleges into which they had been transplanted. Their staff were apparently viewed with suspicion by their academic colleagues because of the practical and commercial orientation of their role, and it is far from clear that they commanded the sort of widespread respect enjoyed by their counterparts in the Land Grant Colleges in the USA. In the reorganisation of the agricultural advisory service, after the Second World War, the advisory functions of the technological departments were transferred out of the English and Welsh universities and colleges[4,5] into a separate government research and extension service[6] under the Ministry of Agriculture, but agricultural economics remained within, although with a much reduced advisory function. This provided a stimulus towards closer integration with academic economics departments. This was particularly so at my own university of Manchester which, following the appointment of Professor W.J. Thomas in 1953, took a leading role in introducing econometrics and advanced economic theory into new degree programmes.

Another landmark in the development of agricultural economics and the orientation of research was the setting up of the nationwide Farm Management Survey in 1936. For this, each centre was required to collect standardised accounting data from a sample of farms in its region. These data were then used to build up a picture of farm incomes and analyses of whole farm and farm enterprise profitability and efficiency, which could be used for advisory work and for the fixing of guaranteed prices and deficiency payments for farm products under the emerging system of agricultural support introduced after the Agriculture Marketing Acts of 1931 and 1933. This material became of critical importance during the Second World War and in the application of agricultural policy following the Agriculture Act of 1947. The collection of Farm Management Survey data has continued to the present day and has been incorporated into the European Community's Farm Accounting Data Network since 1978.

The availability of such data stimulated the teaching of agricultural production economics, farm management and, to an extent, agricultural policy. However the farm accounting data gave rise to remarkably little academic research until relatively recently. In part, this was because of the unwieldiness of the data, requiring months, if not years, of manual analysis (until the advent of the computer). In part it can be attributed to insufficient theoretical and mathematical training of the average professional agricultural economist in the early years. The universities involved based their teaching firmly on neo-classical micro-economics and, although quantitative in a numerate sense, did not develop knowledge of inferential econometric methods.

This situation was to change materially during the late 1950s and 1960s, again influenced significantly by the progress of agricultural economics in the USA. A number of British agricultural graduates were finding their way to study at American universities, where they were being subjected to a more rigorous theoretical and mathematical training. Their return to Britain offered a new opportunity for the broadening as well as the deepening of teaching in agricultural economics.

Another way of tracing the development of British agricultural economics is to review briefly some aspects of the development of the Agricultural Economics Society (AES). The Society had its inaugural meeting at Oxford in 1926 and its Journal made its first appearance in 1928 as 'Proceedings of the Society'. In its early years the Society included as members a good number of prominent farmers, landowners, and economists in industry as well as academics and civil servants, and the Society provided a valuable medium for pulling together influential people (from the standpoint of agricultural policy) from all these spheres. For many years the papers presented to the Society remained accessible to this wide spectrum of membership, its papers were of broad and general interest, and the theoretical and quantitative level was not too taxing. This also changed from the 1960s. Increasingly the papers presented reflected the theoretical and econometric interests of the new academic practitioners of agricultural economics. The number of farming members has since declined, and those whose primary interest is in farm management found less to interest them in the Society's conferences. Hence in 1967 a Farm Management Association was established as a section affiliated to the British Institute of Management, with its own journal, *Farm Management*. Similarly the agricultural marketing economists have begun to focus some of their efforts recently through the Marketing Education Group of the Institute of Marketing. While both farm management and agricultural marketing economists retain their membership of the AES, there is therefore evidence of a splitting up into specialist groups. Increasingly the centre ground of agricultural economics, as represented by the papers presented to and published by the Agricultural Economics Society, and as represented by the contents of agricultural economics degrees, has increasingly been occupied by work involving micro-economics, neo-classical welfare theory, trade theory and econometrics.

The agricultural economics profession and its disciplinary basis

Those in the U.K. who consider themselves to be agricultural economists fall into one or more of the following categories:

1) They are members of the Agricultural Economics Society
2) They currently work in one of the thirteen regional agricultural economics centres in England, Wales, Scotland or Northern Ireland, or in the academic agricultural economics departments associated with the majority of these.
3) They hold posts specifically designated in agricultural economics or farm management at other university departments such as at Oxford (Queen Elizabeth House), Nottingham (Economics Department) and University College of Wales at Bangor; and also in the various colleges connected with agriculture, including Harper Adams, Seale-Hayne and Silsoe.
4) They have a degree in agricultural economics, management or marketing (more commonly a postgraduate one these days) from one of the centres identified in 2) and 3) above. In some cases they may have a comparable qualification from a foreign university, most usually one in North America. They may work as economists in the Agriculture Departments, other public institutions, industry, farming, or the banks.

The profession is thus a relatively cohesive one. That is not to say that it is a homogeneous group or that there is a unity of interests and approaches, but it does seem that there is a fairly widespread adherence to a common disciplinary base, best defined in terms of the contents of contemporary undergraduate and postgraduate degrees in agricultural economics.

As the historical details above indicate, the major influence upon the British approach to agricultural economics has been 'neo-classical' economics and the associated later developments in quantitative methods of statistical inference and econometrics. Micro-economic theory is the foundation on which all British agricultural economics degrees are based. At the undergraduate level the depth of economic theory taught depends to some extent on whether agricultural economics is taught within a general agricultural degree or within a combined degree with economics. In the latter case, there is much more scope for developing a rigorous mathematical and statistical approach to the subject, which is the necessary basis for postgraduate and professional economics research on agricultural problems.

It still remains the case that a majority of the agricultural economists occupying academic posts in the UK hold undergraduate degrees in agriculture (although many of these are from urban rather than farming backgrounds). Indeed this appears to be the most natural route into the profession, with students gravitating towards economics-related issues while in the process of coming to terms with the technical, but more particularly the social and political problems of agriculture. In particular, students develop keen interests in the economics of agricultural policy and Third World development. To succeed, however, these aspiring economists of agriculture have to have an aptitude for abstract and quantitative analysis in order to be able to communicate to general economists and statisticians and to select the appropriate tools of analysis to apply to the agricultural sector. As the focus of agricultural economics has progressively expanded beyond the farm-gate, so its practitioners have increasingly to absorb a knowledge of general economic theory and method.

Thus it is hardly surprising that an increasing number of contemporary agricultural economists have no background whatsoever in agriculture and that their point of departure was a first degree in economics. Given the extent to which general micro-economics still draws examples from agriculture, the teaching of agricultural economics can fill a valuable place in an economics degree, illustrating in a straightforward way how economic theory may be applied. This applied aspect attracts many economics students to futher study, and, with their natural aptitudes for abstract and quantitative analysis, these entrants to the profession contribute much of the most elegant and advanced research. This is a vital role which maintains and refreshes the academic standing of the profession in the eyes of colleagues in related disciplines.

One of the clearest indicators of the methodological approach of British agricultural economists is revealed in the main textbooks which have been written in recent years, since these form the main teaching aids for students. Among the most important of these are a) *The Costs of the Common Agricultural Policy* by Buckwell et al., b) *Agriculture and Economic Development* by Ghatak and Ingersent; c) *An Economic Analysis of Agriculture* by Hill and Ingersent; d) *Agricultural Economics: Principles and Policy* by Ritson; e) *The Demand for Food*, edited by Thomas and f) *An Introduction to the Principles of Agricultural Economics* by Tuck. Any reviewer of this body of core texts (plus supporting ones) could not fail to notice both the use of micro-economic theory to provide the central analysis, and the liberal reference to econometric results to support the theoretical arguments. True, the commentary around the analysis is often accompanied by reservations of a pragmatic or sceptical nature, but the reviewer would have difficulty in finding any major alternative philosophical influences than those already referred to.

In order to avoid giving the impression that there is no room for anything other than micro-economics, welfare economics and econometrics in British agricultural economics, some corrective remarks are needed. First, it must be emphasised that there are agricultural economists concerned with the environment, rural development and Third World agriculture who bring a whole range of perspectives, including Marxism into their teaching. They do not constitute a coherent or major alternative school to that of neo-classical economics (such as Michel Petit (1982) indicates exists in France), but they complement it and give breadth to the profession. Likewise there are marketing and farm management economists (in comparatively small numbers) whose teaching covers much important institutional detail and whose empirical methods seldom require quadratic programming or maximum likelihood analysis applied to non-linear simultaneous systems. They make an essential contribution to the vocational training of professional agricultural economists to perform well-defined types of jobs, and they provide a crucial contribution in demonstrating the immediate practical relevance of our discipline. The steps made in the practical sub-disciplines of marketing and farm management have very much depended upon the advances the profession has made in applying new theoretical and quantitative analytical methods to basic problems relating to agriculture.

Because there appears to be a degree of misunderstanding among non-economists about neo-classical economics, it is perhaps necessary to add a brief rider to explain that employing it does not necessarily require the practitioner to adopt an ahistorical approach or one which ignores institutional factors. It is not a totally rigid, unyielding system of analysis. True, its micro-economic foundations rest upon assumptions that firms maximise expected profits and that households act to maximise their expected utility. These lead to propositions about the way in which consumer expenditure patterns adapt to changes in prices and incomes, trade patterns respond to price and exchange rate changes, and about how product supply and input demand react to economic factors. Above all it is a system for explaining the interrelationships between price formation and the allocation of goods and services. Empirical applications of the theory and its propositions do not require that all firms and consumers maximise profits and utility respectively. At the economy-wide, regional or market level it is no problem that some economic actors adopt behaviour motivated by different objectives, if, as has been very extensively observed, general (total or average) behaviour at market level conforms well to the patterns suggested by the theory. Propositions derived from micro-economic theory – for example, about the impact of price changes upon product supply, demand, substitution of factors of production and consumer expenditure – have been found to be robust tools for explaining actual market behaviour. They may not explain the actions of each individual or firm but at the aggregate level they have repeatedly proved their worth.

Other contributors to the economics of agriculture

True to the picture outlined above, that agriculture has featured centrally in neo-classical economics generally, there are economists who would not wish to be identified with the agricultural economics profession who have continued to make important contributions to current debates. Indeed there are those who are highly critical of agricultural economists, on the grounds that their interests are too closely aligned to those of the Ministry of Agriculture; this they see as stemming from the fact that most academic agricultural economists work in departments associated with regional centres funded by the Ministry and that it is from the Ministry or the Department of Agriculture for Scotland or Northern Ireland that they receive a significant proportion of their research funds and postgraduate scholarships. Graham Hallet (1968 and 1981) has most forcibly expressed this view in public when he states (p.ix) "Agricultural economics", in the UK and some other countries, is a specialised field, organisationally separate from "economics" – a separation which has not, perhaps, raised the intellectual calibre of "agricultural economics" or increased the knowledgeability of economists' forays into agricultural matters'. While this charge may have once had some substance, it has very little force now, after the impact of the postgraduate degree courses introduced during the 1960s and the recruitment at that time of many North American trained agricultural economists; rather it reflects, in my view, Hallett's own insulation from events. Nevertheless, there are other mainstream economists who may well incline towards Hallett's view, and among these are possibly John Bowers and Paul Cheshire who authored among many other things a book entitled *Agriculture, the Countryside, and Land use: An Economic Critique (1983)*. Certainly they and other economists such as Morris at the Institute of Fiscal Studies and Wyn Godley and colleagues at the Cambridge Institute of Applied Economics have entered with gusto into the economic debate about the Common Agricultural Policy of the EEC. In that, they have been joined by others, such as Conservative MP Sir Richard Body, who has written two fierce polemics against the CAP (Body 1982 and 1984).

Changing emphasis in research

As an applied discipline, research in agricultural economics is continually adjusting to changes in the dominant issues. In the early days of the 1920s and 1930s the emphasis was very much on farm management because of the perceived need to adopt a more scientific approach to the choice of enterprises and the use of resources. There was also a good deal of attention spent on the collection of market price data and on interpretation of changes in market conditions. Institutional developments have greatly reduced the role of academic research in these areas: the Ministry's Agricultural Development and Advisory Service became a major force for improving standards of farm management, but in turn some of its role has been officially declared unnecessary as commercial supply firms have increasingly backed up their marketing with sophisticated management advice; and the impressive development of a national farming press has provided farmers with extensive information and analysis of market conditions, prices and new technological developments, making unnecessary the sort of extensive market and policy reviews which used to be published annually by the Institute of Agricultural Economics at Oxford.[7]

Major changes took place in the orientation of agricultural economics research in the late 1950s facilitated and encouraged by the development and spread of large-scale computing facilities. In 1956 G.T. Jones at Oxford was commissioned by the USDA to build a complete econometric model of UK agriculture. This was followed in the late 1960s and 1970s by a number of important studies among which one might instance Cowling, Metcalf and Rayner's (1970) study of agricultural input markets, and the set of studies of food demand edited by Thomas (1972). At the same time other agricultural economists were making use of increasingly sophisticated mathematical programming techniques, and there was a steady flow of publications starting in 1956 (Mackenzie and Godsell);[8] in 1964 Throsby published an important work on dynamic programming; for several years starting from 1970 work continued at Newcastle University on a multi-regional linear programming model of UK agriculture; and there were other noteworthy advances in programming research (e.g. McInerney (1967)).

Into the middle of all this experimentation with new quantitative techniques, was injected a powerful new concern with the quantitative analysis of economic policy (Josling 1969). This has led to an increasing volume of research during the period running from UK accession to the EEC in 1973 to the heated policy debates surrounding the current crisis of the Common Agricultural Policy. There is now so much research of this genre that it is perhaps invidious to single out examples, but the best known is the book *The Costs of the Common Agricultural Policy* by Buckwell et. al. (1982). The approach adopted in this type of research epitomises the role which agricultural economists can and should play in contemporary debates. Their role is to employ the tools of economic theory and econometrics as efficiently as possible to state what the economics discipline (employed in as scientific a mode as possible) can reveal about the costs and benefits of changes in policy. It is only one of several viewpoints, that is for sure, but market forces are remarkably powerful, and it is of considerable importance to point out the consequences of fighting against them and using policy to try and turn or deflect the tide.

With the emergent budgetary and overproduction crises in the EEC in recent years, and their attendant problems, the research agenda in agricultural economics has changed. For several years now there has been a steady expansion of work related to rural employment, environmental conservation, and alternative land uses. There has always been an investment in such work. Professor Gerald Wibberley at Wye College had a particularly notable influence in the study of land and environmental economics; his appointment to a joint professorship at Wye and University Colleges of London University promoted the spread of an interdisciplinary approach to these problems, and the Countryside Unit at Wye which is a legacy of his approach is an important source of contributions to the current debates on land use and rural development. Martin Whitby at Newcastle University with a succession of colleagues has also kept up a constant output of research on rural employment, recreation and rural amenity, and individual agricultural economists in other institutions have continued to make sporadic contributions. But in the last few years it is apparent from research proposals submitted for funding, that agricultural economists in all the academic centres are expressing an interest in 'environmental' issues. Quite a number of studies are currently under way, aginst the background of a possible decline in agriculture, on the links between agriculture and rural employment in other industries and service sectors, and between agriculture and industrial activity at the national level. There is also a major resurgence in research on the economics of forestry as the prospect looms of widespread afforestation on land released from agriculture. Likewise there is a good deal of work taking place on the economics of the new policies, such a Management Agreements, which have emerged for encouraging conservation management by farmers.

For many years the central focus of policy orientated agricultural economics research was to warn against the dangers of excessive price support and overprotection of agriculture. Now that those dangers have become apparent to all, the research agenda has changed to how best to manage the adjustment from high price support to more market-orientated policies, and of how to accommodate positive policies for managing the rural environment and conservation without running into the pitfalls of ever-expanding budgetary cost which have resulted from the EEC's over-commitment to product price support.

While disagreeing strongly with Hallett's condemnation of the intellectual level of contemporary agricultural economics, it is possible to accept that there has been a degree of insularity from some other disciplines. While agricultural economists have always worked closely with agricultural scientists and for the last twenty to twenty-five years with economists, the instances of close linkages with rural sociologists, geographers and ecologists have been confined largely to a few institutions (already referred to) and a handful of individuals. Given the pressures now facing agriculture in Western Europe, it is obvious that much more interdisciplinary research collaboration is needed to achieve the right balance of aims in countryside development. This poses a considerable challenge, since experience suggests that many academics are too fiercely independent to operate comfortably in an interdisciplinary framework. Nevertheless, the very changes which have recently occurred in the agenda of agricultural economics research are indicative of a more open-minded approach, which augurs well for more multidisciplinary collaboration.

Notes

1 The author wishes to thank Professor W.J. Thomas for his valuable comments and his advice over some of the historical details. All errors of omission (particularly) and commission are entirely due to the author.
2 This section draws very heavily upon Whetham's monograph published in 1981.
3 As Giles (1987) records the first three of these were set up in 1923 [at Cambridge University, at Reading (then a college of London University) and Wye College], with the appointment of Provincial Agricultural Economists. By 1926 nine other centres had been similarly created at the universities of Bristol, Leeds, Manchester, Newcastle and Oxford, at Aberystwyth (University College of Wales) and at Harper Adams, Seale Hayne and Sutton Bonnington agricultural colleges.
4 The three Scottish Colleges and Queens University Belfast have retained the advisory role to the present day.
5 In a series of steps, related to reorganising the national Farm Management Survey (see text below) the number of centres in England and Wales has now been reduced to nine. These are at the universities of Aberystwyth, Cambridge, Exeter, Manchester, Newcastle, Nottingham, Reading, Wye College (London University), and at Askham Bryan College of Agriculture and Horticulture.
6 This service is now called ADAS – the Agricultural Development and Advisory Service.
7 The Institute published a series of reviews of the state of agricultural markets and

changes in agricultural policy starting with the Agricultural Register in 1933-34 and culminating with Economic Changes in British Agriculture, 1959-64.

8 A survey of all the early programming studies was published by John Nix in 1969.

Bibliography

Bacon, R. W. Godley and A. McFarquhar, 'The Direct Cost to Britain of Belonging to the EEC', Chapter 5 in *Cambridge Economic Policy Review*, 4, Gower Press, 1979.

Body, R., *Agriculture: The Triumph and the Shame*, Temple Smith, 1982.

Body, R., *Farming in the Clouds*, Temple Smith, 1984.

Bowers, J.K. and P. Cheshire, *Agriculture, the Countryside and Land Use: An Economic Critique*, Methuen, 1983.

Buckwell, A.E. D.R. Harvey, K.J. Thomson and K.A. Parton, *The Costs of the Common Agricultural Policy*, Croom Helm, 1982.

Cowling, K. D. Metcalfe and A.J. Rayner, *Resource Structure of Agriculture*, Pergamon, 1970.

Ghatak, S. and K. Ingersent, *Agriculture and Economic Development*, Wheatsheaf Books, 1984.

Giles, A.K., 'The A.E.S.: A Commentary on its Past, Present and Future', *J. Agric. Econ.*, XXVII (3), 1976.

Giles, A.K., 'No Fixed Address – Presidential Address', *J. Agric. Econ.*, XXXVIII, 1987.

Hallett, G., *The Economics of Agricultural Policy*, Basil Blackwell, 1968 (First Edn.) 1981, (Second Edn.).

Hill B.E. and K.A. Ingersent, *An Economic Analysis of Agriculture*, Heinemann 1977.

Josling, T. 'A Formal Approach to Agricultural Policy', *J. Agric. Econ.*, 20(2), 1969.

Mackenzie H.C. and T.E. Godsell, 'Linear Programming and the Cost of Pig Fattening Rations', *J. Agric. Econ.*, 11(4), 1956.

Marshall, A., *Principles of Economics*, (8th Edition), Macmillan, 1946.

McInerney, J.P., 'Maximum Programming – An Approach to Farm Planning Under Uncertainty', *J. Agric. Econ.*, 18(3), 1967.

Morris, C.N., 'The Common Agricultural Policy', *Fiscal Studies* 1(2), pp. 17-35, 1980.

Nix, J.S., 'Annotated Bibliography on Farm Planning and Programming Techniques', *Farm Management*, 1(7), 1969.

Petit, M., 'Is there a French School of Agricultural Economics', *J. Agric. Econ.* XXXIII (3), 325-338, 1982.

Ritson, C., *Agricultural Economics: Principles and Policy*, Granada, 1977.

Thomas, W.J., (ed.), *The Demand for Food*, Manchester University Press, 1972.

Throsby, C.D., 'Some Dynamic Models for Farm Management Research', *J. Agric. Econ.* 16(1), 1964.

Trevelyan, G.M., *British History in the Nineteenth Century*, Longmans Green, 1922, p. 152.

Tuck, R.H., *An Introduction to the Principles of Agricultural Economics*, Longman, 1961.

Whetham, Edith, H., *Agricultural Economics in Britain 1900-1940*, Monograph of the Institute of Agricultural Economics, University of Oxford, 1981.

Part V: Anthropology

13 Commentary and Introduction

Maryon McDonald

We are accustomed to translational problems between France and Britain. It has taken some time to realise, however, that the translational difficulties are not mere technicalities. Take the example of the Common Agricultural Policy: 'agriculture', we now realise, is not *l'agriculture*. It is not that there is a better translation available by simply hunting through dictionaries and finding a better word, and we know that the two concepts cannot, in the realms of policy, be easily matched up in all-night sessions re-jigging texts, or by a series of technical measures. Rather, agriculture and *l'agriculture* each find their meanings within their own cultural systems, and the rustic in clogs on the one hand, the farmer photographed for *Country Life* on the other, the *agneau* of scarcity value, and the lamb chops of everyday fare, are but a few features of the differences and difficulties involved.

Similarly, 'rural' is not *rural*. This is so in virtually every domain, the political, economic and demographic differences being the most obvious. I shall come back to these differences in a moment. Farmers in Britain are not inclined to tip rural dirt into urban streets as a means of protest. The rural and the urban, and the distance and difference between them, do not match up on the two sides of the Channel, and the transgression of the urban by the rural, which has been so effective in France, cannot have the same force in an industrial nation such as Britain where the urban proletariat tipping itself into the countryside at weekends is likely to raise greater alarm.

These points are important. We have, in Britain taken a good deal from French anthropology (especially in the late 1960s and 1970s). Such ready borrowing should not mislead us into imagining anthropology and its preoccupations, or objects of study, to be the same on the two sides of *La Manche*. As Cohen (Chapter 15) remarks of British anthropologists: 'we know painfully little about social life in the British Isles... and, unlike our French colleagues, have been dismissive or afraid of introspection'. Internal studies can appear to the British to be an oddly embarrassing pastime of self-reflection, if not self-obsession.

It is important to understand here that, beyond anthropology, in social and political life more generally, Britain has not required introspection in the same way; the self-definition of France and the French has been more problematic than has the self-definition of Britain. What can feel to the British like introspection, self-inspection, parochialism (Cohen's 'trap of Britainology') or simple xenophobia, is closer, in France, to a tradition of necessary self-consciousness. A good deal of political reflection in France has been concerned with the very existence of the French nation, and its history is one of insecurity and constitutional volatility in comparison with that of Great Britain. Over the last two hundred years, France has had to define its way through four occupations by foreign forces, and, combining with the impulsion of this external interference, an internal self-consciousness has been fired through two monarchies, one consulate, two empires, five republics, one definitive revolution, the Paris Commune, the Vichy regime, and May 1968. Through this succession of external threat and internal upheaval, France and the Jacobin State gave to the world a model of directive centralisation, and France has developed a strong tradition of preoccupation of the nation with itself.

Certain demographic and economic differences tie in with and confirm the political differences between the two contexts of France and Britain. While modern France was being born in the political upheaval of revolution, England was pioneering its own way through what came to be known as the Industrial Revolution. From the mid-eighteenth century onwards, and with increasing momentum, employment was generated in the new manufacturing towns, and the distribution of the population between country and town changed dramatically. By the end of the eighteenth century, the rural smallholder had declined or disappeared, and the self-sufficient peasant was largely a thing of the past.

France came to industrialise later and more slowly, and, in general, did not know any great move away from agriculture until after the Second World War. It is only in this relatively recent period that France has become conscious of the dwindling of its peasantry generally, and begun to take a significant ethnographic interest in it, as a demographic and occupational reality no longer rendered banal by its very omnipresence. It is no accident that this burst of concentrated interest in the revalued 'rural' and the revalued 'peasant' coincided with a demographically informed sense of their imminent demise.

When we turn away from France to Britain, it is striking how British anthropologists lack comparable enthusiasm for the study of their own society – a society which they are very conscious of as being part of the category of 'industrialised and technologically advanced societies' which Cohen uses here. An anthropology of Britain concentrated itself for a while, predictably enough, in its peripheral areas – but British anthropology has generally found its 'other' elsewhere, in the ready terrains of an Empire which France was not able to match. As Cohen comments 'we' and 'they' in British anthropology have traditionally spanned imperial distances.

The context and manner in which the rural world was discovered, therefore, differed between France and Britain, especially in relation to anthropology. In cultural translation between these two contexts, 'rural' does not easily translate *rural*. One more important element which we need to feed into the complexities of translation is what we know generally under the rubric of romanticism. Much of what anthropology has studied involved, in one way or another, the constructs of romanticism. In France, romanticism was shorter-lived and less influential than in Britain. While a literary Britain was able to celebrate rustic naturality, France was undergoing the Revolution and wars of Napoleon, and throughout the nineteenth century the rural world appeared predominantly as the recalcitrant and unwashed in need of schooling. Moreover, while Britain was able to conjure up and celebrate the Celtic peripheries, there was no comfortable political space in France that a minority could occupy, and the celebration of regional minorities came only with the demographic changes and new political oppositions of the 1960s.

Whenever nineteenth-century, centralised France discovered its own internal variety, the construction of the nation was paramount, and curiosities of 'popular traditions' were noted in an inventory of all that was being lost on the proper path to progress and national unity. It was in museums in France that ethnology or anthropology was institutionalised, and French anthropology was the heir to folklore. British anthropology, on the other hand, found its way into the universities, and was the heir to classics, law, natural science and Empire. French anthropology was inevitably born as rural anthropology, although unselfconsciously so, and that rural world was, similarly, the study of the 'popular' and the 'traditional'.

Some of the topics which have dominated modern French anthropology appear to be very much those of traditional anthropological competence, but with the French pursuing at home what the British generally pursued abroad: 'tradition', oral literature, sorcery, and kinship and inheritance are among the topics noted particularly by the French anthropologists in this volume. The importance of the last two – kinship and inheritance – can be appreciated in a country predominantly rural, landed and *paysan* in a way that France, in self-image, so often still is. Lévi-Strauss's alliance theory both fed off and fed back into this backdrop of preoccupation. In Britain, as Cohen notes, kinship has been closely linked with, if not subordinate to, concepts of class.

Given the different political, demographic, ecomomic and literary backgrounds of the two countries, it is not, I think, surprising that modern British anthropology, when working at home at all, should focus on 'remote areas' or urban ethnicity (Ardener 1987) or on the urban working class. Cohen echoes the sentiments of other British anthropologists in envying France its burgeoning, modern ethnographic literature about itself, not least the concentrated literature on Brittany. It is worth noting here that that clerical and politically troublesome area, with its Breton language, appearing continually to threaten the self-definition of the French republic, and with its overwhelmingly rural population and economy trailing behind changes elsewhere in France, has been an obvious and compelling site for modern French internal ethnography (see McDonald 1987). Eighteenth or nineteenth-century Britain could offer sites similar in some respects, but some of the fascination has worn itself out. French anthropology (see Lenclud, below) is aware that its interest in the national territory is unevenly spread: there has been more interest in the south of France than in the north, more interest in the deepest far west than in the industrial east, and more interest in small-scale agriculture or extensive stock-rearing than in large-scale, intensified agricultural production. All these foci of interest, on which attention has been concentrated, share a common appeal and metaphors of difference within modern

French consciousness. For modern British anthropology, their nearest structural equivalents, if present in Britain, have been found not in remote *rural* areas but in the urban streets and factories.

Both the British and French anthropological contributions to this volume suggest an awareness that the 'rural' world, once taken for granted (especially in the French case), is changing and that the concept needs to be 'problematised'. French research pursuing local units of study within the rural world (such as village and commune) has suffered much the same fate as 'community studies' in Britain, and the search has been not for units of study, but for units of identity or, to use Cohen's phrase, of 'belonging'. There seems to be a shared awareness that the urban/rural divide can no longer be taken as unproblematic, and certainly not as any delineation of different types of study. This point has become especially obvious in France, where the *ville/campagne* dichotomy has in any case been muddled in recent decades by both the 'rural exodus' and back-to-the-countryside enthusiasms. The 'rural' is certainly not a distinct domain, and neither the British nor French contributors seem keen to construct any kind of 'rural anthropology' in the way in which some, more naively, have tried to construct a distinct 'urban anthropology'. It is a relief to hear that the tired debates of 'urban anthropology' are not to be replicated for some reified 'rural' world. Both the French and the British seem keen, instead, to move towards an ethnography of the 'rural' and of all that goes with it, 'urban' included.

References

Ardener, E., ' "Remote areas": some theoretical considerations' in A. Jackson (ed.), *Anthropology at Home*, London and New York, Tavistock, 1987.

McDonald, M., 'The politics of fieldwork in Brittany' in A. Jackson (ed.), *Anthropology at Home*, London and New York, Tavistock, 1987.

14 Rural Ethnology in France

Martine Ségalen, Gérard Lenclud and Georges Augustins

From rurality to locality: 50 years of the ethnology of France *by Martine Ségalen*

For several decades ethnology in France has focused its attention specifically upon the rural milieu. Yet ethnologists have not been responsible for the major syntheses of the French rural world, published since the late 1960s, such as *La fin des paysans* (1967) by the rural sociologist Henri Mendras, the multi-authored *Histoire de la France rurale* (1975-1976) or Weber's *Peasants into Frenchmen* (1976). This chapter seeks to explain the apparent lacuna while reviewing briefly the development of ethnology in France. The following chapter by Lenclud addresses the issue from the perspective of the epistemological status of ethnological studies of rural France and their relationship to the wider enterprise of social anthropology.

Ethnology as a discipline does not possess a particular spatial focus, but rather defines its study area in terms of the existence of cultural areas. Its overall intention is not therefore to cut cross-sections through space. This distinguishes ethnology from rural sociology, as does the latter's objective of constructing models capable of producing frameworks for action and prediction.

Historically, ethnology has developed by heavily specialising in cultural space; its vision is totalising, its approach comparative. Its goal has been to analyse and to understand the diversity of French societies and cultures. Such a broad programme has ultimately coincided, for a range of reasons, with the study of the rural world. If today, ethnology leans less towards rural society than before, the research work and debate carried out by ethnologists since the 1940s have, simultaneously, permitted both a better understanding of social phenomena in the rural world and led to the development of an ethnology of France, whose work can stand on an equal footing to that of its mother discipline, social anthropology. Thus, we shall now turn to look at the conditions under which ethnology developed in France and examine the major themes that have held its attention over the last fifty years.

The birth of folklore and of museology

The ethnology of France is first and foremost an ethnology of rural and agricultural France: in short, the France of the peasant village (though, as shall be seen below, these terms do not always have identical meanings within the various fields of research). Before coming to rediscover the research influence of its mother discipline, social anthropology, a discipline oriented chiefly towards the understanding of non-European cultures, ethnology was initially born out of a double union between folklore and museology, though later it gently parted company from them. These two vocations took as their subject matter 'traditional' and 'pre-industrial' society or, in other words, the rural world; industrial society and the town were excluded as being beyond the field of interest.

At the time of its foundation in 1937, the *Musée national des arts et traditions populaires* sought to promote both the understanding of the rural and pre-industrial world and the reassessment of the cultural and artistic endeavours of the 'common people' (Cusenier and Ségalen, 1986; Chiva, 1987). Working along the lines of the major collections of folk songs and folk tales undertaken by the folklorists, the *Musée* was specifically interested in the material culture of French rural society. Under this interpretation, the 'common people' were identified as those human groups in which knowledge was transmitted orally without being written down, where 'tradition' reigned; the idea being that the culture of these groups, identified through its technology and its general knowledge, advanced only very slowly, incorporating innovation, but avoiding major breaks and divisions, protected from external influences of all sorts. The 'common people' were, above all, the 'peasants' and it is peasant artefacts which have been chiefly studied. The Vichy years saw the questionable ascendancy of moral values associated with the peasantry. Studies were initiated, and then developed after the war, whose objectives were the collection of the facts and 'elements' of rural civilisation. From this period date the major surveys of rural architecture and rural furniture which owed much to collaboration with geography (a collaboration which has since considerably diminished). At the same time, the *Musée* set itself the objective of establishing archives of French rural society.

This rather specific vision of the rural world was nonetheless coherent. It presented a somewhat mythified image of a traditional society which, though facing extinction, provided succour for a national society worried about the growth of its working class and whose bourgeoisie needed to adapt in order to safeguard its material and symbolic social position. The net result can be seen in the fascinating showcases of the *Musée* which illustrate the multivarious cultural aspects and techniques of traditional rural society. Stress has been placed upon technological matters, the sequences and processes of production. The showcases present a society without conflict, without hierarchies, without relations with the town, without commerce or industry in its fields. The work of Menon and Lecotté, published in 1945, proposed a similarly idealised vision of a world, in equilibrium and self-sufficient, closed in upon itself. Their work describes 'the instinctive or learnt gestures of love, of work and of faith: family joys, communal activities, work in the field, workshops, fêtes, agrarian ceremonies, the origins of which have vanished into the mists of time' (p. 196).

In search of the 'village'

Alongside this task of establishing permanent collections, and yet often closely linked to it, there developed research in areas identified first by the teachings of Marcel Mauss before the war and Marcel Maget following it. Ethnological thought thereby turned towards the nature of the village community where André Leroi-Gourhan had stressed the necessity of emphasising the interactions between the elements of a 'society'. This new research direction was equally influenced by the American cultural school, particularly the research work of Robert Redfield on 'community as a whole'; a theme drawn upon as much by rural sociologists as by ethnologists of peasant society.

The confluence with social anthropology, which took place during the 1950s, also helped to bring ethnologists into the rural milieu, for it was in rural societies that ethnologists sought to reproduce research conditions and approaches learned from the experiences gained working in non-European countries. It was thus in the village that they sought an enclosed totality, and attempted to describe it by the expedient of the, so-called, 'intensive' monograph. This form represented a notable conceptual advance from the large-scale and extensive studies undertaken before and immediately after the war (for example, the *Atlas Folklorique* which mapped types of agriculture, agricultural implements and so on), which were not specifically interested in the situational context of the various facts observed.

Marcel Maget wrote in 1955:

> The village is ideally suited for the monographic study. It doesn't have such a size that it reaches beyond the comprehension of a single researcher who, even if specialising in one facet, can retain an individualised general view of the entire community. The limited cultural differentiation permits one to grasp the entirety of meanings having a collective value (p. 380).

The commune offers two convenient illusions: first, of an enclosed unit whose totality can be sufficiently grasped; and, secondly, of a social space structured by finite relations based upon family, residence, work and power. By an implicit hypothesis, the commune is seen as the minimal social unit of shared internal knowledge and inter-relations; its size appears sufficiently small to ensure that a researcher will be able to identify the various economic, social and cultural dimensions necessary to maintain cohesion.

Although there might initially appear to be an abundance of community monographs, these are, nonetheless, not that numerous. *Nouville, un village français*, published in 1953 by Bernot and Blancard looked at social relations and the psycho-social attitudes of a village of 594 people in the north of France. It was therefore the village 'unit' which was studied, and not a specifically 'rural' unit since in this commune, a strong proportion of the inhabitants were employed in the local glass works. This gave the authors the opportunity to contrast the behaviour of farmers on the one hand, with that of workers on the other. *Village in the Vaucluse* (Wylie 1957) brought to its American author the sense of distance, supposedly necessary for all ethnological investigations, and emphasised cultural behaviour and social relations within the village. One could also cite the work of Charles Pelras on *Goulien, commune rurale du Cap Sizun* (1966) and that of Robert Cresswell on an Irish village (1969).

The production of these classic monographs was unconnected with parallel developments in the British and American tradition of social anthropology. Subsequently, in France during the 1960s and 1970s, the growing awareness of the complexity of the social situation at the village level led ethnology into large-scale interdisciplinary exercises. These fed off the earlier studies, and in turn were abruptly superseded when ethnology redefined its field of interest and its subject matter, resulting in the pursuit of specific themes for which the rural world was a framework but no longer a specific object of research. Nonetheless, the experience of collaborative research opened up a new debate, first, on the nature of space and rural society and, secondly, on the applicability and relevance of chosen units of observation in ethnology.

Rural research and interdisciplinarity

Between 1962 and 1967, a large research team went into the commune of Plozévet, located at the extremity of the Pays Bigouden in Brittany, which Pierre Jakez Helias had made famous with the publication of his *Cheval d'orgueil*. The Breton communes in general have very particular characteristics in comparison with other French regions. They are first of all much larger, have more people and, until the beginning of the twentieth century at least, the bulk of their inhabitants lived in dispersed hamlets grouped around individual farms. The question of the appropriateness and suitability of the unit of study was immediately raised by the research team assembled by Dr Sutter, around a hypothesis on human genetics. The prevalence of a congenital dislocation of the hip prompted the assumption that this was an enclosed community characterised by frequent marriage between blood relatives. The unity of the commune, however, was far from proven and the territory could be readily subdivided into a succession of smaller districts some of which were notably more outward-looking towards neighbouring communes than others. Thus linguists, historians, ethnologists, sociologists and geneticists, in making that commune their precise study area, found themselves using neither the same spatial boundaries nor the same time periods (André Burguière, 1975).

Starting in 1963, a second major interdisciplinary survey was established, in a small rural region, the Aubrac, rather than a single rural commune. In spite of its size, Plozévet had been too cramped for the numerous specialists who ultimately descended upon it. In Aubrac a coordinated team was set up consisting of agronomists, sociologists, historians, linguists and, of course, ethnologists. The broad objective was determined largely by a prevailing sense of 'emergency ethnology', the aim being to study an authentic agro-pastoral system whose inevitable end was already in sight. Nevertheless, despite its traditional character, the ethnologists involved could not avoid coming across unmistakable problems associated with modernisation. These were found largely in the transition of a traditional dairy husbandry to one primarily oriented towards beef, under the early influence of the Common Agricultural Policy. The dynamics of change were accounted for at both ends of the spectrum; at one end in the works of Charles Parain (1971) which facilitated the precise dating of the initiation of the cheese producing economy – the 'traditional' thereby being used to define a 'starting point' in time – and, at the other end, in the works of the ethnologists, sociologists and agronomists who, in seeking to engage in a form of 'action ethnology', sought to help the local breeders and farmers in their period of economic transition.

Paradoxically, it was in this isolated region of central France that ethnologists first found themselves having to deal with the influence of the town and, subsequently, they came to denounce the illusion of rural autonomy and tradition. The society of Aubrac was one of emigration, towards the south of the country originally, but then, from the end of the nineteenth century, predominantly towards Paris. Using dance traditions as his example, Jean-Michel Guilcher (1975) demonstrated the importance of the Parisian migrants in maintaining the awareness of the increasingly beleaguered indigenous Aubrac culture, through the revival of local dances performed at Paris Balls. Migrant communities could be genuine reserves of traditional rural culture, often more so than the original rural areas. The paper by Jean-Luc Chodkiewicz, *L'Aubrac à Paris* (1973), also illustrated the way in which the regional social milieu was re-established in the capital and the subsequent boomerang effects this had upon local communities in Aubrac. The paucity of existing French ethnological studies of town-country relations is illustrated by the fact that, in Chodkiewicz's innovatory paper, only Anglo-American references are mentioned.

A third interdisciplinary survey was carried out from 1965 onwards in the Châtillon region, chosen for its contrast with Aubrac. Instead of a traditional economy in the process of mutation, this third region displayed a dynamic economy, based upon cereal culture and animal breeding located around a small active regional centre with both industry and services. There was no overall driving hypothesis here as there had been at both Plozévet and Aubrac, but a sociological survey was undertaken within the *arrondissement* which guided subsequent work. However, the region presented few unifying characteristics which could readily justify its selection, and it was the individual local studies which ultimately brought the most rewarding results. One especially, inspired by the general *problématiques* of social anthropology, and undertaken at Minot, helped revitalise French ethnology.

Forms of social reproduction, ceremonial spaces, the knowledge and the representation of women, kinship relations, mutual aid, neighbourliness, the multiple forms of memory, were all investigated. The village became merely a framework, a theatrical backdrop, while the problems of modernisation were virtually abandoned. The influence of these new directions was far-reaching, reorienting research towards social and symbolic objects, up to that point little studied by ethnographers. It was also out of this Châtillon study that Jacques Gutwirth first paved the way for urban ethnology (1972). What this ultimately meant was that the specifically rural component was even less important in the Châtillon study than in that of Plozévet or Aubrac.

The last major interdisciplinary endeavour focused on the Pyrenean Baronnies and brought together ethnologists, historians and geneticists. The principal impact of this study however was to reopen the whole issue of the village or commune unit while identifying the importance of the 'household' – up to that point largely ignored as a social unit and a significant source of social relations.

Despite these large-scale collective sub-regional studies, interdisciplinarity did not produce the fruits that were expected of it, though other unexpected benefits did undoubtedly result. Since 1975, interdisciplinary studies have no longer been undertaken and the scale of work has shifted towards the micro-level (Bromberger 1987). Consequently, there is now less a truly rural ethnology than ever before. Instead, there is an ethnology of politics, of religion, of symbols and of family relations (see Gérard Lenclud and Georges Augustins, below). There is no ethnology in France that is concerned specifically and exclusively with the rural world. Today ethnology is defined by its field of interest. However, it is important to recognise that despite this current shift in emphasis and, in addition to its general contribution to knowledge as a whole, French ethnology through fifty years of accumulated research work has undeniably contributed significantly to our understanding of the rural world, the nature of its space and its societies.

Rural places: the village, the commune and the village community

The importance of the spatial reference unit first emerged as an issue during the Plozévet study and later, in an even more significant way, during the Aubrac survey. What links exist between the commune, essentially an administrative unit, and the village community, basically a unit of social relations? The fiction that the two were necessarily connected soon became untenable.

The third volume of the Aubrac study, called *Ethnologie contemporaine* (the first examined agronomy and rural sociology and the second, historical ethnology), opens with a discussion of the importance of selecting appropriate units of observation since, during the course of the investigation, researchers had turned increasingly towards particular, meaningful units. Thus, Charles Parain and Corneille Jest wrote:

> The current study considers the existing commune as the equivalent of a village community, for the essential reason that the numerical data used is generally to be found at the communal level, as the smallest administrative unit.
>
> The ethnological reality however is frequently very much more complex, as ethnohistorical research has demonstrated. In Aubrac, and more generally in a major part of central and southern France, the term village (*village*) corresponds not to the commune but to the hamlet (*hameau*) – in the common French use of the term – though obviously a hamlet of some acknowledged local importance. It is at this 'village' scale that the true communities are ordinarily to be found. The most characteristic feature of a village community, and its most binding component, is the existence of common goods and property. However, in Aubrac, the proportion of these common goods belonging either to a fraction only of the commune, or to a single village within it, and thereby known as 'sectional goods', is far greater than the proportion that were genuinely communal. Nonetheless some genuine commune property does exist here and there within Aubrac indicating that the broad trend by which, in the past, commune property has been

fragmented into individual village properties has increasingly given way to a tendency towards a commune-level regrouping of land (1972).

The definition of the village community thus appeared as one of the major preoccupations of ethnology during the 1960s. In 1958, Isac Chiva proposed a general definition of the 'rural' community as:

> 'a limited social unit which exists within a given area and gains its subsistence from the exploitation of this given area through a more or less closed economy. Equipped with social, economic and sometimes judicial organisation, and its own system of ethical values, it forms a whole which is able to assure the longevity of the social group and both the material and moral subsistence of each of its individual members.

Charles Parain (1970) went on to refine this definition further in the light of European examples. He stressed, first, the variation of the territorial base, ranging from the very small to the widely extended; secondly, the dissociation between the village community and the administrative entity, most pronounced in regions of dispersed settlement; and, thirdly, the importance of collectively appropriated economic goods, following the results of the Aubrac example.

Louis Assier-Andrieu summarised the consensus which emerged from and superseded the various opposing positions:

> (1) the village community is a whole whose components, in the case of families linked to their households, must reproduce the conditions of their association in order individually to perpetuate themselves; (2) such conditions are found in the production, in the greater or lesser sense, of the means of subsistence through cooperation between family units, an accord and a collective consensus involving the entire community. Thus there is no 'community' on its own without both a material base and the social relations to justify it' (1986, p. 93).

Going beyond the consideration of purely demographic and economic criteria, this definition reintroduces the cultural dimension. The twin requirements for actual community existence are therefore both social relations and production relations. Notions of autonomy, independent community, isolation and self-sufficiency have all been unequivocally dismissed.

The analysis of power in the village has permitted a radical re-evaluation of the extent to which it is open or closed. On the one hand, Isac Chiva and Marie-Claude Pingaud (1976) have claimed:

> The progressive opening up of the countryside, the involvement of rural inhabitants in national economic and social structures, the increasingly numerous forms of participation in decision-making through the auspices of professional organisations, unions, financial agencies and so on, which parallel political authority, have encouraged the emergence of new forms of competition. Thus today, one stresses the complexity of interdependency relations and, thereby, the ambiguity of modes of expression and of the constitution of the local milieu (p. 7).

Nevertheless, ethnographic studies have demonstrated that the village and the commune are still durable social units. The ideological unity of villages is periodically reawakened during elections. Struggles for power are expressed sharply in permanent, though often latent, tensions within local political life (Bertrand Hervieu, 1976, p. 17). Considering the issue of power in the village has led ethnologists to discover that village cohesion and class struggle, village autonomy and the national political system are not necessarily mutually exclusive. At the extreme, these are false dichotomies. Ethnology allows one to interpret them not as opposites but rather as part of a single, complex reality.

Regions and cultural space

From the discussion of village unity, ethnologists have found themselves drawn into another spatial level, that of the region. A collective work *Régions de la France* (Chiva, 1981) demonstrated that external criteria for subdivision alter according to the otherwise related disciplines of ethnology, history, human geography and linguistics. The boundaries of units of civil and religious administration do not always readily correspond to the region, which is perceived rather as a cultural entity. But the region itself does not necessarily conform any more readily to other types of spatial unit, whether historical, such as the *province*, or cultural, such as the *pays*. In short, spatial simultaneity is far from being evident and any attempt to create interlocking spatial conceptions is altogether too risky.

Moving away from these external criteria for defining and subdividing spatial areas, researchers have turned instead to the analysis of the regional interior: what is the cultural dimension at the regional level? What are the signs of its identity? What activities are associated with it? Thus one comes to examine the collective uses of the spatial area as seen by the individual occupants. Marie-Claude Pingaud, for example, has identified local space in terms of changes of residence, travel for important purchases or family visits, contact or avoidance of neighbours, the political field, the cycles of the movement of people and of merchandise, marriage, fairs and markets, language and ultimately in terms of the sense of belonging to a group (1981, pp. 28–30). The complete change of perspective thereby comes full circle as such an approach seeks, first, to locate the physical and mental experience of place in terms of the collective imagination and, secondly, to define the 'us' as distinct from the 'them'; the components that make up 'belonging' cannot be established without reference to the alternative components of 'not belonging'.

Such studies as these have not been exclusively scientific since they have also met with 'regionalist' claims; what was the 'pays' in which one wanted to live? Could one find spatial units of a common identity from which to found regionalist claims and political action? The issue of rural identity was thus raised by the general movement of the mid-70s towards a more localised conception of rural France symbolised by the slogan 'We want to live in the "pays" ', but its origins can be traced back to the ways ethnologists conceived the regional and rural characteristics of localities during the 1950s.

Social actors in the rural world

Folklore is not interested in man *per se* but in 'facts'. Folklore's knowledge of man comes only through its role as informant, standing between the social actor and the materials that he employs to discover, to analyse and to classify his world.

The early extensive surveys tried hard to establish networks linking all the scales of a territory, from the commune to the region. Such studies portrayed the peasant as entrenched yet comfortable, capable of promoting 'popular' artefacts (by demanding and by consuming them; their actual construction being the work of local craftsmen or even local craft industries).

With the advent of an ethnology devoted to village monographs the social actor appeared, whose behaviour subsequently became the focus for observation and study. Social hierarchies, different social groups and the conflicts between them were placed in the foreground though it is nonetheless true that ethnology concentrated more upon the archaic peasantry than on the modern agriculturalist, the latter having been left to rural sociologists. In this preoccupation, one can see the influence of technological museology, whose particular vocation has been to collect the 'traditional' tools and material culture of peasant society while ignoring, for example, the tractor.

One can also see here the effects of the coming together of ethnology and history both of which have been interested in the fact that not everything has been overcome by division and modernity. One example amongst many is the situation whereby modern breeders combine the use of bouquets containing plants supposed to have medicinal properties against 'Ewe's Thrush' alongside highly modern techniques of vaccination (Anne-Marie Brisebarre, 1984). Rural sociologists have learned from ethnologists the long-term persistence of structures, of culture and of social relations. The position of ethnology, which defines the present in terms of the past, has therefore been critical in the continuity of rural studies. It is thus easy to understand why its focus has been on traditional rather than modern systems of agriculture.

In the village, ethnologists largely restricted their attention to peasants and artisans, from the blacksmith to the woodcutter, but for the last ten or so years, under the notable influence of the *Eco-Musées*, they have developed a growing interest in industrial ethnology, particularly those forms of industry which are found in the countryside, such as mining, steel production or tanning. The community, a notion which seemed suspect in the context of the village, has thereby regained some of its appropriateness; a community of mine-workers or of metal-workers, homogeneous and close-knit, and yet who function in a semi-urban, semi-rural setting.

Attention is also being paid to new rural actors. For example, the study of village fêtes has been reinterpreted in the light of agricultural modernisation and the return of villagers who, having emigrated as youths have since come to occupy the family house as their second home. Ethnologists are no longer particularly concerned with the origins of this or that piece of folklore, but rather with their significance here and now for a new rural population who nonetheless continue to celebrate a 'golden age' of the village which never existed. The study of hunting has provided the opportunity for looking at contemporary land-use conflicts between farmers, the 'back-to-the-land' movement and the urban dwellers. Using a symbolic perspective, researchers have examined the role of this 'madness' that overcomes a large proportion of the male population annually (Hell, 1985). Symbolic anthropology, which has grown notably in France during the last ten years, no longer considers 'rural attitudes' but seeks instead, using a wide range of sources, to identify the coherence of practices and of knowledge. It is, in short, an ethnology of things and of words. The former distinctions between learned knowledge and popular knowledge, between urban and rural and between written and oral have been absorbed into an approach that highlights interconnectivity and heterogeneity. For example, from his studies of local dance customs in the Pays Basque, Jean-Michel Guilcher (1983) has demonstrated the influence of dance masters taught in the army on what was often thought to be a traditional form.

The study of the system of property dispersion is the only one to continue to operate almost exclusively within the rural context; with a focus on the transference and splitting up of land or property attached to an agricultural holding through matrimony and residence. Such a research theme clearly has no sense in the urban setting, characterised by the wage-earning classes. On the other hand, it is relevant to contemporary issues as it illustrates the continuity between ancient ways of exploiting agricultural holdings and more modern forms, such as the *Groupement agricole d'exploitation en commun*. Likewise, it can lead to the study of the rural bourgeoisie and nobility who are still strongly oriented towards land and property inheritance.

Conclusion

Ethnology in France has renounced the grand studies, has never been particularly keen on the village monograph approach and has recognised the illusion of interdisciplinarity. For over 15 years now, the issues dealt with by ethnology can no longer be subdivided according to socio-demographic criteria (excluding, for the moment, those trends in ethnology which claim to work 'in' and 'on' the urban milieu, with their specific *problématiques* and research methods).

Neither explicitly urban nor rural, ethnological research in France has today become 'localised'. It is concerned with identifying, in a specific context, local behaviour and local customs or facts. But this sense of locality is not necessarily self-defining, and the researcher today has allowed himself to detour into history, and even beyond the precise boundaries of his field of observation so as to better construct the meaning of 'local'.

The great upheavals which both agriculture and rural society have faced since the 1950s precipitated, some 20 years later, several major syntheses. This paper has tried to show why, though fundamentally oriented towards the rural world, ethnology was not the discipline to produce them. If the rural world has not been interpreted in a comprehensive sense by ethnologists, the many and varied debates that have developed from their discipline have nonetheless produced temporary syntheses, especially with respect to the issues of, first, the relevant units of observation, secondly, the notion of power and, thirdly, the role of locality and identity. It has not been ethnology's goal, after all, to reflect upon an artificially delineated research field. In drawing attention to the problems which beset the projects of sociologists, activists or politicians, by demonstrating the richness of the ever-present symbolism in social life and stressing the role of social actors, not as the puppets of arbitrary sociological laws but as actors in their own right, has not the ethnological approach made a more useful contribution?

Is there a rural ethnology in France? *by Gérard Lenclud*

The uncertainty which surrounds the relationship between ethnology in France and French rural societies stems largely from the broad ambiguity which characterises the relationship between ethnology in general and its subject-matter. Having been for much of its history devoted to societies very different from our own, should ethnology be regarded as the science of primitive societies? If, in seeking to understand their own country, contemporary French ethnologists have turned predominantly, but not exclusively, to the observation of rural communities, should one then characterise ethnology in France as a ruralist discipline? Furthermore, what of the future if research into urban communities becomes the major focus of ethnological research in modern society? The real issue is the intellectual status of ethnological knowledge. What actually is its conceptualisation of the real-world societies that it studies; such as, in this case, rural societies?

Expressed starkly, our thesis is that although the rural world has been the chosen field of study for ethnologists working in France, rural societies, as a singular social and cultural formation within the overall national context, have never constituted the objects of ethnological research in the strictly scientific sense of the term.

It is well known that there are objects of research and objects of research. They can be defined in the rigorously empirical sense of the word, consisting of the pure and simple designation of a sphere of facts, delineated by observation and experimentation. An ethnological study area is essentially an object of research in this sense. But scientific activity can also be organised around research objects which are associated with particular constellations of issues and ideas. These objects, therefore, are less segments of reality than sets of questions closely linked together into a coherent system.

It appears to us that the ruralness of rural societies, in terms of what characterises them and differentiates them from other types of society, has never really been employed by ethnology to formulate anthropological questions or to contribute to knowledge in general. One can talk of a rural sociology, a rural economics or a rural geography in the sense that they have, more or less, their own institutional basis and specialised *problématiques* concerning the evolution and functioning of, respectively, agrarian societies, agricultural enterprises and markets, and the rural milieu as a whole. Each of these disciplines addresses the specifically rural character of the phenomena observed. One is reluctant to make such claims for rural ethnology for the reason that the rural context, in France at least, has been treated less as an issue in itself than as merely one of the many varied attributes affecting the human groups under study: when apparently rural factors are taken as study objects it is because they stand for other characteristics. When, from its institutional birth in the 1930s, for example, French ethnology went on to become by and large 'rural', this was in pursuit of the 'popular' or 'traditional' character of rural phenomena.

Some of the reasons for this selection of the rural world are fairly obvious when one considers the relative importance of rural areas in the national space and in the economy, the society and the culture of France. Similarly, one cannot help noticing that the 'explosion' of rural studies in French domestic ethnology came somewhat late in the general movement which has inspired the international anthropological community to bring the study of so-called peasant communities into the discipline's fold. The rediscovery by French ethnologists of peasant societies within the French mainland was certainly not dissimilar to the discovery of peasant societies in the Caribbean, Mexico or the Andes by American anthropologists under the auspices of the Smithsonian Institute, and indeed was undertaken largely for the same reasons. Furthermore, one cannot ignore the fact that the development of rural studies in French ethnology was incontestably linked to the strong interest of neighbouring disciplines, especially history and geography, in the rural world.

However, two simple observations suffice to identify exactly the true nature of ethnology's curiosity in this regard. The first is the general impression given by a map of the distribution of ethnological studies. Much more has been done in the south than in the north, more in the remote west than the industrial east, more in areas dominated by small-scale agriculture or extensive husbandry than open, unenclosed regions of intensive production. The amount of work done in the Pyrenees, for example, is utterly unmatched by that done in, say, the Beauce, Brie or Picardy. Yet Nouville is no more rural than the Bigouden region. Aubrac, Châtillon or the Baronnies (three areas subjected to major interdisciplinary studies) are not necessarily representative of peasant France as a whole. The map of rural ethnology is thus curiously unbalanced. Is it an exaggeration to say that French ethnologists have been preoccupied with the plough-share rather than the tractor, the last bastions of self-sufficiency or of small family-farming rather than cash-flow enterprises; in short, with a marginal and underpopulated France, its past, its dialects and indigenous patterns of speech, its cultural autonomy, its judicial idiosyncracies and its political characteristics? It seems almost as if the assumed national trends towards modernity and a more homogeneous society have been rejected or ignored. Certainly, it is clear that ethnologists have not selected the range of study areas necessary to explore in full the diversity of rural societies in France, if this was ever their goal.

The second observation is the relative indifference of ethnologists to the major phenomena by which the influence of wider society is recognised and through which changes in rural societies can be interpreted. Ethnologists have hardly made any attempt to problematise, that is to say to translate into relevant ethnological questions, the overwhelming effects of trends such as the massive rural exodus and the resultant evolution of land use forms, the diffusion of new methods of production and the changing awareness of peasant farmers which have resulted from them and, finally, the transformation of the economic conditions of agricultural production and of markets. Although ethnologists have considered these elements as social realities, as information to be integrated and indeed described, they have not taken them as anthropological realities; i.e., issues which ethnology, as a particular form of knowledge, might help to explain.

In short, therefore, rural societies have been the locations of research more than objects of research in themselves; the rural world being more a pretext than a medium in its own right. In the 1960s, one would have looked in vain amongst the various published works of a supposed 'ruralist' character, for the equivalent of the general observations made by American anthropologists (such as Steward, Redfield, Foster, Wolf, Geertz etc.) with respect to peasantism as specific social and cultural forms, including the co-ordinated attempts to elaborate an ideal 'peasant' type, based upon the complementary notions of relative autonomy and independence. If a generation of French ethnologists dispersed throughout France were witnesses to a crucial period of change in the peasantry, this does not appear to have had any effect upon their intellectual inspiration – if that can be judged from their published works. Topics such as forms of marriage and the transference of property, the nature and extent of customs and their influence on rights, the popular folk tale and witchcraft have been the rallying points for ethnologists far more than have been the major processes of change operating in the rural world. In acknowledging this situation, one does not necessarily express regret but rather invites critical examination of the reasons for it. The principal reason is that the development of an ethnology of France (and thereby an ethnology of rural societies) has been determined largely by an internal disciplinary logic, rather more than by the need to respond to factors in the real world.

What then, have rural societies offered ethnologists in France? – essentially a solution to an epistemological problem and a methodological device. A solution to an epistemological problem? Ethnology is commonly defined as a science of society and culture, looked at from the 'outside'. It is commonly asserted that access to the facts of general social functioning, as Mauss puts it, takes place best through observation at a distance and a detached view. But where in France can one gain sufficient detachment? Rural societies have supplied ethnologists with a social world in which they were not directly important participants, a cultural configuration whose values they did not immediately share. The cultural distance between the observer and the observed is always relative. Yet it is almost as if ethnologists have taken this distance as an heuristic principle, in this case as a means of objectification. Rural societies in France have played, relatively speaking, roughly the same role that Mediterranean societies played for British anthropologists, at a certain period during the history of their discipline, when they offered the researchers a distant, though nevertheless close enough, alternative to their own homeland. Yet, because these societies were nonetheless removed and therefore strange to many people, the British anthropologists were able to apply to them the hypotheses and models of general anthropology with which to test the methods of ethnological investigation, thereby further extending its scope. Peasants have similarly provided French ethnology with a means of re-entering by the back door a society often referred to as modern and complex.

A methodological device? The forms of social organisation found in rural societies reveal local 'communities' which are spatially discrete and, at first sight, homogeneous, and which constitute a sort of 'level of authenticity' (Lévi-Strauss) in the sense that the ensemble of inter-personal relations appears, or can appear, as a social system with a certain completeness. Such societies offer, on account of their spatial distribution and their form of human organisation, relevant units of observation for the extension of anthropological field work beyond its traditional domains. Furthermore, each community appears to be an 'entity at once total, contiguous and concrete' (ibid.), thereby suitable for a style of investigation that is both holistic in its intention and microscopic in its attention to the details to be studied. Although one might undoubtedly dub this an academic fiction, it is no more so than are those descriptions of the tribal world and lineage wherein distinct ethnic groups are distributed on a map in an established order and separated by clearly defined frontiers.

To best understand the status of rural studies in the ethnology of France, it is useful to recall briefly, by way of reference, the way in which knowledge in classical ethnology is traditionally arranged. This starts, first, at the scale of the restricted human group, taken in its most intimate characteristics. Secondly, ethnology has operated at the scale of the cultural unit and its many possible subdivisions. Each monograph study brought its own stone to the edifice constructed from the accumulated information on a culture; a culture whose boundaries have been defined less by the approximate methods of experimentation than by the expedient of comparisons with other cultures. Thirdly, and at the same time, ethnological knowledge has organised itself in what one might term a systematic direction, in the sense that ethnology has incorporated all that is inseparable from social experience in a number of other major institutional fields, which are themselves no more than projections of our own analytic categories – that is to say the various dimensions that we have formed in order to learn about this or that social phenomenon: i.e. technical, economic, familial, social organisation, political, religious and so on. Ultimately, ethnological knowledge endeavours to reach a genuinely anthropological level by establishing valuable propositions for all human societies.

The various intermediary levels of knowledge that lie between ethnology and anthropology are also, in France, relatively institutionalised. There is an African, an American and an Oceanic anthropology, each of which brings together a variety of specific regional specialisations (ethnology of East Africa, of the Bantu, of Volta societies, etc.). At the same time, there is an ethnology of techniques, an economic anthropology, a familial anthropology and so on. In certain circumstances, however, a body of knowledge – more or less institutionalised – summarising a general type of lifestyle will be defined, initially at least, by ecological and techno-economic criteria. Thus, one finds an ethnology of hunter-gatherers and an ethnology of nomadic pastoralists.

This general model of the organisation of knowledge has been more or less carried over into French domestic ethnology. Ethnography has obviously been set up in the same way as in classic ethnology, that is to say, on the basis of monographs concerning groups sufficiently restricted that the bulk of the relevant documentation can be gathered by a single researcher. The majority of these individual monographs are therefore village-based. They are oriented towards the region only in those cases when it sufficiently displays different traits (or, one could add, is sufficiently studied) to enable it to represent a distinct culture in the strict anthropological sense of the term. Researchers working in France have also tended to concentrate their research efforts according to the major institutional fields observed higher up the scale. Without claiming to have attained the actual level of anthropology itself, the monographs dedicated to rural societies within mainland France do nonetheless lie within the 'regionalist' *problématiques* whose presumed context is, in growing order of generality, first French society or culture, then European society or culture, and, finally, society or cultures of the 'modern' or 'complex' type, in contrast to those traditionally studied by ethnologists.

Within this model of the organisation of knowledge, rural society *per se* has not emerged as a focus for analysis. Instead, it is an element that has been, in a sense, overlooked in the processes of organisation, comparison and generalisation. To caricature a little, the villager, as he acts, speaks and thinks, as described in monographic studies, slips from the status of an empirical subject to that of a social and cultural being, who acts as a cypher for either regional ideas and values, or national ones, or even those which are the expression of a more general form of society, of the modern western type.

Why has there been this lack of a specific rural *problématique* in French domestic ethnology? One can perhaps identify three reasons. The first has been the dominant influence of general anthropology, its body of theory, its *problématiques*, its concepts, and its methods, on the establishment and development of an ethnology of France. To return to the classic image of scientific method as being a dialogue between hypothesis and experimentation in which reality is never allowed to have the first word but must instead respond only to the questions asked of it, the French rural reality has responded chiefly to the questions posed of it by general anthropology. Undoubtedly, many of ethnology's weaknesses stem from the resulting temptation to import methods and concepts originally designed to support the analysis of societal situations which contrast very strongly with those of France (one thinks in particular of the mass of analyses, at an institutional dimension, of social stratification). Furthermore, one comes to question the originality of the contribution that ethnology has brought to our understanding of the French real-world situation since, as anthropology asserts, how can one hope to understand a society if one has not submitted it to a comparison with something else? The absence of any *problématiques* that are, strictly speaking, ruralist is the direct consequence of this state of affairs.

The second reason for this lack of *problématiques* lies in the chosen methodology, which has been expressed in the almost exclusive predominance of the monograph and its holistic approach. What might appear to some people as a 'fascination with the local' has led as its logical consequence, first, to the near impossibility of making internal comparisons, so much have the various approaches diverged; and, secondly, to leaving virtually unstated the real importance of the wider contexts and processes which, to a large extent, define the rural reality.

The third and final reason for this relative lack of a rural *problématique* has been, without doubt, the transformation of French rural societies. It is conceivable that the French or European rural world could have achieved an intellectual and institutional status within anthropology equivalent to that attained by certain general societal types, such as hunter-gatherers or pastoral nomadic societies. At a particular point in the history of American anthropology, peasant societies achieved just this status. But contemporary trends have undermined the coherence and distinctiveness of French peasant societies. As the genuinely ruralist disciplines in general have proved, to try and distinguish empirically between what is rural and what is not is a very hazardous enterprise in contemporary France. The town/country dichotomy has surely, by now, exhausted all its heuristic power. Who can tell where the frontier lies between the rural world and the world which encompasses it? Who can still claim that the former is governed by a unique logic, without which localised disciplinary knowledge loses much of its specific *raison d'être*? It is no coincidence that ethno-history has been the preferred approach of ethnologists studying rural France.

This is not to deny that French domestic ethnology has considerably furthered our knowledge of the rural world, its societies and its cultures. It has done so, directly, through the published works which have appeared and continue to appear. It has done so indirectly by the influence it has exerted upon neighbouring disciplines, notably history, in enriching their own *problématiques* and suggesting new areas of investigation. But, by one of those curious paradoxes that pervade the history of the social sciences, its contribution has resulted less from what it has intended to study, in the sense of a deliberately ruralist objective, than in the course of an undertaking that has been of an altogether different nature.

To prevent the argument developed here from becoming too abstract, we offer an example – that of kinship – to illustrate the development of French ethnology and its relationship to rural societies. The reason for the choice is that kinship is quite justly considered to be the foundation stone of ethnology, but for a long time it was erroneously regarded, as being less important in modern societies.

Kinship and social organisation *by Georges Augustins*

It was only when a large number of them had disappeared, or were in the course of disintegration, that European peasant societies – and more particularly those in France – finally became the object of anthropological studies of kinship. For a long time, it seems, it was taken for granted that the most relevant levels of interpretation were, on the one hand, the family (i.e., most commonly, the domestic organisation) and, on the other, the peasant community (i.e. the socio-political organisation). That Western peasant societies could have been the arena for kinship relations and processes, comparable to those encountered in 'exotic' countries, was simply overlooked. In addition, a tradition, which extends back to Frédéric Le Play, encouraged the consideration of the family only within the context of the household, thereby precluding any understanding of the mechanisms of property redistribution and political allegiance operating at any other level. Furthermore, the tendency amongst advocates of the theory of descent (which has become increasingly widespread since the 1950s) to take the domestic group as the chosen unit of investigation, further encouraged the focusing of analysis on the relations between the composition of households, demography and economy.

Nonetheless, ethnology has developed its own research direction in this field and one can summarise current ethnological research into kinship under several key headings:

1 The analysis of the kinship universe

The drawing up of genealogies is not simply a mnemonic exercise. It also relates to a certain conception of social life, indeed even of individual identity. A number of researchers have sought either to expose the underlying systems of representation or to identify the imagery which both social life and individual identity can mask and reveal at the same time. The expressions of kinship (uncle, cousin and so on) have also been looked at through their diverse and varied connotations (social as well as emotional), as cognitive devices in addition to being the support for social relations. Similarly, limits of this kinship universe have been explored (through the semantic analysis of, for example, the duality kin/stranger).

2 The analysis of matrimonial and land inheritance practices

As a reaction against the strictly legalistic approach, which seemed to characterise the theory of descent, some researchers, influenced by Pierre Bourdieu, struggled to demonstrate the various 'strategies' which seemed to lie behind actual practices. In this, they tried to take into account observed regularities; regularities which nonetheless bear witness to numerous distortions between standard and actual practice.

Several meticulous studies have attempted to retrace the history of land inheritance within a given village and to use this in conjunction with reconstructions derived from family histories. Archival material, such as *cadastres*, censuses and other civil records, can yield a rich and prodigious information base. Such studies have allowed researchers to show how certain patterns can be explained either by strategies of land reallocation or by renting out land that has been handed down to emigrants.

3 The analysis of the role of kinship in political life

It has long been well known that municipal elections incite passions which can appear, at least to the outsider, out of all proportion with the actual political issues involved. Various studies have demonstrated, first, that the local political game has frequently been largely symbolic and, secondly and more significantly, that municipal elections have been one of the primary means of exposing blood relations. Consequently, elections can be interpreted as a special arena of rivalry over power and prestige between antagonistic kinship groups, with these cleavages frequently conforming to political or ideological cleavages.

4 The analysis of the complex structure of marriage

The search for consistency in patterns of marriage has, of course, held the attention of a number of researchers whether their aim has been to identify several basic types of matrimonial strategy or to demonstrate the underlying mechanisms of exchange involved. Work carried out in the south west of France and in Brittany has identified instances of cycles of dowry circulation (which also means, obviously, cycles in the exchange of spouses). The interpretation of these results has been delicate, however, as it has proved very difficult, in certain regions, to be precise about what exactly are the units of exchange.

5 The analysis of the relationship between official rights, customary rights and inheritance practices

France is a country which, until the beginning of the nineteenth century, lived under a regime of legal diversity, each region having its own law and each important town having its own 'customary practices'. The south was for a long time under the influence of Roman law which favoured one descendant, while the north, under the influence of first Frankish and then feudal law, was more egalitarian. It has been tempting to try and assess to what degree these multi-secular influences have continued to affect contemporary legal practices. Both extensive and monograph studies have revealed that customary practices have generally been maintained despite the standardisation of the law in 1804. New light has thus been shed on the relationship between, on the one hand, official law and customary practice and, on the other, the nature and extent of opposition between social norms and actual practice.

6 The analysis of mechanisms for the perpetuation of domestic groups

European ethnology has a considerable advantage as a result of the presence of detailed archives, which are, for certain fields and for certain time periods, virtually exhaustive. This asset has prompted several researchers to undertake a reconstruction of the domestic groups of a village over one or more centuries. The results have led to a re-examination of the relationships between domestic organisation and the practices of land inheritance, and comparative research has led to the creation of typologies and the improved delineation of regional variations.

Conclusions

Work done on kinship in France has followed a large number of disparate paths, which can nevertheless be summarised into several major issues:

- What role do kinship relations have in individual imagery and is this role variable according to regions?
- Does the notion of a kinship group have a genuine meaning? Alternatively, does the impossibility of identifying such groups demonstrate a fundamental difference between European societies and others, or does it demonstrate a methodological bias which, while its strength has lain elsewhere, has precluded the understanding of the European situation by reducing kinship to the scale of the household?
- Is the notion of strategy capable of accounting for the observed hiatus between norms and practices? Is it ultimately a valuable tool for investigation?
- Can one tease out patterns of matrimonial practice, the logic of which has not proved

reducible to simple strategies, but rather constitutes a sort of European extension of semi-complex marriage structures?
- Finally, can one detect a logic in the perpetuation of domestic groups; these not being simply the victims of economic or demographic factors.

Bibliography

Assier-Andrieu, Louis, 'Le peuple et la loi', *Anthropologie historique des droits paysans en Catalogne française*, Paris, LGDJ, 1987, 263 pp.
L'Aubrac, étude ethnologique, linguistique, agronomique et économique d'un établissement humain, Paris, CNRS, 7 volumes, 1970–86.
Bernot, Lucien and Blancard, René, *Nouville, un village français,* Paris, Institut d'Ethnologie, 1953, 447 pp.
Bodiguel, Maryvonne, *Le rural en question,* Paris, L'Harmattan, 1986, 183 pp.
Brisebarre, Anne-Marie, 'A propos de l'usage thérapeutique des bouquets suspendus dans les bergeries cévenoles', *Bulletin d'ethno-médecine,* 1984, 32, 4éme trimestre, pp. 129–63.
Bromberger, Christian, 'Du grand au petit. Variation des échelles et des objets d'analyse dans l'histoire récente de l'ethnologie de la France', in Isac Chiva and Utz Jeggle, *Ethnologie en miroir,* Paris, Editions de la Maison des Sciences de l'Homme, 1987, pp. 67–94.
Burguiere, André, *Bretons de Plozévet,* Paris, Flammarion, 1975, p. 383.
Chiva, Isac, *Les communautés rurales. Problèmes, méthodes et exemples de recherches,* Unesco, Rapports et documents de Sciences sociales, no. 10, 1958, p. 48.
Chiva, Isac, 'Entre livre et musée. Emergence d'une ethnologie de la France', in *Ethnologies en miroir,* op. cit., 1987, pp. 9–33.
Chodkiewicz, Jean-Luc, 'L'Aubrac à Paris. Ecologie d'une migration culturelle', in *L'Aubrac,* tome IV, Ethnologie contemporaine II, Paris, CNRS, 1973, pp. 197–223.
Cresswell, Robert, *Une communauté rurale de l'Irlande,* Paris, Institut d'Ethnologie, 1969, 573 pp.
Cusenier, Jean and Ségalen, Martine, *Ethnologie de la France,* Paris, PUF, Collection Que Sais-Je, 1986, 128 pp.
Guilcher, Jean-Michel, 'Les conditions de la culture traditionnelle en Aubrac', in *L'Aubrac,* Tome V, Ethnologie contemporaine III, Paris, CNRS, 1975, pp. 19–30.
Guilcher, Jean-Michel, *La tradition de danse en Béarn et Pays Basque français,* Paris, Editions de la Maison des Sciences de l'Homme, 1983, 727 pp.
Gutwirth, Jacques, 'Les associations de loisir d'une petite ville: Châtillon-sur-Seine', *Ethnologie française,* 1972, 1–2, pp. 140–80.
Hervieu, Bertrand, 'Le pouvoir au village': difficultés et perspectives d'une recherche', *Etudes rurales,* July–December 1976, 63–64, pp. 15–30.
Hell, Bertrand, *Entre chien et loup. Faits et dits de chasse dans la France de l'Est,* Paris, Editions de la Maison des Sciences de l'Homme, 1985, 308 pp.
Histoire de la France rurale, sous la direction de Georges Duby et Armand Wallon (eds), Paris, Le Seuil, 4 volumes, 1975–76.
Jollivet, Marcel and Mendras, Henri, (eds), *Les collectivités rurales françaises,* Paris, Armand Colin, 1971.
Lévi-Strauss, Laurent, Mendras, Henri and Veyssier, Louis, 'Rural community studies in France', in J.L. Durand-Drouhin, L.M. Szwengrub and I. Mihailescu (eds), *Rural community studies in Europe. Trends, selected and annotated bibliographies, analyses,* Vol. 1, Oxford, Pergamon Press, 1980, pp. 255–99.

Maget, Marcel, 'Remarques sur le village comme cadre de recherches anthropologiques', *Bulletin de psychologie*, 1955, VIII, 7-8, pp. 375-82.
Mendras, Henri, *La fin des paysans*, Paris, SEDEIS, 1967, 308 pp., (2ème édition 1984).
Menon, Pierre-Louis and Lecotte, Roger, *Au village de France. La vie traditionnelle des paysans*, Paris, Bourrelier, 1945, 212 pp.
Parain, Charles, 'Fondements d'une ethnologie historique de l'Aubrac', in *L'Aubrac*, tome II, Ethnologie historique, 1971, pp. 18-124.
Parain, Charles, 'Contribution à une problématique de la communauté villageoise dans le domaine européen', *L'Ethnographie*, 1970, 64, pp. 34-60.
Parain, Charles and Jest, Corneille, 'Introduction générale', in *L'Aubrac,* tome III, Ethnologie contemporaine I, Paris, CNRS, 1972, pp. 19-20.
Pelras, Charles, *Goulien, commune rurale du Cap Sizun (Finistère), Etude d'ethnologie globale*, Paris, Masson, 1966, 469 pages.
'Pouvoir et patrimoine au village', *Etudes rurales*, n°. spécial, (eds) Isac Chiva and Marie-Claude Pingaud, 1976, pp. 63-64.
Pingaud, Marie-Claude, ' "Région" et "territoire" dans quelques recherches interdisciplinaires', in *Les régions de la France*: *Le Monde alpin et rhodanien,* n°. spécial, Isac Chiva, 1981, 1, pp. 23-31.
Weber, Eugen, *La fin des terroirs: la modernisation de la France rurale, 1870-1914*, Paris, Fayard, 1983, 839 pp. (English title: *Peasants into Frenchmen 1976*).
Wylie, Laurence, *Village in the Vaucluse. An account of life in a French village.* Cambridge, Harvard University Press, 1957, 375 pp., French translation: *Un village du Vaucluse*, Paris, Gallimard, 1981, 432 pp.

15 The British Anthropological Tradition, Otherness and Rural Studies

Anthony Cohen

In Whalsay, Shetland, where I have conducted research during the last fourteen years, conversation among men, whether in public or private, is often punctuated by lengthy silences. The men may whistle softly and tunelessly through their teeth, or occasionally sigh 'aye, Man!', but it is essentially silence. These breaks in the exchange of words are more than mere pauses. They do not appear to cause any embarrassment or discomfort. They do not betoken the exhaustion of communication. If anything, they seem to signify the very opposite: that 'we do not require the embellishments of talk to validate our relationship'; that there may be as much communion (or *communitas*) in silence as in verbal exchange. In this interpretation, these silences signify intimacy and familiarity. Perhaps they impressed me because I am personally a hesitant conversationalist and so the legitimacy of silence was an unexpected and welcome bonus for the self-conscious fieldworker. But they also struck me as unusual. Chapman remarks that Plouhinec fishing crew-mates express their intimacy in conversational garrulousness (1987). Bailey observes that the villagers of Valloire attempt to *avoid* being seen to converse publicly since they would be presumed to be engaging in malicious gossip; and, in any case, because conversation can waste time and might thus impugn one's reputation as a diligent worker (1971, p. 2).

How should we account for the differences? Until quite recently in Britain we would have answered this question in terms of 'cultural difference'. The problematic behaviour would have been contextualised as an integral element in the cultural pattern. There were methods for this kind of exercise; the ethnographer was judged to have followed them correctly or incorrectly. In either case, the problem was conceptualised as one of how sense should be made and conveyed of the cultural 'Other'. But what of the Self, as something more than a fallible scientific instrument? Should we not include in the equation the attraction to the taciturn ethnographer of silence; of chatter to his loquacious colleague; of gossip to the anthropologist of 'small politics'? And, if we do, then of whom is the observation really being made – and how should we recognise the self-other boundary?

This issue is now central to the discipline of social anthropology. But as far as the anthropological study of Britain (and, perhaps, of other Western industrialised countries) was concerned, it had another dimension for anthropologists. A distinction was made between what, *faute de mieux*, I shall call 'conventional' anthropology (that is, the anthropology of 'elsewhere') and parochial or local studies. In France, the distinction has been rather less marked; both were *l'ethnologie*. In Britain, however, the one was 'anthropology'; the other was resisted by all the taxonomic ingenuity available to a boundary-conscious (and rather incestuous) clan: it was 'community studies', or 'sociology', perhaps 'village studies', but surely not Anthropology? After all, its subjects spoke a language which was recognisable as English; they lived within the same national boundaries and watched the same television programmes as the anthropologists themselves. They did not appear to have rituals of a complexity so arcane as to require the interpretive skills of the anthropologist. How, then, could *they* be Other? And, if they were not, then, by definition, the study of them surely could not be anthropology. Because anthropologists could not recognise, or were not interested in Otherness in people of their own nationality and colour, they also could not perceive any problem about understanding them. It was an arrogance from which most practitioners would now wish to dissociate themselves.

During the late 1960s and 1970s, most anthropologists of Britain, regrettably myself among them, seemed to feel constrained to accept the imperative to discover cultural otherness as a means of legitimising their studies as proper anthropology. Thus, even within our own national boundaries we tended to concentrate our efforts on the most remote communities or on those manifestly distinguished by a vernacular language or dialect. The tendency was evident also throughout the anthropology of the industrialised world. Our mistake was two-fold: first, to confuse Otherness with *manifest* difference; and, secondly, by focusing narrowly on the Other, to neglect the significance of Self. Both matters have now become central topics of debate in anthropology generally, and this belated maturing of our subject has placed studies of proximate societies and cultures at the very top of the anthropological agenda.

Their contemporary importance signals other changes in the discipline. There was a variety of reasons why the study of proximate societies had been disdained. They ranged from the silly – that such work was insufficiently demanding on the intellect, reiterated recently by Leach (1985) – to the misguided: that it would be tantamount to the study of self and, therefore, to what we could be presumed to know already. But underpinning this range of scepticism was the powerful compulsion of anthropologists, inherited from their Victorian forebears, to taxonomy, to distinguish between types of society on the bases of their structural and institutional compositions and of the cultures which they assumed to be thus determined. Taxonomy persists, but its terms have changed. The categories on which we were nurtured – 'modern', 'primitive', 'pre-industrial' and 'traditional' – have largely gone by the board, but we still speak of pastoralists, hunter-gatherers, urban-industrialists, of modes of production and so forth.

Such mediation keeps the empirical relations among people at a distance from the observer making them appear to respond to a cultural logic: the quintessential postulate by an observer about an Other (see Foucault, 1972, pp. 9–10). Perhaps the development which has been most important in bringing about the change in the kinds of society we now study is that this distancing became anachronistic and, to the satisfaction of some scholars, discredited as well. In this age of postmodernism we have recognised the problem of Otherness as one which inheres in 'person' rather than in such abstractions as 'society' or 'culture'. This does not suggest the renaissance of methodological individualism, but the critical reappraisal of the ways in which we have previously coped conceptually with individuality: essentially, by dismissing it in order to satisfy the demands of comparison – the characteristic practice of, what Hobart describes as, our 'salad days' (1987).

Related to this was the similarly fundamental change in the way we have come to think about 'culture'. Interpretive anthropologists, under the influence of their doyen Clifford Geertz, made clear that the primary obstacles to ethnographic and anthropological understanding do not inhere so much in the boundaries of culture as in those of mind. Their intention in this argument was not to dissolve the realities of cultural difference – far from it – nor to privilege any other determining variable such as societal form, relations of production, or whatever. Rather, it was to hammer home an insight which now appears so obvious as to be banal (yet, in its historical context, was quite stunning): that any mind beyond the ethnographer's own is Other and, therefore, requires to have interpretive work done on it. It was entirely consonant with this view that culture came to be seen as providing the means by which interpretations might be made, rather than as being, in the previously dominant neo-Tylorian view, the interpretations themselves. In this earlier functionalist paradigm, people had been thought of as sharing beliefs and meanings by virtue of their common culture. Now they were perceived instead as sharing symbols – that is, the *formal* and imprecise means of expressing beliefs and meanings – but not as necessarily sharing the *contents* of these symbols (namely, the beliefs and meanings themselves). Hence we may identify a subtle *double-entendre* in the English title of Sperber's *Rethinking Symbolism* (1975): symbolism is 're-thought' there as an anthropological category; but the shared symbol is also rethought (reinterpreted) by each ordinary person as he or she makes 'ordinary' use of it.

Thus liberated from its structural and functional connotations in which it appeared as an integrating mechanism, culture was now depicted as an *aggregating* phenomenon whose commonality among the population of any given society should be regarded as problematic (see Cohen, 1985). It is in precisely this way that the individual is re-admitted into the anthropological reckoning as something more than a determinate and pliable refraction of superordinate social forces. At higher analytic levels such as those of workplace, community, region, gender and class, it becomes clear that in a society so manifestly heterogeneous as Britain, the assumption of such commonality can no longer be seriously sustained by anthropologists.

Let me risk a gross generalisation and suggest that the British Establishment was more reluctant to admit heterogeneity of Britain than had been the case in France. Perhaps the different histories and philosophies of the two countries as colonial powers may suggest the reason. But, laying aside such speculation, this reluctance persisted, with enlightenment perhaps only now being forced upon the consciousness of politicians and editors by the results of recent general elections. Anthropologists were a little quicker to see the light. Formerly, such heterogeneity as had been generally recognised in British society had referred principally to gross differences of class, to the distinction between town and country, and to the presence of immigrants among the host population. But in so far as anthropologists accorded any legitimacy to research within Britain, it was to research on ethnicity and race. After all, the ethnic communities were 'other': differently pigmented; linguistically and, perhaps, religiously distinct. They had other 'cultures' (Watson, 1977). But our revision of the concept of culture suggested the existence of a plurality of cultures within the *indigenous* population, as well as within any one ethnic group. Otherness was now all around us, and not marked only by the explicit 'ethnognomomic' signs and 'cultural totems' (Schwartz, 1975) by which we had previously identified cultural boundaries. Apart from research on urban ethnicity, anthropologists of Britain had sought out otherness in remote areas of the British Isles, especially on the 'Celtic fringe', leaving the more central and highly populated areas seriously understudied (an imbalance which, according to Lenclud (this volume, chapter 14) was apparent also in studies of France). However, with our enhanced or enlightened sensitivity to otherness this was also to change.[1] There is now research in progress throughout the British Isles, including urban areas (e.g. Wallman, 1982; 1984) and industrial sites (e.g. Harris, 1987).

This burgeoning of interest is a recent development principally of the 1980s – I shall refer shortly to the earlier history of British anthropological studies – and we do not yet possess the enviable ethnographic and theoretically sophisticated treasury such as that which has already been accumulated in France. We have not had, and certainly will never have, the systematic study of a particular region such as that made over a number of years in Brittany. It remains a matter for optimistic speculation as to where we shall acquire so generally influential and iconoclastic a monograph as Favret-Saada's *Les Mots, La Mort, Les Sorts* (1977), or studies which reveal such meticulous ethnographic history as Ségalen's *Quinze Générations de Bas-Bretons* (1985) and Zonabend's *La Mémoire Longue* (1980). Of course, we lacked the marvellous ethnological foundations so deftly laid by hands as various as those of Van Gennep, Hertz and Mauss, and so sensitively developed in Helias's masterpiece *Le Cheval d'Orgueil* (1975) and in Ségalen's delightful *Mari et Femme dans la Société Paysanne* (1980). British social anthropologists have never accorded appropriately respectful attention to folklore. Social anthropologists often seem to regard the study of 'material culture' as a nuisance on the path to a degree. Whilst anthropologists both of Britain and, more generally, of Europe, have turned ever more seriously to historical research, British historians, lacking a Le Roy Ladurie, and, with a few notable exceptions such as Laslett and Thompson, continue to show a contemptuous disinterest in anthropological studies. British sociology offers us little comfort, since it seems either to confuse anthropology with mere observational methodology, or ignores the advances it has made during the last thirty years.

Thus, despite the flowering of local studies, such anthropology remains a minority activity within the discipline and a relatively isolated one within the social sciences generally. It is still easier in Britain and the United States to find a publisher for an anthropological monograph on Melanesian villagers or aboriginal migrants than on a British local community.

The historical reasons for our failure to develop a tradition of British anthropology – indeed, for our resistance to such studies – are many, various and too speculative to go into further here. That they are deeply rooted in Victorian imperialism with its associated traditions of evolutionary theory and missionary justification cannot, I think, be doubted. There was a brief period during the 1950s and early 1960s when some activity was initiated, for which part of the credit was due to Raymond Firth and Max Gluckman. In what was intended to provide a comparison with David Schneider's project in Chicago, Firth led a study of middle-class kinship in London (e.g. Firth *et al.* 1969), complementing but taking a rather different tack from the studies of working-class kinship and friendship made in East London by Wilmott and Young (e.g. 1957) and Bott's work on kinship, class and social relations (1957). Gluckman did not personally conduct research in Britain, but was the catalyst for a series of studies of locality and workplace. One of these, which, incidentally, he supervised, provided the basis for Frankenberg's classic *Village on the Border* (1957). Of course the genre had originated earlier, independently of British influence, with Arensberg and Kimball's *Family and Community in Ireland* (1948) and Arensberg's *Irish Countryman* (1937). Later, it produced Littlejohn's *Westrigg* (1963); Williams's study of Gosforth (1956) and of Ashworthy (1963); Isabel Emmett's *A North Wales Village* (1964); and a series of sociological and geographical studies in various parts of England and Wales, the best known being the Banbury research, conducted by Margaret Stacey and her colleagues (e.g. 1960), and Alwyn Rees's *Life in a Welsh Countryside* (1951).[2] Reviews of the genre invariably associate with it two studies which have French connections, Wylie's *Village in the Vaucluse* (1957) and Cresswell's *Une Communauté Rurale d'Irlande* (1969). There were similar kinds of study being made in North America but, on both sides of the Atlantic, the genre came to an abrupt end, for apparently similar reasons.

It is not necessary to rehearse here the fierce criticism which was directed at the community study from a variety of theoretical directions. Suffice it to say that it was influenced, on the one hand, by a suspicion of holistic studies which owed more to an animus against functionalism than to the content of these studies themselves; and, on the other hand, by a vulgar form of Marxist polemic which insisted that any analytic category such as community which denied the primacy of class must be a bourgeois mystification. So far as the latter was concerned, the state could be admitted into the equation, but there was little room for any other conceptual baggage. Both critiques were silly. The seminal British community studies, for example, those by Frankenberg, Littlejohn and Williams, all dealt explicitly with class, locating it within the local context without subordinating it to a notion of community-as-structural isolate. Further, the influence of functionalism was general throughout the British and American anthropological traditions, and was hardly limited to studies of Britain. Yet, its demise began to accelerate generally in anthropology *after* British community studies had effectively come to an end, at least so far as the engagement with them of anthropologists was concerned. Some critics of community studies also depicted them as theoretically arid and, in the aftermath of these attacks, there seems to have been a sense of uncertainty about the forms which an anthropology of Britain might take. In the Introduction to his *People of the Sierra* (1971), Pitt-Rivers recalled that few European precedents were available to him when he began his research in Spain. Unlike some other Europeanists of his generation, he properly avoided the temptation to replicate African models in an obviously inappropriate context. With the notable exception of the vibrant tradition of Irish studies which matured earlier, the anthropology of Britain has only recently begun again to find the confidence to behave in a similar manner, and to allow the nature of British cultures to generate its analytical concepts and models.

I will mention briefly two instances of this coming-of-age. In 1978, Robin Fox's monograph, *The Tory Islanders*, was published followed, three years later, by Marilyn Strathern's *Elmdon* (1981). Fox's book brought to fruition an argument he had been constructing since the mid-1960s about the nature of bilateral kinship and cognatic descent. Early in this venture, he had insisted that cognatic descent should not be regarded merely as the detritus of collapsed unilineal systems; and that British forms of famili-hood, far from being impoverished and attenuated expressions of kinship, manifested extraordinary variety and were full of analytical puzzles (1965). His argument contrasted strikingly with other contemporary work which tended to treat variations in British kinship as little more than the epiphenomena of class differences (Firth et al., 1969; Littlejohn, 1963; Wilmott and Young, *inter alia* 1957; Bott, 1957). Above all, he saw that Tory Island kinship was far more than a structure entailing rights and obligations: the structure provided a formal framework of principle which was continuously subverted strategically in the process of social life. It provided a gloss for the adaptability of behaviour which was necessitated by the everyday exigencies of life on the island. He was therefore able to show how, by their very transgressibility, the principles of descent and residence, and the rules of marriage, although appearing to be dogmatic charters of social association, enabled people to maximise their access to the island's severely limited resources. It is an approach to kinship which clearly discriminates between form and content (structure and process; appearance and reality) revealing ideologies as subtle as those to be found elsewhere. In particular, he demonstrates that bilaterialism in kinship can be as effective a principle of closure as it was widely assumed to be of openness.

This somewhat iconoclastic view also underlies Strathern's argument. But she goes on to show that not only does kinship provide a strategic basis for social interaction; in Britain, as elsewhere, it also provides a model for the conceptualisation of social life. Families in Elmdon are even more attenuated than those on Tory. There has been greater mobility, a much greater dispersal of family members; and, above all, Elmdon has been repopulated by outsiders. Nevertheless, there remains a cluster of long-established non-mobile families which have intermarried with each other over the generations and who regard themselves as 'Real Elmdoners'. They may be unable to impute distinctive characteristics to Elmdon itself; but they nevertheless see themselves as its most authentic members. The centrality of kinship to this notion of authenticity – inextricably linked to a sense, reinforced over time, of shared place – provides them, in turn, with models of 'village' and 'class'. They are the immobile rural working class, who might imagine themselves perceived as failures in the struggle for materialistic success and upward mobility; displaced by the middle-class urban commuters who now dominate the community and occupy its better houses. Yet, their conviction in themselves and their families as *real*, authentic Elmdon counter-balances their sense of their own marginality. Here, kinship is clearly revealed as a symbolic resource of the greatest importance, as something to 'think with' rather than just to 'act out'.

In more general theoretical terms, these studies show clearly that despite their appearance of familiarity and similarity the elementary forms of social organisation in the British Isles are characterised by the diversity and heterogeneity of their content, rather than by its uniformity – an argument pursued comparatively by the contributors to *Belonging* (Cohen 1982) and advocated in respect to American kinship by Schneider (*inter alia* 1980). This being so, it was obvious that to talk of British archetypes – 'the family', or whatever – was absurd; and, especially, that to posit a plurality of cultural forms, indeed of cultures, within the British Isles was rather less far-fetched than anthropological sceptics may previously have supposed. Some of the major received categories of anthropological analysis were thereby shown by ethnographic experience of Britain to be inadequate.

This is to suggest that our central concepts should be sensitive to difference, to variety, rather than being merely exclusive in their application. Clearly, one would describe kinship or symbolism in a British community in a manner very different to that in which we would render the family life or ritual processes of a village in inter-lacustrine East Africa. But, if comparison is a viable enterprise at all – an assumption which, it seems, we can no longer make lightly (see Holy, ed., 1987) – then the comparative concepts of kinship and symbolism can only have integrity if they are applicable in both contexts. Earlier anthropologists of Britain tested their powers of comparison largely by trying to locate British data within conceptual matrices of ethnographically extraneous origin. Within the last ten years, the worm has begun to turn: we now dare to suggest that ethnographic experience of research here – and, more generally, in Europe, North America and other industrialised and technological societies – may begin to inform the central conceptual apparatus of anthropology itself.

This brings us back to the central issue of 'Otherness'. I have suggested that anthropologists mistakenly denied the integrity of an anthropology of Britain because its subjects seemed to be insufficiently 'other'. Augé made a similar suggestion, writing that 'our societies are thought to have lost the thing that validates the others, namely, authenticity' (1982, p. 3). The corollary of their misapprehension was their construction of the cultures they *did* study as being *so* 'other' as to require description and interpretation in theoretical terms which were wholly inapplicable to their own cultures and societies. Peacock (1975) was so unwise as to suggest that technological development displaces symbolism: *we*, therefore, have technology; *they* have symbols! Yet, what wondrously complex theoretical devices we have had to invent in order to elicit their symbols. (cf. Sperber, 1980).

One may only presume that, put before the people they purport to describe, they would be greeted with incredulity if not by embarrassed giggling. We require Freud, Sapir, Ricoeur to render the meanings of Ndembu circumcision or Sinhalese exorcism; but the Ndembu and Sinhalese appear to manage quite well on their own. Elaborating on a similar observation, Roy Wagner asks, 'What are symbols that we should be concerned with them? They are certainly not something that "the natives" have told the anthropologist about, though natives are often outspoken about what we call their "content". Rather, it seems, they are something that we often say the natives are all about' (1986, p. 1). Moreover, we present our miraculous feats of systematic interpretation as if we were involved only in the resolution of the problem, rather than in its construction. For whom is the Nuer sacrifice of cucumbers a problem: the Nuer or us? To whom does the meaning of the Kwakiutl cannibal dance present a difficulty: to the Indians who participate in it or look on for entertainment; or to the anthropologist who, perhaps, confuses his problems of understanding with theirs? And so we have imported into the enterprise of interpreting other people's behaviour – obviously one fraught with difficulty – transformational and structural linguistics; Wittgensteinian family resemblances; unconscious cognitive structures; gestalt psychology; semiotics, as if the problems we were thereby trying to resolve were exclusively those of the Other, rather than of our *selves*. It is not until we are brought up short by, for example, Fernandez writing on Bwiti metaphor (e.g. 1974), or Wagner on Daribi ritual, or Barley on Dowayo symbolism (1983) that anthropologists of exotically *other* cultures are cautioned: 'Just a moment. What we are conceptualising or mystifying as a problem may be *our* problem, not theirs'. The conundrums we impute to them for resolution by their ingenious rituals are possibly rooted in our own mentalities. So Wagner concludes his rhetorical question by asking, 'Are symbols, then, a kind of disease of civilization, that we in our ministrations, like so many Typhoid Marys, unwittingly communicate to the natives? Or, conversely, is civilization itself a disease of symbols. . .?' (loc. cit.). When we claim to be working out the meanings of *their* behaviour, we cannot do so by writing our *selves* out of the equation – for our selves constitute variables and unknowns of as much significance as the 'others'.

Our enhanced sensitivity to the problematic nature of ethnographic authority is obviously due to developments in the discipline other than those of parochial studies. I shall touch on some in a moment. But part of the contribution which may be made to anthropology generally by our increasing experience of parochial studies is that our awareness of local heterogeneity and diversity surely calls in to question our monolithic characterisations of 'other cultures' and the imputation to them of 'key' values, cultural logics or uniform characters. Indeed, our alertness to the fallacies of generalisation has made questionable our very representation of peoples as 'societies' or 'cultures'.

The displacement of structural studies by symbolic anthropology, and our recognition of the meanings of symbols as being negotiable, contestable or, at the very least, interpretable has made imperative the elicitation of heterogeneity – or, certainly, the rigorous investigation of the limits of similarity. In part, this changed emphasis can be attributed to 'interpretivism' and Geertz's influence. But these also contributed to the genre known as 'reflexive anthropology': the deliberate linking of the personality and cultural biography of the observer with the subjects of observation. The post-modern reflexivists argued as follows. If we take seriously Geertz's contention that ethnography is an interpretive exercise; that, in purporting to describe the meanings which cultures have for those who bear them, anthropologists are really doing no more than making informed guesses about these meanings, then they must be clear and explicit about the respects in which they are themselves constituting these very cultures. Geertz freely concedes that anthropology is a discipline in which we place our interpretive constructions upon other people's constructions. Therefore, say his post-modern critics, we ought not to allow our constructions to masquerade as theirs. When we offer an ethnography of another culture it should be, they say (following Bakhtin) in 'dialogical' rather than 'analogical' terms. Ethnography, they argue, should be a record of the analytically unprocessed observation (or interaction between ethnographer and 'informant', Self and Other) rather than of the anthropologist's *post hoc* theorised conclusions.

There is a manifest difference here between the post-modernists and the interpretivist school which spawned them. Geertz proposed an analogy between culture and a text. The argument ran thus: we can clearly distinguish between the score of a string quartet, as a symbolic inscription of music, and its musical interpretation, by players and audience, in performance. For Geertz, culture *is* performance; it is interpretation (which is why in his view ethnography must be the interpretation of interpretations). However, the post-moderns seem to be arguing that it is possible to retrieve that interpretation, to record and purvey it, keeping it separate from the secondary interpretations made by the audience: that, somehow therefore, it is possible to isolate what is played from what is heard. Only by keeping the two apart could we properly represent the audience's interpretation/experience of the music as a product of their interaction.

This claim is implausible. Unlike the ethnomethodologists, the post-moderns are not looking for a retreat from analysis; but for, first, a separation of data from analysis – an aspiration which would seem no more capable of accomplishment than the experiential separation of playing music from hearing it – and, secondly, a clear account of how the observer constitutes the data and its subsequent analysis in their conflation as 'ethnography'. They propose that it is ethnography rather than culture which should be treated as 'text', so that it becomes incumbent upon us to provide interpretive directions – crescendo here, diminuendo there – for the manner in which it should be read.

In so far as the post-modernist critique alerts us to the centrality of self in the ethnographic endeavour, it can be applauded. But it fails to accomplish any advance on our means of accommodating this idea within our ethnographic procedures. Leading post-modernist writers like Tedlock (1983), Dwyer (1982), Crapanzano (1980, 1985) and Taussig (1986) have attempted to acknowledge the bias of the self by displaying the materials – conversations, oral poems, life histories, and so forth – from which their texts are assembled. It is a kind of challenge to the reader: 'here are my raw materials, and this is what I have made of them'. But it is a spurious testimony. As author, the ethnographer exercises discretion over what is revealed to us. Even if the ethnographer's field notebooks, photographs and tapes were put on display, we would still be faced with selective items. What is written down, or recorded, or photographed, is necessarily selective. A leading critic refers to "staged" dialogues and to "fictions" of dialogue (Clifford, 1986, p. 14; also Rabinow, 1986, pp. 245–6).

But it is spurious in another respect too. We write down what we see and hear. We may well write down things we have not yet understood, but we cannot suppress the sense-making that goes on while we are watching and, later, when we are writing. It would be odd to make a deliberate attempt to do so. It would be tantamount to neutralising the interpretive skills which are the very *raison d'être* of the observational posture that distinguishes anthropology from other disciplines. In ordinary life we do not defer sense-making: we do not hold stimuli in one figurative hand, our interpretive models in the other, and only bring them together in an explicit manner under controlled conditions. We begin the struggle to render stimuli intelligible even as we experience them. Under ordinary circumstances we have no choice in the matter. The combined forces of our personal experience and of our compulsion to make things understandable to ourselves are irresistible. That is precisely the behaviour which anthropologists have to capture in their ethnographic work, and they do so in a similar manner. Unless they are in an abnormal state of consciousness, they cannot hold sense-making at bay.

The crucial issue for us has always been that of the unconscious influences on our sense-making, and this is where the question of the Self and the Other is central. In the 'classical' British ethnographic tradition, anthropologists coped with the issue by ignoring it or by defining it out of existence. True to Durkheimian positivistic science, they seem to have decided that, provided they observed the proper ethnographic procedures, the self could not intrude at all or, at least, not in a way which would invalidate their observations. Genealogies were mapped, marriage alliances revealed, networks plotted, extended cases 'documented' or 'crafted' (Epstein, ed., 1967). The Other was thereby revealed and science was done. Later, we became bold enough to recognise and admit that, as Boon has so cogently argued (1982), we are trapped as sense-makers within the inherently contrastive proclivities of our own social experience. We consoled ourselves with the thought that we also had our anthropological experience with which to test our own and others' interpretations and with which to place at least a minimal check on our subjectivity. (Consider, for example, Sperber's distinction between 'ethnography' and 'anthropology' (1985, p. 10). In this respect, we complicate the self-other juxtaposition for it becomes apparent that, as anthropologists, we combine *two* selves in our ethnographic 'persons': the analyst and the participant. This is true regardless of where fieldwork is conducted, but our appreciation of it may well have sharpened through our recent experience of parochial studies precisely because when we are 'at home' rather than in the exotic 'field' we have to be deliberately alert to the recognition of our own split personalities.

Good fieldwork must involve the anthropologist in moving continuously between these two selves and the worlds to which they belong (Geertz, 1975; Strathern, 1987). One respect in which the self of the fieldworker may differ from its other manifestations is in the 'self'-consciousness which it perpetually exercises. One may not continue to be consumed by the near-paralysing self-consciousness which infects the early days of one's field research; but it does not disappear. One continues to use one's self to make sense of the society and to verify one's interpretations. Did I behave correctly, or otherwise? Did I understand? Did I anticipate accurately? Did I make myself understood? The self is *the* essential element of anthropological fieldwork. It is largely by observing his own self performing (as the post-modernists would say, 'in discourse') that the fieldworker 'discovers' the culture he studies. Facts, data, documentation are all constituted in this way by the ethnographer's self. That may be scientifically unsatisfactory, but it is both the limitation and the strength of anthropology.

Later, in the *writing* of the ethnography, the ethnographer's self acknowledges a quite different imperative: to present his judgements about one group of people in a manner which will be persuasive to another – that is, to create a 'persuasive fiction' (Strathern, 1987). These two orientations of the ethnographer's self are alchemically resolved by his interpolation into the conceptual mediation of 'an anthropological framework', a peculiar mode of thought which, he supposes, differs from lay analysis. He may go so far as to claim that this conceptual matrix is actually founded on, or has at least been fundamentally influenced by, his need to make sense of a particular society to which, therefore, it must bear some congruence. The self thinks in a manner which it believes and/or claims to have been generated by its experience of those about whom it thinks.

Others may judge this to be a self-induced confidence trick. Credulous though I may be, I disagree. Obviously the discourse between ethnographer and informant is crucial to the anthropological exercise. But I would add another, also crucial – between the selves of the ethnographer: one of which interacts and, hopefully, communes with those among whom he lives (in talk – and in silence!); the second, one which struggles to make and to communicate an intellectual sense of them, which is qualitatively different from (neither inferior nor superior to) the kind of sense appropriate to his interaction with them. The first is a communion; the second, a detachment which feeds on the first. The act of translation, whether between cultures, conceptual schemes or minds (selves) is the essence of anthropology.

The status of the Other as the catalytic and central element in anthropology is thus transformed. Lenclud (this volume) argues that the device of *l'Autre* provided *les ethnologues* with a means of characterising rural France as 'different', in a way which was artificial and over-generalised and which did not comprehend relations between rural society and the rest of France. I think there may well be more honourable exceptions to such inadequacy in the French literature than in its British equivalent. My own concern with the Other has been a little different. It is to recognise that 'otherness' begins with and *within* mind rather than at the abstracted level of culture. This view obliges the anthropologist to accommodate the complexity and subtlety of mind (and, by extension therefore, the awesome diversity to be found within culture) and to see *other* people as being just as complicated, uncomforming, subtle and uncertain as he is himself. In this respect I associate myself with those who maintain that the real potency of anthropology lies in its unequivocal commitment to the interpretive nature of the exercise: by the ethnographer using his own experience of interpretive struggle, among his 'selves' as well as with an *alter*, to temper the theoretical judgements he makes about what inclines other people to do what they do.

The alacrity with which British and American anthropologists have leaped into this maze may be at least partly explained by the absence from their own intellectual midsts of such dominant systematic theorists as Levi-Strauss, Foucault, Barthes or Althusser. Now in Britain, uncertain of ourselves theoretically, we seem to be increasingly tempted by American ethnographic experimentation or by the supposed potentialities of philosophy, linguistics and history. This moment of iconoclasm and flux offers an opportunity not only to rehabilitate parochial studies, but to use them to inform and influence the very central ideas of our discipline. I offer one instance in conclusion.

Social psychologists and sociologists depicted social identity as the product and imperative of interaction between *Ego* and *Alter*. Yet the anthropologist did not locate himself within this interaction: he was merely a detached observer of the interplay between 'other' and 'other'. The interaction itself was the critical variable, rendering identity salient, malleable and expedient. It was a perspective entirely consistent with that of the Generalisable Other which was deducible from a logic perceived to inhere in culture or structure, and which was qualitatively different from the complexity of the anthropological self. The identity of the other was always a matter of relativity – and little wonder, for anthropology generally remained so firmly entrenched in relativistic thinking (cf. Burridge, 1979, p. 8).

In no topic is this relativism more apparent than in the study of ethnic identity. Ever since Barth portrayed ethnic identity as a reflex of boundary transactions (1969), treating ethnicity as a 'front stage' performance (Goffman, 1959), ethnicity studies have ground out ever more instances of the deliberate marking and celebration of cultural difference. But recent writers have advanced on Barth's seminal statement by recognising that the significance of such boundary marking goes beyond the interaction of ethnic *Ego* and *Alter*. For example, both Schwartz (1975) and Paine (1984) refer to ethnic identity as a 'self-reflective' dimension of culture, suggesting that the boundary posture cannot be convincing to members (nor, we may therefore presume, to others) if it cannot also appear to them as an authentic medium for their *internal* discourse. In his fascinating analysis of the London West Indian carnival, Abner Cohen showed how the carnival changed over time from being a reflection of relations between black immigrants and white indigenes into, first, a platform for the rehearsal of relations among the immigrants' islands of origin; and then among different generations and ideological tendencies within the black population. But with particular respect to this latter phase, he also shows how the carnival provides participants with a route to *self*-discovery and definition which has little to do with affective contrasts (Cohen, 1980). This is the dimension of ethnicity to which Epstein directs our attention when he urges that 'a view of ethnic groups "from without", i.e. simply in their external relations and interactions, needs to be supplemented by one "from within" ' (1978, p. xii). Epstein continues to emphasise contextual influences on identity and, on this matter, I am presently more agnostic. It seems to me that if anthropologists are serious in wishing to treat ethnicity as being more than a set of relativities, they have to grapple with the concept of self and not abandon the task to psychologists and philosophers. I concur with the writers I have cited in their view that ethnicity is not just a statement about the self made for the purposes of interactions with others, but is also a statement made by the self to the self. Perhaps I go further than they would wish to in suggesting that this statement may spring wholly, or in part, from a sense of intrinsic, rather than relative, selfhood.

I am not proposing that the self should be fetishised, nor that we should replace the hallowed, but anachronistic Significant Other by the Significant Self. Rather, I would argue, it is only by focusing upon the self in this way that we can hope to understand why certain aspects of culture or collectivity are emphasised in ethnic relations to the exclusion of others even when they may not be peculiar to the group which utilises them, and be less obviously distinctive than some other available items. I have noted this apparent paradox in my own research in Shetland (e.g. Cohen, 1987), and am therefore struck by Schwartz's observation (op. cit.) that, among Admiralty Islanders, many of these kinds of item appear to have a 'sectarian' character, expressing 'distinctions that seem very important to insiders, dividing them into passionate factions', but which 'to outsiders seem like the merest variations on a theme'. The boundary may thus be seen as an expression of internality, as well as of externality.

But for anthropology to have any possibility of access to this boundary, we have to discard our conventional notions of generalisable Others, unless we are to rest content with the grossest simplification. We have to accept the impenetrable complexity of diversity *within* the cultures we study, not least because such diversity has been revealed to us within our *own* cultures. We have therefore to use our experience of self, and especially of 'self' as a sometimes incoherent bundle of selves (or Others) to appreciate the immensity of the task which confronts us in attempting to understand, and to purvey our understanding of, other people. It is with this in mind that we may console ourselves with the suggestion that to see anthropology as not just the study of 'Other', but also of 'self', is not self-indulgence. Rather, it is a recognition that reflexivity may be our most powerful tool. How else could we make sense of silence when it goes unnoticed by its perpetrators, except in the breach – and is then regarded as a more eloquent statement of difference than could be made by words alone.

Notes

*My sincere thanks to Robert Paine, Martine Ségalen and Marilyn Strathern for commenting so helpfully on earlier drafts of this paper.

1. Compare the locations of the studies in *Belonging* (Cohen, ed., 1982) with those in *Symbolising Boundaries* (Cohen, ed., 1986). See also the Appendix to this paper for recent studies of rural Britain.
2. For reviews of these and other studies, see Frankenberg (1966); Bell and Newby (1971); and Allan (1984).

Bibliography

Allan, G., 'A geography of post-War British community studies', presented to the *ESRC Workshop on Community Studies*, University of Aston, 1984.

Arensberg, C., *The Irish Countryman*, New York, Macmillan, 1937.

Arensberg, C. and Kimball, S.T., *Family and Community in Ireland*, Cambridge, Mass., Harvard University Press, 1948.

Augé, M., *The Anthropological Circle: Symbol, Function, History*, Cambridge University Press, 1982.

Bailey, F.G., 'Gifts and poison' in F.G. Bailey (ed.) *Gifts and Poison: the Politics of Reputation* Oxford, Blackwell, 1971.

Barley, N., *Symbolic Structures: An Exploration of the Culture of the Dowayos*, Cambridge University Press, 1983.

Barth, F., 'Introduction', in F. Barth, (ed.), *Ethnic Groups and Boundaries*, London, George Allen & Unwin, 1969, pp. 1–38.

Bell, C. and Newby, H., *Community Studies*, London, George Allen & Unwin, 1971.
Boon, J.A., *Other Tribes, Other Scribes,* Cambridge University Press, 1982.
Bott, E., *Family and Social Network,* London, Tavistock, 1957.
Burridge, K.L., *Someone, No One: An Essay on Individuality,* Princeton, N.J., Princeton University Press, 1979.
Chapman, M., *A Social Anthropological Study of a Breton Village, with Celtic Comparisons* unpublished Ph.D. thesis, University of Oxford, 1987.
Clifford, J., 'Introduction: partial truths', in *Writing Culture: the Poetics and Politics of Ethnography,* (J. Clifford and G.E. Marcus, eds.) Berkeley: University of California Press, 1986, pp. 1–26.
Cohen, Abner, 'Drama and politics in the development of a London carnival', *Man* (N.S.) 15, 1980.
Cohen, A.P., *The Symbolic Construction of Community,* London, Tavistock, 1985.
— *Whalsay: Symbol, Segment and Boundary in a Shetland Island Community,* Manchester University Press, 1987.
— (ed.) *Belonging: Identity and Social Organisation in British Rural Cultures,* Manchester University Press, 1982.
— (ed.) *Symbolising Boundaries: Identity and Diversity in British Cultures,* Manchester University Press, 1986.
Crapanzano, V., *Tuhami: Portrait of a Moroccan,* Chicago: University of Chicago Press, 1980.
— *Waiting: the Whites of South Africa,* New York: Random House, 1985.
Cresswell, R., *Une Communauté Rurale d'Irlande,* Paris: Institut d'Ethnologie, 1969.
Dumont, L., (1983) *Essays on Individualism: Modern Ideology in Anthropological Perspective,* Chicago, University of Chicago Press, 1986.
Dwyer, K., *Moroccan Dialogues: Anthropology in Question,* Baltimore, Johns Hopkins University Press, 1982.
Emmett, I., *A North Wales Village,* London, Routledge & Kegan Paul, 1964.
Epstein, A.L., *Ethos and Identity: Three Studies in Ethnicity,* London, Tavistock, 1978.
— (ed.), *The Craft of Social Anthropology,* London, Tavistock, 1967.
Favret-Saada, J., *Les Mots, La Mort, Les Sorts,* Paris, Éditions Gallimard, 1977.
Fernandez, J.W., 'The mission of metaphor in expressive culture', *Current Anthropology,* 15 (2), 1974, pp. 119–45.
Firth, J.R., et al., *Families and their Relatives,* London, Routledge & Kegan Paul, 1969.
Foucault, M., *The Archaeology of Knowledge,* London, Tavistock, 1972.
Fox, J.R., 'Prolegomena to the study of British kinship', in J. Gould, (ed.), *Penguin Survey of the Social Sciences,* Harmondsworth, Penguin, 1965.
— *The Tory Islanders: a People of the Celtic Fringe,* Cambridge University Press, 1978.
Frankenberg, R.J., *Village on the Border,* London, Cohen & West, 1957.
— *Communities in Britain,* Harmondsworth, Penguin, 1966.
Geertz, C., 'Thick description: toward an interpretive theory of culture', in *The Interpretation of Cultures,* London, Hutchinson. 1975, pp. 3–30.
Goffman, E., *The Presentation of Self in Everyday Life,* New York, Doubleday Anchor, 1959.
Harris, R., *Power and Powerlessness in Industry: An Analysis of the Social Relations of Production,* London, Tavistock, 1987.
Helias, P.-J., *Le Cheval d'Orgueil,* Paris, Librarie Plon, 1975.
Hobart, M., 'Summer's days and salad days: the coming of age of anthropology', in *Comparative Anthropology* (L. Holy, ed.), Oxford, Blackwell, 1987, pp. 22–51.
Holy, L. (ed.) (1987) *Comparative Anthropology,* Oxford, Blackwell, 1987.
Leach, E.R., (1985) 'Observers who are part of the system', *THES,* 29 November 1987.

Littlejohn, J., *Westrigg: the Sociology of a Cheviot Parish*, London, Routledge & Kegan Paul, 1963.
Paine, R.P.B., 'Norwegians and Saami: nation-state and Fourth World', in *Minorities and Mother-country Imagery* (G.L. Gold, ed.) St John's, ISER, 1984, pp. 211–48.
Peacock, J.L. *Consciousness and Change: Symbolic Anthropology in Evolutionary Perspective*, Oxford, Blackwell, 1975.
Pitt-Rivers, J.A., *People of the Sierra*, (2nd. edition) Chicago, University of Chicago Press, 1971.
Rabinow, P., 'Representations are social facts: modernity and post-modernity in anthropology', in *Writing Culture* (J. Clifford and G.E. Marcus, eds.), Berkeley, University of California Press, 1986, pp. 234–61.
Rees, A., *Life in a Welsh Countryside*, Cardiff, University of Wales Press, 1951.
Schneider, D.M., *American Kinship: a Cultural Account* (2nd edition), Chicago, University of Chicago Press, 1980.
Schwartz, T., 'Cultural totemism: ethnic identity primitive and modern', in *Ethnic Identity: Cultural Continuities and Change* (G. de Vos and L. Romanucci-Ross, eds.), Palo Alto, Mayfield Publishing Co, 1975, pp. 106–31.
Ségalen, M., *Mari et Femme dans la Société Paysanne*, Paris, Flammarion, 1980.
— *Quinze Générations de Bas-Bretons: Parenté et Société dans le Pays Bigouden, 1720-1980*, Paris, Presses Universitaires de France, 1985.
Sperber, D. *Rethinking Symbolism*, Cambridge University Press, 1975.
— 'Is symbolic thought pre-rational?' in *Symbol as Sense: New Approaches to the Study of Meaning*, (M. LeCron Foster and S. Brandes, eds.), London, Academic Press, 1980, pp. 25–44.
— *On Anthropological Knowledge: Three Essays*, Cambridge University Press, 1985.
Stacey, M., *Tradition and Change: A Study of Banbury*, Oxford University Press, 1960.
Strathern, M., *Kinship at the Core: an Anthropology of Elmdon, a Village in North-west Essex in the 1960s*, Cambridge University Press, 1981.
— 'Out of context: the persuasive fictions of anthropology', *Current Anthropology*, 28 (3), 1987, pp. 251-270.
Taussig, M., *Shamanism, Colonialism and the Wild Man*, Chicago, University of Chicago Press, 1986.
Tedlock, D., *The Spoken Word and the Work of Interpretation*, Philadelphia: University of Pennsylvania Press, 1983.
Wagner, R., *Symbols that Stand for Themselves*, Chicago, University of Chicago Press, 1986.
Wallman, S., *Living in South London: Perspectives on Battersea, 1871-1981*, Aldershot, Gower Publishing Co., 1982.
— *Eight London Households*, London, Tavistock, 1984.
Watson, J.L., (ed.), *Between Two Cultures: Migrants and Minorities in Britain*, Oxford, Blackwell, 1977.
Williams, W.M., *The Sociology of an English Village: Gosforth*, London, Routledge & Kegan Paul, 1956.
— *A West Country Village: Ashworthy*, London, Routledge & Kegan Paul, 1963.
Wilmott, P. and Young, M., *Family and Kinship in East London*, London, Routledge and Kegan Paul, 1957.
Wylie, L., *Village in the Vaucluse*, Oxford University Press, 1957.
Zonabend, F., *La Mémoire Longue*, Paris, Presses Universitaires de France, 1980.

Appendix: Recent anthropological studies of rural Britain

In 1983 I submitted to the Social Affairs Committee of the Economic and Social Research Council a consultative paper and bibliography reviewing anthropological studies of the rural British Isles published or conducted during the preceding fifteen years (Cohen 1983). Here I append an update to that earlier bibliography (covering work on rural Britain published up to 1987) with the caution that it is not exhaustive.

Although I may reasonably claim to have been an early protagonist of the cause, I was obliged to adopt a rather critical posture in my 1983 report when reviewing existing work on Britain. Indeed, some of my colleagues appeared to be quite gratified that I had disparaged the quality of so much of the anthropology of rural Britain. I speculated about a number of factors which might explain the less than brilliant standard of pre-1983 work. Basic to these was that, during the 1960s and 1970s, the anthropological profession underrated the importance of such studies, regarding them as marginal to the discipline and as a research option to which resort should be made only if fieldwork elsewhere was impossible, for whatever reason. As a consequence, there was only a paltry literature; a lack of experience both in conducting and in supervising research in Britain; a woefully blithe ignorance of the problems of doing anthropological research in such a society; and a lack of confidence and vigour in the propagation of new concepts and models. Fieldwork often seemed to lack the bite and rigour revealed in anthropological research in more conventional stamping grounds; the parameters of argument appeared to be largely derived from those developed elsewhere. It was not just that we focused on the usual topics, but that we tended to do so within the matrices of prevailing anthropological models; and, therefore, inevitably risked misconstruing what was before our very eyes. We seemed to be apologetic for taking up readers' time with descriptions of systems and processes which were manifestly less elaborate, exotic, mysterious and, therefore, intellectually demanding than those to be found in Africa, Asia, the Pacific or the Middle East. In short, we were defensive.

As I have argued in this paper, the moment for such defensiveness has now definitely passed. With the recent expansion in the scope of ethnographic research on Britain, and with our enhanced experience and the methodological sophistication which that brings in its wake, we are now in a position to inform anthropology and ethnographic practice wherever it is conducted. This transformation suggests that there is a certain artificiality now in reviewing British rural anthropology as a specialised area. First, the grounds for distinguishing between urban and rural studies have become much less obvious during the last decade as the conceptual bases and ethnographic foci of urban anthropology have changed. Secondly, anthropologists of Britain have correctly avoided the trap of Britainology. If they acknowledge an area allegiance at all, it is probably to European, rather than to more exclusively British, studies. Because of its considerably longer and more developed tradition, the island of Ireland used to have a more coherent literature than any British region. For obvious reasons, however, there is now a noticeable bifurcation in Irish anthropological studies between those conducted in the Republic and those in the North: with occasional exceptions (e.g., Crozier, 1985, Buckley, 1982), the latter are substantially focused on aspects of sectarian relations. In Scotland, most published work is concentrated on the Hebrides and on the north-east, including the Northern Isles. These are quite different ethnographic regions since the former is predominantly Gaelic, whilst the latter is not; and they are markedly dissimilar in their economic and religious lives. Even within the Western Isles literature, there is little in the way of concerted debate (with the honourable exception of Peter Mewett's work) while the latter area is more notable for its internal diversity than for its uniformity. The Shetland literature has been recently augmented by two books (Byron, 1986; Cohen, 1987) although, again, both authors avoid restricting themselves to parochial comparison but use a much broader frame of comparative reference. Recently published work on rural England is generally oriented primarily (and properly) to topic, rather than to localities as constituents of a cultural area. (There are exceptions, of course: e.g. Phillips, 1984; 1986). Thus, for example, Bouquet (1984; 1986) deals with aspects of gender and of family farming, explicitly addressing the contemporary French literature; Rapport (1983; 1986) is primarily concerned with debates on linguistic and symbolic anthropology; Okely (1983), with ethnicity (and, more recently, with the comparison of social issues related to ageing in English and French milieux); Michaud (1986), likewise with ageing; and James (1983; 1986) with youth and adolescence.

I do not wish to suggest that the authors cited here treat location as incidental; that would be absurd. Rather, like some innovative anthropologists of urban Britain,[1] and although painfully conscious of working in something of an ethnographic void, they have been concerned to contribute to the non-parochial comparative study of their topics in anthropology generally, or with reference to European and other industrialised societies. Obviously, my personal inclination is to applaud this wider view, although it does raise questions about the practical engagement of anthropologists with *British* issues, particularly in respect of policy, an engagement which has grown through political pressures; and which will certainly become increasingly prominent. In urban milieux, anthropologists are already studying planning processes, matters associated with housing, employment and health care, issues related to education, minority languages, religion and various aspects of ethnicity. It is to be hoped that we will soon see work in rural areas concerned with the consequences of changes in agriculture and land use, with rural unemployment, demographic change and with ecological problems. I would not advocate a departure from established anthropological concerns; rather, that they should be directed to new foci which are of obvious empirical relevance. For example, when, at last, there is some public recognition of the difficulties which confront carers, so anthropologists should apply to their investigation their cross-cultural expertise in the study of kinship, friendship and solidary social relations. As ecological problems weigh ever more heavily, so anthropologists must apply the insights gained from the study of other societies which are polarised between indigenous 'users' and extraneous planners and developers. The anthropological literature provides a rich base of ideas and experience for an examination of organisational behaviour, of localism, sectarianism, social deprivation and disadvantage, indeed, of all of the issues which characterise life in contemporary Britain. This is not a plea for 'applied anthropology', whatever that may be; but for the recognition that, as anthropologists, we know painfully little about social life in the British Isles. I have the impression that, in this regard, we have suffered from our own imperialism and, unlike our French colleagues, have been dismissive or afraid of introspection. It may therefore be that this kind of work offers the most fruitful areas for our future collaboration.

Note

1 See, for example, Vered Talai's *Armenians in London: The Management of Social Boundaries* (Manchester: Manchester University Press, 1989) and Sandra Wallman's *Eight London Households* (London: Tavistock, 1985).

Addenda to bibliography

Bouquet, M., (1984a) 'Women's work in rural South-west England', in *Family and Work in Rural Societies* (N. Long, ed.), London, Tavistock, 1984.
— (1984b) 'The differential integration of the rural family', *Sociologia Ruralis,* XXIV (1), 1984.
— *Family, Servants and Visitors: The Farm Household in Nineteenth and Twentieth Century Devon,* Norwich, Geo Books, 1985.
—' "You cannot be a brahmin in the English countryside." The partitioning of status, and its representation within the farm family in Devon', in Cohen, (ed.), 1986.
Bradley, T. and Lowe, P., (eds), *Locality and Rurality: Economy and Society in Rural Regions,* Norwich, Geo Books, 1984.
Buckley, A.D., *A Gentle People: a Study of a Peaceful Community in Ulster,* Cultra, Ulster Folk Museum, 1982.
— 'Playful rebellion: social control and the framing of experience in an Ulster community', *Man* (n.s.), 18, 1983.
Bufwack, M.S., *Village without Violence: an Examination of a Northern Irish Community,* Cambridge, Mass., Schenkman, 1982.
Byron, R.J., *Sea Change: a Shetland Society, 1970-79,* St John's, ISER, 1986.
Cohen, A.P., *Anthropological Studies of Rural Britain, 1968-1983: A Position Paper* (HG 6/27) London, ESRC, 1983.
Cohen, A.P., 'Symbolism and social change: matters of life and death in Whalsay, Shetland', *Man* (n.s.), 20 (2), 1985.
— 'Of symbols and boundaries, or, does Ertie's greatcoat hold the key?' in Cohen, (ed.), 1986.
— *Whalsay: Symbol, Segment and Boundary in a Shetland Island Community,* Manchester, MUP, 1987.
— (ed.), *Belonging: Identity and Social Organization in British Rural Cultures,* Manchester: MUP, 1982.
— (ed.), *Symbolising Boundaries: Identity and Diversity in British Cultures,* Manchester: MUP, 1986.
Crozier, R.M., *Patterns of Hospitality in a Rural Ulster Community,* unpublished PhD dissertation, The Queen's University of Belfast, 1985.
Donnan, H. and McFarlane, G. 'Social life in rural Northern Ireland', *Studies,* 74, 1985.
(and R. Jenkins), *The Sectarian Divide in Northern Ireland Today,* R.A.I. Occasional Paper, 41, London, Royal Anthropological Institute, 1986.
Forsythe, D., *Urban-Rural Migration, Change and Conflict in an Orkney Island Community,* North Sea Oil Panel Occasional Paper, 14, London, SSRC, 1982.

Gilligan, J.H., 'The rural labour process: a case study of a Cornish town', in Bradley and Lowe, (eds), 1984.
James, A., *The Structure and Experience of Childhood and Adolescence: an Anthropological Approach to Socialisation,* unpublished PhD Thesis, University of Durham, 1983.
— 'Learning to belong: the boundaries of adolescence', in Cohen, (ed.), 1986.
McFarlane, G., 'Violence in rural Northern Ireland: social scientific models, folk interpretations and local variations', in *The Anthropology of Violence* (D. Riches, ed.), Oxford, Blackwell, 1985.
— ' "It's not as simple as that": the expression of the Catholic and Protestant boundary in Northern Irish rural communities', in Cohen, (ed.) 1986.
Messenger, J.C., *An Anthropologist at Play: Balladmongering in Ireland and its Consequences for Research,* Lanham, Md., University Press of America, 1983.
Mewett, P.G., 'Economic brokerage and peripheral underdevelopment in the Isle of Lewis', *Sociological Review,* 31, 1983.
— 'Boundaries and discourse in a Lewis crofting community', in Cohen, (ed.), 1986.
Michaud, E., 'The story of Miss P.'. *New Society,* vol. 74, (1197), 1985.
— *Old Age: Attitudes to Ageing and the Elderly in an English village,* Unpublished PhD Thesis, University . . ., 1986.
Nadel, J.H., 'Stigma and separation: pariah status and community persistence in a Scottish fishing village', *Ethnology,* 23, 1984.
Okely, J., *The Traveller - Gypsies* Cambridge, CUP, 1983.
Peace, A., ' "A different place altogether": diversity, unity and boundary in an Irish village', in Cohen, (ed.), 1986.
Phillips, S.K., (1984a) *Identity, Social Organisation and Change: Muker Parish, a Yorkshire Dales Community,* unpublished D Phil Thesis, University of Oxford, 1984.
— (1984b) 'Encoded in stone: neighbouring relationships and the organisation of stone walls among Yorkshire Dales farmers', *J. Anth. Soc. Oxford,* XV (3), 1984.
— 'Natives and incomers: the symbolism of belonging in Muker parish, North Yorkshire', in Cohen, (ed.), 1986.
Quayle, B., 'Images of place in a Northumbrian dale', in Bradley and Lowe, (eds), 1984.
Rapport, N.J., *Are Meanings Shared and Communicated? A Study of the Diversity of World Views in a Cumbrian Village* unpublished PhD Thesis, University of Manchester, 1983.
— 'Cedar High Farm: ambiguous symbolic boundary. An essay in anthropological intuition', in Cohen, (ed.), 1986.
Shanks, A.N., *Families and Places: Social Relations among Northern Irish Gentry,* unpublished PhD dissertation, The Queen's University of Belfast, 1982.
Strathern, M., 'Localism displaced: a "vanishing village" in rural England', *Ethnos,* 49, 1984 (also see 'The social meaning of localism', in Bradley and Lowe, (eds.), 1984).
Thompson, P., et al, *Living the Fishing,* London, Routledge & Kegan Paul, 1983.

Part VI. Sociology

16 Commentary and Introduction

Peter Hamilton

The striking difference between the numbers of active researchers, research organisations and institutions, journals, books, reports and publications devoted to what we can for the sake of convenience call 'rural sociology' in Britain and France requires some explanation. Its considerable presence in France and virtual absence in Britain are not however the result of a straightforward difference between the rural histories of the two countries. To explore the reasons calls for the use of at least two analytical perspectives, to equip us to address a simple question: who is the consumer of the 'rural sociology' in question?

The first perspective is therefore necessarily a *sociology of knowledge*, relating particularly to the different organisational and institutional contexts. The fact that these are intimately connected to wider socio-historical factors dictates that the second analytical element of a comparison directs attention to the different historical experiences of the two rural societies since at least the end of the Second World War.

1 French rural sociology: two paradigms

In France, the emergence and development of rural sociology as a recognisable and institutionalised discipline is closely linked to stages in the evolution of French rural society. By contrast, development and change in the British countryside over the same period did not produce *any* significant body of academic or social scientific work which can be labelled as 'rural' sociology. It is tempting to see in these differences more fundamental divisions between the two countries, in the relationship of rural society to the wider national society.

The rapid post-war transformation of French society and economy had its counterpart in the decline of a rural society which at the eve of the Second World War accounted for about 40 per cent of the French population. Put crudely, this rapid and massive social change created a demand for a rural sociology which was addressed to problems of 'agricultural modernisation' in both their cultural and social structural implications.

The emergence of rural sociology in such circumstancs was not, however, the simple result of academic interest in the effects of social change. French rural sociology reflects to a considerable extent the 'demand' for its products: and this demand has come essentially from a single source – the state and the welter of corporatist institutions with which it has become implicated. The role of the French state in the creation and direction of an institutionalised rural sociology devoted to specifically French concerns is thus of pre-eminent importance to an understanding of the themes and issues with which it has dealt. To a large extent these have been marked by a concern with the impact of socio-economic change on a rural society represented as a 'world' apart from that of modern, urban, industrial society – a world believed (at least initially) by the economic planners to be a brake on the necessary modernisation of France.

In very simple terms the central direction or 'planification' of technical and economic change in France over the forty-odd years to 1985, was designed to render France a 'modern' economy, in which development was depicted as a 'march through the sectors' from primary to tertiary (and arguably today, with the advent of an information-technology driven economy, to the quaternary sector). In such a process, the primary need, viewed from the perspective of the state, was to displace the bulk of the active population from low productivity to high productivity sectors of the economy, and within agriculture to displace the mass of low productivity producers, so as to leave a radically reduced agricultural population of high-productivity producers. The *paysan* would be replaced by the *agriculteur*. The objective was, as one extremely influential study of the first twenty years of this process described it, '*la fin des paysans*'.

In such a context, rural sociology was perceived little differently to plant science as a technical aid to 'agricultural modernisation'. Its particular areas of concern were the problems created by the need for and the consequences of *l'exode rurale*. Its natural counterpart was an urban sociology concerned at least in part with the mirror image of the rural problems: the impact of *l'exode rurale* on the towns and cities.

As the paper by Maryvonne Bodiguel and Bertrand Hervieu indicates, the emergence of French rural sociology as a distinct discipline took two main directions: one concerned more with the cultural impact of change on the society and civilisation of the *paysan*, and the other more directed towards what we could call the 'macro-structural' context of the agricultural sector. But in both cases it is important to note that the 'consumer' of this rural sociology was either the state itself, or the corporatist agricultural organisations – in which the state and a particular constellation of interests were inextricably interlocked.

In the first main tradition of French rural sociology, the theoretical paradigm tended to resemble American 'structural functionalism', but with more affinities to a Mertonian 'theory of the middle range', than to Parsonian grand theory. The approach has also been openly interdisciplinary or perhaps more precisely multidisciplinary. Disciplines such as social anthropology, geography (especially that associated with the Norman geographer and his concept of *l'espace vécu*, Armand Frémont) and economics, were also involved in the creation of a more comprehensive model of the changes which French rural society was undergoing in its 'modernisation'.

The key name here is Henri Mendras, a central figure because his work served as a sort of 'textbook' for this approach, and because he created a node of research activity based at l'Université de Paris X at Nanterre. In this, Mendras followed in the footsteps of Emile Durkheim: creating a school built around a particular conception of rural society (itself Durkheimian in tone), and the elaboration of a specific methodology. His approach emphasises the notion (first found in Redfield) of rural society – typified by the village – as a sort of 'encapsulated collectivity', a small-scale social system which is surrounded by its societal 'environment', what Mendras terms a *société englobante*. The characteristic processes of social change acting upon French rural society in the last forty years fundamentally altered the links between *collectivité locale* and *société englobante*. In simple terms, the local collectivity was no longer characterised by distinctively 'peasant society' structure and values, and its articulating links with the global society had become more extensive and interdependent.

It should be clear that this approach is one which concentrates on the cultural and social brakes on development of a 'modern' rural society and economy: indeed Mendras's first published monograph dealt with the cultural hindrances to the take-up of 'modern' agricultural practices in Alsace, based on research conducted in the mid-1950s. The perspective has developed and become more sophisticated with time, but nonetheless it remains rooted in the idea that one form of society, tied up with a characteristic and distinctive way of life, has been replaced by another, more 'modern' and less 'peasant'. It is an approach which fits well with the 'march through the sectors' concept of societal modernisation – hence its relative popularity with both the state and the wider rural public. Indeed the latter point is not without importance. For in France, the fact that for the majority of the population there is some rural link (a family tie and quite frequently also a *maison secondaire*) has itself generated a market for the popular but also quite serious studies of the history and sociology of the French countryside – witness the *succès d'estime* of such works as Duby's four volume *Histoire de la France Rurale,* Le Roy Ladurie's *Montaillou* and Helias's *Le Cheval d'Orgueil.*

The second main approach has been broadly Marxist in theoretical form, and has emphasised the economic changes involved in the modernisation process. A later trend than the Mendrassian perspective (and clearly linked to *les événements* of 1968) its approach has on the whole been more focused on the issue of the incorporation of (peasant) agriculture into capitalism.[1] As a result, its influence has been more international in scope, Harriet Friedmann's work being the most obviously in debt to this perspective. Claude Servolin (though much less the leader of a 'school' than Mendras) is the key figure here. His central thesis – that the French peasant farmer was a petty commodity producer (*petit marchand capitalist*), but has become progressively 'incorporated' into capitalist economic and social relations – was one which cut directly across the Mendrassian approach. However, it also came into direct competition with a politically influential economic perspective (associated most closely with the work of Denis Bergmann) which stressed the economic advantages of the modern, large farm unit over the peasant smallholding. Servolin's approach came to symbolise the struggle of the small farmer in France, especially in the context of economic and political pressures which could be seen as a progressive proletarianisation of the small or peasant farmer.

The Servolinian approach then was far more concerned than the Mendrassian with the political economy of rural social change, and placed considerable emphasis on the economics of agriculture. Its institutional location was also fundamentally different: where Mendras was a university academic whose 'school' was primarily composed of other academics, with links to the state through CNRS; the Servolinian approach was implanted primarily in the advisory and research arms of the French state agricultural bureaucracy, Servolin himself working as economist at, and for a time director of, the *Département d'Economie et Sociologie Rurales*, of the *Institut National de Recherche Agronomique*, in Paris. The very fact that a number of different institutional locations exists within which separate paradigms of rural society can be developed and propagated (cf. the network of regional research institutes under INRA's umbrella), points up the very clear differences which exist when attempting to make a comparison between French and British approaches to rural sociology.

2 British rural sociology: a theoretical vacuum

Turning now to the British case, a very different set of circumstances is apparent. In simple terms, until the advent of the environmental agencies and organisations in recent years, there has not been a 'demand' for rural sociology in the UK. Without a 'consumer' the resources have not been forthcoming to generate a viable sub-discipline, and the activity of rural sociology has remained marginal and transitory.

It is of course possible to suggest that the rural sector, and especially agriculture, constituted a relatively unproblematic area for post-war British sociologists. The rural population – at least that element working on the land – was a small proportion of the total: an eighth of that in France. Yet post-war Britain *was* concerned about the agricultural sector. But it was a concern focused on the strategic role of agriculture, rather than the social changes accompanying industrial modernisation: the issue was food security. Arguably this generated a completely different spectrum of concerns, in which the sociologist – if he or she did have any role to play – could only play second fiddle to those whose role was to increase agricultural productivity – the scientists and the agricultural economists.

Of course the sociologist never got to put in an appearance in this post-war dream of increasing food output, as the goal of food security came ever closer under the benevolent wing of the Ministry of Agriculture, Fisheries and Food, facilitated by its cosy accommodation with the National Farmers' Union. The only social science deemed relevant to this framework was agricultural economics, a sort of intellectual ghetto maintained by the state in segregated and specially funded university departments, along with various advisory organisations later to become ADAS (the Agricultural Development and Advisory Service).

The issues which should have been treated by sociologists (assuming there would have been enough candidates for the job) – and which were in truth little different from those tackled across the Channel, were hived off into strange culs-de-sac by the agricultural economists and given obfuscatory names such as 'agricultural adjustment' to describe the increase in the size of holdings and the decline in the employed labour force, or even more misleadingly, the 'diffusion of innovations'. Agricultural economists had their own journals, specialised theories and methodologies, and a training which had relatively little to do with mainstream economics and a great deal to do with agriculture: they certainly had virtually nothing to do with rural society, or the impact of changes within agriculture on the society, culture, politics, economics or environment of the rural areas in which agriculture took place.

There seem to be two main reasons for this under-theorising of the sociological dimension of either agricultural or rural change in post-war Britain. At the institutional level, sociology really had no purchase on the British academic world until the early 1960s – and then only as a sort of American import, or somewhat esoteric intellectual dalliance practised largely by central European *emigrés* and their tiny coteries of graduate students.

There was almost no distinctively British tradition of sociology, unlike the situation in France where the Durkheimian influence extended into the secondary school system through the compulsory inclusion of sociological studies in the teacher training syllabus. Sociology was also widely seen in Britain as a science for understanding and resolving social problems. These were deemed largely to exist in the cities, and to be concerned primarily with issues connected to housing, health and education. The few studies of British rural society which do exist from this period attest to this framework of interests, although we must not forget that works such as those of W.M. Williams, Ronald Frankenberg, or James Littlejohn, did attempt to create a distinctively British form of rural sociology, albeit one based very firmly within the prevailing paradigms – essentially a rather functionalist 'community studies' and its derivatives. But there was no 'demand' for this sociology – either from the agricultural sector or rural society, but more significantly, none from the profession of sociology itself.

British sociology was pre-eminently concerned with class and occupational issues which were urban and industrial in their context, and linked quite explicitly to a broader political debate in the late 1950s and early 1960s which revolved around the Labour Party's inability to succeed electorally. The very invisibility of a rural dimension to this debate attests to the preoccupation with male, industrial labour (management, professionals, the service occupations and women's work and social class position were also ignored), from which British sociology has even now not fully recovered. Thus the conceptual agenda had little or no room for work which did not treat questions such as social mobility, class consciousness, or the politics of the local community in terms which required an urban industrial vocabularly rather then one which was rural and agricultural.

The second factor which acted against a distinctively sociological approach to farming or rural society concerns the very nature of the post-war political agenda, and the 'hiving-off' of rural matters to the agricultural lobby. Whereas in France the process of social change was itself deeply politicised as it affected both rural society and agriculture, in Britain the political power of the farming lobby, and its apparent coincidence with wider public desires for cheap and secure sources of food, counteracted any tendency there might have been for rural social change and its problems to appear on the wider political agenda until very recently – and thus to become translated into sociological issues.

The very size of the agricultural sector in the UK meant that it could not be, as in France, a battleground on which wider political battles could be fought, and hence it was not a domain in which the opposition of social interests was at all evident. The very success of the NFU in its corporatist links with the state maintained the fiction that academic attention on agriculture and rural society should be devoted to making the farm sector more 'efficient' and profitable, so that 'society's' interests in having a ready supply of cheap food could be served. But the definition of that societal interest was not in any fundamental sense opened up to scrutiny or debate. Indeed, it seems more plausible in this context to suggest that the very predominance of agricultural economics itself prevented the establishment of a viable rural sociology in the UK: for such a science would have been a competitor in fields (e.g. labour mobility, farm management) in which agricultural economists had accumulated a sizable stake. Thus exclusionary practices – the techniques by which any social group attempts to control access to its privileged resources – were employed to maintain the integrity of the profession. There are to this day no professional sociologists in any of the departments of agricultural economics in the UK.

This situation has meant that it has been difficult for rural sociology to gain any sort of academic or other institutional foothold. Its successes are essentially due to 'spin-offs' from mainstream sociology or to disaffection with the sterility of agricultural economics. Howard Newby's work, as is well known, began as an attempt to test certain ideas drawn from David Lockwood's theories about deference, with an occupational group which seemed most liable to this form of class relationship – agricultural workers. If this work had led to the formation of a well grounded neo-Weberian school of rural sociologists led by Newby, its promise would have been fulfilled. But the lack of institutional locations at a time when the university sector in the UK, and sociology in particular, are contracting has proved a formidable handicap to the formation of a coherent grouping. The tendency of many of its erstwhile members to redefine their interests beyond rural sociology has not helped.

Recent younger exponents of a more Marxist and 'structural' rural sociology such as Michael Winter and Terry Marsden, are in essence shadow-boxing with agricultural economics. And the important and interesting work of Ruth Gasson on the farm family and pluriactivity has always remained marginal in mainstream sociological terms because of a conceptual agenda drawn from the restricted vocabulary of agricultural economics. But while such people will continue to be important in bridging sociological and agricultural domains, their lack of professional standing in sociology is a hindrance in the development of a distinctively British rural sociology which avoids a marginal status as a residual category of agricultural economics.

More recently, the emergence of a new set of structural cleavages in rural society associated with environmentalism and amenity pressures on the countryside has drawn attention to the political context of rural society, in ways which have provided a new agenda for a distinctively British rural sociology. The emergence of a new configuration of interests in the countryside and particularly in relation to conflicts over land use, has at last provided a coherent rural focus for many sociologists. The role of the 'newer' rural agencies and voluntary organisations concerned with amenity and ecological issues has been significant in creating a 'demand' for such a policy-oriented rural sociology. But it must be pointed out that it also coincides with the relative demise of the dominant 'productivist' paradigm in agriculture.

The work of Lowe and Cox and their associates has shown that this new 'environmental' tradition can create a conceptual vocabulary of some richness, and generate new theoretical insight. But it is an approach which is in some respects limited by its grounding in policy issues, and its tendency to be focused on the 'enabling' level in terms of the formulation of policy recommendations. As a result it does not provide the basis from which to construct a coherent and more general model of British rural society, and the changes which it is undergoing – although it clearly focuses on certain critical dimensions of change.

In certain respects, the creation of a coherent and general rural sociology in Britain may not now be possible, for reasons other than the institutional and intellectual constraints alluded to above. For in a more general sense, sociology itself has become less rather than more disciplinary as a social science and far less 'paradigm-orientated' than in the 1960s and 1970s. It is more and more implicated in cross-disciplinary work, and open to theoretical influences from many different intellectual fields.

The Rural Economy and Society Study Group itself is an example of this trend. It derived from a group originally begun by the authors, Howard Newby and Kenneth Thompson in 1978 as a means of encouraging communication between those sociologists and their graduate students interested in the development of agricultural sociology. But it has developed far beyond any disciplinary grounding in sociology, to focus not on theories or methodology, but on issues. Within such a context, it is unlikely that any individual or group will attempt to build a new rural sociology synthesis, because the important questions appear to be those which cross the constraints of disciplinary boundaries.

Conclusions

Without attempting to predict the future, what can we conclude about the conditions in which rural sociology will develop in both Britain and France?

For our French colleagues, the enabling role of *sociologie rurale* within a context of rapid and deep-seated rural change has been at an end for at least a decade. Although there are of course still many social problems associated with change in the French countryside, there appears to be less 'demand' for these to be approached and resolved by the sociologist.

As the 'problem' disappears, a sense of disequilibrium is evident within French rural sociology. It has become a discipline in search of a subject. The paper by Bodiguel and Hervieu suggests that the new avenue for research will be the political identity of the French *agriculteur* of the year 2000, in a context of agricultural concentration and European-wide policy constraints. It can also be suggested that French rural sociology still remains relatively underdeveloped in those areas where town and country are most evidently in conflict – the environmental domain. France is experiencing major land use conflicts in key natural and semi-natural areas (e.g. the mountain regions, and areas where permanent meadows and wetlands constitute an invaluable ecological resource), and these are issues which the British case has shown are effectively handled using the theories and methods of sociology.

To the extent that there is – at long last – some area of convergence between a well-developed French *sociologie rurale* and an underdeveloped British rural sociology this is to be found in an increasing interest in environmental and amenity issues, and their opposition of relatively clearly-defined social groups. As this begins to assume a European dimension, the potential for collaborative work must surely increase. However, the continued marginality of rural sociology as perspective or methodology in Britain (especially set against the context of an increasingly marginalised sociology profession in general) must leave cause for concern. Until British rural sociologists achieve some form of continuous institutional base, and create cumulative research traditions, this problem will persist and maintain rural sociology in an underdeveloped state by comparison with the situation in France. In Britain, rural sociology continues to be a problem in search of a discipline.

Note

1. cf. Peter Hamilton (1984) *The Incorporation of Agriculture Within Capitalism* in K. Thompson (ed.) *Work, Employment and Unemployment*, Milton Keynes, The Open University Press.

17 The Metamorphosis of French Rural Sociology

Maryvonne Bodiguel and Bertrand Hervieu

1 Rural sociology: a discipline? *by Maryvonne Bodiguel*

Although France claims several of the founding fathers of sociology, the discipline only really achieved its independence there towards the end of the 1950s having, up to that point, been largely subsumed by philosophy. Subsequently, however, French sociology has flourished, both diversifying its subject-matter and adapting its approach to new issues.

If one were to define a role for sociology durings its early years, it would be in terms of informing the decisions of public authorities, and social actors in general; explaining the processes of social change; analysing the social mechanisms which facilitate the emergence and actions of the various elements of society; and, finally, by identifying the various ideologies at work in society. Thus, though still young as a discipline, sociology was originally located very much within the political, social and economic environment of the time. Consequently, its subject-matter tended to be drawn from the major issues of the post-war period – a period rich in social problems and conflicts at all levels, including the spread of urbanisation and the rural exodus, which together stimulated the two major fields of sociology: urban sociology and rural sociology. This paper deals exclusively with the latter: its emergence in France, the principal themes and issues that it has addressed and, finally, its methodology.

I The formative years

To a certain extent, the approach adopted by sociologists in France has been determined by the requirements of politicians and the administration. Thus, many of the crucial issues of the early period – the modernisation and growth of the economy, the control of urban growth, education, professional training, housing, lifestyles etc, – were addressed within the framework of maintaining the urban hierarchy and the centralised and sectoral system of allocation.

(i) The institutional context

During the 1950s, the principal policy-makers in Paris juggled with a multiplicity of plans and programmes for the restructuring of a country badly damaged by the war and yet whose regions were differentially receptive to the various remedies proposed. In this way, the conception of regional planning in centralised terms rekindled the embers of regionalism that were still glowing beneath the ashes.

However, should not administrative, economic and social decision-making have been decentralised? Was it enough merely to disperse them (given the difficulty of accepting the possibility of genuine regional autonomy)? The regional structure, established in 1960, was only really a modest attempt at dispersing the Parisian decision-making centres while the fundamental issue of regionalism smouldered, provoking a wide range of different programmes until the 1982 decentralisation law was introduced. During the years of reconstruction following the war, however, the French state could conceive economic and social problems solely in the vertical terms which it itself tended to perpetuate. As a result, the policies it sought to introduce largely ignored the horizontal framework in which such problems occurred.

The future of the country has also been seen to rest in the ineluctable growth of towns and cities. It has been deemed necessary, for example, to limit the expansion of the Paris region and to stimulate the growth of regional centres, thereby building up a general urban network as a prerequisite for local development. According to their size and infrastructure, a certain amount of economic growth has been devolved to French provincial cities and major towns. Indirectly, rural space has also been shaped by this strategy and its socio-economic problems redefined through this centralisation of decision-making, in accordance with an urban and hierarchical model of short to medium-term social evolution.

Otherwise, such problems are treated in a sectoral manner. Agriculture, for example, whose structures have needed modernising and whose productivity has needed increasing, has been viewed predominantly in terms of its contribution to the national and regional economies and the balance of trade. In 1954, farmers amounted to around 31 per cent of the active population. This proportion had to be considerably reduced if national policies were to meet their general goals. The problem for this period thus became that of introducing and making acceptable to rural communities, policies which, by their very nature, would bleed such communities white and relegate them to second place; this in a country whose population had, until then, been at least half rural.

These basic themes provoked during the 1950s and 1960s a series of lively debates involving, amongst others, the regional nationalists who, in the optimism of the post-war years, had cultivated high hopes of having a more effective voice particularly with the introduction of specific regional policies. Yet, it was for the towns that the bulk of concern was expressed; 'rural space' seeming to be some sort of appendage, of little interest other than for its agricultural potential. In this way, the region – the small economic region or the historic regions of France – became the model onto which was projected a national development programme, the effect of which was often to mask the region's real existence.[1] This political situation was a major factor in polarising the town-country divide.

(ii) An induced sociological approach
The traditional terms of town and countryside, largely used by historians and geographers to denote interactions identified in the course of their practical studies, have been replaced by the concepts of urban and rural, which denote above all social processes.

The process of urbanisation is one of the major dynamics of contemporary France. It is a co-ordinated set of social and economic changes which leads both to the concentration of populations and their associated activities, and to profound changes in social differentiation, in the norms and modes of social behaviour and, finally, in the prevailing system of values. Urbanisation is thereby the motor in a process of change which has relegated the rural mode of social organisation, which for previous centuries had dominated the national economy, to a largely vestigial position. Furthermore, urbanisation as a process has attracted the attention of politicians and policy-makers because of its capacity to sustain their particular visions of growth and a national, or even international, balance including an expanding and competitive agricultural sector and a new organisation of social and economic life around an urban hierarchy.

Nevertheless, as Fernand Braudel has written in *L'Identité de la France*, it soon becomes clear: 'that one cannot have spatial organisation without an accompanying social organisation which is its essential keystone'. This notion, which counters the scorn held for rural communities, was quickly impressed, during the 1960s, upon local political leaders and the architects of regional planning who were increasingly faced with the unforeseen effects of policies which had paid too little attention to local life and local people. Regions were being abandoned, ill-equipped towns were swamped, and provision of urban infrastructure was proving too costly as territorial, economic and demographic imbalances became increasingly pronounced. It was therefore time to re-examine the processes of change as they affected the rural world, in order ultimately to achieve more co-ordinated development.

In responding to such socio-political contingencies, sociology has tended uncritically to reinforce an urban-rural dichotomy which has been largely promoted by public agencies. Thus urban sociology has been based in the town, and rural sociology in the countryside. The expanding significance of the urban phenomenon has given urban sociology the leading role while the rural phenomenon, with its backward-looking connotations, has tended to inspire in rural sociology a sense of special pleading and defensiveness.

From the end of the 1950s when specific demands for research in rural areas became more and more frequent, until the middle of the 1970s, two distinct research directions held pride of place in France. The first was inspired by the work of American anthropologists who, following the example of primitive societies, took the rural community and the village as a self-centred and relatively autonomous unit and, using this framework, sought to analyse processes of change. The second was influenced by Marxist analysis which interpreted the processes of change in terms of a rampant capitalism and class conflict.

The years which followed 1968 and its political and ideological upheavals, helped to break up a debate whose superficiality was demonstrated by the force of circumstance and events. With the economic and social crises of the time, the glorious thirty years were finally over. Since 1975, rural sociology, attracted by the economic and social issues of daily life, has begun to abandon its initial models and evolutionary schema and to turn instead to thematic studies. Faced with the various issues posed by the changing rural world, rural sociology has also begun to question its own approach to French rural society.

II The foundation of the issues

(i) 'Rural' as the object of sociological investigation
One element in particular has influenced the approach French sociology has had to rural studies; what might be called 'the abstraction of the subject'. The urban-rural conflict, seen predominantly in terms of processes of change within contemporary society, has led to a particular conceptualisation of rural space in the sense that a broad and abstract idea *has become conceptualised as an object of theory*.

Until the middle of the century, history and geography largely monopolised the countryside as a subject for study. The analysis of towns and rural areas and the links between them through the centuries was largely covered by historians though few considered the daily activities and the humdrum aspects of life that allow one fully to characterise a bygone period. On the other hand, the geographical tradition, despite the existence of many varied schools, has always, by definition, stuck to space as its focus of research.

Sociology, in its turn, is endowed with the ability to synthesise and, according to Auguste Comte, searches for 'its own fundamental laws governing social phenomena'. Carried along by the socio-political tide of the time, both 'urban' and 'rural' became established as key concepts, and basic sociological laws of change and reproduction were brought to bear in the analysis of the underlying social processes.

Other approaches could have been envisaged: the sociology of religion or the sociology of the family, for example, both transcend the urban-rural divide. They would also have avoided the ambiguities of the adjective 'rural'. According to the Larousse dictionary, it can refer to the countryside, peasants, farming or a sector of the economy. Furthermore, the word *'rural'* is often used as a plural noun in France, denoting those who live in the countryside. There is seemingly nothing in this to suggest that the word ought to be the specific object of a discipline. Nevertheless, *the sociology of the 'rural'* does imply that it is an independent socio-economic and cultural entity. This is not always made explicit, which can lead to confusion. Even so, the sociology of non-urban space has been accorded a more pronounced scientific status in France than anywhere else. In the USA, in contrast, though rural sociology has a long tradition, its objects of study tend to be more sectoral.

(ii) The rural concept in action
Indeed, early French rural sociologists were initially inspired by American sociological studies of farming as they sought to respond directly to the political situation of the immediate post-war years. Agriculture had to develop rapidly in order to respond both to growing internal demand and to the need to improve exports. Such a development was only possible if farmers themselves became

more competitive and this, in turn, entailed more information, the adoption of new techniques and changes in traditional ways of thinking and, ultimately, in value systems.

Most of the relevant literature available at that time was American and directed predominantly towards the study of agricultural extension. In the main, however, it neglected the local socio-economic context. In France, though, the rural community seemed a predominant and variable factor. The acceptance of economic and social structures as important elements in the process of information diffusion of agricultural decision-making gave rise to the village monograph studies.

These monographs crystallised the French approach to the rural 'object' of study. In encompassing everything local within the remit of the study, in order to ascertain the internal logic of village societies, research began to adopt a particular conception of rural communities, derived from the work of American anthropologists on, so-called, primitive societies. Such work, which treated these societies as a totality, inspired the style of a dozen or so monograph studies, led by Henri Mendras. The research on social cohesion, on community self-sufficiency, on value systems, on internal checks and balances, held in place by an essentially inward-looking social organisation, fell largely within the field of 'Folk Societies'. The theory of the relative autonomy of village societies was also conceived at this time and this approach has had a considerable impact over the last twenty years, a fact illustrated by the number of monographs inspired by it and, above all, by the major theoretical reflection published in 1974 (Jollivet 1974).

The various theoretical debates have increasingly focused on processes of change. The Mendrassian school has suggested that rural communities are organised in order to maintain an internal equilibrium which allows them to incorporate innovation while retaining their own status. Alternatively, those inspired by Marxist interpretations have shown how rural 'societies' are integral parts of an evolutionary process within capitalist society and are thereby subject to its laws. Yet both these convictions also affirm, on the one hand, that village society, because it has persisted as long as it has, remains, in part, a guarantor of the French national identity and, on the other, that the village, as the nation's most basic unit, cannot escape the onward march of history.

A number of authors have positioned themselves at the margins of these debates and have striven instead, with a more empirical methodology, to explore, through the use of local monograph studies, processes by which local communities absorb, adapt and submit to a rapidly changing national environment. In this regard, the work of Placide Rambaud and his team has been particularly important during the 1970s.

Despite their various theoretical disagreements, all French rural sociologists implicitly agree that there exists a social and economic specificity in rural space which, in turn, demands specific treatment. This specificity emerges from rural studies as being so self-evident as to be unquestioned. It is rooted in the diversity of the French countryside, with its tremendous regional differences and, even within the same region, one village displaying very different behaviour from another. To these contrasts and polarities, one can add the town-country dichotomy. Against an urban France undergoing a process of homogenisation, therefore, stands a rural France often difficult to characterise, existing, as it does, in so many contrasting forms. Inevitably, this diversity favoured the notion of particularism.

Since the late 1960s, a critical debate, led predominantly by geographers, has emerged regarding the conceptualisation of rural space. Although there is widespread agreement as to the convenience of INSEE's definition of rural communes based on population size (see Chapter 3), it clearly lacks any sociological rationale. A sizeable village, classified as a town by INSEE, can be similar in economic structure and the ways of life within it to a commune classified as rural. In underpopulated regions, the larger rural communes perform similar functions to small towns. Indeed, statistical criteria, by themselves, cannot offer a valid definition of rural: if population density is one variable, economic and social functions are equally significant, and crucial for the sociologist. A regional approach to the definition of rural has been attempted which determines a threshold according to the extent of the existing urban network and whether or not there is a large town present. Even more recently, studies of household consumption have tried to distinguish between 'urban' and 'rural' modes of behaviour.

The tendency today, however, is for the abandonment of any threshold concept to allow the perspective to switch readily, if necessary, from one 'world' to another. A theory of relative autonomy has emerged which parallels the evolution of the rural *problématique* itself. The study of rural societies as a 'totality', from the 1950s to the 1960s, has increasingly given way to research themes that are less specifically rural: for example, social life, family life, inheritance, women's roles, forms of collective identity, local associations and so on. These themes, which extend equally to town and country, are differently expressed according to their spatial incidence but nevertheless remain part of the same sociology.

This cross-sectional sociology is clearly replacing its predecessor which is increasingly seen as having been only a stage in the discipline's evolution. However, current preoccupations have certainly not wiped the slate clean. The study of rural communities, whatever the prevailing ideas, has contined to emphasise the importance of *localisation* in all social processes. Thus, although a study of social interaction in a rural housing estate and in a quarter within a major town might yield similar results, it stands to reason, on the other hand, that the broader environment in which this social interaction takes place, including its origins and likely changes, is of considerable and variable importance. More than simply an urban-rural distinction, these are regional contrasts which appear to be the results of history, culture, morphology, the local economy and so on. Perhaps we are therefore moving towards a sociology of regional differences.

III *The method of rural sociology*

The fecundity of French rural sociology over the last thirty years is equally due to its methodological variation. The *problématique* which has dominated rural studies generally has been embodied in the particular way in which study areas have been conceived. In considering the 'rural world' as a distinct and complete entity, each particular facet needed to be related to and understood in terms of the broader framework. Thus, the monographic method, which analysed communities as societies, involved history, geography, anthropology and economics, not just sociology. Indeed, the bringing together of disciplines is certainly one of the characteristic strengths of rural studies in France. A formative event, in this regard, was a 1953 conference on the theme of 'Towns and Countryside', which brought together historians, sociologists, psychologists and others, and demonstrated a pluridisciplinary approach to the social microscosm, whether past or present.

(i) The search for a 'global' explanation
The search for a 'global' explanation is thus not original to rural sociologists who have worked within a general intellectual climate dominated, in the post-war period, particularly by the historians of the *Annales* school (see Chapter 5) and the Marxists. Thus in the works of rural sociology one comes across the same ideas which have preoccupied historians – particularly the impossibility of tracing a problem or event without recourse to the society in which it occurs, and the necessity of studying it holistically.

Studies of the diffusion of technical innovations amongst farmers, which were amongst the first works of French rural sociology, provide an interesting example. Any explanation of such social processes demands an analysis not only of the relations between individuals and their economic environment, but also their political, social and symbolic environments. Where the sociological approach has diverged from the historians' is in establishing a particular 'rural object of study'. This would have been contrary to historical method which strives to take account of all influences on social reality including, for example, town-country and state-civil society relationships.

Thus, while rural sociology has been strongly inspired by the new historical method, it has applied it to an altogether differently defined field of analysis. Perhaps this has also been an unstated response to the difficulties involved. To address a contemporary problem as a microcosm, i.e. to take account of all the structures which it reveals in addition to the technological, symbolic and ecological context in which it occurs, is an extremely exacting challenge. The model proposed by Henri Mendras has proved convenient in containing the field of analysis. The criticisms it has drawn, particularly from Marxist researchers, have focused less on the definition of the social formation than on its described mode of operation (Bodiguel 1986).

Mendras, in an approach rooted in Weberian method, sought to establish a theory of peasant society based upon a structural-functional conceptualisation of local rural communities as independent social microcosms (Bodiguel 1986). His analysis was grounded upon five fundamental suppositions: the relative autonomy of peasant communities with respect to wider society; the structural importance of the domestic group in the social and economic life of the community; the relatively closed and internal economic system, with little distinction between production and consumption; the existence of a local social system defined by personal relationships and shared knowledge; and the key mediative role of local notables in linking the community with the outside world (Mendras 1976). With the ample evidence provided by the local monographs, Mendras and his followers were able to analyse accordingly the changing nature of post-war French and European rural communities. However, where

Mendrassian analysis failed was in providing a satisfactory explanation of change in terms of either the class struggle or relation to the means of production. Furthermore, in confirming that rural social stratification, despite the survival of certain distinctive forms, is essentially similar to that of urban society and subject to the same determinants within a capitalist state, his analysis dealt itself a further blow.

It is interesting to note, nevertheless, a parallel between this intellectual tradition and the Marxian one, in the same search for a dominant factor which might explain processes of change across the entire social formation under investigation. For Henri Mendras this explanatory factor is to be found in one or other of the constituent systems within local society which ultimately provide a key to the explanation of social change in the society as a whole (for example, in the west of France, in the local value systems that are strongly influenced by both the Catholic Church and the local aristocracy). For the Marxists, the dominant explanatory factor is the evolution of forces of production and the class relations which they engender. Thus, although individual *problématiques* might be totally different, there is a certain congruency in the *explanatory method*.

As an alternative to the Mendrassian approach, Marxian rural sociology sought, in the late 1960s, to introduce a dialectal analysis of rural changes based upon a far wider conception of social and economic forces. Responding to the socio-political changes of the 1960s and in particular to the failure of Mendrassian analysis to examine the relationship between the persistent family farming sector and developing agrarian capitalism, Servolin (1972), among others, developed, on the one hand, a detailed critique of the Mendras approach and, on the other, a Marxist rural sociology. He and other Marxian sociologists have interpreted rural community change in terms of the impact of agrarian capitalism, changing production and class relations and the role of the state and other powerful interests (Jollivet 1974). Rural communities and agricultural enterprises were redefined according to the sort of class analysis more often associated with urban sociology; farming assumed a new status as a specific mode of production, with small-scale family farming pitted against the growing power and influence of agrarian capitalism and the food production industry. However, although Marxist approaches, like the 'all-embracing' *problématiques* of the historians, have had a profound influence on research into the principles of change in contemporary rural communities, there remain relatively few theoretical texts by Marxian sociologists. Furthermore, in the last few years, the importance of the Marxist approach, not only in rural sociology, has undoubtedly waned as researchers have abandoned all-embracing, global theorising for more detailed and more applied analysis of the particularities of local change.

(ii) Towards a thematic approach
Whether as a product of the economic crisis, or as a consequence of the more or less explicit criticism of the treatment of rural communities as specific wholes, or even as a result of the fragmented yet insistent rise of structural analysis and the accompanying interest in the symbolic and ideational dimensions of social life, the orientation of rural research is now changing. Rather than identifying the factors that will explain general processes of change within an encapsulated society, research is currently directed towards analysing the behaviour and

practices of specific social groups within their context, and in direct contact with the changing structures of French society as a whole. Thus, there is no differentiation in the study of a social group in a town or in a village, other than in the broad contextual elements.

Hence the question now frequently asked is: does a distinct rural sociology exist? Is there an object of research which gives rise to distinctive issues, or is there only the study of social life and, rather, a multiplicity of possible vantage-points: large cities, small towns, market towns, villages, densely-populated areas and underpopulated areas? If the latter is the case, then one essential factor becomes the *localisation* of observed processes, the crucial relationship, in all its complexity, which maintains individuals within their immediate environment. The scope for a pluri-disciplinary approach, already common practice, is thereby widened. For rural sociologists still retain one of their earliest convictions – that one cannot effectively study elements of social life without taking account of all its dimensions and the local and national context in which it occurs.

This gentle change, which has been taking place for over a decade now, has, in depriving rural researchers of an alternative theoretical model, left them in some disarray. Thematic studies have grown, however, and it would be satisfying to award them some general interpretive capabilities. Is this the case though? Their accumulation might lead only to a fragmented systemisation. Though not a specifically rural issue, it is nonetheless particularly important for the rural researchers' field of study. There is a confusion of methods and approaches; and the sociologist, striving to be a geographer, historian and economist when not being a jurist, is always aware of having missed something for want of a theoretical model. Even so, although rural sociologists in France are going through a 'crisis' of their own, they are not yet so exhausted as to turn wholly to empiricism.

2 From the end of the peasantry to the return to nature: an annotated bibliography *by Bertrand Hervieu*

Estimated today as accounting for 6–7 per cent of the economically active national population, the number of French farmers will soon reach what is believed to be the fatal level of 5 per cent. Unlike other European countries, this is a completely new experience for French society. Throughout the first half of the twentieth century, the active agricultural population in France was always in the region of 40 per cent of the total active population. Since then the proportion has fallen from 31 per cent in 1954 and 17 per cent in 1970 to its present level. It is against this background of profound change that French rural sociology was born over thirty years ago and has since developed.

I *The modernisation of French agriculture and the 'End of the Peasants'*

The study of the diffusion of technical progress in agriculture marks the beginning of French rural sociology. However, although such studies sought to understand how the modernisation of agriculture took place, 'the necessity of treating the issue of innovation as a component of the more general issue of economic and social change in local communities' (Bodiguel 1975) soon became apparent. To this end, the monographic approach achieved a considerable success. Many of these studies were concerned predominantly with the processes by which the individuality of local social life and attitudes were being eroded and the various ways in which 'village culture' resisted external pressures. Thus, their main focus has been the analysis of the transition from one culture (rural) to another (industrial and urban). The body of work which sought to identify the true reality of 'local social systems' in terms of their specific autonomy ultimately supported a perspective, that was culturalist as well as necessarily agrarian, which has profoundly influenced France's self-image.

It has also left its mark on the social sciences themselves which have adopted as their own the traditional polar opposites of town/country and worker/farmer as both objective and conceptual distinctions. Furthermore, concerning rural matters generally, the social sciences have noted the progressive attenuation of rural activities to little more than agriculture. Rural sociology has largely been the sociology of the peasantry and, in defending it, has thereby reinforced the myth of peasant unity. Thus Maurice Halbwachs asserts that:

> Certainly there are both rich and poor amongst rural inhabitants of different classes. Concern at remaining at their existing level or for raising themselves up the social ladder explains a large part of their social behaviour. But, above all this, they are aware of being *paysans*, in contrast to the inhabitants of towns, and what is specific in their motivations is ultimately explained by the conflict which exists between these two types of civilisation' (*Halbwachs 1955, p. 88*).

A review and critical assessment of the monographic tradition has been the subject of two major works, entitled: Les Collectivités Rurales Françaises (Jollivet (ed.) 1974; Jollivet and Mendras (eds) 1977). A complementary tradition lay in studies of the rural exodus, interpreted in a general sense as the passage from agriculture to industry, from the countryside to the town, and analysed principally from the perspective of the adaptation, the progress and indeed the future of a population leaving one world to enter another (Rambaud and Vincienne 1969 and 1973).

During this period, Henri Mendras attempted to theorise the functioning of rural societies through the notion of key individuals or notables (Mendras 1971 and 1976). Mendras's proposition might be summarised as follows: 'The village, the "local community", forms a single entity but this entity is included, in a structural-functional way, within a "wider society" and together, they make up a "global society". The rapport between the local community and the wider society takes place through particular individuals, the *notables*, who perform the key function of mediation' (Robert 1986, pp. 100–101).

Recognition of the disappearance of the peasantry as a way of life, indeed as a civilisation, is one of the major contributions of this period: *La Fin des Paysans* (Mendras 1967; 1970; 1984), *Une France sans Paysans* (Gervais, Servolin and Weil 1965), *La Fin de la France Paysanne* (Gervais, Jollivet and Tavernier 1976). The titles of these works, amongst the most widely read of French rural sociology texts, speak for themselves.

II The persistence and the disappearance of peasant farming

A critique of approaches which stress the individuality of rural societies and agricultural structures is offered by those writers inspired by Marxist analysis, the key texts of which are articles by Claude Servolin and Marcel Jollivet. Whereas Servolin (1972) demonstrates the persistence of petty commodity production in the midst of a capitalist mode of production, Jollivet claims that:

> ... the capitalist mode of production cannot develop without delivering mortal blows to the rural commune, despite the many ideological and practical reasons it may have for preserving it. What is true for the rural commune is also true for petty commodity production: although its close ties with the supremacy of private property make it necessary, it is also, at the same time, destined to be dismantled and ultimately, to fade away ... (Jollivet 1974, p. 262).

Like the monographic tradition, the critical approach has also stimulated, and provided a background for, a new wave of research across rural areas. Themes have included:

- the development of contractual economic relations in agriculture;
- the closer and progressive observation of social change; and
- local power.

From this return to the field, rural sociologists have drawn two major findings:

a) the persistence of family farming in French agriculture during the current phase of market internationalisation. Sociologists have joined the economists in seeking to understand this phenomenon, particularly by considering the role of the family and, within the family, the role of women in the agricultural enterprise. They have also sought to develop a comparative international perspective on this issue. Agricultural politics have also been examined within this context (Servolin 1985) at the same time as studies were being published on the farming lobby (Berger 1975; Maresca 1983; Boussard 1982);

b) the discovery of the importance of non-agricultural activities in rural areas.

III Return to nature and the revitalisation of French rural societies

The phenomenon of neo-ruralism,[2] growing out of the death-throes of rural society and of particular importance between 1968 and 1975, has played a key role in attracting attention to the importance of non-agricultural activities in general. Research on neo-ruralism itself includes that by Champagne (1977), Eizner, Hervieu and Jollivet (1978), Hervieu and Leger (1979 and 1983) and Mendras (1979). Research on other aspects of non-agricultural activities in rural areas include Eizner and Hervieu (1979) on industrial workers in rural areas and Cadoret (1985) on the 'production' of nature. The 1982 census revealed that the rural population had grown at almost double the national rate and it had become significantly diversified.

The inventiveness and faculty for adaptation displayed by rural communities has introduced a new sensitivity to rural sociology. The movement towards local development, enshrined in the administration's *Contrat de Pays*[3] and regionalisation policies and animated on the ground by local politicians and a network of active local development associations, has given rise to a number of studies, debates and conferences on the themes of local vitality, local upheaval and, ultimately, the revitalisation of rural areas, by Agulhon and Bodiguel (1981), Viard (1981), Hervieu and Maclouf (1983) and Chassagne (1979). Thus the question of the modernisation of the countryside, or the reconciliation of the twin concepts of Modernity and Rurality, is raised once more.

In a postscript to the second edition of his book *La Fin des Paysans* (1984), Mendras asks himself:

> ... should one now put a question mark after the title of this book – La Fin des Paysans? – and thereby imply that some degree of uncertainty would perhaps have been more appropriate?
>
> As it stands, the book is a testament to the death of a civilisation after centuries of existence. It is a scientific diagnosis and not a speculative debate. In twenty years, events have proved me right: in France, a generation has witnessed the disappearance of what amounts to an ancient civilisation and an integral part of itself. Nevertheless, even today, many still refuse to acknowledge the evidence of its passing ... as though it was improper to say to a family gathered around a deathbed; 'Ssh, he is at rest'.

Likewise, as if to apologise for the end of 'Peasant France', should the sociologist maintain that Rural France somehow persists. But isn't there a danger here that French rural sociology might remain confused between signing the former's death certificate and submitting itself to the ideological enthusiasms of the time?

Notes

1. The basic territorial units of administration of the French state are the 82 *départements*. Under the Vichy regime of the early 1940s, neighbouring *départements* were linked together for the purposes of economic administration and policing. In the 1950s, more systematic grouping of *départements* for the purposes of regional planning and administration yielded 22 'regions'. To regionalise the sixth and subsequent national plans, these were further aggregated into 8 macro-regions.
2. The term 'neo-ruralism' has been used to describe the emergence of a new rural 'ideal' amongst back-to-the-land ex-urbanites. More than merely counterurbanisation, neo-ruralism implies a search for traditional rural values and experiences. The bulk of neo-ruralists, in distinction to second-home owners, have sought an active social and economic role within rural communities (as small farmers or craftsmen) and, mainly in the south, have made a significant contribution to rural renovation and local economic diversification (see Chapter 2, this volume).
3. A *Contrat de Pays* is a contract established between a locality and the state or region for the financing and implementing of a specified series of planned development projects within a defined area (see Chapter 2, this volume).

Bibliography

This bibliography is necessarily selective. On the whole, preference has been given to books rather than journal articles. Only some monographs have been included but the reader will find an exhaustive bibliography of these village studies in *Villages en Développement*, edited by Henri Desroche and Placide Rambaud (Recherches Coopératives 4, Paris, Mouton, 1971).

More detailed information on individual subjects can be obtained from two bibliographies, one edited by M.-L. Marduel and M. Robert, *Les Sociétés Rurales Françaises: élements de bibliographie* (CNRS, Paris, 1980); and the other contained within *La Fin de la France Paysanne: 1914 à nos jours* by Michel Gervais, Marcel Jollivet and Yves Tavernier (1977), which makes up the fourth volume of *Histoire de la France Rurale*, edited by Georges Duby and Armand Wallon, Seuil, L'Univers historique, Paris, 1975.

Agulhon, Maurice, Bodiguel, Maryvonne, *Les associations au village,* Le Paradou: Actes Sud, 1981, 107 pp. (Bibliothèque des ruralistes).
Allaire, Gilles, Blanc, Michel, *Politiques agricoles et paysanneries,* Paris, le Sycomore, 1982, 116 pp. (Actuels).
Association française de science politique, Paris, Colloque, 1970, *L'univers politique des paysans dans la France contemporaine,* (eds) Yves Tavernier, Michel Gervais and Claude Servolin. Paris, A. Colin, 1972, 653 pp. (Cahiers de la FNSP; 1984).
Association des ruralistes français, *La pluriactivité des familles agricoles,* Paris, ARF éditions, 1984, 343 pp.
Barthez, Alice, *Famille, travail et agriculture,* Paris, Economica, 1982, VI, 192 pp.
Berger, Suzanne, *Les paysans contre la politique: l'organisation rurale en Bretagne, 1911-1974,* trans. from English, Paris, Seuil, 1975, 345 pp.
Billaud, Jean-Pierre, *Marais poitevin: rencontres de la terre et de l'eau,* Paris, l'Harmattan, 1984, 265 pp.
Bodiguel, Maryvonne, *Les paysans face au progrès,* Paris, Presses de la FNSP, 1975, 177 pp. (Travaux et recherches de sciences politiques; 37).
Bodiguel, Maryvonne, *Le rural en question,* Paris, L'Harmattan, 1986, 183 pp. (Collection Alternatives Paysannes).
Bourdieu, Pierre, 'Célibat et Condition Paysanne', *Etudes Rurales* Av. Sept., Sept. 1962, p. 56, pp. 32–135.
Cadiou, Lefebvre, Lepape, Mathieu-Gavorot, Oriol, *L'agriculture biologique en France, Ecologie ou Mythologie,* Grenoble, PUG, 1975, 189 pp.
Cadoret, A., *Protection de la nature. Histoire et Idéologie de la Nature à l'Environnement,* Paris, L'Harmattan, 1985, 245 pp. Coll. Alternatives Paysannes.
Calmes, R. et al., *L'espace Rural Français,* Paris, Masson, 1978, 171 pp.
Centre National de la Recherche Scientifique, Paris, Groupe de Sociologie Rurale, *Les collectivités rurales françaises,* Paris, A. Colin, 1971.
1: 'Etude comparative de changement social', (eds) M. Jollivet and H. Mendras, 1971, 224 pp.
2: 'Sociétés paysannes ou Lutte de classes au village: problèmes méthodologiques et théoriques de l'étude locale en sociologie rurale, (ed.) Marcel Jollivet, 1974, 266 pp.
Centre National de la Recherche Scientifique, Paris, Programme observation du changement social. *L'esprit des lieux - Localités et Changement social en France,* Paris, ed. CNRS, 1986, 350 pp.
Champagne, Patrick, 'La restructuration de l'espace villageois', *Actes de la recherche en sciences sociales,* 3 May 1975, pp. 43–67.

Chiva, I., Rambaud, P., *Les Etudes Rurales en France Tendances et Organisations de la Recherche,* Paris-Mouton, 1972, 369 pp.
Clerc, François, (ed.), 'Le monde paysan', *Les Cahiers Français,* 187, July–September 1978, Paris La Documentation Française, 1978, 72 pp.
Dumont, René, Ravignan, François de, *Nouveaux voyages dans les campagnes françaises,* Paris, Seuil, 1977, 317 pp. (L'Histoire immédiate).
Eizner, Nicole, Hervieu, Bertrand, *Anciens paysans, nouveaux ouvriers,* Paris, L'Harmattan, 1979, 246 pp.
Eizner, Nicole, *Les paradoxes de l'agriculture française,* Paris, L'Harmattan, 1985, 159 pp. Préface de Pierre Coulomb, Collection Alternatives Paysannes.
Farcy, Henri de, (ed.) *Un million d'agriculteurs à temps partiel?* Paris, le centurion, 1979, 167 pp. (Faire notre histoire. Propositions).
Friedmann, Georges, (ed,) *Villes et campagnes: civilisation urbaine et civilisation rurale en France,* Paris, A. Colin, 1953.
Gervais, Michel, Servolin, Claude, Weil, Jean, *Une France sans paysans,* Paris, Seuil, 1965, 128 pp. (Société; 7).
Gravier, Jean-François, *Paris le désert Français en 1972, Décentralisation. Equipement. Population,* Paris, Flammarion, 1972, 285 pp. (1ère édition 1947).
Gueslin, André, *Le Crédit Agricole,* Paris, La Découverte, 1985.
Grignon, Claude, 'L'enseignement agricole et la domination symbolique de la paysannerie,' *Actes de la Recherche en Sciences Sociales,* n°. 1, janvier 1975, pp. 75–98.
Halbwachs, Maurice, *Esquisse d'une Psychologie des Classes Sociales,* Marcel Rivière, Paris, 1955, 2ème éd. 238 pp.
Houée, Paul, *Les étapes du développement rural,* Paris Economie et humanisme, ed. ouvrières, 1972, 2 vol. (Développement et civilisations):
  1. *Une longue évolution: 1815-1950,* 192 pp.
  2. *La révolution contemporaine: 1950-1970,* 269 pp.
— *Coopération et organisations agricoles françaises,* Paris, ed. Cujas, 1970, 127 pp.
Jegouzo, Guenhaël, Brangeon, Louis, *Les paysans et l'école,* Paris, Cujas, 1976, 287 pp.
Klatzmann, Joseph, *L'Agriculture française,* 2ème éd, Paris, Seuil, 1980, 250 pp. (Points. Economie; 10).
Lagrave, R. M. (ed.), *Celles de la terre. Agricultrice: l'invention politique d'un métier.* Paris, édition de l'Ecole des Hautes Etudes en Sciences Sociales, 1987, 254 pp.
Lamarche, Hugues, Rogers, Susan C., Karnoouh, Claude, *Paysans, femmes et citoyens: luttes pour pouvoir dans un village lorrain,* Le Paradou: Actes Sud, 1980, 215 pp (Ecrits et travaux du groupe de sociologie rurale du CNRS; 4).
Langlois, Françoise, *Les Salariés agricoles en France,* Paris; A. Colin, 1962, XII-223, pp. (Etudes et mémoires/Ecole pratique des hautes études, 6ème section, Centre d'études économiques: 54).
Leger, Danièle, Hervieu, Bertrand, *Des communautés pour les temps difficiles: néo-ruraux ou nouveaux moines,* Paris, 1983, 216 pp. (Faire notre histoire. Propositions).
— *Le retour à la nature: 'au fond de la forêt... l'Etat',* Paris, Seuil, 1979, 240 pp.
Le Roy, Pierre, *Le problème agricole français,* Paris, Economica, 1982, 151 pp.
Lefebvre, H., *Du rural à l'urbain.* Paris, Anthropos, 1970, 285 pp.
Maho, J., *L'image des autres chez les Paysans. Méthodologie et analyse de Sept villages français,* (Preface by P. Naville) Paris Le champ du possible, 1974. 220 pp.
Maresca, Sylvain, *Les dirigeants paysans,* Paris, les Ed. de Minuit, 1983, 294 pp. (Le Sens commun).
Mendras, Henri, *La fin des paysans: suivi d'une réflexion sur 'La fin des paysans', vingt ans après,* Henri Mendras, Le Paradou, Actes Sud, 1984, 370 pp.

— *Sociétés paysannes: éléments pour une théorie de la paysannerie*. Paris: A. Colin, 1976. 235 p. (Collection U).
Mendras, Henri and Tavernier, Yves, (eds) *Terre, paysans et politique: structures agraires, systèmes politiques et politiques agricoles: études rassemblées et présentées par un Groupe de recherches sous la dir. de Henri Mendras et Yves Tavernier*, Paris, SEDEIS, 1969–70, 2 vol.: 611, 304 pp. (*Futuribles*; 12; 14).
Mollard, Amédée, *Paysans exploités: essai sur la question paysanne*, Grenoble, Presses universitaires de Grenoble, 1977, 244 pp.
Morin, Edgar, *Commune en France. La métamorphose de Plodemet*, Paris, Fayard, 1967, 278 pp.
Pernet, François, *Résistances paysannes*, Grenoble, Presses Universitaires de Grenoble, 1982, 189 pp. (Influences).
Rambaud, Placide, *Un village de montagne. Albiez le vieux en Maurienne*, Paris I, de la Nouvelle Faculté, 1981, 298 pp.
Rambaud, Placide, *Société Rurale et Urbanisation*, Paris, Seuil, 1969, 316 pp. Collection 'Esprit'.
Segalen, Martine, *Mari et femme dans la société paysanne*, Paris, Flammarion, 1980, 211 pp. (Bibliothèque d'ethnologie historique).
Servolin, Claude, 'Les politiques Agricoles', *Traité de Sciences Politiques*, Tome IV, Paris, PUF, 1985, pp. 156–260.
Wylie, Laurence William, *Chanzeaux, village d'Anjou* (trad. de l'anglais) Paris, Gallimard, 1970, 196 pp. (Collection Témoins).
Wylie, Laurence William, *Un village du Vaucluse* (trad. de l'anglais), Paris, Gallimard, 1968, 409 pp. (Collection Témoins).
Zonabend, Françoise, *La mémoire longue: temps et histoires au village*, Paris, PUF, 1980, 314 pp.
'Avec nos sabots: la campagne rêvée et convoitée'. *Autrement*, 14, juin 1978, 247 pp. (N. Eizner, B. Hervieu et M. Jollivet ed.).
'Le local dans tous ses Etats: décentralisation et développement: la grande bataille du septennat', *Autrement*, 7 février 1983, 249 pp. (B. Hervieu, P. Maclouf et P. Merlant ed.).

18 Recent British Rural Sociology

Graham Crow, Terry Marsden and Michael Winter

The community studies tradition of research

The images which we have of the changing social structure of the British countryside in the post-war period continue to be influenced to a significant degree by the series of rural community studies which were produced between the 1940s and 1960s. These monographs form part of a broader genre of research which saw a variety of approaches to the investigation of an impressive range of issues in both urban and rural localities accepted. The abundance of empirical material generated appeared to offer the basis on which more general models of community or local social systems could be constructed. The promise of these syntheses, however, was never fully realised in practice, and the attempt served more than anything else to emphasise the serious methodological and theoretical problems which had dogged many of the old studies. As awareness of these difficulties grew, community studies lost much of their former popularity among researchers. They have not been replaced by any recognisable successor; rather it is the case that 'Community studies have ... gone out of fashion ... although the *genre* continues in fits and starts accompanied by, perhaps, a more realistic appraisal of their limits and possibilities' (Newby 1980cc: 78–9).

The relevance of the old tradition of community studies to more recent research in rural sociology has been left somewhat ambiguous. The shortcomings of the genre have to be set against the particular merits of individual studies, and their provision collectively of an historical benchmark (however rough) by which current developments and trends can be gauged. The old studies present us with a detailed and in many ways compelling picture of the past, but there are several counts on which their felicity might be questioned. These criticisms need to be examined if this image is to be used constructively in comparisons with the present.

In the urban community studies by far the greatest amount of attention was devoted to aspects of working-class life, and in particular the demise of the traditional working-class community. In the rural studies there is more diversity of focus, but the investigation of family farming certainly stands out as one of the principal objectives. In part this reflects the fact that it is easier to 'study down' than to 'study up' the social structure (Bell 1978), family farmers, like urban workers, being much more open than the locally-powerful to sociological investigation. However, this alone does not explain why family farmers had significantly more attention devoted to them than farm workers, a more powerless group yet one substantially neglected in the literature of post-war rural sociology (Newby 1977: 101). The researchers who conducted the rural community studies tended to work with a model of the rural social structure in which family farmers occupied a key position. In this model the family farm was taken to be the embodiment of traditionalism, resistant to change, and the backbone of communities desribed as 'truly rural' (Frankenberg 1969: chs. 1–3). In consequence, family farmers were adopted as the most useful group in the countryside for the analytical purposes of showing how local social systems operated, illuminating the processes of social change, and elucidating rural-urban differences.

The community studies genre of research which dominated British rural sociology in the two decades following the Second World War was exemplified in the work of Alwyn Rees – 'the founding father of the British community study' (Bell & Newby 1971: 140) – and of his pupil W. M. Williams. Rees's *Life in a Welsh Countryside* (1951) reported on extensive fieldwork in the Montgomeryshire parish of Llanfihangel yng Ngwynfa, while Williams's two studies, *The Sociology of an English Village: Gosforth* (1956) and *A West Country Village: Ashworthy* (1963) were again of upland villages, respectively, in Cumberland and Devon. Such community studies had much in common. Their authors were all concerned to establish a clear picture of the place being investigated and of the social structure of the community which, for better or for worse (and it was more often understood to be the latter), was undergoing profound change. Rees, for example, wrote of urbanisation, industrialisation, and commercialisation as processes which were all at work in bringing about the decline of the old order. Different writers attached varying emphasis to each of these aspects of modernisation, but the uniting theme running through all of them was the loss of an essentially traditional social order. Emphasis was placed upon conventional sociological ideas about *gemeinschaft* – 'internal solidarity, kinship ties, generational continuity, and traditional face to face society' (Marsden 1984: 206). As a result, the orientation of the community studies was backward-looking rather than forward-looking. In the context of a plethora of studies of groups and communities which were becoming marginalised, the need for research which had a greater contemporary relevance forced a change in the research agenda.

Williams's *Ashworthy* stands at something of a watershed in post-war British rural sociology, being perhaps the last major rural community study of the traditional type. There are, of course, connections between *Ashworthy* and the research which followed it. J. S. Nalson's study *Mobility of Farm Families* (1968), for example, follows up some of the implications of the recognition found in *Ashworthy* that the movement out of agriculture is proportionally much faster among farm workers than it is among family farmers (ibid.: 211), a policy 'problem' to which Williams's findings, on farmers' attachment to their occupation and the reproduction of family farming over the generations, clearly have relevance. In addition, Williams's work does recognise the need for micro-sociological investigation of people and places to be integrated with macro-sociological research, and the dynamic model of rural development which he proposes promises to take into account the fact that there is a wide range of factors influencing emerging patterns in the countryside: 'Tradition, the character and outlook of the individual farmer, his capital resources, government policy and a number of external economic pressures bring about changes from time to time' (Williams 1963: 13). The arrival of 'Up Country Johnnies' (ibid.: 14) – farmers who have come to the parish from some distance – can for example be seen as one of the ways in which agricultural policy has had an impact, by making it possible for people other than 'real farmers' to secure holdings more easily than was the case in the past.

Williams wrote that the parish was not 'typically English' (Williams 1963: 43), although it was chosen for its suitability for study as a community suffering the effects of rural depopulation, and Williams is able to make some useful comparisons with other such areas; he also felt able to generalise to some extent about the continuity of family farming on the basis of his research, in an article entitled 'The Social Study of Family Farming' (1973). Frankenberg's response to this situation was to call for more research, especially in 'the highly specialized, mechanised, and industrialised agricultural areas' (1969: 252). He contrasted upland areas of predominantly family farming with what he called 'a real industrial agricultural economy' where 'the farm *is* like a factory, and the farmer has an office where he calculates his profits and losses. Farmers in such a system compete rather than cooperate, sons feel demeaned by working for wages, and labourers eat in the kitchen' (ibid.: 49).

Problems in the community studies tradition type of research

When Williams recommended the multi-disciplinary approach which he adopted in his analysis of family farming, he was suggesting that a broad outlook on the part of the researcher was superior to narrow specialism; he recommended using 'the techniques and data of several disciplines, notably of the geographer, the economist and the rural sociologist' (1973: 132). The practice of this disciplinary, theoretical, and methodological pluralism in community studies has, however, been subjected to a good deal of critical scrutiny. To begin with, there is no single community studies method, and in practice the methods used were adopted in a rather unsystematic way. Kent suggests that these problems help to account for the decline in popularity of the community studies genre among sociologists:

> All these studies were largely descriptive, and for the most part presented non-quantitative, often impressionistic, data ... Generalisations would be derived inductively, but on a low level of abstraction and specific to the community concerned. The result was that these studies were non-comparable and non-cumulative as far as empirical sociology was concerned (Kent 1981: 137).

These shortcomings were compounded by theoretical problems. Many of the community studies were conducted by investigators 'trained principally in the structural functionalist traditions of social anthropology' (Elliott 1978: 18). It is true that Williams did abandon the assumption of earlier writers concerning the static nature of rural communities, but his model of 'dynamic equilibrium' is still broadly functionalist, with the result that divisions within the community are analysed within the framework of social integration and the reproduction of the overarching social structure. Functionalist influences are also detectable in Frankenberg's attempt to synthesise the community studies monographs into a general model of community stretching from 'truly rural' to urban, but, as has often been pointed out, such a model falls down in its attempt to specify what is sociologically significant about rural and urban location, or to address the central theoretical question of what we mean by the terms 'urban' and 'rural' when applied to communities (Saunders 1981: 10).

The new rural sociology of the 1970s

Given the difficulties of drawing generalisations and theoretical conclusions from studies of places which were often unique, it is not surprising to find community studies research being displaced by investigation with very different and sometimes more ambitious theoretical objectives. The work of Howard Newby and his colleagues in the 1970s has done more than anything else to reinvigorate rural sociology in Britain, not only because of its coverage of new issues but also because of the fact that it broke with the community studies approach to rural sociology in several important respects. To begin with, the work is much more identifiably sociological, seeking to address theoretical issues such as the ways in which the highly unequal relationship between farmers and farmworkers is mediated and reproduced (Newby 1977). There is a concern to draw upon the discipline of sociology as a whole, and as a result the findings of the research conducted among farmworkers (ibid.) and subsequently among farmers (Newby et al. 1978) are discussed in terms of general sociological concepts such as class rather than being treated as being somehow uniquely rural. Conversely, this approach has challenged the theoretical status of a distinct rural sociology, and while Newby does not claim to have resolved what he calls rural sociology's 'basic definitional problem – namely, what constitutes the "rural" ' (Newby 1978: 5), he does suggest that its resolution requires a more 'holistic' approach (ibid.: 5, 26) than was adopted in the past.

What this has meant in practice is a greater attention to and awareness of the relationship between economic and social factors. Previously, although the potential for profitably combining rural sociology with agricultural economics had been recognised (Gasson 1971), the potential had all too rarely been achieved. In the light of this Newby concluded that 'Sociological variables have largely been relegated to residual factors by many agricultural economists, while much rural sociology has been carried out in almost total isolation from a consideration of the economic context of modern agriculture' (1978: 25).

It goes without saying that Newby's own works sought to give due attention to economic factors, and the investigation of the market situations of farm-workers, large-scale capitalist farmers, and small farmers are prominent aspects of the research conducted in East Anglia (Newby 1977; Newby et al. 1978, 1981). As a result, whereas Williams could write of economic pressures bringing about change in agriculture 'from time to time' (Williams 1963: 13), Newby et al. take the persistent tendency of social relations in the agricultural industry to be rationalised as their starting point. The background to their work is the recognition that agriculture has been transformed during the post-war period, a process captured in the popular idea of the transition from farming as a way of life to farming as a business (Newby et al. 1978: 145). This transformation has produced a wide range of effects, but it is essentially an economic phenomenon, albeit one hastened in its arrival by government policy. Thus, Newby writes:

> The encouragement of fewer, larger and more efficient capital-intensive farms has resulted eventually in all of the catalogue of changes which we associate with rural life today: the mechanisation of agriculture, the 'drift from land' of farm workers, rural depopulation, the changing social composition of rural villages and widespread changes in the rural landscape and other environmental aspects of the countryside (Newby 1980a: 115).

What agricultural policy has done is to speed up the transition to a capitalist agriculture, and in particular to encourage the growth of 'agribusiness'. It is in this context that the choice by Newby et al. of East Anglia as the area of study is significant. The contrast with the upland areas of Britain focused on in the community studies is obvious, but while no claims are made regarding East Anglia's greater typicality of the country as a whole, there is a sense in which the area's agriculture is presented as prototypical, a model of rational farm organisation towards which things are tending.

Newby is careful not to suggest that rural sociology and the sociology of agriculture are synonymous, but he does claim that the latter must be a primary concern of the former. Thus 'The "rural" need not, of course, be regarded as coterminous with the "agricultural" but all meaningful definitions of "rural" have at least a basis in agriculture and so a consideration of the development of agriculture remains at the heart of any rural sociology' (Newby 1978: 25).

It is for this reason that Newby et al.'s work on aspects of rural life other than agriculture, such as the urbanisation of the rural class structure (Newby 1980b) and the exercise of power in the countryside (Newby et al 1978: ch. 6), always draws out the links between changes in these areas and developments in agriculture. The holistic approach adopted by Newby can be criticised here for presenting a kind of agricultural fundamentalism which underestimates the wider (non-agricultural) social, economic and political forces shaping rural regions.

This is the gist of the critique from a Marxist or neo-Marxist standpoint. Given its focus on attitudes, its Weberian approach to class and market situations and to social relations built around status, and its use of ideal-typical methodology, Newby's work can be characterised as Weberian. While there are some ways in which Weber's theory of agricultural rationalisation coincides with ideas found in the Marxist tradition, there are also important differences (Crow 1987: ch. 2). Hence, writers such as Urry (1984) have argued that rural sociology (in so far as it can remain a distinctive academic enterprise) needs to concern itself more with macro-level forces of economic restructuring in the context of a changing national and international division of labour. Significantly, Newby himself, in his subsequent writings has tended to pay more attention to theorists in the Marxist tradition such as Kautsky (Newby 1978; Buttel and Newby (eds.) 1980). If it is accepted, however, that the rural/urban distinction is becoming obsolete with the industrialisation of the countryside and the de-industrialisation of urban centres, then the role of a specifically rural sociology must once again be brought into question.

In the context of this uncertainty relating to its scientific basis and more practical issues relating to its marginal position within the academic establishment, it is perhaps unsurprising that the impact of the new rural sociology inspired by the work of Newby has not been as great as it merits. Since Newby et al.'s research of the 1970s, few sociological farm studies of any sort have been undertaken, reflecting the fact that British sociology continues to have an overwhelmingly urban orientation. The other side of this coin is the continued predominance of agricultural economics in the analysis of agricultural and more generally rural matters. As part of sociology in general, rural sociology has sustained considerable denigration in recent years, and this has had its inevitable effect on research funding, particularly where sponsoring agencies are close to government. Agencies seeking information of a sociological type are more likely to look outside sociology for an understanding of 'social factors', which are often presented with scant regard for sociological theory or methodology.

Some comments on farm survey research in Britain

Due largely to rural sociology's institutional weakness within the UK, separate traditions of farm survey research exist providing a competing paradigm to sociological analysis. These have grave weaknesses as sociological accounts but the best of them perhaps merit a closer consideration from sociologists than they have received. Broadly there are two rather similar traditions: a socio-psychological tradition, with an emphasis on the goals and values determining farmer decision-making, with a number of exponents in farm management studies; and a very similar behaviourist tradition within rural and economic geography. Both place tremendous importance upon methodology, particularly the construction of questionnaires and analysis of survey data, to the exclusion of sociological insight at two levels. First, the emphasis upon the articulated views and attitudes of respondents has diverted attention from broader structural questions and the absence of what can be termed a political economic dimension to research. Secondly, a very different failing has been the surprising neglect of ethnographic possibilities in behavioural research.

New issues in rural sociology: beyond the sociology of agriculture

During the last decade sociological interest has been brought to bear upon a number of issues not hitherto central to a rural sociology dominated by community studies and studies of agriculture. These new developments in rural sociology fall into two main areas, the environment and rural social and economic change. It is important to emphasise that the work which has been undertaken around these topics has not always been self-consciously rural sociology. Sociology as a discipline was established only very late in Britain (Bulmer 1985), and its development in the post-war period, while spectacular in terms of the speed of its growth, was also notably patchy. No 'centres of excellence' of rural sociological research have been established in the way that they have for other branches of sociology, and in consequence most rural sociological work has been undertaken by isolated researchers with a concern for rural matters as an *individual* interest. Howard Newby can thus be considered an exceptional figure in British sociology for his sustained interest in rural sociology and his ability to generate collective research (for example Newby et al. 1978), but even here it is instructive to note that he sustains other interests beyond rural sociology, most obviously sociological methods (Bell and Newby (eds) 1977) and social stratification (Newby et al. 1985).

Over the post-war period, rural sociology's poor relation status within sociology as a whole is probably the result of mainstream sociologists' limited interest in rural matters more than a limited interest in mainstream sociology among those rural sociologists that there have been, although the latter charge is not entirely unjustified, in particular when the earlier genre of community studies is considered. It was in this earlier period that patterns of institutional support were established, or, in the case of rural sociology, not established. Because of the paucity of institutional support and sponsorship for rural sociology in Britain, much work which is clearly influenced by ideas from sociology is produced within other disciplines with a strong tradition of rural studies, for example rural and social geography, planning and social anthropology. This inevitably makes the task of selection in such a review very difficult, and we may be open to accusations of trespass in the choice of new work presented here. However, we feel that many of the authors cited would acknowledge some identity, although not exclusively so, with a loosely structured rural sociology network in Britain primarily centring on the Rural Economy and Society Study Group.

The environment

The rapid rise of environmental awareness in recent years, particularly regarding changes resulting from agricultural intensification, has inevitably excited some sociological interest. Two strands of concern are of particular note. First, there has been some survey research among farmers regarding the processes leading to environmental change upon farms. Secondly, some researchers have directed their attention to the political dimensions of the subject and sought to develop the beginnings of a political sociology of rural policy.

Farm survey work to unravel the complexities of the decision-making and socio-structural context of environmental change in agriculture has been attempted by only a small number of workers. It might have been expected that the crisis in confidence in the direction of UK agricultural policy in the 1980s would have led to a much greater increase in the number of such studies. As Clive Potter (1986a; 1986b) has argued, the incidence of environmental change in agriculture cannot be analysed solely with reference to macro factors. Moreover, where a small number of sites of particular ecological interest may be at stake, the actions of individual farmers assume a greater importance than when national farm productivity alone is the issue. Macro-modelling of the agricultural economy would seem to be of less relevance for analysing processes of change in such circumstances.

Potter (1985; 1986a; 1986b) has studied farmers in Shropshire, Suffolk and Norfolk, focusing on the determinants of investment behaviour as a major influence on landscape change on farms. He develops a useful account of alternative investment styles adopted by farmers, based on the interaction of three levels of explanation. First, he cites the influence of changes in policy, technology and macro-economics; secondly, the influence of changes within the farm family, notably succession; and thirdly, the motives of farmers. In spite of this ambitious programme, Potter's primary concern remains that of providing an explanation of environmental change, with the consequence that much of wider sociological interest is not fully explored. Certainly he makes no attempt to extend his analysis into a general sociology of agriculture. By contrast, Marsden, Munton, Whatmore and Little have concentrated upon developing a broad-ranging conceptualisation of the sociology and political economy of British agriculture as a prelude to understanding landscape change (Marsden et al., 1986a; Marsden et al 1986b; Whatmore et al. 1987). Their work offers an essentially Marxist challenge to the earlier work of Newby, and is certainly a significant development in the sociology of agriculture.

A rather different stimulus for rural sociology has arisen from the environmental debate in the revival of interest in agricultural and environmental policy and politics. Although much of this work is discussed in Wyn Grant's chapter on politics in this volume, the work of Cox, Lowe and Winter is also rooted in political sociology and the sociology of agriculture. Indeed corporatism, the central theoretical concept in much of their work, has provided a meeting ground generally for sociology and political science in recent years. The team has continuing research interests in the political sociology of the Farming and Wildlife Advisory Group (1985a), in the history of corporatism in British agriculture (1985b; 1986a), and in the ideologies and political strategies of the various conservation and agricultural agencies (1986b; 1987). If some of the recent work by Paul Cloke (1986; 1987) on rural policy implementation is put alongside the work of Cox, Lowe and Winter it is clear that rural social science in Britain is currently enjoying something of an invigoration from an infusion of political science theory. In view of the theoretical sterility of much rural policy work, previously emanating from planning and geography perspectives, this is much to be welcomed.

Rural social and economic change

A number of studies in the 1960s and early 1970s which were loosely connected with the community studies genre moved away from the concern with remote rural communities and with family farming which had previously been dominant. Instead they focused on communities where rural population levels were not dramatically declining and where agriculture had become a minority pursuit. The works of Ambrose (1974), Connell (1974; 1978), Crichton (1965), Pahl (1965), and Thorns (1968) are all worthy of mention.

Interests have been broadened in the 1980s in a number of new studies exploring what can be termed 'rural revival'. The new studies are based on the realisation that only the remotest of rural locations are currently losing population and that large areas of rural England now exhibit a rich diversity of economic life, including examples of the new high-technology industries. At the same time this raises questions about the consequences of rapid change for the remaining local working-class residents. Three lively areas of research warrant particular mention: counterurbanisation, rural deprivation, and the position of women in rural society.

There are two quite distinct strands to the research in the area of counterurbanisation. The first is the attention accorded to rural change within the largely empirical tradition of rural geography. It is in this tradition that the term 'counterurbanisation' has been coined (see Dean et al. 1984; Perry et al. 1986). A more theoretical, and sociological, strand to the debate has centred on notions of spatial relations and capital restructuring. Here a concern merely with social and economic change within rural communities has been infused by a much wider interest in the operational relocation of industrial and financial capital. A renewed attention to capital movements, regionalism, the spatial division of labour and the relations between spatial and social structures has led to a number of useful publications (Gregory and Urry 1985; Massey 1984; Rees 1984; Urry 1984).

In mentioning these two contrasting traditions we are pointing to a gap which needs to be filled by rural sociology. Neither of the traditions comprises many researchers who would readily adopt the rural sociology label. The counterurbanisation specialists tend towards an atheoretical rural/social geography, while the macro-structural approach encourages Marxian theory as against empirical investigation. It is perhaps indicative of the parlous state of rural sociology in the UK that, to date, work to bridge the gap has not been undertaken (with the exception, perhaps, of insights offered by Tony Bradley, whose work is discussed further below). Remarkably little is known in detail about the social and economic changes in villages accompanying the broad parameters of population movement and industrial restructuring. A new generation of theoretically-informed community studies would do much to fill the gap.

One topic which has excited a certain amount of theoretically informed empirical work is that of rural welfare and rural poverty and deprivation. In particular the work of Tony Bradley shows that rural sociology possesses some powerful tools for the critical analysis of a key policy area (Bradley 1984, 1985, 1986; Bradley, Lowe and Wright 1986). Bradley brings to his work a determination to avoid falling into the trap of defining rural deprivation as a specifically spatial problem of service provision. Rather he insists upon the centrality of the notion of poverty as opposed to deprivation and a class analysis as opposed to a spatial analysis as the central methodological tool. His painstaking analysis of local labour markets offers many pointers to future work and it is to be hoped that this may become a resurgent area of rural sociology taken up by other researchers, the more so because Bradley is no longer involved in social research.

An emergent interest among rural sociologists is the issue of gender and the possibilities for a feminist perspective in rural studies. It is really too early to make more than a passing reference to the work and to indicate the likelihood that the topic will assume increasing importance in the future. The work of Mary

Bouquet (1985) provides a useful starting point and the debate has been taken up by both Little (1986), with respect to the recomposition of gender divisions and ideologies in the economic restructuring of rural localities, and Whatmore (1988 and forthcoming), in the changing household relationships within family farming.

Beyond structure: modified political economy approaches

It is quite evident from the last section that in the 1980s British rural sociology underwent something of a deconstruction of interests. This, we would suggest, is by no means a negative feature and should not be interpreted as a decline in the significance of rural sociological concepts. Rather, emphasis has focused upon a set of related themes which are by no means the sole preserve of the rural sociologist but demand multidisciplinary attention in which he/she assumes a significant role.

The growth and activity centred upon the Rural Economy and Society Study Group, a body containing over a hundred active researchers from a variety of social science disciplines, has demonstrated the continued need for a critical rural sociology which embraces concepts and ideas from several subject areas. The restructuring of rural areas associated with, for instance, counterurbanisation, new industrialisation (see Healey and Ilberry (eds), 1985), the entrenchment of rural deprivation (McCloughlin 1983), and the consequences of overproduction and intensive agriculture (Symes and Marsden 1985), have presented researchers with a new and challenging agenda which has necessitated both a re-examination of theoretical approaches and detailed (particularly longitudinal) empirical work. Also, the burgeoning of interest in the sociological interpretation of the production and consequences of technological change in the United States is now stimulating parallel interest in Britain (see Goodman et al. 1987).

The overall emphasis in this work shows a tendency towards a broadening political economy approach which prioritises the linking of economic analysis within specific social formations and queries the costs and benefits for particular social groups. In the agricultural field, this attempts to balance a concentration upon the activities of the state and capital with their specific manifestations over time and space (see Marsden et al. 1987). The work is attempting to go beyond the structuralist analyses developed in the early 1980s (see, for instance, Buttel and Newby (eds), 1980). The application of a Marxian political economy to agricultural relations brought with it a series of theoretical and methodological problems which tended to thwart development (see Marsden et al. 1986). Writers tended to view agricultural development in unilinear terms. Also, due to the unevenness and specificity of agricultural production over time and space, methodological and definitional confusion has occurred, as with the case of recent debates surrounding the status of the family farm in capitalist societies (see Goodman and Redclift 1985; Friedmann 1986). Similarly, but perhaps more surprising given the priorities assumed by political economy approaches, a comprehensive understanding of the role of the state, first in terms of agricultural production and reproduction, and second, in terms of 'rural' society more generally, has been lacking. Writers have all too easily attempted to identify the singular objectives of state action, overestimating the rationality of government 'policy' towards these issues (Buttel 1982; Cloke 1987). Such weaknesses in theoretical approach and understanding now present a major project to those concerned with rural sociological work in Britain. The structuralist reactions to the inadequacies of the rather idiosyncratic community studies, while significant and rewarding, have now started to give way to a central focus upon the interaction of structural processes and agents, for instance in the dialectical relations linking farm households' production and reproduction with the wider circuits of industrial and finance capital which impinge upon them.

Such shifts towards post-structuralist Marxism raise important methodological issues. For example, if the pitfalls of the earlier rural community studies and much of agricultural economics are to be avoided, the re-emphasis upon both agency and specificity embedded within wider social formations would suggest the re-emergence of theoretically-informed locality studies. Linkages also need to be made between different levels of research inquiry which attempt to relate the ethnography of specificities with the analysis of broader longitudinal change. The recent emergence of debates surrounding the application of realist methodologies (Sayer 1983), which emphasise categorisations reflecting the structured relations between groups rather than taxonomies based upon the particular characteristics of the object of study, provides one fruitful methodological way forward. These have yet, however, to become firmly-established lines of action amongst the three major foci of research effort outlined above (but see Whatmore et al. 1987).

A further dimension to a post-structuralist rural sociology must incorporate the sets of linkages between international, national and local factors in the understanding of rural social change in Britain. The valuable insights now being developed concerning the international farm 'crisis' and its national dimensions provide one contemporary example of this (Goodman and Redclift (eds), 1989). The increasing mobility of finance and, to a lesser extent, of industrial capital but, almost in ironically contradictory ways, the entrenchment experienced by farm families and employees during a period of overproduction, and the readjustments in national policy, necessitate an examination of the intended and unintended consequences of, as well as the motives for, transnational capital shifts. How these eventually are manifested in localities and hence affect and reorientate individual life worlds again cannot be fully understood without recognition of the significance of national and local state structures.

As in other branches of British sociology, the gradual incorporation of the significance of gender and generational power relations and how these cross-cut some of the issues raised above require more comprehensive research effort than has so far been established. While rural sociology has never found a cosy institutional home amongst the traditionally established disciplines of agricultural economics, geography and anthropology, nor in many cases within mainstream sociology itself, it would be a naive mistake to underestimate the significance of the rural sociological work which this review has outlined. Indeed, its very vibrancy in the late 1980s was due to individuals and groups associated in name at least with other academic departments.

Bibliography

Abrams, P. (ed.), *Work, Urbanism and Inequality: UK Society Today,* London, Wiedenfeld & Nicolson, 1978.
Ambrose, P., *The Quiet Revolution,* London, Chatto & Windus, 1974.
Bechhofer, F. and Elliott, B. (eds), *The Petite Bourgeoisie: Comparative Studies of the Uneasy Stratum,* London and Basingstoke, Macmillan, 1981.
Bell, C., 'Studying the locally powerful', in Bell, C. and Encel, S. (eds), *Inside the Whale: ten personal accounts of social research,* Rushcutters Bay NSW, Pergamon Press, 1978, pp. 14-40.
Bell, C. and Newby, H., *Community Studies,* London, George Allen & Unwin, 1971.
— (eds), *Doing Sociological Research,* London, George Allen & Unwin, 1977.
Bouquet, M., 'Women's Work in Rural South-West England', in Long, (ed.), 1984, pp. 142-59.
— *Family, Servants and Visitors: The Farm Household in Nineteenth and Twentieth Century Devon,* Norwich, Geobooks, 1985.
Bradley, T., 'Segmentation in local labour markets', in Bradley, T. and Lowe, P. (eds), 1984, pp. 65-90.
— 'Reworking the quiet revolution: industrial and labour market restructuring in village England', *Sociologia Ruralis,* 25 (1), 1985, pp. 40-60.
— 'Poverty and dependency in rural England', in Lowe, P., Bradley, T. and Wright, S. (eds), 1986, pp. 151-74.
Bradley, T. & Lowe, P. (eds), *Locality and Rurality,* Norwich, Geobooks, 1984.
Bradley, T., Lowe, P. and Wright, S., 'Introduction: rural deprivation and the welfare transition', in Lowe, P., Bradley, T. and Wright, S. (eds), 1986, pp. 1-39.
Bulmer, M., 'The development of sociology and of empirical social research in Britain', in Bulmer, M. (ed.), *Essays on the History of British Sociological Research,* Cambridge, Cambridge University Press, 1985, pp. 3-36.
Buttel, F., The political economy of agriculture in advanced industrial societies, *Current Perspectives in Social Theory,* 3, 1982, pp. 27-55.
Buttel, F. and Newby, H. (eds), *The Rural Sociology of the Advanced Societies: Critical Perspectives,* London, Croom Helm, 1980.
Cloke, P. (1986b), 'Implementation, intergovernmental relations, and rural studies: a review', *Journal of Rural Studies,* 2 (3), 1986, pp. 245-253.
— (ed.), *Rural Planning: Policy into Action?,* London, Harper & Row, 1987.
Cohen, A. (ed.), *Symbolising Boundaries: Identity and diversity in British cultures,* Manchester, Manchester University Press, 1986.
Connell, J., 'The metropolitan village: spatial and social processes in discontinuous suburbs', in Johnson, J.H. (ed.), 1974.
Connell, J., *The End of Tradition,* London, Routledge & Kegan Paul, 1978.
Cox, G., Lowe, P. and Winter, M. (1985a), 'Land use conflict after the Wildlife and Countryside Act: the role of the Farming and Wildlife Advisory Group', *Journal of Rural Studies,* 1 (2), 1985, pp. 173-83.
— (1986b), 'Changing directions in agricultural policy; corporatist arrangements in production and conservation policies', *Sociologia Ruralis,* 25 (2), 1985, pp. 130-154.
— (1986a), 'From state direction to self regulation: the historical development of corporatism in British agriculture', *Policy and Politics,* 14 (4), 1986, pp. 475-90.
— (1986b), 'Agriculture and conservation in Britain: a policy community under siege', in Cox, G., Lowe, P. and Winter, M. (eds) pp. 181-215, 1986.
— (eds), *Agriculture: People and Policies,* London, George Allen & Unwin, 1988.

— 'Private rights and public reponsibilities: the prospects for agricultural and environmental controls' *Journal of Rural Studies*, 4, 1988, 323-37.

Crichton, R., *Commuter Village*, Newton Abbot, David & Charles, 1965.

Crow, G., *Agricultural Rationalization: The fate of family farmers in post-war Britain*, Unpublished PhD, University of Essex, 1987.

Dean, K., Shaw, D., Brown, B., Perry, R. and Thorneycroft, W., Counterurbanisation and the Characteristics of Persons Migrating to West Cornwall, *Geoforum*, Vol. 15 (2), 1984, pp. 177-90.

Elliott, B., 'Social change in the city: structure and process', in Abrams, P. (ed.), 1978.

Errington, A. (ed), *The Farm as a Family Business: An annotated bibliography*, University of Reading, 1986.

Frankenberg, R., *Communities in Britain: Social life in town and country*, Harmondsworth, Penguin, 1969.

Friedmann, H., Patriarchy and Property: a reply to Goodman and Redclift, *Sociologia Ruralis*, XXVI, 2, 1986.

Gasson, R., 'Use of sociology in agricultural economics', *Journal of Agricultural Economics*, 22 (1), 1971, pp. 28-38.

Gasson, R., Crow, G., Errington, A., Hutson, J., Marsden, T. and Winter, M., 'The farm as a family business', *Journal of Agricultural Economics*, 1988.

Goodman, D. and Redclift, M., Capitalism, petty commodity production and the farm enterprise, *Sociologia Ruralis*, 25 (3/4), 1985, pp. 231-47.

Goodman, D. and Redclift, M. (eds), *The International Farm Crisis*, London, Macmillan, 1989.

Goodman, D., Sorj, B. and Wilkinson, J., *From Farming to Biotechnology*, Oxford, Basil Blackwell, 1987.

Harvey, D.R., Barr, C.J., Bell, M., Bunce, R.G.H., Edwards, D., Errington, A.J., Jollans, J.L., McClintock, J.H., Thompson, A.M.M., and Tranter, R.B., *Countryside Implications for England and Wales of Possible Changes in the Common Agricultural Policy*, Centre for Agricultural Strategy, University of Reading, 1986.

Healey, M. and Ilberry, B. (eds), *The Industrialisation of the Countryside*, Norwich, Geobooks, 1985.

Johnson, J.H. (ed.), *The Geography of Suburban Growth*, London, John Wiley, 1974.

Kent, R., *A History of British Empirical Sociology*, Aldershot, Gower, 1981.

Lang, T. and Wiggins, P., 'The industrialisation of the U.K. food system: from production to consumption, in Healey, M. and Ilberry, B. (eds), 1985.

Little, J., 'Feminist Perspectives in Rural Geography: An Introduction', *Journal of Rural Studies*, 1 (2), 1986.

Long, N. (ed.), *Family and Work in Rural Societies: Perspectives on non-wage labour*, London, Tavistock, 1984.

Lowe, P., Bradley, T. and Wright, S. (eds), *Deprivation and Welfare in Rural Areas*, Norwich, Geobooks, 1986.

Marsden, T., 'Capitalist farming and the farm family: a case study', *Sociology*, Vol. 18, No. 2, 1984, pp. 205-24.

Marsden, T., Munton, R., Whatmore, S. and Little, J. (1986a), 'Towards a political economy of capitalist agriculture: a British perspective', *International Journal of Urban and Regional Research*, 10 (4), 1986, pp. 498-521.

— (1986b), 'The restructuring process and economic centrality in capitalist agriculture', *Journal of Rural Studies*, 2 (4), 1986, pp. 271-280.

Marsden, T., Whatmore, S. and Munton, R., 'Uneven development and the restructuring process in British agriculture: a preliminary exploration, *Journal of Rural Studies*, 3, 1987, pp. 297-308.

McCloughlin, B., *Rural Deprivation*, Report to the Department of the Environment, 1983.
Nalson, J., *Mobility of Farm Families: a study of occupational and residential mobility in an upland area of England*, Manchester, Manchester University Press, 1968.
Newby, H., *The Deferential Worker: a study of farm workers in East Anglia*, London, Allen Lane, 1977.
Newby, H., 'The rural sociology of advanced capitalist societies', in Newby, H. (ed.), *International Perspectives in Rural Sociology*, London, Wiley, 1978, pp. 3–30.
Newby, H. (1980a), *Green and Pleasant Land? Social Change in Rural England*, Harmondsworth, Penguin, 1980.
— (1980b), 'Urbanization and the Rural Class Structure: Reflections on a Case Study', in Buttel and Newby, (eds.), 1980, pp. 255–79.
— (1980c), 'Rural Sociology', *Current Sociology*, Vol. 28, No. 1, 1980, pp. 1–141.
— (1982), 'Rural Sociology and its Relevance to the Agricultural Economist: A Review', *Journal of Agricultural Economics*, 33 (2), 1982, pp. 125–65.
Newby, H., Bell, C., Saunders, P. & Rose, D., 'Farmers' attitudes towards conservation', *Countryside Recreation Review* 22, 1977, pp. 23–30.
Newby, H., Bell, C., Rose, D., Saunders, P., *Property, Paternalism and Power: Class and Control in Rural England*, London, Hutchinson, 1978.
Newby, H., Rose, D., Saunders, P. and Bell, C., 'Farming for Survival: The Small Farmer in the Contemporary Rural Class Structure', in Bechhofer, F. and Elliott, B. (eds), 1981, pp. 38–70.
Newby, H., Vogler, C., Rose, D. and Marshall, G., 'From class structure to class action: British working-class politics in the 1980s', in Roberts, B., Finnegan, R. and Gallie, D. (eds), *New Approaches to Economic Life*, Manchester, Manchester University Press, 1985, pp. 86–102.
Perry, R. et al., *Counterurbanisation*, Norwich, Geobooks, 1986.
Potter, C., Countryside Change in Lowland England: A Survey of Farmer Investment Behaviour, Unpublished PhD., University of East Anglia, 1985.
Potter, C. (1986a), 'Investment styles and countryside change in lowland England', in Cox, G., Lowe, P. and Winter, M. (eds), 1986.
— (1986b), 'Processes of countryside change in lowland England', *Journal of Rural Studies*, 2 (3), 1986, pp. 187–195.
Rees, A., *Life in a Welsh Countryside: A social study of Llanfihangel yng Ngwynfa*, Cardiff, University of Wales Press, 1951.
Saunders, P., *Social Theory and the Urban Question*, London, Hutchinson, 1981.
Sayer, A., *Method in Social Science*, London, Hutchinson, 1983.
Symes, D. and Marsden, T., 'Industrialization of agriculture: intensive livestock units in North Humberside', in Healey, M. and Ilberry, B. (eds), *Industrialisation of the Countryside*, Norwich, Geobooks, 1985.
Thorns, D.C., 'The changing system of rural social stratification', *Sociologia Ruralis*, 8 (2), 1968, pp. 161–177.
Urry, J., 'Capitalist restructuring, recomposition and the regions', in Bradley and Lowe, (eds.), 1984, pp. 45–64.
Whatmore, S., 'From women's roles to gender relations: developing perspectives in the analysis of farm women, *Sociologia Ruralis*, 28, 1988, pp. 239–47.
Whatmore, S. (forthcoming) *Home Farm: Women, Work and Family Enterprise*, London, Macmillan.
Whatmore, S., Munton, R., Marsden, T. & Little, J., 'Towards a typology of farm businesses in contemporary British agriculture', *Sociologia Ruralis*, 26 (1), 1987, pp. 21–37.
Williams, W., *The Sociology of an English Village: Gosforth*, London, Routledge & Kegan Paul, 1956.

Williams, W., *A West Country Village: Ashworthy, Family, Kinship and Land*, London, Routledge & Kegan Paul, 1963.

Williams, W., 'The social study of family farming', in Mills, D. (ed.), *English Rural Communities: the impact of a specialised economy*, London & Basingstoke, Macmillan, 1973, pp. 116–33.

Part VII. Politics

19 Commentary and Introduction

Jean Charlot

A simple comparison of the syntheses presented by Wyn Grant and Isabel Boussard reveals, beyond each researcher's own interests, the different approaches typical of the national environment and intellectual tradition of rural and political studies in France and Great Britain. In this introduction, we shall try and illuminate these differences, looking successively at rural politics and power, agricultural politics and the choice of the frame of reference for studies of rurality and politics.

Rural politics and power

The two specialists deal with the question of rural politics and power in different ways: Grant sets it mainly in terms of *local power*, and Boussard mainly in terms of the *relationship between central and local power*.

Grant takes account of studies of local political life (organisations, historical evolution, role perceptions, who has power?) in rural areas:

- according to types of local community; and
- according to types of local government constituency.

In particular, he addresses the development of local power, the recent 'nationalisation' of rural political life, the political deference of agricultural labourers, etc. Such a viewpoint bears witness to a fine tradition of decentralised power and of the study of local power in itself.

Boussard, in contrast, almost always places local power within the national context, covering:

- administrative and political divisions;
- the electoral behaviour of rural inhabitants (union elections, local elections, national elections);
- national crises provoked by agricultural disputes;

- the image of farmers in French public opinion;
- coverage of agricultural issues in party political programmes; and
- the strength of farmers and other rural people in national elites.

She considers, in some detail, the existence of a 'farmer vote', the nature of farmer protest (men of progress or men excluded from progress?), the conditions favourable for the introduction of technical innovations to agriculture (the integration of local society within wider society) and changes in rural society (secularisation, the development of formal associations, etc.).

These two spotlights on rural politics and power complement one another without actually meeting, particularly as Grant incorporates relevant material from other social sciences, including sociology, anthropology, and history, while Boussard makes a point of separating political science from history, economics and the like to preserve its individuality.

Agricultural politics

In this field, there is a common theme – of political decision-making (notably, in the adoption of major pieces of agricultural legislation) – and a common *problématique*, linked to the study of pressure groups (neo-corporatism, etc), as well as similar actors (the FNSEA and the NFU, the Agricultural Ministries, the European Commission, the specialist organisations). Even so, the accent is placed on different issues.

Boussard organises her critical review around two recurrent yet essential themes:

- the modernisation of agriculture; and
- the debate on the unity of the farmers' movement.

Moreover, her examination is focused more on the centre (the Ministry of Agriculture, the posts held there by members of the agricultural elite) than on the periphery of the decision-making structure, or its context.

Grant notes, above all, the external changes and pressures which have destabilised established decision-making processes:

- the shift in agricultural policy, from narrowly productivist objectives to incorporate conservation aims under the influence of the environmental lobby and the new rural middle classes;
- the growing preoccupatin with the costs of agricultural policy; and
- the Europeanisation of agricultural policy/politics.

The choice of the frame of reference

The European context of all agricultural policy, whether French or British, lies beneath the surface in the two reviews. Grant deliberately excludes it while Boussard dedicates only a paragraph to it. It is as if agricultural policies were still solely decided in Paris or in London. This insular vision no longer corresponds well to contemporary political reality. Of course, the blame does not reside with those who have set out to identify the state of current research, but represents a challenge to the whole research community.

Towards a rural political science

Overall, one is struck by the much greater volume of French work in rural political studies and the greater coherence and unity of the research tradition. This probably is a reflection of the relative political importance of rural issues in the two countries. Perhaps because France became both urbanised and industrialised much later, and at a slower rate, than Great Britain, it maintains, in its political life, a considerable sensitivity for the rural world. Amongst senior political leaders, many have passed through the Ministry of Agriculture and make much of it (Chirac, Rocard, etc.) while almost all have a rural background (Mitterrand, Chirac, etc.). In Great Britain, despite its Cabinet status, the Ministry of Agriculture is not a stopping point in an ascendant career, indeed, just the opposite, and David Lloyd George is the only Prime Minister of this century popularly associated with an agricultural region. Therefore, unlike their British colleagues, French political scientists all have to be ruralists whatever their field of study, if only to integrate the rural dimension into their work. Thus, the French school of the study of electoral behaviour is marked by André Siegfried and electoral geography – in contrast to British psephology which is animated by the industrial and urban debate on class-voting. Thus, also, the study of ideology in France cannot afford to neglect rural myths (the eternal order of the fields, the return to the land, the value of nature, etc.).

The interest shown by politicians in rural issues and thus by political scientists should not, however, be confused with the intellectual strength of rural political science. Its progress depends crucially upon methodological advances on three fronts: clarification of its subject-matter; adaptation of the framework of analysis to current realities; and refinement of the study of demands upon rural politics and the institutional and political responses.

1 Clarification of the subject matter

Rural political studies have a double subject – the *agricultural* and the *rural*. Though the difference between the two is well brought out in descriptive accounts of the contemporary reality of rural society, the confusion between the two, and indeed the reduction of 'rural' to 'agricultural', remains common in the study of agricultural policy as well as in political discourse (except for the new political discourse of the ecologists, which is little heeded in France). The reductionism is, without doubt, largely due to the phenomenon – well known to specialists on pressure groups – whereby groups linked to production (in this case, agriculture) are always more prominent, more powerful and more ubiquitous than those which are not.

2 The appropriateness of the framework of analysis

Rural society and agriculture in Britain and France remain relevant objects of study. The problem is knowing whether one can understand the constraints and pressures upon them and their freedom of action, without placing them within a dual political context – the national and the European. The latter dimension must not be regarded as a necessary specialisation only in certain rural fields (notably economics), but as an integral component of all.

3 Rural politics: the variety of demands and responses

External agencies tend to aggregate and stereotype rural politics. The divisions of the French agricultural lobby and the varieties of regionalist movements in Great Britain point instead to the variegation and heterogeneity of rural politics. Research must come to terms with and reinstate the ideological complexity of conflicting goals for rural areas, the debate on partisan politics and, finally, the diversity of influences and mediating bodies.

20 French Political Science and Rural Problems

Isabel Boussard

Although it is not the intention of this paper to define political science, one nevertheless needs to delineate a field of interest not only in relation to other disciplines, but also in terms of the intended subject-matter. The rural world is ubiquitous and strict boundaries are difficult to define. Land policy, regionalism and territorial conflicts all have their rural dimensions. Yet they have been systematically excluded here, and the chapter deals only with those works for which rural problems make up the specific field of interest and principal focus of study.

It is clearly even more difficult to draw boundaries around a field of interest in relation to other disciplines. Political science, the supreme example of a discipline at the confluence of others, involves history, sociology, law, geography etc. Renouncing a doctrinaire definition of this science, the approach adopted here is completely empirical, and is based on a systematic review of the activities of the *Association Française de Science Politique* (AFSP) since its foundation in November 1949, and the publications that have emerged more or less directly from it: the *Revue Française de Science Politique* (RFSP), works of the *Fondation Nationale des Sciences Politiques* (FNSP) and those published by authors whose areas of study are very close.[1]

The studies included group themselves around three main perspectives, which reflect the traditional perspectives of political science. The first of these – covering the agricultural sector as a whole, the socio-professional categorisation of farmers, their reactions, demonstrations, behaviour and attitudes – is the behavioural perspective. Secondly, agricultural policy, the subdivision of public policy, the principal laws, land reform, genesis and processes of development; this one might call the decision-making perspective. Finally, the functional perspective comprises studies of professional organisations – either as pressure groups or in terms of their leaders. To the works included in this third perspective, one needs to add those of the Ministry of Agriculture, or its external agencies. This more administrative aspect complements the functional perspective.

The behavioural perspective: rural people in the rural world

This perspective comprises those studies which take account of both the agricultural sector and rural inhabitants overall and looks at things from their point of view. It can be subdivided into four branches: local or national monographs, studies of crises, those concerning formal political behaviour and, finally, relations with the wider world.

1 Local or national monographs

These studies present and describe the agricultural sector of a region or country. The first edition of the RFSP (May 1951) included such a monograph concerning the Départements of the Côtes du Nord. The author, Alain de Vulpian, working in the tradition of André Siegfried, distinguished two politically opposed regions on the basis of their history, agrarian structure and economy: a western sector whose people had moved away from Christianity and who were more open to Marxist influences, and an eastern one, more submissive to the influence of the Church. The same preoccupations inspired the examination of the Creuse by Derruau-Boniol (1957) and one finds likewise in his study, a more restrained western sector with *radicales* tendencies, and an eastern one where the Communist Party had become progressively installed, particularly since the Second World War.

Maryvonne Bodiguel (1975) concentrated on the examination of the reactions of local farmers to the introduction of such technical innovations as the tractor, artificial insemination and industrial chicken farming. The conclusion was that the acceptance of change will largely be a function of the degree of integration of the local community within wider society.

In 1956, the AFSP held a meeting on *Les paysans français et la politique* (Fauvet and Mendras 1958). It included four monographs concerning the *arrondissement* of Ambert, the Haute-Maurienne, the canton of Orgères-en-Beauce and the transformations of a canton of Santerre. All four employed the same method and were complemented by the overview of Charles d'Aragon on the most desirable administrative and political structures.

In 1973, the Association held a meeting on the study of local power (AFSP 1973) from which one might highlight the paper by Laurent Levi-Strauss (1975) on the respective workings of the economy and kinship patterns on local municipal power. Jean-Pierre Houssel (1980) has described the development of *la vie associative* (voluntary associations) in the upland regions of Lyonnais and Forez – a development resulting largely from an awareness of the need for comprehensive planning within the context of the smaller region. Studies of local power are particularly numerous but usually fall more within the realm of sociology (Association des Ruralistes Français 1983).

The interest of French political science is clearly not confined to France and, as we shall see below, there are numerous studies concerning developing countries. Some of these take the peasant class as a whole as the focus of study, such as the village community within the Owa political area in West Africa (Savonnet-Guyot 1975) or the *'relance paysanne'* (peasant revival) during the Greek political crisis of the summer of 1965 (Chartier-Yannopoulou 1967).

2 Studies of crises

Examining the general attitude of farmers and rural people leads one naturally to consider their particular behaviour when faced with the various crises that can affect them – crop destruction, demonstrations, uprisings etc. Suzanne Quiers-Valette (1962) has looked at the economic causes of the discontent amongst French farmers during the summer of 1961 and in doing so has been led towards more psychological considerations, particularly in comparing the effort spent and the results achieved. Henri Mendras (1962) saw these same demonstrations as expressions not of poverty but of crises in economic growth, resulting from the disquiet of progressive farmers who, having made investments, feared for their returns.

A similar conclusion was reached by Jean Meynaud who maintained that the triggering off particularly of the protest movements in Brittany 'was due to the aspirations of the advanced farmers and not the desperation of the impoverished ones' (Meynaud, 1963, p. 14). Fanch Elégoët (1984) also studied the Breton demonstrations and showed their influence on the organization of produce-markets, notably that of St-Pol-de-Léon.

Alternatively, Jean-Pierre Bernard (1969) believed that the deterioration of the economic situation of farmers engendered protest movements and struggles that resulted in land reform, at least in the cases of Peru and Bolivia. In more general terms, Silas Cerquiera in considering revolutions in Latin America has insisted on the fact that it is the 'fusion of national agrarian movements – urban and peasant – their mixture, that becomes explosive' (Cerquiera 1969, p. 1021).

3 Politicisation, depoliticisation?

One can group together, under this heading, all those studies that have dealt directly with the political divisions and relations of the rural world, including the question raised by Henri Mendras (1962) of its possible depoliticisation Marie-Elisabeth Handman and Yves Tavernier (1970) have analysed the special role played by the *Fédération Nationale des Syndicats d'Exploitants Agricoles* (FNSEA) in the Presidential election campaign of 1965. Before the first ballot, it advised against voting for the outgoing candidate, but as the champion of the Left remained its most dangerous adversary, unprecedentedly it gave no orders for the second ballot.

The first person to pave the way for electoral studies as such was Joseph Klatzmann. Using an ecological method and applying it to the results of the elections of 2 January 1956 at the cantonal level, he concluded that the status of farmers had only a marginal influence on the outcome (Fauvet and Mendras 1958). Daniel Derivry extended this type of study up to the legislative elections of 1968 but was able to conclude that there was a specific 'farmer vote' (Tavernier et al. 1972). Supplementing the ecological method with a systematic analysis of public opinion surveys, Boussard (1982) examined the five presidential and legislative elections from 1973 to 1981 and found that, despite the renowned conservatism of rural people, the Socialist Party did not do too badly in the countryside.

The municipal elections of March 1983 have been studied from two different perspectives. On the one hand, the voting patterns of communes of less than 3,500 inhabitants were analysed and the spatial structure of political allegiances was found to compare closely (particularly for the Right) with that discovered by Joseph Klatzmann in 1956 (Boussard 1983c). Jean-Pierre Houssel (1983) has done similar but more detailed work on the rural communes of the Roanne *arrondissement*. On the other hand, the 1983 elections have been compared to the elections to the Chambers of Agriculture which took place later the same month (Boussard 1983a; Crissenoy 1985; Faure 1983). Placing the two types of election side by side is perilous but not without value. One can see that the policy of Edith Cresson, the Socialist Minister of Agriculture between 1981 and 1983, did not succeed in its goal of weakening the FNSEA, and, significantly, its strongholds coincided with those *départements* where farmers voted mainly for the Right. Pierre Bartoli (1985), descending to the detailed level of small agricultural sub-regions with the four *départements* of Languedoc, remarked upon the success of the FNSEA and concluded that this was concomitant with a weakening of the viticultural movement.

The last cantonal elections, of 1985, were studied from the point of view of those elected in cantons with fewer than 3,000 voters (Boussard 1985a); and the legislative elections of 1986 were the subject of the meeting of the AFSP held in December 1987 (Ranger 1987).

4 Relations with the wider world

The relations between rural people and the wider world are mediated politically by parties and elected officials, but the role of the Church and other socio-professional institutions may also be significant.

Party manifestoes have their importance, even if they are rarely put into practice, and it is instructive to look at the significance they give to the countryside. Take, for example, the elections of the 2 January 1956 – probably the first to be studied using the methods of modern political science though one needs to bear in mind that they were rather untypical, precipitated as they were by the dissolution of the National Assembly. Georges Dupeux (in Duverger et al. 1957) considered the party platforms and demonstrated that agriculture and rural issues were not central to the programmes of the parties, which were preoccupied instead with Algeria and reform of the constitution. Nevertheless, two organisations accorded rural issues a higher position. First, the Radical Party, which made them the third point in its manifesto (after 'democratic reform' and 'social problems'), intended to set up *'Assises Nationales de l'Agriculture Française'* charged with initiating programmes and drawing up collective contracts between farmers and the state. The other case was the Communist Party which placed the 'defence of the working farmer/worker peasant' as its second priority (after the improvement of the standard of living of workers). The party's motto has always been, 'Give the land to those who work it', and its sympathies were clearly with them.

Since its creation, the AFSP has held two conferences on *Les paysans et la politique*. The one in 1956 gave considerable attention to the role of the political parties. Almost the entire political spectrum was dealt with, with the notable omission of Gaullism (Fauvet and Mendras 1958). The 1970 conference in part made good this omission but only for the Fifth Republic (Tavernier et al. 1972). Otherwise, there exists surprisingly no study of the relationship between the *Rassemblement du Peuple Français* (RPF, i.e. the Gaullists) and the rural world. The other parties examined at the 1970 conference were the unified Socialist Party and the Communist Party.

Turning to the study of politicians, what proportion have an agricultural background? In 1889 30 per cent of deputies had links with agriculture; by 1910 there were no more than 18 per cent; and, during the inter-war years and under the Fourth Republic, between 9 and 13 per cent. Mattei Dogan has established that amongst the candidates of the 2 January 1956 elections, almost a fifth 'came from agriculture' (Fauvet and Mendras 1958). In 1967, however, only 8.4 per cent of deputies declared themselves 'farmers' (but sometimes simply for electoral reasons) while farmers still formed over 16 per cent of the working population (Tavernier et al. 1972). In 1985, about thirty deputies came more or less directly from agricultural backgrounds – around 6 per cent – and roughly the same proportion were returned to the Assembly in the 1986 elections. Now that farmers represent only between 7 and 8 per cent of the total working population, the margin of their underrepresentation has greatly narrowed (Boussard 1985b). Dogan has extended this analysis to include senators, amongst whom there has been a better representation of rural people. In 1936, they comprised 24 per cent of the Senate (i.e. twice the proportion as in the Chamber); in 1956 the figure was 25 per cent; and by 1986 it was just over 20 per cent.

Beyond the formal political world, but with a significant historical influence, are the churches, most especially the Catholic Church (Fauvet and Mendras 1959). In 1970 Bertrand Hervieu and André Vial looked at 'the Catholic Church and the 'peasantry'. They painted a large and historical picture. But of the present they talked of 'rupture', of 'being out of touch', of 'the identity crisis amongst rural clergymen', adding that: 'it seems difficult today to be able to rely, for any length of time, upon the Catholic Church to maintain the established order' (Tavernier et al. 1972, p. 314). But this is only one aspect of a more profound problem. Religious observance has declined precipitously and at a much greater rate than the rural exodus, so that it no longer seems possible for the Church to play a major role in rural affairs.

Finally, farmers are not as isolated as some would maintain (Clerc 1984). They live amongst other Frenchmen and are in frequent contact with them. It seems useful, in that case, to look at how these 'other Frenchmen' regard farmers. We have gone systematically through all the public opinion surveys carried out in France since 1945. At least a hundred dealt with this issue. The overall conclusion to be drawn is that the general image is not unfavourable and that it contradicts what the farmers themselves think – that they are not well liked, are misunderstood, treated with condescension, regarded as being 'boorish', 'doltish', 'bloody minded', in short *'bouleurs de terre'* (sods of the earth) to use the colourful expression of Emile Guillaumin. In contrast, the French public actually sees farming as a major national asset, finds farmers to be dynamic and practising one of those rare jobs in which risks have to be taken and is sympathetic of support for farms which are no longer profitable (Boussard 1981).

The decision-making perspective: public policy

The issue that dominates this section on policies for the countryside is that ubiquitous process – the modernisation of agriculture. The work of Pierre Barral, *Les Sociétés Rurales du XXe Siècle* (1978), is difficult to classify, but serves as a good introduction. It tackles a number of particularly historic themes and seeks to characterise the state of rural society at the turn of the century and then under the successive impacts of the 'great upheavals' – the First and Second World Wars, the financial crisis of 1929, and the various revolutions, Russian, Mexican etc. Otherwise, the field can conveniently be split into developing countries studies, the situation in France and, finally, the problems of the EEC.

1 Rural policies in developing countries

The first article on the subject to appear in the RFSP (Plessz 1954) argued that the study of contemporary agrarian reform offers an enormous scope to the different social sciences, each with their particular methodologies, such as demography, economics, cultural anthropology and so on. For political science, not least, it offers considerable possibilities since the aim is to ascertain which political forces can bring about agrarian reform, to the detriment of which social groups, etc. This calls for quantitative and qualitative studies of the media, propaganda, political parties, electoral results and opinion polls. Such methods have been applied, at least in part, in several specific cases: for example in Yugoslavia (Castellan 1958), in Mexico (Chevalier 1969) and Latin America overall (Chevalier, 1969), in Algeria, (Villers 1980) and in Colombia (Gilhodès 1974). These works highlight the balance of opposing forces, their links with the countryside and the different possible levels of explanation. Yet, there remains relatively few such studies in comparison to the enormous amount of literature on developing countries from such perspectives as economics, demography, ethnography or geography.

2 The French case

As early as 1950, Michel Augé-Laribé paved the way in the study of French agricultural policy, though he chiefly described existing policy measures and the extent of their implementation. Gaston Rimareix and Yves Tavernier (1963) rose above this in examining the decision-making processes which brought about the *Loi Complémentaire* of 1962, highlighting the frequent contacts between the Minister of Agriculture and the agricultural unions, notably the FNSEA and the *Centre National des Jeunes Agriculteurs* (CNJA).

Pierre Muller (1985) stressed the role of this latter group in drafting the law of

1960; he identified in particular the direct approaches of its leaders to the advisers to the the Prime Minister and President, effectively by-passing the Minister of Agriculture. Chombard de Lauwe (1979) also examined the two *Lois d'Orientation*, their context, the lengthy parliamentary debate they provoked and the resultant opposition to change.

In my own work, I have investigated the procedures which led up to the adoption of the law of the 2 December 1940, establishing the *Commission Nationale d'Organisation Corporative* (Boussard 1980). This was a unique situation since Parliament had been adjourned and, as a consequence, the normal channels were no longer functioning. Nevertheless, the various interests found the means to express themselves through other channels, and a genuine debate was effected through a series of communications between the unions, the office of the *Chef de l'Etat*, that of the Ministry of Agriculture and the administration.

Pierre Muller (1981) has considered French agricultural modernisation policy as a whole and has linked it closely with the appearance of the CNJA as a viable national force. For this author, the Third Republic was a period of stagnation and conservatism. Likewise, André Fel (1985) maintains that the 'true agricultural revolution' dates from the 1960s. I would want to challenge these assessments. First, it seems right to concur with Eugen Weber that agricultural modernisation first took place around the 1880s. Secondly, agriculture was not neglected under the Third Republic; it enjoyed strong protection and innovative policies (Boussard 1985c and 1987). It seems preferable therefore to talk of a second period of modernisation after 1945, or a 'second agricultural revolution (since 1950)', as does Pierre Barral (1968, p. 293).

3 The European economic community

In the study of decision-making processes, the establishment of the Common Agricultural Policy is no less interesting. In 1964, Pierre Gerbet described the negotiations and the respective positions of the different partners, suggesting that the CAP was forged through a succession of conflicts. Five years later, Hélène Delorme and Yves Tavernier (1969) summed up the situation in terms of new generations confronting traditional forces, though some of the producers' associations were more favourable than others to the setting up of the CAP. Amongst French farmers they found general support for a peaceful and inclusive European bloc to be widespread, but such support 'diminished rapidly when the actual form of its organisation was proposed' (p. 141). In 1978, Hélène Delorme and Laurence Tubiana posed the problem of the southward enlargement of the Community; 'one step forward two steps backwards' was how they described it. The immediate enlargement seemed to them to be explosive and a long transitional period would be necessary in order to finalise market reforms in Mediterranean products, i.e. fruit and vegetables but chiefly *vins de table*.

If this section of the paper seems much shorter than the one before it, it is because here the disciplinary boundaries are less well defined. The political scientist must guard against straying into the domain of the economist, or encroaching upon the territory of the historian. The distinctive contribution of political science lies in the study of decision-making, of motives, of opposing

The organisational perspective: agricultural movements

In the 1950s and early 1960s, pressure groups were very much in fashion, particularly under the influence of Jean Maynaud, and a large number of works on this subject appeared, especially on professional agricultural organisations (Mathiot 1952; Meynaud 1957; Meynaud and Meyriat 1959 and Meynaud 1962). Agricultural movements continue to attract scholarly attention but not as much as twenty or thirty years ago. One might distinguish those studies dealing with the organisations themselves and their roles; secondly, those concerned with their leaders and agricultural elites; and, finally, those papers dealing specifically with the Ministry of Agriculture.

1 Agricultural associations

Just as public policies have been dominated by questions relating to agricultural modernisation, so studies of professional organisations have been oriented towards a central theme: the question of agricultural unity. The political scientist cannot afford to ignore the historical aspect of this.

Agricultural unity had, in fact, been attained by the Vichy Government through the Acts of 2 December 1940 and 16 December 1942 which not only established sectoral and representational unity but also brought together separate bodies dealing with insurance, cooperation and credit under the single authority of a *Conseil National Corporatif*. Specialist organisations were also included as well as the proposed *Chambres Régionales d'Agriculture* which were never actually created (Boussard 1980). With the Liberation the whole lot was abolished though the Socialist Minister of Agriculture, Pierre Tanguy-Prigent, wanted to preserve that unity in creating the *Confédération Générale de l'Agriculture* (CGA). He failed completely but the idea remained as a dream, a paradise to be regained for some, a hell for others. It needs to be said that the problem was not a simple one, that the differences were not only political and that, on top of it all, a certain ambiguity existed over the very terms used.

As early as 1955, Henri Mendras denounced the idea of farmer unity: 'There exists a myth of farmer unity analogous to the myth of worker unity. This unity has only ever been achieved superficially or by imposition . . . Nevertheless, the dream of uniting all farmers under a single professional body or under a single political party which would represent a third of the nation and would thus be in a position to impose their demands, persists' (p. 755). After the war, however, the FNSEA became so clearly a majority that a certain *de facto* agricultural unity was achieved, at least from the trade union point of view, but then only for a short while.

In September 1962, the RFSP devoted an edition to 'Farmers and Politics under the Fifth Republic'. Yves Tavernier (1962) studied the relationships between agricultural unionism and government policy. He maintained that instead of political differences, an inter-generational conflict appeared which penetrated to the very core of the FNSEA. He also examined the 1964 Congress of the FNSEA (Tavernier 1964) and impartially confirmed that 'One sole union organisation, the FNSEA, represents in France all farmers irrespective of the scale of their enterprise, the mode of tenure or the type of their production. This unity is the fruit of recent change'.

The same author extended his research until 1965 and, with reference to the presidential elections, noted that the FNSEA prudently incited its members not to vote for the Gaullist candidate (Tavernier 1966). He also pointed out that the Left and the extreme Left, although not represented on the administrative council of the FNSEA, did 'control numerous *départemental* federations'. In June 1968 he turned his attention to the *Mouvement de Coordination et de Défense des Exploitations Agricoles Familiales* (MODEF) which had drawn together members who had been excluded from the FNSEA (Tavernier 1968). The hostility of MODEF to the agricultural policies of the Fifth Republic was even stronger than that of the FNSEA. MODEF's principal aim was to protect the family farm but not quite in the manner which the government of the time would have liked. In 1969, Tavernier also published a useful twin study of the FNSEA and the CNJA which modestly claimed to be primarily a 'research guide' including documentary sources.

In 1970, Pierre Coulomb and Henri Nallet entered the fray with a piece entitled 'Testing the unity of union organisations' (Tavernier et al. 1972). They believed that the fragile unity had been saved by incorporating new elements through the CNJA. Nevertheless, unity was still threatened, mainly by the existence of MODEF and the *Fédération Française de l'Agriculture* (FFA). Philippe Gratton, (1971), however, attacks the notion of unity as a pernicious illusion and, with it, Barral's cautious and qualified position: 'This myth has always been upheld by researchers and historians, with Barral striving to give it validity, nobility and credibility by conceptualising it under the term *'agrarisme'* . . . In seeking to guarantee its scientific character, Barral adds that he will use the term "in a purely objective sense excluding all value judgments" ' (Grattan 1972, p. 9).

This is, in some ways, a similar view to that found in the special edition of the journal *Pour* on *'Paysans: la fin du corporatisme?'* (*Pour* 1985). Pierre Coulomb and Hélène Delorme maintain that union unity is 'considered to be less and less adequate for the protection of farmers whose situations and prospects are developing at different rates'. They note a growth in the power of other unions at a time of self-questioning within the FNSEA. François Colson believes that the diversity of French agriculture calls for a similar diversity in union representation. Finally, examining 'farmers' political strength and the Common Agricultural Policy', Delorme (1969) looked for the demand for unity to be restored but now within the context of an international union.

To summarise, at the present time, there exist amongst French agricultural unions the FNSEA and its 'youth' branch, the *Cercle National des Jeunes Agriculteurs*, set up in 1947 and becoming *'Centre'* in 1957. In 1959, MODEF was constituted close to the Communist Party and in 1969, the 'right wing' FFA came into being. In 1981, the *Conféderation Nationale Syndicale des Travailleurs-Paysans* (CNSTP) was formed from several small 'left-wing' unions and in 1982, the *Fédération Nationale des Sydicats Paysans* (FNSP) was established with close ties with the ideas of the Socialist Minister of the period, Edith Cresson. In May 1987, these last two bodies fused to form the new *Confédération Paysanne*. To these organisations one needs to add the *Assemblée Permanente des Chambres d'Agriculture* (APCA) and the *Confédération Nationale de la Mulualité, de la Coopération et du Crédit Agricole* (CNMCCA, the so called 'Boulevard-St-Germain'). Agricultural unionism has often been studied at the local level: the paper by Serge Mallet on Finistère, which appeared in 1961 was, to some extent, a landmark study.

Apart from trade unionism, the other professional agricultural organisations have been relatively little studied. Before the war, the Dorgères[2] movement attracted the attention of Louis Gabriel-Robinet (1937), an already well-known young journalist. In 1970, Pascal Ory wrote a master's thesis on the subject. Jean-Michel Royer has compared the Dorgères and Poujade[3] movements (Fauvet and Mendras 1958); and Stanley Hoffmann (1956), these two movements with the position of the FNSEA. Only one specialist organisation has been the subject of a detailed investigation – the *Association Générale des Producteurs de Blé* (AGPB) by Henri Roussillon (1970) who, after a historical section, analyses its organisation and activities.

The *Jeunesse Agricole Catholique* (JAC) has been better studied. In 1983, Marie-Josèphe Durupt produced a doctoral thesis on the *Mouvements d'Action Catholique Rurale*. In it, she showed the originality of the JAC, the training of its militants and its progressive assumption of political responsibilities, and studied, in considerable depth, their own press coverage of their activities, its contents, presentation, distribution and use. The personal awareness of members of the movement stimulated by their involvement in their work, by the support of adults, etc. was highlighted by Marcel Faure (1967). In 1980, at a seminar in Rennes on 'La JAC et la modernisation de l'agriculture de l'Ouest' (INRA 1980), Paul Houée distinguished three major phases, Yves Lambert focused particularly on its role in the Ancenis regions and Roger Le Guen, on the growth and development of agricultural operations in Maine-et-Loire. The JAC, CNJA and CETA (*Centres d'études techniques agricoles*) were held responsible, by Pierre Muller (1982), for the 'birth of a new farmer ideology'. He differentiated a 'time of missionaries', one of 'militants' and a 'time of politics', when the new political ideology had become established.

Most of the agricultural press is the mouthpiece of professional associations or political parties. In 1956, Bertrand Labrusse drew up a sort of catalogue of this press, differentiating between the news-sheets of one organisation or another; those publications not linked to either a party or a movement; press bulletins; periodicals like Agra-Presse; and professional and technical publications (Fauvet and Mendras 1958), Jean-Michel Royer (Duverger et al. 1957) in examining 'several pressure groups through their newspapers and magazines' covered a range of agricultural periodicals, including the 'political' (such as *La Terre, L'Unité Paysanne*); the 'Catholic' (*Foyer Rural, Jeunes forces rurales*); and the 'professional'. Amongst the latter one can distinguish the specialist publications (*Le Bouilleur de France, La Vie Laitière*) from those which are not, such as *l'Information Agricole*', the organ of the FNSEA. A final category is the 'information press', about which Royer comments: 'In this group, where the principal is to be apolitical, one is not surprised to find that political choices are perhaps even more precise than in the others' (Duverger et al. 1957 p. 148) – an example is *L'Affiche Agricole* which supported the civic activities of René Blondelle.[4]

2 Agricultural elites

These studies form only a relatively recent fraction of that branch of political science which ranges from Vilfredo Pareto to Pierre Birnbaum. A survey was undertaken in 1966 of those one might call 'budding elites' – the students of the *grandes écoles d'agriculture* in Paris, Grignon, Montpellier, Nancy, Rennes, Toulouse and Versailles. The journal *Paysans* (1967) published a series of tables showing their fathers' and paternal grandfathers' profession, the percentage of these who had themselves passed through a *grande école*, their place of residence, etc.

The person who has done the most work in this field is Sylvain Maresca. In 1979, he published five biographies of farmers' leaders chosen to illustrate the successive stages in the careers of different types of leader in Meurthe-et-Moselle: the rich cattle baron, the original JACist, one who represents the second wave of JACists, the new inheritor (who represents the knell of the JAC) and a representative of the *'parvenus'*, the wealthy newcomer farmers. In 1981, Maresca looked at the timetable, the profile and the accessibility of three leaders who had responsibility at the *départemental*, regional and national levels respectively. He then traced, step by step, so to speak, the career of François Guillaume, the FNSEA President. The culmination of these various studies was a book entitled *Les Dirigeants Paysans* (Maresca 1983), which examined the accountability *(les propriétés sociales)* and representativeness of these leaders as well as the local elites in Meurthe-et-Moselle and Charente.

Maresca too believes that true union unity is unachievable. In Charente, inter-union rivalry is strong since the dissident federation of this *département* was one of the first to seek affiliation to MODEF. In a recent paper analysing the power game in rural communes, Maresca suggests that local cohesion can be maintained but only according to a new unitary principle. This principle has become 'selective' by striving 'continually to create the conditions of its own reinforcement, by selecting its members according to their conformity to an already dominant definition, one that is essentially professional' (Maresca 1984, p. 457).

The Ministry of Agriculture

The Ministry combines professional elites and civil servants. In a series of articles, René Chatelain, one of its senior civil servants, argued that all the important posts within the Ministry had been taken up by agricultural engineers or 'agros', even in those areas 'where agronomics does not appear to have any role to play' (Chatelain 1934–55, p. 278). A similar critical observation was made by Charles Vincent de Vaugelas, a Treasury Inspector who also held a post in the

Ministry for a while. He concluded that such a situation prevented people from having 'friendships, developed at school or university, with high civil servants of other ministries' (Fauvet and Mendras 1958, p. 256). In short, a ministry which has insufficient contacts with the rest of the administration, is badly placed for taking action and, therefore, bad for the farmers themselves.

As these conclusions were not based upon any systematic empirical evidence, I conducted a survey of the top civil servants from 1936 to 1976. Of the 162 individuals covered, only 29 per cent had come from the *grandes écoles d'agriculture* or *veterinaries*. If one adds the ministers and the members of ministerial cabinets, the proportion falls to a sixth, though they still remain the largest group (Boussard, 1983c). This counting exercise has been taken further by the addition of rural 'notables', who were selected through the biographical notes appearing in the first three editions of *Who's Who in France*. Three short conclusions can be drawn: that these are well-educated people who often have a secondary residence in Paris and who simultaneously hold a large number of professional and political positions.

In the published proceedings of the 1956 conference, a documentary annex provided a summary history of the Ministry, showing its structure and areas of involvement and briefly describing its main leaders (Fauvet and Mendras 1958). Yves Tavernier has looked at ministerial reform, the so-called 'Pisani reform', the difficulties of which he clearly saw as stemming essentially from the differences in outlook between the two corps that ideally should be fused together: rural engineering, comprised of modern, dynamic men, 'the pourers of concrete', in contrast to whom the '*ingénieur des Eaux et Forêts* appears as a stick-in-the-mud traditionalist' (Tavernier 1967, p. 900).

These are the two most prestigious corps in agriculture and rural affairs. Of the first, about half have emerged from the *Institut National Agronomique* (the 'agros') and half from the *Ecole Polytechnique*. The second group are almost all 'agros'. One cannot stress enough the importance of this career pathway in France; from the *grandes écoles* and *grand corps* to high administrative and possibly political responsibilities. This is the same subject, albeit in a much wider sense, that has been dealt with by Pierre Blanc-Gonnet (1969): he has produced a historical survey of agricultural administration in France and has looked at the extent of the reforms as a whole including, amongst other things, the difficulties experienced by the *Directeurs Départementaux de l'Agriculture* (DDA) and the *Office National des Forêts* (ONF).

Whether it be in the organisations and the professional elites or in the Ministry of Agriculture, the rural sphere forms a relatively closed world. This characteristic has often been deplored and has sometimes been exaggerated. In the leading circles, everybody knows one another but this does not mean that the rest of society can be ignored, nor indeed the rest of the world. A good example of this is provided by François Guillaume, still President of the FNSEA, who has been described as the most 'well-connected' French 'lobbyist' in the USA.[5]

Furthermore, the integrated lifestyle is more developed in the countryside than in the town. Communes of less than 1,500 inhabitants can count up to 25 associations, and these are not only economically oriented (Bodiguel 1986, p. 168). There are historical societies, archaeological societies, amenity groups etc. In short, rural people have learnt how to adapt to isolation.

Conclusion

The list of works identified here certainly has not exhausted the subject but it has indicated the major directions. A brief review of the articles appearing in the RFSP shows that between 1951 and 1970 almost 3 per cent of the articles dealt with rural issues, but the proportion has fallen by about half in the period since then. Why? Was it a change in direction of the *Revue*? A change in mood? A change in the intellectual fashion? Some ideas, strongly supported for several years, are sometimes subsequently abandoned.

But there is also the evolution of the rural sector. Are we really approaching *Une France sans Paysans* (Gervais et al. 1965), *La Fin de la France Paysanne* (Gervais et al. 1976) or *La Fin des Paysans* (Mendras 1984)? One is aware that the rural exodus is being attenuated and that there could even be a certain revival of rural life. The vast urban agglomerations have ceased to grow, to the advantage of the small towns or the larger market towns. One talks now of an urban exodus. It is perhaps the object of study itself that is changing.

It is the appeal of nature, of an alternative environment, which attracts urban workers, doctors and senior executives. But even if the farmers have become minorities, they remain the 'great architects' of the countryside. Political science cannot forget this double emphasis: to study the entirety of rural problems while keeping in mind the fact that farmers are always the most active 'gardeners of France, guardians of the soil and protectors of nature', as one of our Deputies put it rather colourfully.[6] Finally, let us not forget also the job description provided by the minister who remained longest in the Rue-de-Varenne: 'A Minister of Agriculture is, in the end, nothing more than an attentive and vigilant gardener, who works the land with a constant passion'.[7]

Notes

1. Also excluded are works dealing with France, but written by foreign authors: such as Gordon Wright, Charles K. Warner, Bernard E. Brown, Lawrence Wylie etc.
2. *Le Mouvement de Revendications Paysannes* (the Movement for Farmers' Demands) was very active between 1928 and 1939. Henri Dorgères led the fight against obligatory social insurance, taxes and the 'reds'. His 'green shirts' (the youth wing of the movement) are considered as a close parallel to fascist organisations of the same period.
3. Starting in 1953, Pierre Poujade, a small-town shopkeeper, led violent protests against the authorities, focusing resentment at the increasing interference of the state, particularly through taxation. About 50 of his supporters were elected in the legislative elections of 2 January 1956. It proved to be a hollow victory and the movement disintegrated in the political crisis of 1958 with the advent of Gaullism.
4. The career of René Blondelle is so rich and varied that it is difficult to summarise. In charge of the union of agricultural unions in Aisne before the war, the *Union Corportiste* in 1941, he was Secretary General, then President of the FNSEA from 1946–54, President of the *Assemblée des Chambres d'Agriculture* in 1952, an independent senator in 1955, etc.

5. Chavelet (Elisabeth), 'François Guillaume a saisi les subtilités du lobbying', *Le Figaro-Economie*, 6 January 1986.
6. Emmanuel Hamel, 2nd sitting of 22 April 1976 *Journal Officiel* Parliamentary Debates, 23 April 1976, p. 2063.
7. Henri Queuille, *Annales de l'Académie d'Agriculture*, ceremonial sitting of 22 February 1939, p. 257.

Bibliography

Association des ruralistes français, *Pouvoirs dans la commune, pouvoirs sur la commune en milieu rural*, Montpellier, 24–5 novembre 1983, pagination multiple, multig.
Association française de science politique, *Journée d'études sur le pouvoir local*, Paris, 10 février 1973, pagination multiple, multigr.
Augé-Laribé, Michel, *La politique agricole de la France, 1880-1940*, Paris, Presses Universitaires de France, 1950, 483 pp.
Barral, Pierre, *Les agrariens français de Méline à Pisani*, Paris, Presses de la FNSP, 1968, 386 pp.
— *Les sociétés rurales du XXème siècle*, Paris, Colin, 1978, 327 pp.
Bartoli, Pierre, 'Evolution du mouvement viticole et élections aux Chambres d'agriculture', *nouvelles campagnes,* 35, octobre 1985, pp. 55–77.
Bernard, Jean-Pierre, 'Mouvements paysans et réformes agraires. Réflexions sur les cas péruvien et bolivien', *RFSP,* XIX (5), octobre 1969, pp. 982–1017.
Blanc-Gonnet, Pierre, *La réforme des services extérieurs du ministère de l'agriculture*, Paris, Cujas, 1969, 118 pp.
Bodiguel, Maryvonne, *Les paysans face au progrès*, Paris, Presses de la FNSP, 1975, 178 pp.
— *Le rural en question. Politiques et sociologues en quête d'objet*, Paris, l'Harmattan, 1986, 185 pp.
Boussard, I., *Vichy et la Corporation paysanne* Paris, Presses de la FNSP, 1980, 414 pp.
— 'L'image socio-politique des agriculteurs dans l'opinion publique française depuis 1945', *Economie rurale*, 145, septembre-octobre 1981, pp. 25–31.
— 'Le comportement électoral des agriculteurs français de 1973 à 1981', *Economie rurale*, 149, mai-juin 1982, pp. 2–12.
— (1983a), 'Elections aux Chambres d'agriculture et municipales: le vote des agriculteurs', *Revue politique et parlementaire*, 85 (903), avril 1983, pp. 79–94.
— (1983b), 'Fonctionnaires et notables agricoles en France', rapport au colloque organisé par l'Institut d'Histoire du Temps présent et l'Instituto Nazionale per la storia del Movimento di liberazione in Italia: les élites en France et en Italie, de la guerre à l'après-guerre: renouvellement ou permanence, Le elites in Francia e Italia negli anni quaranta, Rome, 14–6 avril 1983, *Italia contemporanea*, 153, et *Mélanges de l'Ecole française de Rome*, tome 95, 1983–2, pp. 51–68.
— (1983c), 'Le comportement des ruraux lors des élections municipales de mars 1983', rapport au colloque de l'Association des ruralistes français: *Pouvoirs sur la commune. Pouvoirs dans la commune*, Montpellier, 24–5 novembre 1983, 20 p. multigr.
— (1985a), 'Le vote dans les cantons à dominante rurale', *Revue politique et parlementaire*, dossier: cantonales 1985, 87(918), juillet-août 1985, pp. 32–4.
— (1985b), 'Les agriculteurs et la représentation proportionnelle', 8 p. dactyl. (Extraits dans *Agri-Sept.*, 13 décembre 1985, pp. 38–9).
— (1985) 'Les radicaux face à l'évolution de l'agriculture française', *Cahiers d'Histoire du radicalisme*, 2, décembre 1985, pp. 21–35.

— 'Henri Queuille et la France rurale', rapport au colloque de la Société des 'Amitiés d'Henri Queuille' et de la Société d'Histoire du radicalisme: *Henri Queuille et la République*, Paris, 25-6 octobre 1984, 64 pp., multigr., Presses Universitaires de Limoges, 1987.
Castellan, Georges, 'La paysannerie dans la Yougoslavie socialiste', *RFSP*, VIII (2), juin 1958, pp. 336-357.
Cerquiera, Silas, 'Mouvements agraires, mouvements nationaux et révolution en Amérique Latine', *RFSP*, XIX (5), octobre 1969, pp. 1018-41.
Charlier-Yannopoulou, Tatiana, 'La crise politique grecque', *RSFP*, XVII (1), fevrier 1967, pp. 47-64.
Chatelain, René, 'Ministère de l'agriculture', *Revue administrative,* série d'articles de mai-juin 1954 à janvier-février 1955, pp. 278-9, 527-9, 651-4, 57-60.
Chevalier, François, ' "Ejido" et la stabilité au Mexique', *RFSP*, XVI (4), avril 1966, pp. 717-52.
— 'Décolonisation et réforme agraire en Amérique Latine', *RFSP* XIX (5), octobre 1969, pp. 973-81.
Chombard de Lauwe, Jean, *L'aventure agricole de la France*, Paris, Presses Universitaires de France, 1979, 376 pp.
Clerc, François, 'Les agriculteurs et l'opinion publique: une information à améliorer', *Paysans*, 168, octobre-novembre 1984, pp. 6-13.
Coulomb, Pierre, 'Feu les offices fonciers', *Etudes foncières*, 22 mars 1984, pp. 1-11.
Crisenoy, Chantal de, 'Chambres d'agriculture: les vrais résultats', *Nouvelles campagnes*, 35, octobre 1985, pp. 38-42.
Delorme, Hélène, 'Le rôle des forces paysannes dans l'élaboration de la politique agricole commune', *RFSP* XIX (2), avril 1969, pp. 356-91.
Delorme, Hélène and Tavernier, Yves, *Les paysans français et l'Europe*, Paris, Presses de la FNSP, 1969, 152 pp.
Delorme, Hélène and Tubiana, Laurence, 'L'élargissement vers le sud du Marché commun agricole', *RFSP*, XXVIII (4), août 1978, pp. 698-716.
Derruau-Boniol, S. 'Le département de la Creuse. Structure sociale et évolution politique', *RFSP*, VII (1), janvier-mars 1957, pp. 38-66.
Durupt, Marie-Josèphe, *Les mouvements d'action catholique rurale, facteur d'évolution du milieu rural*, Thèse de IIIème cycle sous la direction de René Rémond, Paris X-Nanterre, 1983, 2 vol., 413-165-41 pp. 2.
Duverger, Maurice, Goguel, François and Touchard, Jean, *Les élections du 2 janvier 1956*, Paris, Presses de la FNSP, 1957, 505 pp.
Elégoët, Fanch, *Révoltes paysannes en Bretagne: à l'origine de l'organisation des marchés*, Plobennec, éd. du Léon, 1984, 504 pp.
Faure, Marcel, 'Pourquoi la JAC?', *Paysans*, 66, juin-juillet 1967, pp. 43-9.
— 'Après les élections aux Chambres d'agriculture', *Paysans*, 158, février-mars 1983, pp. 81-8.
Fauvet, Jacques and Mendras, Henri (eds.) *Les paysans et la politique dans la France contemporaine*, Paris, Presses de la FNSP, 1958, 532 pp. (Tiré de la journée AFSP du 30 juin 1956)
Fel, André, 'Les révolutions vertes de la campagne française', *Vingtième siècle*, 8, octobre-décembre 1985, pp. 3-17.
Gabriel-Robinet, Louis, *Dorgères et le Front paysan*, Paris, Plon, 1937, 93 pp.
Gerbet, Pierre, 'La mise en oeuvre du marché common agricole', *RFSP*, XIV (4), août 1964, pp. 761-73.
Gervais, Michel, Servolin, Claude and Weil, Jean, *Une France sans paysans*, Paris, Le Seuil, 1965, 128 pp.
Gervais, Michel, Jollivet, Marcel and Tavernier, Yves, *La fin de la France paysanne*, tome

IV de *L'Histoire de la France rurale*, Paris, Le Seuil, 1976, 672 pp.
Gilhodes, Pierre, *La question agraire en Colombie*, Paris, Presses de la FNSP, 1974, 541 pp.
Gratton, Philippe, *Les luttes de classe dans les campagnes*, Paris, Anthropos, 1971, 483 pp.
— *Les paysans français contre l'agrarisme*, Paris, Maspéro, 1972, 224 pp.
Handman, Marie-Elisabeth and Tavernier, Yves, 'Le syndicalisme paysan et la campagne électorale', pp. 285–308, in Centre d'étude de la vie politique française ed., *L'élection présidentielle de décembre 1965*, Paris, Presses de la FNSP, 1970, 548 pp.
Hoffmann, Stanley, *Le mouvement Poujade*, Paris, Presses de la FNSP, 1956, 417 pp.
Houssel, Jean-Pierre, 'L'association du village à la petite région dans les pôles de résistance du monde rural: l'exemple des monts du Lyonnais et du Forez', *Cahiers du centre interdisciplinaire d'études rurales appliquées,* (CIERA) 3, Université de Lyon II, juin 1980, pp. 89–104.
— 'Gauche et droite dans les petites villes et communes rurales de l'arrondissement de Roanne', *Cahiers d'Histoire*, XXVIII (213), 1983, pp. 133–48.
Institut national de la recherche agronomique, *La JAC et la modernisation de l'Agriculture de l'Ouest*, station d'Economie et de Sociologie rurales, Rennes, octobre 1980, 208 pp.
Lévi-Strauss, Laurent, 'Pouvoir municipal et parenté dans un village bourguignon', *Annales,* 30 (1), février 1975, pp. 149–59.
Mallet, Serge, 'La réforme syndicale en Finistère', *Les Temps modernes,* 183, juillet 1961, pp. 130–63.
Maresca, Sylvain, 'Ebauche d'une analyse sociologique des élites paysannes. Cinq biographies de dirigeants paysans', *Etudes rurales*, 76, octobre–décembre 1979, pp. 51–81.
— 'La représentation de la paysannerie. Remarques ethnographiques sur le travail de représentation des dirigeants agricoles', *Actes de la recherche en sciences sociales*, 38, mai 1981, pp. 3–18.
— *Les dirigeants paysans*, Paris, Ed. de Minuit, 1983, 294 pp.
— 'Le territoire politique', *RFSP*, XXXIV (3), juin 1984, pp. 449–66.
Mathiot, André, Les 'pressure groups' aux Etats-Unis, *RFSP*, II (3), juillet–septembre 1952, pp. 429–73.
Mendras, Henri, 'Les organisations agricoles et la politique', *RFSP*, V (4), octobre–décembre 1955, pp. 736–60.
— 'Politisation, dépolitisation, repolitisation du milieu rural', pp. 251–65 in: Vedel, Georges, (ed.), *La dépolitisation, mythe ou réalité?*', Paris, Presses de la FNSP, 1962, 288 pp.
— 'Les manifestations de juin 1961', *RFSP*, XII (3), septembre 1962, pp. 647–71.
— *La fin des paysans. Suivi d'une réflexion sur la fin des paysans. Vingt ans après*, Paris, Actes Sud, 1984, 372 pp.
Meynaud, Jean, 'Les groupes d'intérêt et l'administration en France', *RFSP*, VII (3), juillet–septembre 1957, p. 573–93.
Meynaud, Jean and Meyriat, Jean, Les 'groupes de pression' en Europe occidentale: état des travaux, *RFSP*, IX (1), mars 1959, pp. 229–46 et XII (2), juin 1962, pp. 433–55.
Meynaud, Jean, 'Les groupes de pression sous la Vème République', *RFSP*, XII (3), septembre 1962, pp. 672–97.
— *La révolte paysanne*, Paris, Payot, 1963, 308 pp.
Muller, Pierre, 'Un exemple de politique française de modernisation de l'agriculture', 11 pp., rapport au colloque de l'AFSP, Grenoble, table ronde no. 4, *L'analyse des politiques publiques*, 22-4 octobre 1981.
— 'Comment les idées deviennent-elles politiques? La naissance d'une nouvelle idéologie paysanne en France', *RFSP*, XXXII (1), février 1982, 173 pp.
— *Le technocrate et le paysan*, Paris, Ed. Ouvrières, 1984, 173 pp.
— 'Les limites du volontarisme: le cas des politiques rurales', 19 pp., rapport au colloque de

l'AFSP: *Alternances et changements politiques,* Paris, 17-8 janvier 1985.
Ory, Pascal, *Henri Dorgères et la Défense paysanne des origines à 1939,* mémoire de maîtrise sous la direction de René Rémond, Université Paris X-Nanterre, 1970, 250 pp.
Paysans, 'Origine sociale et passé scolaire des étudiants en agronomie', 66, juin-juillet 1967, pp. 83-7.
Plessz, Nicolas, 'Méthodes d'étude des réformes agraires dans les pays insuffisamment développés', *RFSP,* IV (1), janvier-mars 1954, pp. 56-69.
Pour, 'Paysans: la fin du corporatisme?', 102, septembre-octobre 1985, 108 pp.
Quiers-Valette, Suzanne, 'Les causes économiques du mécontentement des paysans français en 1961', *RFSP,* XII (3), septembre 1962, pp. 555-98.
Ranger, Jean, 'La fin des cultures politiques regionales?' rapport au colloque de l'AFSP: *Les agriculteurs et la politique,* Paris décembre 1987.
Rimareix, Gaston and Tavernier, Yves, 'L'élaboration et le vote de la loi complémentaire à la loi d'orientation agricole', *RFSP,* XIII (2), juin 1963, pp. 389-425.
Roussillon, Henry, *L'association générale des producteurs de blé,* Paris, Presses de la FNSP, 1970, 180 pp.
Savonnet-Guyot, Claudette, 'La communauté villageoise comme système politique: un modèle ouest-africain', *RFSP,* XXV (6), décembre 1975, pp. 1112-44.
Tavernier, Yves, 'Le syndicalisme paysan et la politique agricole du gouvernement', *RFSP,* XII (3), septembre 1962, pp. 599-646.
— 'Le XVIIIème congrès de la FNSEA, 25-27 février 1964', *RFSP,* XIV (5), octobre 1964, pp. 972-88.
— 'Le syndicalisme paysan et la Vème République', *RFSP, XVI (5),* octobre 1966, pp. 869-912.
— 'Une nouvelle administration pour l'agriculture: la réforme du ministère', *RFSP,* XVII (5), octobre 1967, pp. 889-917.
— 'Le mouvement de coordination et de défense des exploitations agricoles familiales', *RFSP,* XVIII (3), juin 1968, pp. 542-63.
— *Le syndicalisme paysan.* FNSEA-CNJA, Paris, Presses de la FNSP, 1969, 227 pp.
Tavernier, Yves, Gervais, Michel and Servolin, Claude (eds), *L'univers politique des paysans dans la France contemporaine,* Paris, Presses de la FNSP, 1972, 651 pp. (issu du colloque de l'AFSP des 29-30 mai 1970).
Villers, Gauthier de, 'L'Etat et la révolution agraire en Algérie', *RFSP,* XXX (1), février 1980, pp. 112-39.
Vulpian, Alain de, 'Physionomie agraire et orientation politique dans le département des Côtes-du-Nord. 1928-1946', *RFSP,* I (1-2), mai 1951, pp. 110-132.

21 Rural Politics in Britain

Wyn Grant

The study of rural politics is much more weakly developed in Britain than in France. Such work as has been carried out has been undertaken largely by isolated individuals located in geographically peripheral universities such as Aberdeen, Aberystwyth and Exeter. There is really no national institutional support for such work; even informal networks are weakly developed. This situation can be attributed to a number of factors. First, Britain is a highly urbanised society, and rural issues are of marginal importance in national politics. This marginalisation has probably been enhanced by the Labour Party's loss of the parliamentary seats it used to hold in rural areas. Although there are distinctive regional political cultures in Wales and Scotland, British politics has a strong metropolitan focus, an orientation particularly reflected in the treatment of politics by the mass media. Even so, these considerations have not prevented the development of a relatively strong tradition of rural geography. One factor in the case of political science must be that what are generally regarded as the strongest political science departments are located in major urban centres such as Manchester. Even when there was a stronger general interest in British political science in the study of local politics, reflecting the influence of the American 'community power' debate, studies concentrated on urban locations, perhaps because the exercise of power was more visible there.

The scope and structure of the chapter

In the space available here, I shall not attempt to discuss the definition of 'rural', or such issues as whether or not there is an urban-rural continuum. Such a discussion, if pursued thoroughly, could well take up all of the available space without reaching a firm or acceptable conclusion. The usual escape route in such situations is to use a dictionary definition, but, on this occasion, the Concise Oxford Dictionary is not very helpful. It defines rural as 'in, of suggesting, the country (opp. urban), pastoral or agricultural'. My problem is that I do not see a straight opposition between urban and rural; their social relationship is, at least in principle, a complementary one. Many smaller urban centres (and even some medium-sized ones) derive a considerable amount of prosperity from acting as service centres for the surrounding countryside. One might speculate that cities which do not perform this function might be defined as urban in the dictionary sense. Thus, in Devon, Plymouth's development has been based on its role as a naval centre; it does not have the kind of relationship with the surrounding countryside that one might find in the case of the county town, Exeter.

These few lexicographical remarks already serve as a hostage to fortune. Rather than add to them, and divert attention from the main purpose of the paper – to provide a bibliographical review of the available material – I shall simply explain the structure of the chapter. I have divided the material into four main topics: the pattern of politics in rural communities; agricultural policy and politics; regional nationalism; and environmental politics, particularly in relation to 'the politics of the countryside'. The inclusion of the first two topics is not, I think, controversial, even if there are boundary problems. Regional nationalism is covered because it is present in parts of the country (Scotland, Wales and Cornwall) which have substantial 'rural' populations (however defined), and because a considerable portion of Nationalist support has been derived from the countryside and small towns. Environmental politics is an area in which there has been a growing amount of work: much of it relates to industrial pollution, but there is also a concern with pollution from agricultural sources, and with the spoilation of the countryside by modern farming methods.

The pattern of politics in rural communities

Studies of local government and constituency politics in Britain have focused largely on urban or semi-urban areas. The then Social Science Research Council provided considerable sums of money for work on local government and politics in the late 1960s and early 1970s, but most of this money was spent on studies of cities. Centres such as London, Birmingham, Bristol and Sheffield have been carefully studied.

One of the classic studies of rural local politics is that by Madgwick (1973) of the county of Cardiganshire (Ceredigion) in Wales (Cymru), now part of the post-reorganisation county of Dyfed (cyngor sir Dyfed). Madgwick's study is particularly interesting because it covers both local government and constituency politics, the Cardigan constituency being held by Labour and then by the Liberals. The study also contains a considerable amount of information about 'Welshness' and about support for Plaid Cymru (the Welsh National Party) which is shown to be concentrated among the young at the time of the study. The study is a careful blend of historical and survey analysis; one wishes that studies of a similar scope had been attempted elsewhere. Some of the difficulties of studying rural politics are revealed by a remark by a party secretary quoted in the acknowledgements: 'If you give me a tenth of your grant I'll try to see that there's some politics going on for you to study?'

There is no comparable study for a Scottish constituency: Grimble, writing in Butler and King (1966) offers a vignette of Caithness and Sutherland, surely a unique parliamentary constituency in that, since the Second World War, it has successively returned a Conservative, Independent, Liberal, Labour, and Social Democratic MP (to complete the picture, the MEP for the Highlands and Islands, of which Caithness and Sutherland forms a part, is a Scottish Nationalist). Dyer (1973) does, however, provide an interesting account of politics in the county of Kincardineshire (south of Aberdeen).

Within England, Lee's (1963) study of the evolution of local government and politics in the county of Cheshire remains a classic. Lee traces the replacement of a traditional social elite by a more modern type of office-holder. The leading members of the council and the chief officers formed a 'ministerialist' party. There was a follow up study of the urbanising county in 1974 (Lee et al. 1974). Stanyer (1967) provides an analytical framework for the study of county government. He was not concerned just with county councils as such, but with the complex relationships of the county with central government, and with the district authorities within its boundaries. He examines patterns of cooperation and conflict between county and district authorities, and considers links between them such as dual membership of both types of authority and officer relationships. Stanyer has also carefully examined the development of politics in Devon. Much of this work remains unpublished, or available in conference papers, but a useful account by him can be found in Stanyer (1975). Johnson (1972) analyses the gradual 'nationalisation' of the rural politics in Norfolk.

Grant (1977a, Chapter 1) provides an account of two district councils in rural areas which at the time had a preponderance of 'independent' members – 'Westward' (Penwith in Cornwall), and 'Central' (Stratford-upon-Avon in Warwickshire). A separate account (Grant 1977b) provides additional material on the 'role perceptions' of rural councillors. They placed considerable emphasis on individual judgement, on assessing a problem on its merits in the light of local conditions as part of a commitment to a philosophy of nonpartisanship in local politics. This led to a less predictable form of decision-making than on partisan councils. Other studies have emerged from an anthropological tradition, in which some attention is given to political questions. For a useful summary of earlier studies, see Frankenberg (1965, Chs. 1–5). A later example of this genre, although not by a professional anthropologist, is again from Devon (Martin 1965).

The Essex 'school' of rural sociology has produced some interesting studies, not least for the fact that they are based on empirical research in the intensive farming area of East Anglia, rather than 'upland Britain'. Newby (1977) is an important exploration of the phenomenon of deference among farm-workers. Making careful use of interview material and participant observation data, Newby provides an in-depth analysis of the farm-workers' experience of their jobs, their relations with employers, workmates and neighbours, and the impact of recent changes in the rural community. Deference is seen as a form of relationship, rather than a set of attitudes, in which economic power rests with the farmer, and the farm-worker is relatively powerless. This general theme is also pursued in Chapter 6 of Newby et al. (1978) which provides an account of 'the rural power structure'. They show how an ideology based on common interests defined in terms of a common area of residence swamps potential conflicts of interest, with propertied interests enjoying a hegemony. Their analysis is less convincing when they try to explain why West Suffolk County Council was prepared to enter overspill agreements, unlike East Suffolk. (For a discussion of this point, and a more general review of the Essex work, see Grant 1980). Saunders et al. (1978) provides a more general theoretical review of rural community power, leading to the conclusion that rural areas have one of the *most* successful ruling classes still extant.

Although the nature of the subject means that particular studies, especially those in a conference or working paper format, may have been missed, the general impression that emerges is one of some very good works, but also of the general thinness of the coverage. In particular, there would appear to be scope for further work on Scotland, for example on the regional and island councils in rural areas (although there has been some scattered interest in the subject of 'island government': see, for example, Gronneberg 1975; Kermode 1979, but the Isle of Man is not, of course, part of the UK). The emphasis in work on local government and politics has, in any case, switched to central-local relations, or the study of particular policy areas, and works like that of Madgwick may seem hopelessly old-fashioned, not least to students of electoral politics. If that is the case, it is a pity.

Agricultural politics

In this section, I shall not deal with the extensive literature on the CAP (see, for example, Fennell 1979; Neville-Rolfe 1984) but rather concentrate on domestic agricultural politics. This is an area which has attracted quite a lot of attention from political scientists and other social scientists because of a widespread belief that the National Farmers' Union offers a classic example of a successful pressure group. Self and Storing (1962) is rather dated now because it offers an analysis of agricultural politics centred around the price review process under the 1947 Agriculture Act. However, it remains a classic of the pressure group literature, offering many enduring insights into agricultural politics. Williams (1965) gives an account of the events leading up to the 1947 Act from the viewpoint of the responsible Cabinet Minister. More generally, Flynn (1989) examines the competition between the Labour and Conservative Parties and the role of party ideologies in shaping post-war agricultural and rural policy-making.

Wilson (1977, 1978) looks at the National Farmers' Union in comparison with American farmers' organisations and concludes (1978, p. 31) that it is 'arguably the best and organizationally strongest of western agricultural interest groups.' Richardson, Jordan and Kimber (1978) provide an analysis of a successful attempt by a group of interests concerned with water reorganisation during the early 1970s to prevent a radical change in administrative arrangements for land drainage. The article concludes that the 'agricultural MAFFia' won the day with a network linking the Ministry of Agriculture, Fisheries and Food (MAFF), the Country Landowners' Association and the National Farmers' Union. Grant (1983a) looks at the NFU within the terms of a corporatist perspective. An important article by Cox, Lowe and Winter (1985a) looks at the pressures on agricultural 'exceptionalism' which have resulted from the shift in political attention from production to conservation policies. This analysis is taken further in Cox, Lowe and Winter (1986) where they point out that the conservation issue is now firmly on the main political agenda with no prospect of its being marginalised again. Chapter 4 of Lowe et al. (1986) provides one of the most up-to-date accounts of the 'farming, landowning and timber-growing lobbies'; and Grant (1987) includes a section on agricultural politics. In Cox, Lowe and Winter (1987), the authors examine the factors which are transforming the policy agenda in agricultural politics: questioning of the basic objectives of agricultural policy both reduces the external influence of the leaders of farmers' organisations, and undermines their internal authority with their own members.

What has been relatively neglected is the organisation of the farming lobby at the regional and local level. The separate farmers' unions in Scotland and Northern Ireland (linked with the NFU) and the breakaway Farmers' Union of Wales have received scant attention. Grant (1978) provides some information on the activities of the Scottish union. Murdoch (1988) examines the formation and development of the Farmers' Union of Wales. At the local level, apart from some interesting material in Newby et al. (1978), the only systematic studies are those by Walters (1975) on Cheshire and Stanyer (1975) on Devon. Walters suggests (1975, p. 270) that 'The county executive is in a sense a safety valve for expressing and containing the zeal of Union militants'. Stanyer argues (1975, p. 275) that 'though farming politics in Cheshire was a part of the group politics of the county, the political roles of farmers had a much wider significance in the government of Devon.' However, the 1972 reform of local government destroyed a traditional political system and extended urban politics to the rural areas of the county.

The politics of the dairy sector has received a certain amount of attention, particularly as the arrangements there have come under greater strain as a result of the imposition of quotas and other changes. Much of the work has been influenced by a corporatist perspective (Grant, 1983b, 1985a, 1985b; Winter, 1984). The changes being experienced in this sector are the focus of the research project being conducted, as part of the ESRC corporatism and accountability initiative, by Cox, Lowe and Winter (1990).

Forestry is a sector which might repay greater attention, particularly with the prospect of a major expansion of afforestation in the lowlands. Critiques of existing policy are to be found in Grove (1983), Stewart (ed.) (1985), and British Association of Nature Conservationists (1987). However, the academic literature is rather limited. A compilation of material is to be found in Grant (1975), and Grant (forthcoming) will contain comparative material on the forestry and forest products industry in Britain, Canada and the US.

Compared with the analysis of rural local politics, political scientists have been relatively active in the study of agricultural politics. In part, this has been because agriculture has seemed to offer a classic example of a 'closed' and stable policy community in which the principal participants can readily be identified, there is little intrusion from external actors, and, therefore, patterns of influence can be studied with relative ease. However, the underlying theme of recent work has been the disturbance of this policy community by a number of external factors: principally, membership of the EEC; a greater emphasis on conservation; and growing concern about the cost of subsidising agricultural production. This concern has been reflected in polemical books such as Body (1982, 1984). For academics, it offers the opportunity to study a policy-making system in transition, although it is uncertain how long the transition process will take, and how far reaching its effects will be.

Regional nationalism

Britain has Nationalist parties in Scotland (the Scottish National Party), Wales (Plaid Cymru) and Cornwall (Mebyon Kernow). In the 1983 Parliament, the Scottish and Welsh Nationalists each had two seats in the House of Commons. The Cornish Nationalists have only won seats at local government level; in parliamentary elections, they poll small but respectable votes. One of the few accounts of Cornish Nationalism is to be found in Thayer (1965); he also has material on Welsh and Scottish Nationalism.

One feature of the Scottish and Welsh Nationalist movements has been their relative success in seats made up of rural areas interspersed with small towns. All the seats that Plaid Cymru have held, or might realistically hope to win, are in such areas, although it has had some support in the urbanised valleys of South Wales. The SNP has been more successful at attracting support in urban areas, although it has been particularly unsuccessful in the capital city, Edinburgh. If one looks at the October 1974 results, the most successful election for the Nationalists, three of the seats won by the SNP (Aberdeenshire East, Banff and Galloway) were among the ten most agricultural seats in Britain (measured in terms of percentage employed in agriculture; of the other seven, three were won by Liberals and one by Plaid Cymru). Another four of the eleven seats won, making seven in all, might reasonably be defined as relatively rural (Argyll, Moray and Nairn, Perth, Western Isles). Commenting on SNP performance in October 1974, Steed (1975, p. 349) notes, 'The only consistent element in these figures is weakness in the cities'.

In one of the pieces on Scottish nationalism which has best stood the test of time, Mansbach (1973) notes (p. 88) that 'in the Highlands, islands and borders, and in the village and small town culture in central Scotland, the party experienced a steady rise in strength'. Data collection by Mansbach shows that branches had larger memberships in rural areas, and that the ratio of branches to population was higher in sparsely populated rural and semi-rural counties. Kellas (1975, p. 130) notes that 'In the north of Scotland, where the SNP did particularly well, its strength was massed in the small towns which made up a considerable proportion of the constituencies'. He refers to work published in newspapers by Dr M. Dyer of Aberdeen University in which Dyer argues that the SNP vote represented the realisation of a latent anti-Conservative majority. According to Dyer, Liberals and Labour 'could make little headway in a society which distrusted trade unions and industrialisation. But it was anti-landlord and anti-deferential, as well as strongly parochial' (Kellas, 1975, p. 130).

The literature on Nationalism reached its peak output in the 1970s when, as Miller (1980, p. 118) comments, 'nationalism, both as a constitutional and political force, threatened to ignite British politics'. A few pieces were published in the early 1980s, representing the culmination of research carried out in the 1970s, but after than, interest died away, despite a revival indicated by the SNP coming second in the 1986 Scottish regional elections and in the 1989 European elections in Scotland. A welcome exception to the recent paucity of the literature is Levy (1986) who examines SNP strategies over the period of the 1974-79 Parliament. One important point that Levy makes is that the earlier literature concentrated on the electorate rather than the party. Like Mansbach (1973), he shows the SNP to be an incoherent and fragmented party. He provides a cogent analysis of the strategic problems facing the SNP, arguing that the SNP leadership cannot be viewed as a coherent entity which consistently pursues a vote-winning strategy. Its structural weaknesses and internal rivalries were particularly apparent in its attempts to cope with the 1970s devolution debate.

Another feature of the literature is that relatively few published works seek to compare the SNP and Plaid Cymru. A dated exception is Grant and Preece (1968); Coupland (1954) is useful as a quarry of historical material. Rawkins (1978) places the phenomenon of minority nationalism in a broader theoretical context. Nairn (1977) provides a neo-Marxist perspective on the nationalist phenomenon which is unique in covering not only Scotland and Wales, but also English and Irish/Ulster nationalism. Greenberg (1979) covers Scottish, Welsh, Cornish and Manx nationalism, but this book is not a serious academic study. The best comparative analysis is provided by McAllister (1981) who covers not only the SNP and PC, but also the SDLP in Northern Ireland.

More comparative analyses would be interesting, because the two parties are of a rather different character. Plaid Cymru is fighting to defend a threatened culture; hence its difficulty in extending its appeal outside the Welsh-speaking heartland. This has led to a greater emphasis on civil disobedience within the broader nationalist movement. In the Scottish case, Schwarz (1970) discusses how a separatist movement could exist without eliciting violence. One of the characteristics of the SNP is that it has placed a greater emphasis on 'economic' nationalism (Gaelic is very much a minority language in Scotland), symbolised by the 1970s slogan 'It's Scotland's oil'. Plaid Cymru has leaned more towards a socialist version of nationalism; the SNP, although troubled by right and left fringes, has been more eclectic, appearing vaguely social democratic in outlook. Relations between the two parties have not always been as good as one might expect.

Not surprisingly, the literature on Scottish Nationalism is more extensive than that on the Welsh case. There are a number of historical analyses (Hanham 1969; Harvie 1977; Kellas 1968); the difficulty with these, as Mansbach (1973, p. 187) points out is that they 'begin with an analysis of historical Scottish resistance to English control and go on to imply that current enthusiasts for Scottish devolution or independence share common historical myths and symbols'. From a political science perspective, a more interesting approach is offered by Keating and Bleiman (1979) who provide a historical analysis of the impact of nationalism on the Labour Party. This book was written by two Labour activists, one opposed to devolution, one in favour of it. Brand (1978) provides an account of the nationalist movement from the viewpoint of an academic sympathiser. Wolfe (1973) gives an insider's view of the development of the SNP.

Webb (1978) would be a good place for the reader unfamiliar with the subject to start. He provides a historical perspective, plus a useful chapter on alternative explanations of the Nationalist revival. The usefulness of the select bibliography is enhanced by the fact that it includes references to a number of unpublished dissertations and papers.

Successive Nuffield election studies have charted the growth of the SNP, with particularly useful information in the appendices. The volume on the 1970 election contains a useful account by Kellas (1971) of the initial revival period after 1966. McLean's (1970) piece on 'The Rise and *Fall* of the Scottish National Party' seems in retrospect to have been a little premature in its perspective. Bochel and Denver (1972) seek to provide an alternative account of the *decline* of the SNP two years before its leap forward in the Februrary 1974 election. To be fair, however, two of their points look sound in a longer-run perspective: SNP voters retained a psychological commitment to their old parties; and the SNP failed to develop a secure social base by making nationality more important than class (one exception, as has been noted, was in northern rural areas, although by 1983 four of the five most northerly seats in Scotland were held by the Alliance – two SDP, two Liberals – with the SNP's only privy councillor holding the fifth). Roger Mullen (1979) provides a useful summary of the emergence of the SNP from the political shadows. Miller (1977) explores the relationship between SNP voting and the demand for Scottish self-government. Miller (1980) provides a useful retrospective on the Scottish dimension of British politics from 1974 to 1979. For a more general analysis of the ways in which the Scottish electorate differs from that of the rest of Britain, see Miller (1981).

Of accounts of Welsh Nationalism, Butt Philip (1975) remains one of the most comprehensive treatments. As mentioned in an earlier section, Madgwick (1973) provides some valuable insights. Rawkins (1979) is one of the few accounts of the political sociology of Welsh Nationalism. He discusses how potentially divergent groups are able to coexist within Plaid Cymru. Information on the nature of the support for Plaid Cymru is also found in Balsom (1979a, 1979b). For those interested, Davies (1983) deals with the early history of Plaid Cymru. A nationalist perspective on the development of Welsh Nationalism is to be found in Beresford Ellis (1968).

Environmental politics

Over the last decade or so, concern has been growing about the impact of modern agriculture on the rural environment: the intrusiveness of modern farm buildings; the effect of the extensive use of fertilisers and agrochemicals on animals, plants and, for that matter, human beings; the impact of the grubbing up of hedges on the visual appearance of the countryside, and habitats for wildlife; the ploughing up of 'wetlands', or other sites of special ecological significance; all these and other concerns form part of an interrelated package of issues. The underlying theme is the need for a greater emphasis on conservation, as distinct from production, in agricultural policy. The pressures being felt by government and the agricultural lobby on these issues reflect a wider 'greening' of politics also found in concern about such issues as the civilian use of nuclear power. For a number of reasons, this 'greening' of politics has not gone as far as in West Germany. Although I have no direct knowledge of France, I would hazard a guess that the environmental movement is less well developed there than in the UK.

Once again, a good place to start for an account of the current debate is Lowe et al. (1986). This places changing conflicts in the countryside in context, provides an account of the conservation movement, and deals with the significant 1981 Wildlife and Countryside Act and its implementation. There are a number of case studies, followed by a review of proposals for reform.

There are a number of books which provide information on the development of the environmental movement. Of the earlier studies, Allison (1975) is particularly useful on more traditional groups such as the CPRE. Kimber and Richardson (1974) provide a mixed, but nevertheless interesting, bag of case studies. However, the key book in this area is undoubtedly Lowe and Goyder (1983). Providing a mix of systematic chapters and case studies, I rank it alongside Self and Storing as a significant contribution to the literature on pressure groups.

Bowers and Cheshire (1983) provided a critique of existing agricultural support policies as inefficient, unjust and environmentally damaging; a rather more polemical account is to be found in Shoard (1980). Newby et al. (1978) discuss the threat to dominant landowning and farming interests posed by an influx of middle-class ex-urbanites with rather different priorities; and Newby (1979) provides a useful general discussion of such tensions, and of the growing disillusionment with agriculture as a force for rural conservation. Cox and Lowe (1983a, 1983b, 1984) discuss the changing context of countryside politics in terms of a relatively closed agricultural policy community characterised by corporatist relationships coming under increasing pressure from environmental groups more typically involved in pluralist relationships with government.

Looking at this field from the outside, my impression is that a lot of good work has been done and is being done. However, continued funding will be necessary if existing and highly productive research groups are to be kept together. This is important, because the debate has not run its course, and there are a number of important changes in progress which need charting and analysing. In the future, one might see such developments as the merger of the Ministry of Agriculture and the relevant parts of the Department of the Environment in a Department of Rural Affairs with somewhat different priorities from MAFF. Whatever happens, the research impetus must be maintained.

Conclusion

What general conclusions can be reached about the adequacy of the available literature? The least well-developed area is on patterns of politics at the local government and constituency level in rural areas. Attention has been focused on more urbanised areas, because conflict there is more overt, and more often canalised on party lines. Moreover, urban authorities are seen as both more important and more politically innovative. It is not easy to carve a middle path between a kind of political Arcadianism which glorifies the apparent absence of conflict in rural locations, and a belief that rural politics is simply a backward version of what happens in more urbanised areas.

The research effort on regional nationalism is very much influenced by levels of support for the Nationalist parties. There was an initial research boom in the late 1960s, followed by a falling away in the early 1970s, apart from articles explaining the 'decline' of Nationalism. Nationalist successes in the 1974 elections, and the consequent devolution debate, led to a new period of intense research activity. Since the beginning of the 1980s, relatively little has been done. One might hope that academics would be less influenced by political fashions and would regard minority nationalism as repaying some more consistent attention. Signs of an apparent Nationalist revival in 1985 do not appear to have attracted much research interest; moreover, journalistic discussions about what might happen in a 'hung' parliament concentrated on the Alliance parties, and neglected the potential balancing role of the Nationalists.

The literature on agricultural politics is well developed, but continuing research is necessary to assess the very significant changes taking place in the 1980s. There is an overlap here with the research on environmental politics, as environmental considerations start to have a greater influence on agricultural policy making. Environmental politics is a vigorous research area; it is important that the momentum is not lost.

Bibliography

Allison, L. *Environmental Planning*, London, Allen & Unwin, 1975.
Balsom (1979a), 'The Nature and Distribution of Support for Plaid Cymru', University of Strathclyde Studies in Public Policy, 36, 1979.
Balsom (1979b), 'Plaid Cymru' in H.M. Drucker (ed.), *Multi-Party Britain*, London, Macmillan, 1979.
Beresford Ellis, *Wales a Nation Again*, London, Library 33, 1968.
Bochel, J. and D. Denver, 'The Decline of the SNP: an Alternative View', *Political Studies*, 20, 1972, 311–16.
Body, R., *Agriculture: the Triumph and the Shame*, London, Maurice Temple Smith, 1982.
Body, R., *Farming in the Clouds*, London, Maurice Temple Smith, 1984.
Bowers, J.K. and P. Cheshire, *Agriculture, the Countryside and Land Use: an Economic Critique*, London, Methuen, 1983.
Brand, J., *The National Movement in Scotland*, London, Routledge & Kegan Paul, 1978.
British Association of Nature Conservationists, *Forests for Britain*, Chichester, Packard Publishing, 1987.
Butler, D. and A. King, *The British General Election of 1966*, London, Macmillan, 1966.
Butt Philip, A., *The Welsh Question*, Cardiff, University of Wales Press, 1975.
Coupland, Sir R., *Welsh and Scottish Nationalism*, London, Collins, 1954.
Cox, G. and P. Lowe (1983a), 'Countryside Politics: Goodbye to Goodwill?', *Political Quarterly*, 54, 1983, 268–82.
— (1983b), 'A Battle Not the War: The Politics of the Wildlife and Countryside Act', in A. Gilg (ed.), *The Countryside Planning Yearbook*, Vol. 4, Norwich, Geo Books, 1983.
— (1984), 'Agricultural Corporatism and Conservation Politics' in T. Bradley and P. Lowe (eds) *Locality and Rurality*, Norwich, Geo Books, 1984.
— (1985a), 'Changing Directions in Agricultural Policy: Corporatist Arrangements in Production and Conservation Policies', *Sociologia Ruralis*, 25, 1985, 130–54.
— (1985b), 'Land Use Conflict after the Wildlife and Countryside Act 1981: the Role of FWAG', *Journal of Rural Studies* 1, 1985, 173–83.
— (1986) 'Agriculture and Conservation in Britain: a Policy Community Under Siege', in

G. Cox, P. Lowe and M. Winter (eds), *Agriculture: People and Policies*, London, Allen & Unwin, 1986, 181-215.
— (1987) 'Farmers and the State: a Crisis for Corporatism', *Political Quarterly*, 58, 1987, 73-81.
— (1990) 'Agricultural regulation and the politics of milk production' in C. Crouch and R. Dore (eds) *Corporatism and Accountability*, Oxford, Clarendon Press, 1990, 169-98.
Davies, D.H., *The Welsh Nationalist Party, 1925-45: A Call to Nationhood*, Cardiff, University of Wales Press, 1983.
Dyer, M., 'Independent Politics in Kincardineshire', University of Aberdeen PhD thesis, 1973.
Fennell, R., *The Common Agricultural Policy of the European Community*, London, Granada, 1979.
Flynn, A., 'Rural Working Class Interests in Party Policy Marking in Post-War England', University of London, PhD. thesis, 1989.
Frankenberg, R., *Communities in Britain*, Harmondsworth, Pelican, 1965.
Grant, W., 'Forestry Policy in Britain', in D. Murray, R. Thomas, W. Grant, N. Smith (eds) *Agriculture*, Milton Keynes, Open University Press, 1975.
— (1977a), *Independent Local Politics in England and Wales*, Farnborough, Teakfield, 1977.
— (1977b), 'The Role Perceptions of Rural Councillors', University of Warwick Department of Politics Working Paper, 1977.
— (1978) 'British Interests and the European Community: the Representation of Industrialists and Farmers', *West European Politics*, 1, 1978, 194-211.
— (1980) 'The New Rural Sociology and the Study of Local Politics in Britain', *Public Administration Bulletin*, No. 32, 1980, 62-71.
— (1983a) 'The National Farmers' Union: the Classic Case of Incorporation?', in D. Marsh (ed.) *Pressure Politics*, London, Junction Books, 1983.
— (1983b) 'Corporatism, the public and the private and the milk marketing system in Britain', *Sussex Working Papers in Corporatism*, No. 2, 1983, University of Sussex.
— (1985a), 'Corporatism and the Public-Private Distinction' in J-E Lane (ed.), *State and Market: The Politics of the Public and the Private*, London, Sage, 1985.
— (1985b), 'Private Organisations as Agents of Public Policy: the Case of Milk Marketing in Britain', in W. Streeck and P.C. Schmitter (eds), *Private Interest Government*, London, Sage, 1985.
— (1987) *Business and Politics in Britain*, London, Macmillan, 1987.
Grant, W., *Government and Industry: a Transatlantic Comparison*, Upleadon, Edward Elgar, forthcoming.
Grant, W. and R.J.C. Preece, 'Welsh and Scottish Nationalism', *Parliamentary Affairs*, 21, 1968, 255-65.
Greenberg, W., *The Flags of the Forgotten*, Brighton, Clifton Books, 1979.
Gronneberg, *Island Governments*, Sandwich, Thuleprint, 1975.
Grove, R., *The Future for Forestry*, British Association of Nature Conservationists, 1983.
Hanham, H., *Scottish Nationalism*, London, Faber, 1969.
Harvie, C., *Scotland and Nationalism*, London, Allen & Unwin, 1977.
Johnson, R.W., 'The Nationalisation of English Rural Politics: Norfolk South-West, 1945-70', *Parliamentary Affairs*, 26, 1972, 8-55.
Keating, M. and D. Bleiman, *Labour and Scottish Nationalism*, London, Macmillan, 1979.
Kellas, J.G., *Modern Scotland*, London, Pall Mall, 1968.
— *The Scottish Political System*, 2nd edition, London, Oxford University Press, 1975.
Kermode, D., *Devolution at Work: A Case Study of the Isle of Man*, Farnborough, Saxon House, 1970.
Kimber, R. and Richardson, J.J. (eds), *Campaigning for the Environment*, London,

Routledge & Kegan Paul, 1974.
Lee, J.M., *Social Leaders and Public Persons: A Study of County Government in Cheshire since 1888*, Oxford, Clarendon Press, 1963.
Lee, J.M., B. Wood, P.W. Solomon and P. Walters, *The Scope of Local Initiative*, London, Martin Roberston, 1974.
Levy, R., 'The Search for a Rational Strategy: the Scottish National Party and Devolution, 1974-9', *Political Studies,* 24, 1986, 236-48.
Lowe, P. and J. Goyder, *Environmental Groups in Politics*, London, Allen & Unwin, 1983.
Lowe, P., G. Cox, M. MacEwen, T. O'Riordan, and M. Winter, *Countryside Conflicts: the Politics of Farming, Forestry and Conservation,* Aldershot, Gower, 1986.
McAllister, I., 'Party Organization and Minority Nationalism: a Comparative Study of the UK', *European Journal of Political Research*, 9, 1981, 237-55.
McLean, I., 'The Rise and Fall of the Scottish National Party', *Political Studies*, 18, 1970, 257-69.
Madgwick, P. with N. Griffiths and V. Walker, *The Politics of Rural Wales,* London, Hutchinson, 1973.
Mansbach, R.W., 'The Scottish National Party: a Revised Political Profile', *Comparative Politics,* 5, 1973, 185-210.
Martin, E., *The Shearers and the Shorn*, London, Routledge & Kegan Paul, 1965.
Miller, W. et al., 'The Connection between SNP Voting and the Demand for Scottish Self-Government', *European Journal of Political Research*, 5, 1977, 83-102.
Miller, W., 'The Scottish Dimension' in D. Butler and D. Kavanagh, *The British General Election of 1979*, London, Macmillan, 1980.
Miller, W., *The End of British Politics?*, Oxford, Clarendon Press, 1981.
Murdoch, J., *State Intervention and Agriculture in Wales*, Unpublished PhD thesis, University College of Wales, Aberystwyth, 1988.
Nairn, T., *The Break-Up of Britain*, London, New Left Books, 1977.
Neville-Rolfe, E., *The Politics of Agriculture in the European Community*, London, European Centre for Political Studies, 1984.
Newby, H., *The Deferential Worker*, Harmondsworth, Penguin, 1977.
— *Green and Pleasant Land?*, Harmondsworth, Penguin, 1979.
Newby, H., Bell, Rose and Saunders, *Property, Paternalism and Power: Class and Control in Rural England,* London, Hutchinson, 1978.
Rawkins, P.M., 'Outsiders as Insiders: the Implications of Minority Nationalism in Scotland and Wales', *Comparative Politics,* 10, 1978, 519-34.
Rawkins, P.M., 'An Approach to the Political Sociology of the Welsh Nationalist Movement', *Political Studies*, 27, 1978, 440-57.
Richardson, J.J., G. Jordan and R. Kimber, 'Lobbying, Administrative Reform and Policy Styles: the Case of Land Drainage', *Political Studies*, 26, 1978, 47-64.
Roger Mullen, W.A., 'The Scottish National Party', in H.M. Drucker (ed.) *Multi-Party Britain*, London, Macmillan, 1979.
Saunders, P., H. Newby, C. Bell and D. Rose, 'Rural Community and Rural Community Power', in H. Newby (ed.), *International Perspectives in Rural Sociology*, Chichester, John Wiley, 1978.
Schwarz, J.E., 'The Scottish National Party: Nonviolent Separatism and Theories of Violence', *World Politics*, 22, 1970, 496-517.
Self, P. and H. Storing, *The State and the Farmer*, London, Allen & Unwin, 1962.
Shoard, M., *The Theft of the Countryside*, London Maurice Temple Smith, 1980.
Stanyer, J. *County Government in England and Wales*, London, Routledge & Kegan Paul, 1967.
Stanyer, J., 'Farming Politics: Devon and Cheshire compared', in D. Murray et al. (eds),

Agriculture, Milton Keynes, Open University Press, 1975.
Steed, M., 'The Results Analysed', in D. Butler and D. Kavanagh, *The British General Election of October 1974*, London, Macmillan, 1975.
Stewart, P. (ed.), *The Wood from the Trees: the Developing Debate about British Forestry*, Chichester, Packard, 1985.
Thayer, *The British Political Fringe*, London, Anthony Blond, 1985.
Walters, P., 'Farming Politics at the Grass Roots: the Cheshire County Branch of the National Farmers' Union', in D. Murray et al. (eds), *Agriculture,* Milton Keynes, Open University Press, 1975.
Webb, K., *The Growth of Nationalism in Scotland*, Harmondsworth, Pelican, 1978.
Williams, Lord, *Digging for Britain*, London, Hutchinson, 1965.
Wilson, G., *Special Interests and Policy-Making: Agricultural Policy and Politics in Britain and the USA, 1956-70*, Chichester, Wiley, 1977.
— 'Farmers' Organizations in Advanced Societies', in H. Newby (ed.), *International Perspectives on Rural Sociology*, Chichester, Wiley, 1978.
Winter, M., 'Corporatism and Agriculture in the UK: The Case of the Milk Marketing Board', *Sociologia Ruralis*, 24, 1984, 106-19.
Wolfe, B., *Scotland Lives*, Edinburgh, Reprographical, 1973.

Index

(Figures in italics indicate the pages on which an article by the author so annotated appears.)
academic posts, 170
Aberystwyth, 167 *see also* University College of Wales
Act
  Agricultural Marketing, 168
  Agriculture (1947), 11, 28, 168, 289
  Hill Farming (1946), 29
  Local Government (1888), 41
  New Poor Law (1834), 84
  of 1789, 39
  Town and Country Planning (1947), 11, 41
  Wildlife and Countryside (1981), 294
  see also loi.
ADAS *see* Agricultural Development and Advisory Service
Admiralty Islanders, 215
advisory centres, 167
Africa, 106, 208, 209
Agrarian History of England and Wales, 55, 76, 77, 81, 83, 85
agrarian socialism, 65
agrarianism, 147
agrarisme, 277
agricultural
  associations, 276-9
  bureaucracy, 228
  capital, 100
  corporatists, 13
  crisis, 143
  Development and Advisory Service (ADAS), 228
  economics, 44, 139-43, 144-64, 165-75, 229-30, 253
  Economics Research Institute, 167
  Economics Society (AES), 168-9
  elites, 279
  engineers, 145-8
  enterprises, 72, 73
  extension, 237
  growth, 25
  History Review, The, 86
  holdings, 192
  innovation, 266
  interests, 33
  land-use, 117
  lobby, 147, 149
  machinery, 24, 270
  marketing, 169
  modernisation, 26, 148
  movements, 276-80
  organisations, 14, 44, 58, 150, 226, 269
  periodicals, 278
  planning, 104
  policy, 22, 25-6, 154-5, 157, 159, 166, 252, 254, 266-7, 269, 274-5
  politics, 289-91
  practices, 227
  production, 67-9, 151, 155-8, 161-2
  rationalisation, 252
  raw materials, 158
  reform, 59, 160-1
  revolution, 60, 74, 78, 79-80, 155
  sector, 22-7, 230
  statistics, 154-5
  systems, 43-4
  unity, 276
agriculture
  British, 27-33
  capitalist, 6-8, 16
  Chambers of, 272
  commercialised, 3-4

300 *Index*

    contrast between Britain and France, 21–2
    Department of, 172
    -food production sector, 159
    government policies towards, x, 32
    history, 77–81
    improvements in, 78
    interest groups, 13
    Minister (French), 23, 85, 149
    modernisation, 155, 241–2, 266
    peasant, 6–8, 12
    post-war developments, 21
    review of, 122
    slow increases in productivity, 4
    studies, 129
    see also farmers, farming
agronomists, 149
Agulhon, Maurice, 60, 65, 67
Alsace, 46, 227
analytical methods, lack of, 125
ancien regime, 4
Annales d'histoire économique et sociale, 47, 48
Annales school, 47, 48–9, 61–5, 70, 72, 239
anthropology, 44, 50, 71, 179–82, 183–202, 203–20, 235
applied geography, the state, policy-making and, 129–30
archival material, 199
aristocracy, declining position of the, 84
aristocratic land ownership, 6–8, 10, 84
arrondissements, 17, 109, 187, 109, 187, 270, 272
art of the possible', 130
Asby, Arthur, 167
Assier-Andrieu, Louis, 189
Association des Producteurs de Blé (AGPB), 278
Association des Ruralists Françaises, 106
Association Française de Science Politique (AFSP), 269, 270, 273
Atlas Folklorique, 185
Aurbrac, 186, 187, 188, 189
Augé-Laribé, Michel, 274
Augustins, Georges, *183–202*, 213
Auvergne, the, 26
Aveyron, 25

'back-to-the-land' movement, 191
Bailey, F.G., 203
ballot, 271
Balzac, Honoré de, 12
Barral, Pierre, 60, 65, 69, 274, 275, 277
Barth, F., 214
Beckett, J.V., 85
Bedford, Duke of, 85
beef, ix, 158, 187
behavioural perspective, 270–4
Bergmann, Denis, 227
Bernard, Jean-Pierre, 271

Bernot, L., 185
Berr, Henri, 62
Bertrand, G., 101
Birnbaum, Pierre, 279
Black Death, the (Bubonic Plague), 55, 57, 77–8
Blanc, Michel, 140, 141, 142, *144–64*
Blan-Gonnet, Pierre, 280
Blancard, R., 185
Bloch, Marc, 47, 58, 61–5, 70, 98
Blondelle, René, 281
blue collar workers, 27, 34, 38, 107
Bodiguel, Maryvonne, *37–52*, 226, *233–47*, 270
Body, Sir Richard, 172
Bois, Paul, 64
Bonaparte, Napoleon, 17
Bonnamour, J., 102, 113
Bontron, J.-C., 100
Boon, J.A., 212
Bouquet, Mary, 256–7
Boulevard-St-Germain, 278
Bourdieu, P., 71, 199
Boussard, Isabel, 265–6, *269–85*
Bouvier, Jean, 59
Bradley, Tony, 256
Braudel, Fernand, 63–4, 70, 235
Bretagne/Manche, 26
Bristol, 42
Britain
    development, organisation and orientation of agricultural economics in, 165–75
    post-war, 21–36
    rural geography in, 117–35
    rural policy-making in, 26
    rural politics in, 286–98
British
    agricultural economists, 140–2
    agricultural graduates, 168
    Agricultural History Society, 86
    anthropological tradition, 203–20
    aristocracy, 8
    Association, 10
    beef, ix
    countryside, 40–3
    Establishment, 205
    rural history, 76–89
    rural sociology, 228–31, 248–62
    society, 7, 268
Brittany, 111, 186, 199, 206, 271
Brun, André, 139–43
Brunet, Pierre, 102, 109
Brunhes, Jean, 98
Buller, Henry, *3–20, 21–36, 37–52*, 126–7

Caen, 106
cannibals, 210
CAP *see* Common Agricultural Policy
Capital, 48

capital
  accumulation, 127
  devalued, 158
  goods, 157
  investment, 32
  restructuring, 127
capitalism
  agrarian, 71-2, 152, 153, 154, 235, 243
  industrial, 3, 127, 145
  origins of, 72
Carrière, P., 104
Catholic clergy, 12 see also Church, the
Cawson, A., 131
Celtic fringe, 206
Celtic nationalism, 32
census, population, 11, 38, 43, 107
Central Landowners' Association see Country Landowners' Association centralisation, 31, 130
Centre National
  de la Recherche Scientifique, xi, 49
  des Jeunes Agriculteurs (CNJA), 23, 274, 275, 277
'centres of excellence' lack of, 254
Cerquiera, Silas, 271
Chambres Régionales d'Agriculture, 276
Chapuis, Robert, 109
Chapman, J., 81
Chapman, M., 203
Charlot, Jean, 265-8
Charver, J.P., 103
Chatelain, René, 279
Châtillon, 187
Chaunu, Pierre, 64
Chef d'Etat, 275
Chiva, Isac, 189
Chodkiewicz, Jean-Luc, 187
Cholley, André, 99
Church, the, 39, 148, 240, 270, 272, 273 see also catholic clergy
Clark, G., 118, 121, 131
class
  British ruling, 7
  composition, 132
  middle, 27-33, 132
  struggle, theory of, 141, 154, 189, 240
  residential middle, 31
  system, agrarian, 7
  -voting, debate on, 267
  working, 30, 130-1
Cleary, Mark, 93-6
climatic zones, 3
Cloke, Paul, 42, 94, 95, 96, 117-35, 255
Clout, Hugh, 93-6, 117-18
CNJA see Centre National des Jeunes Agriculteurs
CNRS, 104, 106, 111, 228
Cobden, Richard, 165
Cohen, Abner, 214

Cohen, Anthony, 179-182, 204-20
Collins, E.J.T., 80
Colman, David, 141, 142, 165-75
Colson, François, 277
combine harvester, 28
comfort, intellectual versus material, 142
Commission d'histoire économique et sociale de le Révolution française, 62
Commission Nationale d'Organisation Corporative, 275
Commissariat Général du Plan, 148
Committee on Land Utilisation in Rural Areas, 11
Common Agricultural Policy (CAP, 29, 139, 149, 159, 166, 172, 173, 179, 187, 275, 277, 289
common fields, 56, 82
common people, 184
Commune Charter, 39
communes, 17, 26-7, 38, 39-40, 107, 109, 111, 185, 186, 238, 272
Communist Party, 270, 272-3, 277
communists, 154
community power, 286
community studies, 44, 248-62
commuting, 38
Compagnie nationale d'aménagement du Bas-Rhône-Languedoc, 25
compoix, 72
computer analysis, 81, 96, 102
Comte, Auguste, 236
concepts, 15-18, 125, 132, 139
concepts, definitions and research traditions, 37-52
Confédération Générale de l'Agriculture (CGA), 276
Confédération Nationale Syndicale de la Mutualité, de la Coopération et due Crédit Agricoles (CNMCCA), 278
Confédération Nationale Syndicale des Travailleurs-Paysans (CNSTP), 277
Confédération Paysanne, 278
conflict, 123
Conseil National Corportif, 276
conservation, 123
Conservative Party, 289
contrasting traditions, 93-5, 179
contributors to the economics of agriculture, 171-2
Contrats de Pays, 26
convergence, a tendency towards, 143
Corbin, Alain, 65, 67
Corn Laws, 29, 165-6
Corporation Paysanne see Peasant Corporation
corporatism, 255, 290
Corsica, 26
Côte-d'Or, 57
Coulomb, Pierre, 277

Council for the Preservation of Rural England (CPRE), 10, 11
counterurbanisation process, 33, 34, 122, 127, 244, 256
Country Landowners' Association (CLA), 10, 289
countryman, 15, 16
countryside, the,
  appreciation of, 125
  changes in, 97–101, 107–8
  concept of, 9, 14, 28, 29, 33, 40–3
  French, 227
  movement into, 30, 38
  opening up of, 68–9, 101
  pressure on, 230
  significance of, 61
  study of, 43–4, 248–50
  uniqueness of, 46
  unpeopled, 15
Cox, G., 231
CPRE *see* Council for the Preservation of Rural England
Credit Agricole Mutuel, 59
Cresson, Edith, 278
Cresswell, Robert, 186
crisis, studies of, 271
Crow, G., 252
Cuisenier, J., 50
cultural context, 3–20
cultural space, 183

diary husbandry, 187, 290
DATAR *see* Délégation pour l'aménagement du territoire et à l'action régionale
Dear, M., 131
decision-making, 122, 131, 149, 162, 266, 274–6
decline of rural landscape, 15
Défense Paysanne, 13
definitions, 15–18
d'Aragon, Charles, 270
de Gaulle, General Charles, 23, 148
de la Blanche, Vidal, 63
de Lauwe, Chombart, 275
de Planhol, Xavier, 101
de Vaugelas, Charles Vincent, 279–80
de Vulpian, Alain, 270
Délégation pour l'aménagement du territoire et à l'action régionale (DATAR), 25, 32, 33
Delorme, Hélène, 275, 277
Demangeon, Albert, 63, 97
democracy, central government view of, 39–40
demographic approach, 38, 42–3
département, 16–17, 24, 57–8, 68, 69, 73, 244, 272, 279
Départment d'Economie et Sociologie

Rurales, 140, 145, 146
Department of the Environment, 294
depopulation, 25, 30, 32, 34 *see also* population, migration
Derivry, Daniel, 271
Derruau-Boniol, S., 270
developing countries, rural policies in, 274
development agencies, 25–6, 32, 172
Development Commission, 32, 167
development of rural geography, conceptual, 125–33
Directeurs Départementaux de l'Agriculture (DDA), 280
Direction départmentale
  de l'agriculture, 25
  de l'equipement, 25
Dion, Roger, 98
discipline, 172
distribution of food, 158–9
Diry, J.P., 103
Doctorat d'Etat, 60
Dogan, Mattei, 273
domestic groups, 200
Dorel, G., 103
Dorgères, Henri, 13, 278, 281
Dunleavy, P., 128, 130
Dupeux, Georges, 272
Durkheim, Emile, 46, 63, 227
Durupt, Marie-Joséphe, 278
Durkheimian rationalism, 47, 48, 212, 229
Dyer, M., 228, 291
dynamic equilibrium, 251

East Anglia, 251–2
Eco-Musées, 191
Ecole Française de Géographie, 97
Ecole des Hautes Etudes en Sciences Sociales, 47
Ecole Normale Superieure, 106
ecological consciousness, 10
Economic and Social Research Council, xi, 218
economic
  crisis, 157, 159
  decline, 21
  dependence of farm workers, 83
  diversification, 31
  liberalisation, 160
  management, 160
  neo-classical, 169, 171
  renewal, 31
  restructuring, 132
  stagnation, 5
  structures, 158
  trends in Britain, 37
economics
  commentary and introduction, 139–43
  in France, rural, 144–64

economy, French, 4, 226
Edinburgh, 291
education, state, 13
educational and institutional structure, 167–9
EEC (European Economic Community), 29, 159, 174, 275–6, 290
Ego and Alter, 214
electoral college system, 15
elections, municipal, 272
electrions, national, 273, 291–2
Elliott, B., 250
employment
  decline in, 31, 122
  generation of, 180
  tertiary, 27
enclosures, parliamentary, 56, 77, 79, 81–2, 141
engineering
  British, 4
  French, 4, 144–64
England, 31, 56, 82, 83, 167, 207, 219, 256, 288
English Farming Past and Present, 85
Enlightenment, the, 4
environmental
  agencies, 228
  awareness, 254–5
  change, 253, 254
  management, 95
  movement, 14
  politics, 95, 293–4
  recomposition, 128
Environmentally Sensitivity Areas, 33
Epstein, A.L., 214
Ernle, Lord (P.E. Prothero), 76, 85
ESRC, 43
Essex school, 288–9
estate agents, 85
estate management, study of, 85
ethnology, 50, 71, 183–202
ethnographers/ethnologists, 70, 112, 181, 183, 187, 203–20
European Community (EC),
  form of, ix
  French agricultural domination of, 23
  rural policy of, 96, 266–7
  transnational framework of, x–xi
Everitt, Professor Alan, 83

factories, growth of, 3
factory system, 3, 127
Fairbrother, Nan, 5
family, the, 140–1, 152, 198, 209, 230, 243, 249, 250
famine, 78
farm(s)
  Accounting Data Network, 168
  business, 102
  capital, sources of, 81
  comparison with other farms of individual enterprise, 162
  crisis, 258
  implements, study of, 80–1
  income, 105
  labour, 83
  large, 59
  management, 156, 172, 253
  Management Association, 169
  Management Survey, 168
  size of, 29, 72–3, 80, 86, 156
  specialisation, 157
  structure of, 80, 86
  tenants, 81
farmers
  backbone of French nation, 14–15
  British, 27–33, 77–81, 82
  categorisation of, 269
  compared to wage-earners, 152–3
  competitiveness of, 237
  as consumers, 99–100
  and the ecosystem, 108
  and farm servants, 83
  finances of, 156
  French, 14–15, 16, 22–7, 227, 234, 241
  investment behaviour, 255
  movement, unity of, 266
  movement, young, 22–3, 148
  place in contemporary society, 152, 154
  rationality of, 156
  vote, 266, 271, 273
farming
  areas, upland, 44
  changed methods in, 22, 33, 77–81, 219
  co-operatives, 158
  demesne, 77–8
  dominance of, 22–7
  family, 140–1, 152, 209, 230, 243, 249, 250, 255, 258
  finance, 258
  industry, 10–11
  large-scale arable, 83
  mechanisation, 28, 30, 79
  organic, 33
  output and productivity, 86
  policies, 96
  recession in, 11
  and Wildlife Advisory Group, 255
Farm Management, 169
Faure, Marcel, 278
Faucher, Daniel, 97
Favret-Saada, J., 206
Febvre, Lucien, 58, 61–5, 70
Fédération Française de l'Agriculture (FFA), 277
Féderation National des Syndicats d'Exploitants Agricoles (FNSEA), 13,

304 *Index*

266, 271, 272, 274, 276-7, 278
Fédération National des Syndicate Paysans (FNSP) 278
Fel, André, 275
Fernandez, J.W., 210
feudal law, 200
field systems, 77-8
fieldwork, 218
Fifth Republic, the 23, 24
First Empire, 39
Firth, Raymond, 207
Fifth Republic, 273
Flatrès, P., 104
FNSE *see Fédération National des Syndicats d'Exploitants Agricoles*
'Folk Societies', 237
folklore and museology, birth of 184-5, 206
Fondation Nationale des Sciences Politique (FNSP), 269
Fontenay, 106
food
  chains, 162
  cheap, 9, 230
  cheese ix, 187
  commodities, 4, 149
  demand, studies of, 173
  'economic miracle', 22
  exports of, xi, 29
  industry, 149
  imports of, xi, 28
  processing industry, 158-9
  production, 144, 148-9, 240
  production chains, 158, 162
  products, 158-9
  purity, 33
  shortages, 22, 29
  sources of, 229
  supply, domestic, 29, 228
  supply problems, 13-14
  survey research, 253
forestry plantations, 111, 290
Fothergill, S., 127
Foucault, M., 204
Fox, Robin, 208
France
  modernisation, 23
  Peasant, 244
  post-war, 21-36
  rural ethnology in, 183-202
  rural economics in, 144-64
  reconstruction and modernisation, 22
Frankenberg, R., 249, 250, 251
Frémont, A., 103, 226
French
  agricultural economists, 140
  cheese, ix, 187
  Commission on Agricultural Geography, 106

economic management, 32
economy, 21, 60, 194, 236
geography and the rural world, 97-116
historiography, 61-75
ideology of peasantism, 11-14
national identity, 237
political economy, 155
political science and rural problems, 269-85
rural sociology, 225-8, 233-47, 268
rural world, 107-8
Senate, 15
wine, ix
Friedman, Harriet, 227
Front Paysan, 13
functionalist, 251

Gabriel-Robinet, Louis, 278
Gachon, Lucien, 97
Gasson, Ruth, 230, 251
Gaullism, 273
Gavignaud, Geneviève, *55-60, 61-75*
GDP *see* gross domestic product
Geertz, Clifford, 205, 210-11
gemeinschaft, 249
genealogies, 198, 212
geography, 49, 63, 70, 93-6, 97-116, 117-35, 238
Gerbet, Pierre, 275
German
  forces, 21
  occupation of France, 14
  sociology, 48
Gilg, Andrew, 118, 126
Ginter, Professor Donald, 81
glass works, 185
global explanation, 239-40
Gluckman, Max, 207
GNP *see* gross national product
Goffman, E., 214
Goubert, Pierre, 68, 70
government, local, 41-2, 45, 131
government support for agriculture, 29, 160-1
Gourou, P., 98
Grandes Ecoles, 51, 145-7, 148, 279, 280
Grant, Wyn, 255, 265, 266, 286-98
Gratton, Philippe, 277
Great Depression
  of the 1880s, 9, 56, 80-1
  of the 1930s, 12
Great War *see* War, First World
green belts, creation, of, 10
gross domestic product (GDP), 28
gross national product (GNP), 24
Gudgin, G., 127
Guellec, Agnès, 104
Guermond, Yves, 98, 103
Gueslin, André, 59

Guilcher, Jean-Michel, 187, 192
Guillaumin, Emile, 274
Guillaume, François, 279, 280
Gutwirth, Jacques, 187

Habakkuk, Sir John, 56, 84–5
Halbwachs, Maurice, 47, 63, 242
Hamilton, Peter, 225–32
Hallet, Granham, 172, 174
Hammond, J.L. and Barbara, 76
Handman, Marie-Elisabeth, 271
harvesting, 80
Hasbach, W., 76
hegemony, 139–40
Helias, Pierre Jakez, 186
Hervieu, Bertrand, 226, *233-47*, 273
heterodox currents, 154–5
historical
    background to agricultural economics, 165–7
    context, 3–20
    school, emergence of a, 61–5
historians, 55–60, 62, 70, 72, 82, 86, 236, 239
history
agrarian, 55–60
    of British anthropological studies, 206
    Départemental, 69–70
    French rural, 65–70, 193
    in perspective, 61–75
    political upheavals in, 47
    structural, 64
    themes in agricultural and rural, 76–89
Hobart, M., 205
Hobsbawn, E.J., 83
Hoffman, Stanley, 278
Hoggart, K., 126–7
homo economicus, theory of, 141
Horn, Pamela, 83
Houée Paul, 278
House of Lords, 15
housing
    distance between, 38
    investigation of rural, 86, 122, 188
    pressure, 30
    urban, 219
Houssel, Jean-Pierre, 270, 272
Hubscher, Ronald, 55, 57, *61-75*
husbandry, convertible, 79

ideology
    agrarian, 69
    of deregulation, 130
    in France, study of, 267
    in national cultures, rural, 14–15
    of Peasantism, French, 11–14
    of rurality in Britain and France, 37–52
imperialism, 207, 220
income, changes in, 120

Indians, 210
industrial sectors, French, 5, 191
industrialisation, 3–6, 21, 26–7, 59, 145, 253
industry, ruralisation of, 31
information-gathering, 161, 199
Institut National de la
    Recherche Agronomique (INRA), 140, 142, 145–8, 228
    Statistique et de l'Economie (INSEE) 38, 109, 238
Institute
    of Agricultural Economics, 167, 169, 172
    of Applied Economics, 172
    of British Geographers, 94, 118
    of Fiscal Studies, 172
    of Marketing, 169
institutional context, 234
'insurance' theory, 82
interdisciplinary geographers, 111–14
integration, process of, 67
International
    Association of Agricultural Economists, 144
    Congress of Geography, 102, 104
    Geographical Union, 106
    Yearbook of Rural Planning, 118

Jacobins, 12, 180
jacquerie, 14
Jaurés, Jean, 62
Jessua, Claude, 141
Jest, Corneille, 188–9
Jeunesse Agricole
    Catholique (JAC), 14, 278–9
    Chrétienne (JAC), 23
Jollivet, Marcel, 243
Journal of Rural Studies, 118
Jones, G.T., 172
Juillard, Etienne, 98
Justices of the Peace, 41

Kayser, Bernard, 94–6, *97-116*
Keeble, D.E., 127
Kellas, J.G., 291, 292–3
Kent, R., 250
Kerridge, Professor E., 55, 78–9
Key concepts, 236–256
kinship, 198–201, 209
Klatzmann, Joseph, 271, 272
Knafou, R., 104
Kostrowcki, J., 102
Kussmaul, Ann, 83

l'aménagement du territoire, 25
l'Année Sociologique, 46
la fin des paysans see peasantry, end of
l'exploitation, 16
Le Guen, Roger, 278
Le Play, Frédéric, 198

Labour Pary, 229, 286, 289, 292
labour
  child, 83
  exploitation of, 16
  female, 31
  force, 28, 77, 83
  market, 127
  mobility of, 4
  spatial divisions of, 129
  studies of farm, 83
Labrousse, Ernest, 64, 70
Labrusse, Bertrand, 278
Lacombe, Philippe, 140, 141, 142, *144-64*
Ladurie, Emmanuel LeRoy, 64, 72, 206
'lamb wars', ix
Lambert, Yves, 278
land
  consolidation, 13
  fragmentation, 71
  Grant Colleges, 167
  holdings, 24
  inheritance, 199, 200
  market, 82, 84, 156, 256
  -owners, 80, 81, 82, 85, 111
  -ownership, 6-7, 77, 84-5, 86
  purchase, 4-5
  reforms, 24
  rents, 73, 166
  -scape, 97-8, 99, 100, 122, 128
  stewards, 85
  tax, 81-2
  -use maps, 102
  -use planning, 25, 29-30
  -use policy, 10, 25, 27, 95, 99, 122
Languedoc, 104, 110, 272
language, 15-18, 179, 181, 204
Larousse dictionary, 236
Latin America, 105, 271
Laurent, Robert, 57, 65
Leach, E.R., 204
Lecotte, Roger, 184-5
Lee, J.M., 288
Lefebvre, Georges, 57, 62
legal rights, 200
Lenclud, Gérard, *183-202*, 206
Leroi-Gourham, André, 185
Lévi-Strauss, Claude, 64, 181, 195, 270
Levy, R. 292
liberalism, economic, 8, 152
Limousin, 26
Limouzin, P., 104
literature, 12, 112, 120, 128, 170, 206-10, 211, 213, 218-20, 237, 274, 292
Little, J., 257
livestock, 79, 100
Lloyd George, David, 267
local
  authorities, 41, 131
  government, 41-2, 45, 131
  studies, 110-11
  localisation, 238, 241
Lockwood, David, 230
Loi (laws)
  complémentaire (1962), 23, 274
  foncière (1962), 102
  d'orientation agricole (1960), 23
  d'orientation foncière (1967), 25
  on research (1982), 146
Loire, the, 6
London, 3, 207, 214, 267
Lord Lieutenant (of a county), 41
Lowe, Philip, *3-20, 21-36, 37-52*, 231

McCloskey, Professor Donald, 82
Madgwick, P., 287, 289, 293
Maget, Marcel, 185
Making of the English Working Class, The, 83
Maitland, F.W., 76
Mallet, Serge, 278
Malthus, T.R., 165
Management Agreements, 174
Manchester, 286
Manchester School, 166
manors, 84
Mansbach, R.W., 291, 292
manufacturing
  activity, 31
  employment in, 31
  growth in, 27
  maps, 102, 109, 194
Maresca, Sylvain, 279
market
  centres, small, 5
  domestic, 21
  economy, 13
  European, 99
  'free' produce, 158
  protection against fluctuations in, 28
  reforms 275
  regulation, 140
  single European, xi
  structures, 150
  towns, 31, 281
Marsden, T., 249
Marshall, Alfred, 166
Marshall Aid, 22
marriage, 186, 195, 199-200, 212
Martin, J.M., 81
Marx, Karl, 8, 48, 77, 152
Marxism, 47, 48, 147, 149, 160, 258
Marxist
  analysis, 48, 50, 65, 152, 154, 235, 243
  approach, 152-3, 227, 252, 270
  challenge, 255
  historians, 77, 239

interpretations, 57, 141, 237
polemic, 207
politics, 62, 257
rural sociology, 230
theory, 256
tradition, 157, 240
vogue, 51
Massey, D., 128
Massif Central, 25, 111
Mathieu, N., 100
Mauss, Marcel, 50, 58, 63, 185, 195
Mendés France, Pierre, 148
Mendras, Henri, 49, 183, 227, 228, 237, 239–40, 242, 244, 271, 276
Menon, P.L., 184–5
Métailie, J.P., 101
methodological developments, 102
Mewett, Peter, 219
Meynaud, Jean, 271, 276
Mill, John Stuart, 165, 166
milk, 153, 157
Miller, W., 291, 293
Mingay, Gordon, 55–7, 76–89
Minister of Agriculture, 23, 85, 149, 272, 274–5, 276
Ministry of Agriculture
  and agricultural economics, 44
  background of administrators, 267, 279–80
  and economists, 147
  merger with Department of the Environment, 294
  and the provincial advisory centres, 167, 171–2
  study of, 266
  training of civil servants for, 145
  works of, 269
Ministry of Agriculture, Fisheries and Food (MAFF), 228, 289
Ministry of Research and Technology, 146
Minot, 187
Mitchell, Peter Chalmers, 10
models, 117, 131, 150, 151, 156, 218, 227, 234, 236, 248, 251
modernisation, 148, 160, 187, 226
Monnet, Jean, 22
monographs, local or regional, 67–9, 73–4, 77, 93–4, 110, 112, 191, 196–7, 227, 237, 239, 243, 270–1
Montpellier, 106
Moreau, Jacques, 40
Moseley, Malcolm, 94, 95, 96, *117–35*
motorways, 30
Mouvement de Coordination et de Défense des Exploitations Agricoles Familiales (MODEF), 277
Mullen, Roger, 293
Muller, Pierre, 274–5, 278
municipal elections, 199

Munton, R. J.C., 120, 121, 123, 126
Musée national des arts et traditions populaires, 184
museums, 181

Nallet, Henri, 149, 277
Nalson, J.S., 249
Napoleonic code of equal inheritance, 4
Napoleonic period, 4
National
  Assembly, 272, 273
  Economic Plan, 22
  Farmers' Union (NFU), 228, 230, 266, 289–90
  Health Service, 30–1
  Trust, the, 10
national parks, 10
nationalism, 32, 291, 294–5
nationalisation of key industries, 27
nature conservation, 29
nature, return to, 241–4
neo-classical concepts, 127, 139–40, 149, 150–2, 154
neo-classical paradigm, 139–40, 140–1, 142
neo-realism, 243, 244
new issues in rural sociology, 253–5
Newby, Howard, 230, 231, 249, 251–5, 288
NFU *see* National Farmers' Union
Northern Ireland, 29, 167, 290

occupation of France, 21
Office Interprofessional du Blé, 158
Office de las Recherche Scientifique Technique d'Outre Mers (ORSTROM), 104, 106
Office National des Fôrets (ONF) 280
Office of Population Censuses and Surveys, 43
opportunity cost, 151
oil, imported, 22
ORSTOM *see* Office de la Recherche Scientifique et Technique d'Outre Mers
Ory, Pascal, 278
Other/otherness (cultural), 203–20
out-migration, 30
Oxford, 167, 168

Pacione, M., 23, 124, 127
Paine, R.P.B., 214
Parain, Charles, 187, 188, 189
Pareto, Vilfredo, 279
Paris
  Balls, 187
  centre for science and culture, 4
  commercial agriculture developed around, 23
  Commune, 180
  national growth centred on, 25

308 Index

policy-makers in, 234, 267
secondary residences in, 280
parish, 39
parochialism, 180
Parti Agraire, 13
party manifestoes, 272
Pas-de-Calais, 65
pastoralisation, 4
patriotism, 15
pays, 16–17, 190
Pays Basque, 192
paysan, 16, 181, 226, 242
peasant
  civilisation, 71
  Corporation, 13
  'democracy', 8
  farmers, 4–5, 12, 227, 243
  French, 11–14
  politics, 14
  purchasing power of, 5
  Republic, 66
  society, 6–8, 194, 198, 239
  village, 184, 185–6, 188–90
peasantism, 11–14
peasantry, end of, 22–7, 60, 94, 226, 241–4
Pelras, Charles, 186
Perpillou, A., 102
Perroux, F., 99
perspectives, 269, 270–80
Petit, Michel, 49, 144, 171
Peyon, J.-P., 103
Pfister, Dean, 62
Philip, Butt, 293
Phillips, D., 120, 128, 129
philosophy, 233
phylloxera, 67
Piaget, Jean, 64
Pingaud, Claude, 189
Pinguard, Marie-Claude, 190
Pisani, Edgar, 23
Pitt-Rivers, J.A., 207–8
Plaid Cymru, 287, 291, 292, 293
planification, 226
planning
  and policy-making, 130
  rural, 25–7, 106
  system, 30
Plans d'aménagement rural, 26
Plozévet, 186, 188
Plans d'occupation des sols, 26
pluralism, 126
pluridisciplinarity, 46–7, 48–9, 50, 51, 143, 241
policy communities, 133
policy-makers
  British, 41, 130
  French, 22, 25, 37, 51
policy-making, 43, 157, 234, 290, 295

policy networks, 133
political
  approach, 39–40, 40–3
  decision-making, 266
  economy, 128, 132, 149–55, 162, 163, 166, 257–8
  life, local, 265
  life, role of kinship in, 199
  lobbies, 69
  power, 157
  science, rural, 267–8, 269–85
  sociology of rural policy, 254
politicisation, depoliticisation, 271–2
politics
  agricultural, 266
  British, 8
  commentary and introduction, 265–8
  and concentrated land ownership, 7
  French, 8
  pattern of, 287
  and power, rural, 265–6
poor law, 83
Poor Law, New, 84, 85
poor relief, 83
Popular Front, 13, 158
population
  black, 214
  British, 4, 5, 9, 28, 214
  density, 42–3, 100, 238
  fluctuations in, 77, 78
  French, 4, 5, 21, 99, 241
  growth, 38
  increasing, 4, 79, 107–8
  indigenous, 206
  migration, 11–12, 21, 22, 30, 187
  rural, 4, 11, 38, 98
  and social change, 122
  urbanised, 9
  village, 113
positivism, applied, 126–8
post-Darwinian years, 9
post-structuralist rural sociology, 258
post-war
  Britain, 21–36, 248
  France, 21–36, 234, 236–7
  immigration, 14
  years, 17
Postel-Vinay, Gilles, 59
Potter, Clive, 254–5
Poujade, Pierre, 281
power relations, 130, 154, 157, 265–6
Prefect, the, 39
Presidential election, 271, 277
preservation movement in Britain, 8–11, 14
price fluctuations, 158
primary sources, 76, 199
privatisation, 130
problématique

of agricultural policy, 157, 161, 266
economic, 143, 144, 160
focus of research, 17, 63, 103, 105
of historians, 240
of local studies, 110, 187
and the monograph, 59
regionalist, 196
of rural history, 66, 70, 73, 198
rural sociology, 193, 197, 238
trends in ethnology, 192
production methods, 153, 157-8
productivist paradigm, 231
productivity, 73
profession, agricultural economics, 169-71
protectionism, 11, 57, 142, 166
Proudhonian tradition, 148
public policy, 274-6
quangos (quasi-autonomous non-government organisations), 45
Quiers-Valette, Suzanne, 271

Radical Party, 272
Radnor, 42
railways 5, 10
Rambaud, Placide, 237
rapprochement, a, 33-4
Rassemblement du Peuple Français (RPF), 273
rational behaviour, 150
recession, 31
Redfield, Robert, 44, 185, 227
Rees, Alwyn, 249
reform
  agricultural, 24, 59, 160-1
  institutional, 96
  land, 7
  modernising, 4
  Pisani, 280
regional
  centres, 45, 234
  nationalists, 234, 287, 291-3
  policy-mechanisms, 26
  studies, 70
regionalism, 117, 234
regions and cultural space, 190
regions, politically opposed to, 270
Reinhard, Marcel, 70
relations with the Wider world, 272-4
remembrement, 13
Renard, J., 103
renewal zones, 26
rents, 82
Republicans, 12
research, x
  applied, 129-30
  changing emphasis in, 172-4
  community studies tradition of, 248-62
  and extension services, 29

focus of, 17, 87, 103, 185
French rural, 46-51, 97-116, 144-64, 186-8, 193-8
management of, 161
methods, 102
modern, 56
neo-ruralism, 243
organisation of, 94-5
quantitative, 96
rural, 43, 45, 240
subjects of rural geography, 121
and teaching not linked in France, 142
themes, x, 46, 97-116, 117-35, 155-9
restructuring, 132
Revolution
  of 1789, 39
  of 1848, 12
  French, 4, 39, 59-60, 65, 181
  Industrial, 180
  July, 39
  Russian, 48
  'silent', 21
Revue Française de Science Politique (RFSP), 269-70, 274, 276-7, 281
Rhône, 26
Ricardo, David, 165, 166
Rimariex, Gaston, 274
Rogers, J.E. Thorold, 76
Roget's Thesaurus, 16
Roman Law, 200
Rougerie, J., 69
Roupnel, Gaston, 98
Roussillon, Henri, 71, 278
Royal Commissions, 81
Royer, Jean-Michel, 278-9
Rudé, George, 83
rural
  Areas Database, 43
  Britain, 15, 27-33
  change, 34
  community, 16, 237
  concepts, 236-8
  culture, ix
  deprivation, 122, 127, 256
  development, 21-36
  Development Areas, 40
  Development Boards, 32
  Development Commission, 122
  district council, 42
  economics in France, 144-64
  Economy and Society Study Group, 45-6, 126, 231, 254, 257
  employment, 173
  ethnology in France, 183-202
  exodus, 11, 242, 252
  family, changes to, 108
  France, 22-7
  geography, 93, 97-106, 107-14, 117-35

geography, identity of, 118–25
housing, 14
images, 15, 179–82
industry, 5
lineages, 6–8
migration, 11, 101, 104, 226
mileu, 61, 183
people in a rural world, 270–4
phenomena, 129
places, 188
political science, 267–8
politics, 7, 265–6, 268, 286–98
preservation movement, 8–11
preservation of established roles and positions, 72
resource management, 122–3
revival, 256
society, ix–x, 3–6, 15, 17, 27, 72, 77, 103, 184, 192, 193–8, 225–6
social history, 81–5
sociology, 45, 191, 193, 225–8, 233–47
space, 38–40
studies, 17, 42, 43–6, 61–75, 99, 102–4, 117–18, 129, 193–8
and urban, 179
unrest, 7
rurality, 118, 128–9

Sahels, two, 105
'salad days', 205
Samuel, Raphael, 83
Saunders, P., 131, 251
Schema directeurs d'aménagement et d'urbanisme, 26
Sautter, Gilles, 94, 96, *97–116*
scales of reality, 103, 107
Schneider, David, 207
Schumpeter, Joseph, 154
Schwartz, T., 206, 214, 215, 292
science, neutrality of, 141–2
scientific work, conditions of, 159–61
Scotch whisky, ix
Scotland, 15, 29, 167, 218–19, 286–92 *passim*
Scott, Lord Justice, 11
Scottish
  Highlands, 30
  National Party, 291, 292–3
Self, 211–13, 215
Ségalen, Martine, *183–202*
Senate, the, 273
Service de l'Enregistrement, 58
service provision, 122
Servolin, Claude, 227–8, 240, 243
Shetland, 203, 215, 219
shopkeepers, 73
Sibdore, 101
Siegfried, André, 64, 267, 270
Simmel, 47–8

Sites of Special Scientific Interest, 33
Smith, Adam, 165, 166
Smithsonian Institute, 194
Snell, K.D.M., 83
Soboul, Albert, 58, 65
social
  actors, 190–2
  anthropology, 44, 50
  change, 240
  and economic change, 44, 121, 253, 255–7
  factors, 253
  framework of rural economics, 145–9
  group, 241
  history, rural, 81–5
  life, 179–80, 219–20
  organisation, 198–200, 235
  recomposition, 128
  relations, 68, 125, 151, 163
  Science Research Council, 287
  theory, 125–6, 128
  stratification, 66, 153
  welfare, 122
Socialist Party, 272, 273
Société englobante, 227
Société Française d'Economie Rurale, 144
socio-cultural activities, 128
socio-economic
  change, 38, 154
  characteristics, 128
  composition, 26
  conditions, 126
  structures, 154
socio-political analysis, 57, 96, 153, 235, 240
socio-spatial system, 110
sociological investigation, 236
sociology, 44, 45, 46–7, 174, 191, 206, 223–32, 233–47
space, conceptualisation of, 102–4, 107–8, 113, 128–9, 234
Spain, 208
'spatial fetishism', 118
specialisation (in historical topics), 76
Speenhamland system, 84
Sperber, D., 205, 212
Stanyer, J., 288
state
  and applied geography, 129–30
  apparatus, 39, 146
  bureaucracy, 228
  local, 131
  planning, 130
  role of the, 121, 122, 132–3, 226, 257
  -society relationship, 130
  support, 30
Strathern, Marilyn, 208–9, 213
structural-functionalism, 44, 226
structuralism, 64, 257–8
Sutter, Dr., 186

sufferage, universal, 12
Suffert-Carcenac, G., 101
surveys of rural architecture/furniture, 184
symbols/symbolism, 205, 209, 210
synoptic studies, limitations of, 108–11

Tanguy-Prigent, Pierre, 276
tariffs, introduction of, 9
Tavernier, Yves, 274–7, 280
Tawney, R.H., 56, 84
tax relief, 120
technical progress, 105
technological change, 257
terms, 15–18
textiles, fall in output of, 4
text see literature
Thatcher, Prime Minister Margaret, 32
thematic approach, 240–1
themes in agricultural history and rural social history, 76–89
thése d'Etat, 65–6, 93–4, 103
Third World studies, 94, 97, 103, 104–6, 170, 171
Thirsk, Joan, 55, 76
Thomas, Professor, W.J., 168, 173
Thompson, Kenneth, 231
Thompson, Edward, 83
Thompson, Professor F.M.L., 84–5
Thorold Rogers, J.E., 76
threshing machine, 80
Throsby, C.D., 173
Tönnies, 44, 48
tourism, ix, xi, 31, 113
town centre, 38
town and countryside, 234, 235, 239
tractors, 22, 28, 191, 270
trade union
  agriculture, 51, 278
  conflict, 7
translational difficulties, 179
transport, 122
Treaty of Rome, 22
Tubiana, Laurence, 275
Turner, M., 81
twinning of French and British towns, ix

Union National des Syndicates Agricoles, 13
United States, 81, 86, 103, 107, 166–7, 168, 236, 257, 289
universities, 44, 45, 86, 142, 145, 166, 168, 169, 181
University
  of Aberdeen, 286
  College of Wales, 167, 169, 286
  of Essex, 45
  of Exeter, 286
  of Manchester, 168
  of Newcastle, 173

  of Nottingham, 169
  of Oxford, 169, 172
  of Paris X at Nanterre, 227
  of Strasbourg, 46–7, 62

Up Country Johnnies, 250
urban
  Code, 40
  dwellers, 100
  growth, 9
  rural conflict, 236
  -rural population, 33, 127
  -rural shift, 31, 42, 127
  sociology, 44, 235
  studies, 117, 129
  units, 38
urbanisation, ix, 3–6, 21, 101, 235, 252
Urry, J., 128–9, 252

Val d'Anniviers, 98
value system, 9
Vial, André, 273
Vichy Corporation see Peasant Corporation
Vichy government, 13, 14, 39, 180, 184, 244, 276
Victorian Countryside, The, 85
Vigier, Philippe, 65
Vietnam, 98
Vilar, Pierre, 64
village community, the, 108, 113, 227, 237, 242, 271
vine growers, 57
Vinogradoff, P., 76
vocabularies, 16–17, 229, 230, 231

wages
  industrial, 9
  relationship, 152–3
  subsidising, 84
Wagner, Roy, 209–10
Wahl, A., 71
Wales, 15, 31, 167, 207, 249, 286, 293
war
  Agricultural Executive Committees, 28
  Algerian, 23
  First World, 12, 62, 76, 85, 274
  Napoleonic, 4, 81, 166, 181
  Second World, 10, 21, 28, 44, 87, 155, 167, 168, 180, 225, 249, 270, 274, 288
water meadows, 79
Watson, J.L., 206
Webb, K., 292
Weber, E., 74, 183, 275
Weber, Max, 48
Weberian relativism, 47, 48, 71, 239, 252
welfare of the rural population, 121–2, 131
Welfare state, 30
Wetham, Edith, 86, 165

Whalsay, 203
Whatmore, S., 257
wheat, price of, 166
Whitby, Martin, 173
white collar workers, 38
Who's Who in France, 280
Wibberly, Professor Gerald, 173
Williams, A., 120, 128, 129
Williams, W.M., 249–52
women, position of in rural society, 256–7

workhouse, the, 84
working class, rural, 30, 130–1, 184, 248, 256

Yelling, J.A., 81, 82

Zola, Emile, 12
Zones de Peuplement Industriel ou Urbain (ZPIU), 38
Zoological Society, 10